This is a collection of original essays on the relationship between property and power, a fundamental theme in medieval history. It is produced by largely the same team responsible for the acclaimed *The Settlement of Disputes in Early Medieval Europe* (1986), and – like its predecessor – is founded on the study of charter material. It aims to reveal the complex realities underlying the standard observation that property, especially land, was the source of power in the middle ages.

The essays examine the following themes: the role of central authority in determining property relationships; what power over property actually meant; how property could be turned into political power; and the extent to which the development of immunities (islands of separate jurisdiction) affected the balance of power in European societies. The geographical range of the discussions, and their spread over time, are wide enough to allow comparisons to be made across *different* medieval societies, although there is a solid core of material from Frankish contexts. A sustained comparison of the key issues forms the conclusion, and there is also a glossary, intended to make the arcane world of medieval property relations more accessible to the non-specialist reader.

PROPERTY AND POWER IN THE EARLY MIDDLE AGES

PROPERTY AND POWER
IN THE EARLY
MIDDLE AGES

EDITED BY

WENDY DAVIES

and

PAUL FOURACRE

CAMBRIDGE
UNIVERSITY PRESS

Published by the Press Syndicate of the University of Cambridge
The Pitt Building, Trumpington Street, Cambridge CB2 1RP
40 West 20th Street, New York, NY 10011-4211, USA
10 Stamford Road, Oakleigh, Melbourne 3166, Australia

First published 1995

Printed in Great Britain at the University Press, Cambridge

A catalogue record for this book is available from the British Library

Library of Congress cataloguing in publication data

Property and power in the early middle ages / edited by Wendy Davies and Paul Fouracre.
p.   cm.
Includes bibliographical references (p.) and index.
Contents: The ideology of sharing: apostolic community and ecclesiastical property
in the early middle ages / David Ganz – Teutsind, Witlaic and the history of
Merovingian *precaria* / Ian Wood – Eternal light and earthly needs: practical aspects of
the development of Frankish immunities / Paul Fouracre – The wary widow /
Janet Nelson – Lordship and justice in the early English kingdom: Oswaldslow revisited /
Patrick Wormald – Adding insult to injury: power, property and immunities in early
medieval Wales / Wendy Davies – Property transactions and social relations between
rulers, bishops and nobles in early eleventh-century Saxony: the evidence of the
Vita Meinwerci / Timothy Reuter – Monastic exemptions in tenth- and eleventh-century
Byzantium / Rosemary Morris – Property ownership and signorial power in twelfth-century
Tuscany / Chris Wickham – Property and power in early medieval Europe.
ISBN 0 521 43419 X
1. Land tenure – Europe – History.   2. Property – Europe – History.   3. Power (Social
sciences) – Europe – History.   4. Privileges and immunities – Europe – History.
5. Europe – Social conditions – To 1492.   6. Middle Ages.   I. Davies, Wendy.
II. Fouracre, Paul.
HD141.P76   1995
333.3'22'0940902 – dc20   95-3006   CIP

ISBN 0 521 43419 X hardback

WV

Contents

vii

Maps

Preface

This book, like its predecessor *The Settlement of Disputes in Early Medieval Europe*, is meant to be read as a book and not as a collection of separate essays. It arises from the ongoing collaboration of the group and from our agreement to look at some key issues concerning property, and power over property, in different parts of early medieval Europe. As before, we have talked over each other's contributions at length, and agreed the content of introduction and conclusion.

Charter weekends have gone on. We have continued to meet regularly, in Bucknell, to discuss old and new approaches to the early middle ages and to find some healthy criticism for our individual work in hand. We share a common approach but have plenty to learn, and we each benefit from the interaction. Tim Reuter and David Ganz, who were part of the original group although unable to contribute to *Disputes*, came to meetings from the late 1980s and have written papers here. Richard Sharpe has come regularly to meetings, and contributed to discussion and to the shape and content of this book, but does not have a named paper in it.

We want our ideas to be accessible and are anxious that students should read and use this volume as well as scholars and specialists. We have therefore again included a glossary of early medieval words and concepts; this is a simple guide – intentionally so – and is not a comprehensive survey.

We all owe debts of gratitude to friends and colleagues for their assistance; of these, Barbara Rosenwein's special interest has been much appreciated, and we look forward to publication of her own book on immunities. Since we first began to meet, several of us have married and some of us have raised children; we are grateful for family tolerance of our weekend absences and for their continuing support. We plan a third volume, and trust that it will be ready more quickly than the second.

BUCKNELL
13 November 1994

Abbreviations

ChLA   *Chartae Latinae Antiquiores*, ed. A. Bruckner and M. Marichal; vol. 14, ed. H. Atsma and J. Vezin, Zurich, 1982; cited by number.

DB   *Domesday Book seu Liber Censualis Wilhelmi Primi Regis Angliae*, ed. A. Farley, 2 vols., London, 1783.

D C II   *Die Urkunden Konrads II.*, ed. H. Bresslau, *MGH Diplomata regum et imperatorum Germaniae*, vol. 4, Vienna, 1909.

D H II   *Die Urkunden Heinrichs II. und Arduins*, ed. H. Bresslau, H. Bloch and R. Holtzmann, *MGH Diplomata regum et imperatorum Germaniae*, vol. 3, Vienna, 1900–3.

D O I   *Die Urkunden Konrad I., Heinrich I., und Otto I.*, ed T. Sickel, *MGH Diplomata regum et imperatorum Germaniae*, vol. 1, Hannover, 1879–84.

D O II   *Die Urkunden Otto des II.*, ed. T. Sickel, *MGH Diplomata regum et imperatorum Germaniae*, vol. 2, pt 1, Vienna, 1888.

D O III   *Die Urkunden Otto des III.*, ed. T. Sickel, *MGH Diplomata regum et imperatorum Germaniae*, vol. 2, pt 2, Vienna, 1893.

GAF   *Gesta sanctorum patrum Fontanellensis coenobii*, ed. F. Lohier and R. P. J. Laporte, Rouen, 1936.

LL   *The Text of the Book of Llan Dâv*, ed. J. G. Evans with J. Rhys, Oxford, 1893; cited by number.

MGH   *Monumenta Germaniae Historica.*

MGH AA   *MGH Auctores Antiquissimi.*

MGH Capit.	*Capitularia Regum Francorum*, vol. 1, ed. A. Boretius; vol. 2, ed. A. Boretius and V. Krause, *MGH LL in quarto*, sectio 2, vols. 1–2, Hannover, 1883, 1897.
MGH Conc.	*Concilia aevi Karolini*, ed. A. Werminghoff, 2 vols., *MGH LL in quarto*, sectio 3, *Concilia*, vol. 2, pts 1–2, Hannover and Leipzig, 1906, 1908.
and	*Die Konzilien der karolingischen Teilreiche, 843–859*, ed. W. Hartmann, *MGH LL in quarto*, sectio 3, *Concilia*, vol. 3, Hannover, 1984.
MGH SRG	*MGH Scriptores Rerum Germanicarum in usum Scholarum separatim editi.*
MGH SRM	*MGH Scriptores Rerum Merovingicarum.*
MGH Form.	*Formulae Merowingici et Karolini Aevi*, ed. K. Zeumer, *MGH LL in quarto*, sectio 5, Hannover, 1886.
Reg.	*Regesta Regum Anglo-Normannorum*, vol. 1, ed. H. W. C. Davis; vol. 2, ed. C. Johnson and H. A. Cronne; Oxford, 1912, 1956; cited by number.
RHW	H. Erhard, *Regesta Historiae Westfaliae, accedit Codex diplomaticus*, 2 vols., Münster, 1847–51.
S	P. H. Sawyer, *Anglo-Saxon Charters: An Annotated List and Bibliography*, London, 1968.
VM	*Vita Meinwerci episcopi Patherbrunnensis*, ed. F. Tenckhoff, *MGH SRG*, vol. 59, Hannover, 1921.

Introduction

Nine years ago, we completed the predecessor to this volume, *The Settlement of Disputes in Early Medieval Europe.*[1] The present book is the work of substantially the same group of people, and it starts from the same two premisses: first, that the early medieval period has to be understood in its own terms, not in those of the better documented periods before and after it, the late Roman Empire and the 'high' middle ages of the twelfth and thirteenth centuries; second, that its political and social structures are best appreciated, not through the study of laws and other normative texts, but through charters.

Although charters evidently relate to the world of written law, they are much closer than are laws to the daily practices of the men and women of the early middle ages. Indeed, they are as close as we can normally get to such practices, at least in so far as the latter involve the possession of land. In our previous book, we looked at the records of court cases and other disputes, as a guide to these practices at the point where they came closest to the world of law. In this one, we look at the relationship between landed property and political power. This is a huge topic; it cannot be encompassed in a single work, and we have not tried to. In addition, we are all nine years older and nine years busier; we have thought it best not to try to weld our work into a single line of argument, as was our intention in *The Settlement of Disputes.* The present book should, therefore, be seen as separate articles on a common theme, property and power, rather than as a homogeneous survey. At the core of the book, nonetheless, is a single set of presuppositions. This introduction will sketch some of them, as a framing for what follows; they will be picked up again in the

[1] Ed. W. Davies and P. Fouracre.

conclusion. As with the previous book, although these sections were drafted by individuals, they stand as an expression of the group approach.[2]

Historians, whatever their differences, tend to agree that in the early and central middle ages, land equalled power: that, within limits, the amount of land one controlled correlated with the amount of power one wielded. One of the main problems comes with working out how one got from the first to the second, for having land did not automatically generate power in pre-industrial society, any more than having money automatically generates power in industrial society. Close to automatically; but not quite. Different political systems produce different sets of procedures for moving from one to the other, then as now. And this is made more complex by the other main problem: of exactly how 'power' could be defined. What mattered most, local power or power in the framework of public politics (the world of kings and princes)?[3] What were the procedures which made it legitimate? This brings us into the arena where rules mattered, just as the last book did. But, again as in the last book, we will argue that local procedures, and the practical knowledge of how far one could go without losing the support of others, were more important than abstract legal norms.

Land, in a pre-industrial society, was the source of (very nearly) all wealth; put simply, wealth brought you power because it allowed you to reward armed men who in turn allowed you to acquire further wealth in a variety of ways and defend the wealth you had. Marc Bloch famously argued that, in a world where wages were impracticable – because coin was relatively uncommon and/or of too high a value for ordinary transactions, and because markets were too unreliable to be the medium for turning coin into food and clothing – the only ways of keeping these armed men were as an immediate retinue, who lived in one's hall and were fed from one's rents, or else as tenants, who lived on parts of one's estates and took the rents directly.[4] The first method was an impermanent procedure, for retainers sought

---

[2] The introduction was written by Chris Wickham and Timothy Reuter; the conclusion by Wendy Davies and Paul Fouracre.

[3] For a discussion which makes explicit the possible relationships between different kinds of power in the early middle ages see W. Davies, *Patterns of Power in Early Wales*.

[4] M. Bloch, *Feudal Society*, pp. 68–9.

to marry and settle down; the second immediately produced problems of control, for armed tenants might not be loyal for ever, and might be hard to uproot. Bloch's work focussed on what he called the 'feudal' period in the post-Carolingian world, roughly the tenth to thirteenth centuries, when the state was mostly weak and when most political power operated in a sort of zero-sum way: that is to say, the more land (and thus power) I control, the less you do. But he certainly, and rightly, regarded the earlier medieval period as one when money was equally – indeed, still more – hard to use; the same logic, which has come to be known as the 'politics of land', applied.

Even in the central middle ages, the issues were not as simple as that. Feudal lords were not Hobbesian individualists; they operated in a framework of rules, legitimations and rituals, which were complex enough to fill hundreds of pages in Bloch's work, and the works of many successors.[5] If your power was not capable of being legitimated, it did not exist; your armed men would not follow you, or not for long. But in the early middle ages, it was more complex still, for the local powers of landowners still stood in apposition to wider public powers wielded or granted by kings and princes, which together made up what we can call the 'state'. This was the arena in which fully legitimate power resided in the early middle ages; local lordship seems not to have had anything like the same authority that it came to do in eleventh- and twelfth-century France. But this does not mean it had none; only that the nature of political legitimation was, in the early middle ages, even more complex than later – as well as, in a period of very poor documentation, far more obscure.

THE EARLY MEDIEVAL STATE

Early medieval public power was paradoxical: both weak and strong. Even in the areas where it derived directly from the ruins of the Roman state, it was immeasurably poorer and weaker than that state, as the notorious poverty and sparseness of its surviving material culture (both standing buildings and

---

[5] See most recently H. Fichtenau, *Living in the Tenth Century*; G. Althoff, *Verwandte, Freunde und Getreue*; and G. Koziol, *Begging Pardon and Favor*; and on these and other works T. Reuter, 'Pre-Gregorian mentalities', *Journal of Ecclesiastical History*, 35 (1994). T. Bisson, 'The "feudal revolution"', *Past and Present*, 142 (1994), is an important new survey.

archaeological remains) bear witness. The Roman Empire provided a very clear set of means by which one could turn wealth
into power. The state was independently wealthy, both as a
landowner and, above all, thanks to its capacity to extract large
proportions of the surplus of the Empire directly in tax.[6] Most
of that tax was spent on a standing army; but the amount of
wealth that regularly went through the state's coffers was so
great that participation in public political activities was hugely
profitable, outweighing even the enormous private wealth possessed by the richest late Roman aristocrats. Private wealth was,
here, quite explicitly seen as an entry-permit into the arena of
legitimate political activity, which was entirely restricted to members of the hierarchies of state officials, whether in central
government or in the local government of the cities. The dominance by the senatorial aristocracy over their own private properties certainly could be extended in the direction of informal
networks of patronage (*patrocinium*) over neighbours, some of
which were pretty coercive; but this was never regarded as
legitimate by public authorities. Even when patronage was sufficiently locally stable to constitute a normative framework in
practice, it was never important enough to act as a *substitute* for
public power.

Such was the situation up to the fifth century in the West –
and indeed for many centuries to come in the Byzantine East.
But, in the disruption of the invasion period, the tax base of
the Western Empire collapsed; only fragments remained to benefit the Frankish kings in Gaul and the Visigothic kings in
Spain, and in Britain and Lombard Italy not even that. Exactly
how much taxation remained in the West in (say) 600 is disputed, more than ever in recent years; but the majority view is
still that the last vestiges of the land tax were by that date
fading fast.[7] Early medieval states were largely, and increasingly,
based on landowning; in the relationships between kings and
aristocrats, the zero-sum game could begin. And sprawling political systems like those of the Merovingian Franks were very hard
to control in depth. What a local count, or bishop, or private

---

[6] The most interesting recent discussion of this topic is J. Haldon, *The State and the Tributary
Mode of Production*.
[7] See the debate cited below by Paul Fouracre, in his nn. 4, 6, 18, 19.

landowner did in his locality was for the most part impossible to police, and most kings barely attempted to do so; indeed, except where their own interests were affected, they were perhaps not even concerned to.

Under these circumstances, private landowning might easily, and quickly, become the basis for a real local political authority that might rival that of kings. Already for the 570s and 580s Gregory of Tours could describe the brutal exercise of local private authority by lay aristocrats such as Rauching, and the feuding and private settlement engaged in by Tours nobles such as Sichar and Chramnesind.[8] In the next century, immunities from the activities of public officials, including judges, on ecclesiastical estates begin to appear as part of our earliest surviving charter material in Francia; such immunities, it has been often argued, are the original form of the local judicial power, based directly on landholding, that is so characteristic of the eleventh- and twelfth-century *seigneurie* in the world Bloch described. It has been further argued that public power was increasingly restricted to the level of rhetoric; only the military aggregation of the first three Carolingians, from Charles Martel to Charlemagne (714–814), reversed the trend, and even then only temporarily. In the end, the early medieval state would fail, utterly: it would be swallowed up in the steadily growing importance of private, local, landed power.

Much of this is a true picture, particularly of Francia. But it is incomplete; on its own it gives a false image of how power itself was constructed. Above all, it undervalues the continuing political force of wide-ranging public authority throughout the early middle ages:[9] until the late eleventh century in East Francia (slowly becoming what we call Germany); until after 1100 in northern Spain; until 1066 in England (and, in a different way, afterwards as well). Indeed, in Byzantium and at the level of the city state in northern Italy it never went away; and in the Celtic lands it was

---

[8] Gregory of Tours, *Decem Libri Historiarum*, V. 3 and IX. 9 (Rauching); VII. 47 and IX. 19 (Sichar and Chramnesind). The latter feud has had many surveys, notably J. M. Wallace-Hadrill, *The Long-Haired Kings*, pp. 121–47; E. A. James, '*Beati pacifici*: bishops and the law in sixth-century Gaul', in J. Bossy (ed.), *Disputes and Settlements*. For more on local mediations, see any of the articles in our own *The Settlement of Disputes*.

[9] See the survey by P. Fouracre, 'Cultural conformity and social conservatism in early medieval Europe', *History Workshop Journal*, 33 (1992); and P. Bonnassie's classic analysis (focussed on its breakdown), in *From Slavery to Feudalism in South-Western Europe*, pp. 104–31.

actually increasing. All the articles in this book in fact deal with societies where public authority had a real political presence, and are indeed devoted to explaining how it interfaced with local landed power. In this context, some remarks about how the ruler's power did indeed remain relevant as an independent political force and as a source of legitimacy need to be made.

The basis of this continuing public relevance was, as already said, landed wealth. The Merovingians and Carolingians, and the Visigothic and Lombard kings, all possessed immense landed resources, which did not necessarily decrease much across time. The kings of Italy were never generous with land until after 900; and, if the Frankish kings were, they seem to have been able to recoup their gifts through confiscation from the unfaithful until the later ninth century. Landed wealth did not bring in as much as taxation had done, but since the army was landed, there was less for rulers to spend it on; early medieval kings were at least rich by the standards of their time, with considerable reserves of treasure and other movables, and thus continued to be highly attractive as patrons. The king's court was a focus, then, in all the major continental kingdoms, throughout our period; tenth- and eleventh-century English kings gained a similar role (eleventh-century kings even taxed), and there are, as we shall see, signs in Wales of similar developments, at least on a local scale, after 950 or so. As a result, the power provided by office-holding remained of crucial importance; the prestige of royal courts meant that no-one could hope to achieve a widely recognized position through local dominance alone, however complete.[10] Even Rauching was a duke; indeed, at the end of his life he claimed Merovingian descent. Sichar was a royal *fidelis*, at least. The Merovingian court, despite its dangers (few major secular political figures died natural deaths in Gregory's time), remained a magnet for the high-stakes gamblers that Frankish aristocrats in all periods seem to have been. And, in Francia

---

[10] A counter-example is the local power of machtierns in ninth-century Brittany, which seems to have no central origin; but Brittany, with a central power brand new in that very century (and borrowed from the Franks, at that), can be regarded as an exception that proves the rule. See W. Davies, *Small Worlds*, pp. 163–87; J. M. H. Smith, *Province and Empire*, pp. 28–31. Leaders in many marginal and border areas had ambiguous legitimizations: but they all had some sort of claim to official authority. It is extremely difficult to identify any powerful political figures in the main early medieval kingdoms who were *only* private landowners.

and Lombard Italy for sure,[11] and elsewhere very probably, what local wealth provided was the right to try for this patronage – just as in the Roman Empire. Kings, despite their reputation, raised few from the dust.

This continued uninterrupted involvement in public power and office-holding in our period thus counterbalances the fact that kings and princes could only intervene locally with some difficulty: aristocracies *wanted* to keep links with public power. Indeed, the local dominance that lay aristocrats had was itself legitimized by office-holding, as dukes and counts and the like. This had one important result, which will recur in our material: that when kings wanted to grant protection to their other clients, churchmen, they granted them immunities from precisely this dominance of secular officials. Immunities were a sign of public strength, not public weakness. They had the disadvantage, from the ruler's point of view, of being irrevocable (at least, churchmen said they were, often vocally); but their appearance, as we shall see, tends to be a sign of the invasion of public authority, not its evasion. Here, as elsewhere, we need to understand the nature of early medieval political realities in their own terms, not those of other periods. The private justice of rural *seigneuries* or *signorie* in the eleventh century was indeed a sign of public weakness; but not all local judicial protections functioned in the same way. Local office-holding, the immunity and the *seigneurie* do, nonetheless, have one feature in common, the public legitimation of local landed power: a theme which permeates the whole book.

One further comment needs to be added in this context: the articles in this book are not all about Francia. This is not in itself surprising, but it does have one implication that is worth spelling out. General interpretations of the politics and society of the early and central medieval periods have long tended to be dominated by the history of Francia (and, when the latter split up in the late ninth century, by the history of France). This 'Francocentric' model, as we shall call it, has been influential partly because Francia was indeed the major polity in Western Europe under the Merovingians and Carolingians, and partly because of the prestige

[11] An admirable survey is G. Tabacco, 'La connessione tra potere e possesso nel regno franco e nel regno longobardo', *Settimane di studio*, 20 (1972).

and importance of at least three generations of historians writing in French. These are perfectly good reasons for its influence, in fact; but it is wrong to conclude from the dominance of the model that Frankish/French developments were 'normal', and that other areas were 'atypical' or 'peripheral'. In the period before 900, there were many different ways in which political and social structures developed in different parts of post-Roman Europe; those chosen by the Franks were simply associated with greater military success than some of the others. After 900, the Francocentric model is even more misleading, for it can easily be argued that the tenth- and eleventh-century collapse of public power in France, as immortalized by Georges Duby's book on the Mâconnais,[12] was itself atypical of developments in most of Western Europe: in Germany, England, Spain and even in parts of France itself. One can go too far in attacking this image of collapse, as is argued later in Chris Wickham's article; but it certainly cannot be generalized to the rest of the West. In this book, then, Francia is certainly a major focus of attention, but it is not the only one. We should like to replace the Francocentric model by a more complex picture, one which reflects more exactly the range of historical developments in the whole of Europe.

LAND LAW: WORDS AND THINGS

Two more specific questions need to be set out in an introductory way, before we move into our detailed research: the problem of land law; and the general history of the immunity. Why is land law a problem? Because it has hitherto been seen by too many historians simply as an issue of Roman survival into the early middle ages. This is not surprising, for continental Western European concepts of land tenure were indeed inherited, for the most part, directly from 'vulgar' Roman law.[13] But this does not mean

---

[12] G. Duby, *La société aux XIᵉ et XIIᵉ siècles dans la région mâconnaise*. The general interpretation of the post-Carolingian epoch as one of 'feudal anarchy' pre-dates Duby's book by decades, if not centuries; but his book provided a detailed account of the breakdown of public power in tenth- and eleventh-century Burgundy which seemed to revalidate the interpretation in modern and highly sophisticated terms. As indeed it did; but for Burgundy, not for everywhere else in Europe as well.

[13] For some exceptions, see C. J. Wickham, 'European forests in the early middle ages', *Settimane di studio*, 37 (1989), at pp. 481–99. England, Ireland (but not Wales) and Scandinavia were also not areas of Roman land law.

that we can apply a simple, legalist, interpretation of the rules of land tenure directly to the early middle ages; we have to be more careful.

Our knowledge of 'vulgar' law and its early medieval Western analogues essentially goes back to Ernst Levy's masterpiece of 1953.[14] He showed with crystal clarity both how fourth- and fifth-century vulgar law, the legal practice of the late Empire, differed both from the 'classical' period of the jurists and from the reworking of juristic materials in Justinian's *Digest*; and, furthermore, what its internal logic as a legal system was. He went on to show that the main elements of Romano-Germanic property law derived from vulgar, not classical, Roman law. In particular, the sharp theoretical distinctions between different kinds of rights in land that were a crucial feature of classical law had become blurred in vulgar law, and this blurring continued into the early middle ages. The jurists distinguished between *dominium* (or *proprietas*), the absolute right to landed property, *possessio*, the actual physical control over that property at any one time, and *ius in re aliena*, limited rights in another's property (this in practice included many forms of tenancy). Vulgar law increasingly saw all these as forms of *possessio*, which became an umbrella term covering all landholding. It is not that late Roman or early medieval lawyers did not know quite well that ultimate ownership, simple possession and tenancy were different; it is just that, unlike the classical jurists, they saw no need to apply conceptual precision to the differences:

Like plain people anywhere they found it difficult to think of possession unaccompanied by ownership or of ownership not embodied in possession. In the overwhelming majority of instances they saw possession and ownership coincide, and for more they did not care. If there was a sporadic case deviating from this standard, they felt confident that its particularities could be established in court.[15]

This common-sense attitude, a feature of very many societies, as Levy himself noted, was carried over without difficulty into

---

[14] E. Levy, *West Roman Vulgar Law. The Law of Property*.

[15] E. Levy, *West Roman Vulgar Law*, p. 62; see more generally pp. 61–7, 96–9. Even Levy, for all his concern for understanding the vulgar tradition in its own terms, could not avoid being moralistic about its ignorance; see, for example, *ibid.*, p. 71. For further discussion of late Roman law and its successors in the West, see most recently J. D. Harries and I. N. Wood (eds.), *The Theodosian Code*. The Byzantine Empire followed its own route, on the basis of the *Digest*.

the legislation of the Germanic kingdoms, and survived for a
long time: the seisin of twelfth-century England is not that
different.

Now, one could follow the implications of Levy's approach,
and try to establish an internal legal logic for each early medieval
system of land tenure, with a set of definitions for each of its
classic elements, *proprietas* (or, later, *alodium*), *precarium*, *beneficium*
(or, later, *feudum*), and all the different types of lease: definitions
that would not be as sharp as a classical jurist would have
made them, but would presumably have had force in courts.
This is by and large what people do who interest themselves in
early medieval land law. Sometimes they misread Levy, and
claim that early medieval people could not *distinguish* between
different forms of possession; this Levy certainly never thought,
and indeed no one who looked closely at the above-mentioned
primary elements of early medieval land tenure could seriously
believe it. But even when they do not, they do follow Levy in
looking for what one could think of as quasi-theory: for sets of
rules, even if unarticulated, that governed transactions and could
be drawn on, at least implicitly, in courts.

This is the point at which we differ from legal historians,
even those as subtle as Levy. Levy knew well that practice did
not necessarily follow theory, but he did not pursue the matter;
not all other legal historians have even recognized it. Our researches on court cases, however, reveal arrays of local procedures and practical assumptions that are a world away from
even the relatively common-sense distinctions of the authors of
the average Germanic law code. Such practical assumptions were
often normative: they could be drawn upon in argument, including public legal argument. We must never make the error of
supposing that, when people departed from written law, they
consciously deviated from publicly known normative restrictions.
We should also not conceive of these local procedures and
practical assumptions as simply an overriding law of essentially
the same kind except for being unwritten. It would be better to
see them as practical restrictions on human behaviour. The
penalty for going beyond them was nonetheless well known: it
was the loss of support from others, which would itself result
in failure, whether in court or elsewhere. What mattered was
the knowledge of acceptable local practice, including how far one

could go in manipulating it, as much, or more, than knowledge of
any more abstract set of rules, written or otherwise.[16]

The workings of these practical procedures pervade the articles
in this book. One particularly neat illustration of them can
serve, however, as an introductory example; it is taken from Ian
Wood's article on the *precaria* of the monastery of St Wandrille
in the eighth century. Wood describes how Abbot Teutsind gave
a *precarium* to Count Ratharius in 734 that was a textbook
example of what such a gift should be in vulgar and Romano-
Germanic law: a grant of usufruct of property in return for rent.
This grant was sharply criticized by members of the community
in later years, however. Why? Wood argues that, in other
seventh- and eighth-century Frankish texts, *precaria* had taken
on a new role: as one element in a network of gift-exchange
between secular donors and churches. *Precaria* from churches
were indeed very commonly, even by now normally, granted to
the original donors to the church of the property in question,
or else to near neighbours of the church and relatives of local
monks – people in the friendship network of the church, that
is. Teutsind's *precarium* was strictly legally valid, but it was not
to someone in that network, so it was immoral. Wood is cautious
about the detail of this interpretation, warning that it is circumstantial.[17] But, as an image of how early medieval societies
worked in practice, it functions very well. The monks of St
Wandrille were not interested in the legal theory of the *precarium*;
they were interested in social relationships. The same tenurial
form was right or wrong only in so far as it led, or did not
lead, to relationships that benefited the monastery. Indeed, an
'unjust' *precarium* was not only wrong; it could be argued, in
certain cases, to be invalid. The logical extension of this would,
in the end, become the rules surrounding *beneficia* and fiefs,
which were explicitly valid only in so far as they brought political

---

[16] See Davies and Fouracre, *The Settlement of Disputes, passim.* For the anthropological theory
behind it, see P. Bourdieu, *The Logic of Practice.* Since our book, there have been some
good applications of the same principles in works on central medieval France: S. D.
White, 'Feuding and peace-making in the Touraine around the year 1100', *Traditio*, 42
(1986); *idem*, 'Inheritances and legal arguments in western France, 1050–1100', *Traditio*,
43 (1987); P. Geary, 'Vivre en conflit dans une France sans état', *Annales E.S.C.*, 41
(1986); Koziol, *Begging Pardon and Favor*; D. Barthelémy, *La Société dans le comté de Vendôme
de l'an Mil au XIVe siècle*, pp. 652–706.

[17] See below, pp. 47–8.

loyalty; but, long before feudal law was formalized in these terms, the practical expectations of land grants of all kinds worked in a similar way.

This book, like its predecessor, will for these reasons not spend much time on legal rules. Some brisk, rough definitions will be found in the glossary; but, for the real meaning of social practices, readers will have to look at the specific contexts of the examples we set out. These contexts were more significant than legal theory, for all but the most diligently intellectual members of early medieval elites, and intellectuals were, as in many societies, in most cases pretty marginal to the patterns of events as they occurred on the ground.

IMMUNITIES

Immunities, which granted exemption from one or more of the operations of government and frequently by extension conferred the right to conduct these oneself, have often been seen as the capitulation of rulers in the face of 'over-mighty subjects', converting the *de facto* power inevitably associated with substantial property into fully legitimate power over localities. Immunities and related phenomena are touched on repeatedly in this volume, and are the main theme of several contributions. They will be discussed in detail later in the book; but they need preliminary introduction here too, to give them some conceptual and historiographical context.

Though the word *immunitas* or *emunitas* was used in late Roman government, the immunity was a phenomenon first seen in the Frankish kingdom;[18] there are no exact Visigothic, Lombard, Celtic or Anglo-Saxon analogues. The grant of *emunitas* by the ruler, who alone could grant it, meant freedom from taxation and/or the right to collect taxation from dependants. This was usually coupled with a prohibition of entry to the immune property against tax-collectors and other officials. By the mid-seventh century, however, when

---

[18] For its early history see the discussion by Paul Fouracre, below, pp. 56–60, which may be supplemented by A. C. Murray, 'Immunity, nobility and the edict of Paris', *Speculum*, 69 (1994). More general surveys with full bibliographies are provided by D. Willoweit, 'Immunität', in A. Erler and E. Kaufmann (eds.), *Handwörterbuch der Deutschen Rechtsgeschichte*, vol. 2, *Haustür–Lippe*, cols. 312–30, and C. Schmitt, H. Romer and Lj. Maksimović, 'Immunität', *Lexikon des Mittelalters*, vol. 4, *Erzkanzler-Hide*, cols. 390–3.

records of such grants begin to survive, they had taken on a wider meaning. The prohibition of entry was directed against officials who might enter the immunist's lands in order to hear lawsuits or to arrest accused or suspect persons. This does not necessarily mean that the immunist henceforth exercised judicial rights himself; it may be that he was responsible for bringing offenders before the courts and in return received the king's or count's share of fines. Even from the late ninth century onwards, by which time immunists certainly were providing their own courts, this financial aspect will have remained important, since such courts would have imposed mainly financial rather than corporal penalties.

The ninth and tenth centuries saw significant further developments. Carolingian grants of immunity became common rather than exceptional and began to cover more than the immunists' own lands; in East Francia and Italy in the tenth century, grants of immunity were often coupled with grants of full judicial and regalian rights (*districtus*, *bannus*), so that immunists came to look more and more like counts and to act more independently of the local count.[19] Yet it is important to note that the Frankish immunity was almost an ecclesiastical monopoly; grants to the laity are ill-attested and, where known of, small-scale.[20] Even the back-door approach through proprietary churches was closed. From Louis the Pious's reign (814–40) grants of immunity were no longer made to ecclesiastical bodies unless these had first been made over to the

[19] The formulation in the text above should not be taken as implying that all counties were contiguous closed territories, since in tenth-century Germany many were certainly not (as arguably already in ninth-century Germany); for the problems see T. Reuter, *Germany in the Early Middle Ages, c.800–1056*, pp. 92–3, 218–20; H. Hoffmann, 'Grafschaften in Bischofshand', *Deutsches Archiv für Erforschung des Mittelalters*, 46 (1990); and on 'banal immunity' see the references given by P. Fouracre, below, nn. 34–5.

[20] See the arguments adduced by Paul Fouracre, below, pp. 62–3. Most recently Murray, 'Immunity', at pp. 30–4, basing himself on Clothar II's *Edict*, cc. 13–15 (*MGH Capit.*, vol. 1, no. 9, pp. 22–3), has argued that late sixth-century Merovingians distributed immunities widely to powerful laymen as well as to ecclesiastics, as part of a law and order programme aimed at keeping down brigands and maintaining *pax et disciplina*. This interpretation cannot be discussed in detail here, but it should be said that Murray's reading does not receive much support from earlier Merovingian legislation, which appears to assume that law enforcement directed against brigandage will be carried out exclusively by public authorities. Even those living on ecclesiastical lands are not exempt from local courts, while provisions on the pursuit of *latrones*, especially across administrative boundaries, imply that this is normally the responsibility of 'state' officials (*agentes [publici], iudices*) and refer only once to the role of *potentes* in the suppression of brigandage. In any case, even if his early lay 'police' immunities did once exist, they have left no later traces.

ruler. If monastic proprietors wanted their foundations to enjoy immunity, they had to surrender proprietorship (though of course rulers themselves might later lose effective control of such royal monasteries, as of other royal rights).[21] Lay magnates nonetheless benefited from ecclesiastical immunities, even if in a rather different way. Ecclesiastical immunists, since they were clerics, were not supposed to operate their immunities themselves, in so far as this meant holding or appearing in courts; instead they were to have a lay advocate to do this for them. The advocate was thus well placed to cash in on much of the power implicit in the immunity.

The Frankish immunity of the seventh century with its later extensions has provided a paradigm for the development of the phenomenon outside Francia; but this has usually been framed simply in terms of the Francocentric model, with Francia seen as typical (or advanced), and other parts of Europe as atypical (or backward). Indeed, the concentration by historians on the formal aspects of the Frankish immunity – words used, kinds of grant – has often prevented the real structural parallels (and structural differences) between Frankish immunities and immunity-like phenomena elsewhere from being understood properly. Immunity conceived primarily as freedom from taxation is not all that different from Byzantine tax exemptions (see Rosemary Morris's article below), or from the beneficial hidations and sokes found in the late Old English kingdom (see Patrick Wormald's article below), or from the remissions of tribute obligations found in parts of the Celtic and Scandinavian periphery of Europe. Even immunity conceived primarily as the right to the profits of justice (rather than the right to carry out law enforcement and judicial work) appears to be found over a much wider area than that of the Frankish Empire.[22] All these patterns point as much to governmental power as to its avoidance.

---

[21] J. Semmler, 'Traditio und Königsschutz', *Zeitschrift der Savigny-Stiftung für Rechtsgeschichte. kanonistische Abteilung*, 45 (1959); I. Heidrich, 'Die Verbindung von Schutz und Immunität', *Zeitschrift der Savigny-Stiftung für Rechtsgeschichte. Germanistische Abteilung*, 90 (1973).

[22] Not discussed at length in this book, but also found over a much wider area than Francia are more strictly ecclesiastical institutions such as the exemption of monasteries etc. from episcopal power, the right of asylum, and the enhanced protection given to the areas immediately surrounding churches, e.g. the cathedral close or cemeteries, which is *inter alia* part of the right of sanctuary (see the comments by Wendy Davies below, pp. 140–7). These things are often mentioned in the same breath as immunity – for example in the handbook articles cited in n. 18 above. But they are only indirectly related to it and more comparative work needs to be done on them.

This raises a general point of crucial relevance for the rest of the book: that the importance of immunity for the relationship between public and private power is easily overestimated. The privatization of public jurisdiction from below, which plays such a large role in the Francocentric model of post-Carolingian constitutional history, was hardly ever the product of immunity. Exemption from the activities of the ruler's agents has primary meaning in a context where he *has* such agents – local officials actively engaged in taxing and/or judging on its behalf – as well as the ability to supervise and control their activities. Exemption means closeness to the centre, not distance from it. Only when local officials and supervision have vanished can an ancient grant of immunity take on the secondary function of legitimating a local authority no longer directly linked with the present ruler. This may perhaps have happened here and there in late Carolingian and early Capetian West Francia/France; but immunity did not contribute much to the general decline of public power even there, not least because immunists were ecclesiastics, as we have seen, whereas the privatizers of the Francocentric model were laymen whose power did not rest primarily on advocacies. It was in the East Frankish/German kingdom that the immunity/advocacy combination remained most important in the tenth and eleventh centuries, precisely because royal authority continued to exist there.[23]

The relationship between public authority and ecclesiastical immunity is, in fact, the most pervasive theme of this book. It recurs in the two Merovingian articles (Paul Fouracre, Ian Wood), and those on Wales (Wendy Davies), England (Patrick Wormald), Germany (Timothy Reuter) and Byzantium (Rosemary Morris). The other face of local power, the *seigneurie*, appears in Chris Wickham's article on its weakness in parts of communal Italy, which thus emphasizes public authority as well, in negative, as well as in Wendy Davies's on its development in Wales. Ian Wood's article focusses in addition on the political relationships between the laity and churches as represented by *precaria*; this third theme is taken further by David Ganz's article on the ideology of ecclesiastical

---

[23] For the weakness of advocacy as an institution in west Francia see F. Senn, *L'Institution des avoueries ecclésiastiques en France*. For territorialization and advocacies in east Francia, see T. Mayer, *Fürsten und Staat*, pp. 1–49, B. Arnold, *Princes and Territories in Medieval Germany*, pp. 71, 82–4, 167–8, and the discussion by Timothy Reuter, below, pp. 174–5.

landowning, and Timothy Reuter's on the politics of land donations in Ottonian-Salian Saxony. Fourth and finally, the *precarium* issue leads on to the problem of what determines power *over* land; this is developed in Janet Nelson's article on how much control female landowners had over their land. These themes do not exhaust the issues, obviously; but they are a start. We ourselves intend to develop them further in due course.

CHAPTER I

The ideology of sharing: apostolic community and ecclesiastical property in the early middle ages

David Ganz

The Acts of the Apostles record how the church at Jerusalem grew to 'a multitude of them that believed who were of one heart and of one soul; neither said any of them that aught of the things which he possessed was his own, but they had all things in common. Neither was there any among them that lacked: for as many as were possessors of lands or houses sold them and brought the prices of the things that were sold and laid them down at the Apostles' feet; and distribution was made unto every man according as he had need' (Acts 4: 32, 34). While ancient philosophers had discussed societies without private property, and Luke's vocabulary in this passage has been linked to Aristotle,[1] the Christian church claimed that at its origin it had actually instituted a new attitude to property: private ownership was replaced by a singlenesss of heart which required property to be shared. Luke goes on to tell how Barnabas sold his fields and laid the proceeds at the feet of the Apostles, while Ananias and Saphira kept their property in order to swindle the church and were put to death.

Despite the conversion of post-Roman rulers to Christianity, they and their subjects did not share their wealth with their chosen church following this apostolic model.[2] The first urban Christians

---

This paper owes much to discussions with Glen Olsen, who has been preparing a major study of the Primitive Church since his article 'The idea of the *Ecclesia Primitiva* in the writings of the twelfth-century canonists', *Traditio*, 25 (1969). It could not have been written without the use of the CETEDOC CD ROM.

[1] Aristotle, *Nichomachean Ethics*, 1168 b, cf. *Politics*, 1261–2, 1265, criticizing Plato, *Laws*, 740–4. Cicero, *De Republica*, I. 32, Seneca, *Epistolae*, letter 90, para 3. On Acts cf. E. Haenchen, *The Acts of the Apostles*. The Dead Sea Scrolls reveal that at Qumran goods were held in common. For a good introduction see the articles 'Gemeinschaft' and 'Gütergemeinschaft' by W. Popkes and M. Wacht respectively, in the *Reallexikon für Antike und Christentum*.

[2] For an anthropological account of reciprocity in society M. Sahlins, *Stone Age Economics*, pp. 210–17. For a historian's reactions, the excellent pages by Barbara Rosenwein in her *To be the Neighbor of St Peter: The Social Meaning of Cluny's Property, 909–1049*, pp. 116–38.

never maintained their ideal of common property.[3] To explain their changed priorities they developed a theory of property and of history, primarily through reading those patristic authors who had explored the role of wealth in Christian society and by adapting their teachings in their own ecclesiastical legislation and patristic exegesis. The study of these texts helps to explain how and why churches were endowed: the power of property was always open to justification. But the variations in the modes of that justification reveal changes in ideology, and remind us that ecclesiastical property exists within a scheme of ideology. Other essays in this volume treat practical aspects of church ownership of property, but the practice depended on different ways of locating the legacy of the ideal of the apostolic church and of common ownership in the frameworks of local traditions of ownership and of ecclesiology.[4]

In exploring the afterlife of the apostolic ideal in the Frankish realms we can trace stages in the search for origins and the creation of traditions. The theology of Augustine was to prove less influential in shaping these traditions than the writings of another African Late Antique grammarian, Julianus Pomerius.[5] The endowments of the church were held to sustain a community, and both Pope Gregory I and Bede used the ideals of Acts to define how that community should share its wealth. Chrodegang of Metz, in his Rule for Canons, linked the apostolic ideal with actual landholding practices, and his Rule was adopted as a norm in the Carolingian Empire. Beside their inherited traditions, the Carolingian authors of the collection known as the Le Mans forgeries and of the canonical collection of Pseudo-Isidore developed pseudo-historical records to justify their own visions of church property. This paper will focus on these diverse interpretations as stages in the growth of ideology.

Augustine recognized that a Christian society would keep two systems of property, human and divine. Emperors and kings inherited and administered an earthly system of property rights. 'By human law a man says "this is my villa, this is my house, this

---

[3] A. J. Malherbe, *Social Aspects of Early Christianity*; W. Meeks, *The First Urban Christians: The Social World of the Apostle Paul*.

[4] E. Troeltsch, *The Social Teaching of the Christian Churches*, pp. 58–65, 133–8, gives categories for the nature of religious equality in the early church. O. von Gierke, *Das Deutsche Genossenschaftsrecht*, vol. 3, pp. 113–29, remains essential.

[5] For a biography see R. Kaster, *Guardians of Language*, pp. 342–3.

is my slave." By human law, the law of emperors. Why, because
God has given these human laws to mankind through emperors
and kings of the world.'[6] And Christ, like earthly rulers, has His
own treasury with its rules of property.[7] Augustine is eloquent on
the nature of that treasury: to flee from the approaching ruin of
this world a rich man should give up his wealth to the celestial
treasury, for God is the only true possessor of all wealth.[8] And to
endow God, in this world, means to endow the church. In his *City
of God* Augustine tells Christians not to be conceited about their
sharing of property 'since they do this to attain to the fellowship
of the angels, while Roman worthies did much the same to preserve
the glory of their country'.[9]

'Cain, whose name means possession, is the founder of the
earthly city. This indicates that this city has its beginning and end
on this earth, where there is no hope of anything beyond what can
be seen in this world.'[10] The worldly empire is based on property.
The material territorialization of the church is in opposition to the
values of Augustinian Christianity.[11] In his monastic rule Augustine referred to Acts as the model for his injunction to his monks
to distribute food and clothing, not equally, but to each according
to his needs.[12] Augustine said in a sermon that Acts 4 'gives me
more delight than anything I could say to you myself'.[13]

The ideal of a communal society was traced by Augustine and
Jerome back to Pythagorean communities, but it was no longer fully
achieved in the urban church of the Christian Roman Empire.[14] In
his 'Conferences' John Cassian explained how the apostolic church

---

[6] Augustine, *Tractatus in Joh.*, no. 6, paras 25–6. For an excellent brief introduction to
Augustine's views, cf. M. Wilks,'*Thesaurus Ecclesiae*', in *The Church and Wealth, Studies in
Church History*, vol. 24.

[7] Augustine, *Enarrationes in Psalmos*, psalm 146, para 17.

[8] Augustine, 'Sermo' I (*Patrologia Latina*, vol. 38, col. 327) and *idem*, *Enarrationes in Psalmos*,
psalm 38, para 12, where God is not only *paterfamilias* but also *dominus*.

[9] Augustine, *De Civitate Dei*, V. 18.

[10] Augustine, *De Civitate Dei*, XV. 17.

[11] R. Koselleck, 'The historical-political semantics of asymmetric counterconcepts', in his
Futures Past, on the Semantics of Historical Time, pp. 159–97, is helpful on this and related
polarities in Augustine and lesser historians.

[12] Augustine, *Regula tertia*, p. 418. Possidius (*Vita Augustini*, ch. 5) implies that Augustine's
own community was modelled on the church at Jerusalem.

[13] L. Verheijen, 'Spiritualité et vie monastique chez St Augustin. L'utilisation monastique
des Actes des Apôtres 4, 31, 32–35 dans son oeuvre', in C. Kannengiesser (ed.), *Jean
Chrysostome et Augustin*, and his *Saint Augustine's Monasticism in the Light of Acts 4, 32–35*.

[14] Augustine, *Confessiones*, VI. 14, 24; Jerome, 'Adversus Rufinum', III. 39.

had lost its ideal perfection.[15] After the Council of Jerusalem the church was invaded by the tepid and the lukewarm, and those who remembered the pristine perfection of the church immediately after Pentecost left the city for the countryside, where in secret they kept the original observances of the church alive. They were called *monachi*, because they lived alone, and monastic communities, rather than solitary ascetics, preserved that original perfection.[16] One view of Christian history therefore saw the apostolic ideal as restricted to the monastic community.

When Augustine of Canterbury asked Gregory the Great how the offerings brought by the faithful converts to the altar were to be apportioned, Gregory urged him to 'institute that manner of life which our fathers followed in the earliest beginnings of the Church: none of them said that anything he possessed was his own, but they had all things in common. If, however, there are any who are clerics but in minor orders and who cannot be continent, they should marry and receive their stipends outside the community; for we know that it was written concerning those fathers whom we have mentioned that division was to be made to each according to his need.'[17] Augustine was dealing with a new community, but he was a monk, and Gregory's ideal was akin to Benedict's prescription for the monastic life where no one would own any possessions,[18] echoed by Cassiodorus and Isidore, who explicitly saw the saints in Jerusalem at the time of the Apostles as the model for monks.[19]

But in practice monks often wished to retain individual control of their own property even after it had been given to the monastery.[20] The highly influential Rule of the Master from early sixth-century Italy explained that monastic property belonged to everyone and no one, and prescribed that oblates had to give away their

---

[15] Cassian, *Institutiones*, II.5; cf. *Conlationes*, XII. ii.5, XVIII. v. 2–3. For a full account of the influence of the ideal of Acts, cf. P. Bori, *Chiesa primitiva. L'immagine della communita delli origini- Atti 2, 42–47; 4, 32–37 – nella storia della chiesa antica.*

[16] R. Markus, *The End of Ancient Christianity*, pp. 181–5. For the origins of monasticism the chapter 'Be ye perfect', pp. 63–83, is an eloquent synthesis which recognizes that sharing of property was only a small part of this ideal.

[17] Bede, *Historia Ecclesiastica Gentis Anglorum*, I. 27. That this was Gregory's own monastic ideal is shown by his *Epistolae*, XIV.14.

[18] Benedict, *Regula*, ch. 33, 6.

[19] Cassiodorus, *In Psalmos*, psalm 132; Isidore, *De Ecclesiasticis Officiis*, II. 16.

[20] M. P. Blecker, 'Roman law and consilium in the *Regula Magistri* and the *Regula Benedicti*', *Speculum*, 47 (1972).

property before probation, making an inventory and placing it on the altar.[21] All of the brethren were to be consulted concerning the disposition of the monastic endowment, so that a modern commentator has suggested that the Rule of the Master regards the monastic patrimony as a corporation.[22] Justinian legislated to ensure that the private property of those who entered monasteries was automatically passed on to the monastery, and this was echoed in the Rule of Ferreolus.[23]

The growth of monasticism, and its domination of forms of social memory, furthered the development of an ideology of the common community. In the mid-sixth century the Roman deacon Arator, in his verse paraphrase of Acts, had contrasted the generous man who gives away his possessions so as to gain them for eternity with the greedy man who holds tight to his wealth to lose it in the end. He explained that this is why the Christians placed their wealth at the feet, rather than the hands, of the Apostles, to show how all money ought to be forsaken.[24] In discussing Acts, Bede quoted Arator and stressed that community of property was an indication of how the love of God was shed abroad in mens' hearts.[25] But in his commentary on Acts 11: 29 he assumed that not all of the Christians at Jerusalem had abandoned private property.[26] In the *Retractatio* on Acts Bede was able to compare the Greek and the Old Latin texts of Acts, and when commenting on how 'everything was shared in common' he explained that *communia* corresponds to the cenobites, who live in common, not simply with all men, but with all things in common in the Lord.[27] It was not the shared life, but the shared investment in the celestial treasury, which was the apostolic model. Bede was not unaware of how difficult it might be to maintain such perfection. Seventh-century ecclesiastical

---

[21] *Regula Magistri*, ch. 2, derived from *Regula Basilii*, ch. 29.

[22] This doctrine is called a *regulae sententia*, which Blecker would translate 'a legal maxim'.

[23] Justinian, *Novellae*, V. 5 and CXXIII. 38.

[24] Arator, *De Actibus Apostolorum*, I, lines 383–416.

[25] M. W. Laistner, *Bedae Venerabilis Expositio Actuum Apostolorum et Retractatio*, p. 21.

[26] Laistner, *Bedae Venerabilis Expositio*, p. 53.

[27] Laistner, *Bedae Venerabilis Expositio*, pp. 113–14. My discussion of Bede is heavily indebted to G. Olsen, 'Bede as historian: the evidence from his observations on the life of the first Christian community at Jerusalem', *Journal of Ecclesiastical History*, 33 (1982). Bede also discusses Acts in his *Commentaries*: on Mark, Prologue and III. 10; on Luke, IV. 12; and on Luke V. 18. In Bede, *De Tabernaculo*, II, the community of the faithful is compared to the living stones in the house of God, placed in their orders and joined to one another in a bond of divine and mutual love.

legislation had attempted to enforce common property for monks at the Council of Leodegar of Autun,[28] and in the *Collectio Canonum Hibernensis*.[29] But alongside those who attained the ideal monastic life were cathedral clergy living together but not sharing property, and the private family monasteries described by Bede in his letter to Archbishop Egbert, and attacked by Boniface and Pippin III on the continent.

Bishop Chrodegang of Metz, faced in his own see with the same problems of ecclesiastical organization and ecclesiastical property as Boniface and Pippin were attacking, returned to the model of the primitive church in his Rule of Canons.[30] He sought to organize the officials of the cathedral into a communal life, and explained the theoretical basis for such a life, in contrast to the situation which prevailed in much of Francia. Chrodegang specified that in apostolic times each person had sold their estates (*praedia*) so that none of them dared to say that he had anything of his own.[31]

But because in our time it is not possible to be persuaded to do this, let us agree at least in this: we ought to draw our spirit in some small measure to their way of life. Because it is hardly devout to be tepid inert and remiss; and because every community should be in harmony for the sake of the name of God, we, who ought to live by our own particular rules should consent not merely a little to this perfection.

And if we are unable to abandon all things, let us hold our possessions for their use only, so that, whether we will or no, they will descend not to our heirs of the body and our relatives but to the church, which, with God as our witness, we serve in common. We have our support from these possessions, but let us leave them to this place by inheritance. So that, if the crown of salvation is not given to us along with those perfect

---

[28] 'Concilium Leodegarii', ch. 15, *Concilia Galliae A511–695*, ed. C. de Clercq, p. 320. *Collectio Canonum Hibernensis*, XXXIX, in *Die irische Kanonensammlung*, ed. H. Wasserschleben (a quotation from Isidore, *De Ecclesiasticis Officiis*).

[29] On the *Hibernensis* in the Carolingian realms, see R. E. Reynolds, 'Unity and diversity in Carolingian canon law collections: the case of the *Collectio Hibernensis* and its derivatives', in U. R. Blumenthal (ed.), *Carolingian Essays*.

[30] Chrodegang was *referendarius* to Charles Martel, and was bishop of Metz in about 747 and archbishop in 754. His rule is dated between his episcopate and his death in 766; cf. J. Semmler, 'Chrodegang Bischof von Metz. 747–766', in *Die Reichsabtei Lorsch: Festschrift zum Bedenken an die Stiftung der Reichsabtei Lorsch 764*, vol. 1.

[31] Chrodegang, 'Regula Canonicorum', ch. 31, ed. J.-B. Pelt, *Études sur la liturgie de Metz*, at pp. 24–5. My discussion of Chrodegang owes much to the papers on Chrodegang and the 'Regula Canonicorum' by M. Claussen and R. Gerberding given at Sewanee in 1992. Professor Claussen kindly allowed me to read his 1992 Virginia doctoral dissertation 'Community, tradition and reform in early Carolingian Francia: Chrodegang and the canons of Metz Cathedral'.

ones because of their perfect renunciation and contempt of the world, then at least forgiveness of sins and divine mercy may be conceded to us as to the least of humans. Thus St Prosper and the other holy fathers have established, according to divine law, that clerics who desire to live from ecclesiastical goods should confer their possessions by charter to God and to the church which they serve; and thus they will have license to use ecclesiastical goods without incurring grave fault.[32]

Chrodegang's text offers his own interpretation of the account in Acts. His vocabulary restricted the possessions sold by the apostolic church for the common good to property in land (*praedia*). He also recognized that the apostolic ideal was no longer applicable, and so accepted the *precarium*, the estate held from the ruler or the church for a life, but not heritable.[33] The canons of Metz were to endow the church so that they might receive an income from their land during their lifetime, and the income from such endowments might be used for almsgiving. The canons cannot diminish, sell or commute their *precaria*.[34] They are the possessors, the cathedral is the owner. After the death of the canon 'without the confirmation or *traditio* [record of transfer] of anyone, the property will revert whole and entire to the church to which it has been given, or to the congregation itself'.[35]

Describing how local families and the mayors of the Merovingian palace took over bishoprics while there was little defence against usurpations Walter Goffart explained that 'the lands applied to God's service were secularized partly because of clerical worldliness and partly too because the institutional framework of ecclesiastical government made no allowance for less than conscientious administrators'.[36] Chrodegang's Rule belongs in the context of the ecclesiastical reforms of Pippin, Carloman and Boniface, designed to improve the quality of such

---

[32] Chrodegang, 'Regula Canonicorum', ch. 31; cf. Claussen, 'Community, tradition and reform', pp. 158–61. The reference to Prosper is to the writings of Julianus Pomerius, as Claussen has shown. For a masterly analysis of Chrodegang's debt to Julianus, cf. Claussen, 'Community, tradition and reform', pp. 365–97.

[33] See Wood, below, pp. 43–9, for the *precarium*. The best treatment of the history of the *precaria* remains H. Voltelini, 'Prekarie und Benefizium', *Vierteljahresschrift für Social und Wirtschaftsgeschichte*, 16 (1922).

[34] Chrodegang, 'Regula Canonicorum', ch. 31.

[35] *Ibid*.

[36] W. Goffart, *The Le Mans Forgeries, A Chapter in the History of Church Property in the Ninth Century*, p. 8; E. Ewig, 'Milo et eiusmodi similes', in H. Büttner (ed.), *Sankt Bonifatius: Gedenkengabe zum 1200 Todestage*.

administrators, amongst other things.[37] *Precaria* have a part to
play in the Rule of Canons. Chrodegang had probably attended
the council of Verneuil, which allowed laymen to keep such
precaria once the church concerned had enough property to meet
its essential needs, if they paid an annual rent to the church to
which it had belonged. Recent studies of donations to Bavarian
churches suggest that the situation may have been more complicated; the donation was a means of recording noble possessions
which the owners retained as benefices and were sometimes able
to make hereditary possessions.[38] Donations for one's soul could
have the effect of benefiting an owner at the expense of his
heirs. How far this was true of grants in the Frankish heartlands,
like the *precaria* in the Polyptique of Irminon of St Germain or
the Wissembourg donations deserves to be explored.[39]

Chrodegang's vision of church property draws on the *De Vita
Contemplativa* of Julianus Pomerius, the fifth-century teacher of
Caesarius of Arles. He stated that 'It is expedient to hold the
goods of the church, while one's own goods should be despised
on account of love of perfection'.[40] Both Paulinus of Nola and
Hilary of Arles are praised for abandoning their own possessions
but, as bishops, augmenting the property of their churches.
Julianus urged clerics to leave their goods to relatives, to the
poor or to the church to be a poor man among the poor. Those
who lived a common life at the expense of the church do so to
reduce their own expenditure and avoid taking care of the poor.
Those unable to renounce their own goods should at least
renounce their inheritance. The cleric is only the *praepositus* and
the *dispensator* of the common goods of the church.[41] Poverty is
essential to possessing God. Chrodegang anchors Julianus's
defence of ecclesiastical possession of property, as long as it is
entrusted to a bishop, in a biblical and historical context, the
poverty described in Acts.

[37] W. Levison, *England and the Continent in the Eighth Century*, pp. 84–93.
[38] J. Jahn, 'Tradere ad Sanctum: Politische und gesellschaftliche Aspekte der Traditionspraxis im agilolfingischen Bayern', in F. Seibt (ed.), *Gesellschaftsgeschichte. Festschrift
für Karl Bosl zum 80. Geburtstag*, vol. 1. W. Hartung, 'Adel, Erbrecht, Schenkung: Die
strukturellen Ursachen der frühmittelalterlichen Besitzübertragungen an die Kirche', in
Seibt (ed.), *Gesellschaftsgeschichte*, vol. 1. See also Reuter and Nelson below, pp. 171, 108.
[39] See further Wood and Reuter, below, pp. 48, 185.
[40] *De Vita Contemplativa*, II. 9, *Patrologia Latina*, vol. 59, col. 452.
[41] *De Vita Contemplativa*, II, *Patrologia Latina*, vol. 59, cols. 453–4.

The reformers could not repossess the church, but they did provide for royal protection of monasteries.[42] This protection was intended to prevent heirs from revoking the pious donations of their parents. Royal authority was greater than the rights of those heirs, though on occasions the sovereign might restore lands to them.[43] Most ecclesiastical property was held in such *precaria*.

Under Charlemagne clerical and lay assemblies developed the doctrine that 'those who hold benefices from churches should give a ninth and a tenth from them to the church which owns the land. Those who hold such a benefice by *métayage* [share-cropping] should give tithes from their portion to their own priest'.[44] Louis the Pious allowed the commutation of ninths and tenths into a money rent.[45] His 816 legislation extended the practice of Chrodegang's Rule from Metz across the Empire, and buttressed it with substantial patristic authorities.[46] Charles the Bald attempted to enforce payment from property which had become alienated from the church and the councils of Langres and Savonières justified this. 'For, if tithes should be offered to God from one's own property, by a much more divine legal precept, after the oblation of giving back a fifth part over and above should rightly be offered to His ministers.'[47] The attempt to recover ecclesiastical estates went hand in hand with demands for ninths and tenths from those in possession. The ninths and tenths were paid to the bishop, but might support canons, as at a cell of St Riquier which supported twelve canons, or at the cathedral of St Vincent at Mâcon.[48] Tenure by the *precaria verbo regis* (*precaria* held at the command of the king)

[42] J. Semmler, 'Traditio und Königsschutz', *Zeitschrift der Savigny Stiftung für Rechtsgeschichte. Kanonistische Abteilung*, 45 (1959).

[43] K. Voigt, *Die karolingische Klosterpolitik und der Niedergang des westfrankischen Königtums*, pp. 21, 78.

[44] *MGH Capit.*, vol. 1, no. 81, p. 179, as translated by G. Constable, '*Nona et decima*, an aspect of Carolingian economy', *Speculum*, 35 (1960), at p. 234. Constable suggests that *nona et decima* may go back to Pepin.

[45] *MGH Capit.*, vol. 1, no. 150, p. 307.

[46] R. Schieffer, *Die Entstehung von Domkapiteln in Deutschland*, pp. 232–61. Schieffer gives a helpful account of the early history of cathedral canons in Gaul and Spain at pp. 100–6. For a survey cf. J. Semmler, 'Mönche und Kanoniker im Frankenreiche Pippins III. und Karls des Großen', in *Untersuchungen zu Kloster und Stift, Veröffentlichungen des Max-Planck-Instituts für Geschichte*, vol. 68.

[47] *MGH Conc.* vol. 3; Constable, '*Nona et decima*', p. 236.

[48] Hariulf, *Chronique de l'abbaye de St Riquier*, p. 96; *Recueil des Actes de Charles II le Chauve*, ed. G. Tessier, vol. 2, p. 22.

was regarded as temporary, until the land should be restored to the church. But some have maintained that such *precaria* were in effect permanent alienations for we cannot quantify how much of what had been alienated was restored.[49] Carolingian churches held landed estates, and ensured that if those estates were alienated, the holder was treated as a rent-paying tenant.

The apostolic ideal of common property was a part of the extensive reform legislation of Louis the Pious. In 817 Chrodegang's Rule was incorporated into the *Institutio canonicorum*, along with a large collection of supporting texts which were approved by a council held at Aachen and designed to be applied throughout the Carolingian Empire.[50] In 829 the Council of Paris described ecclesiastical property as 'the offerings of the faithful, the penitential payments of sinners and the patrimony of the poor'.[51] This definition goes back once again to Julianus Pomerius, whose writings had also been quoted by Boniface, Alcuin, Hrabanus and Halitgar of Cambrai, and at the 813 Council of Chalons (ch. 6), at Aachen in 816 (ch. 35), at Paris in 829 (cc. 10, 15 and 18).[52]

This stance was adopted in the reign of Louis the Pious to affirm the rights of the church to property which was no longer in its control. The most cogent statement of the problem of such rights is Maitland's: 'Law must define this vague idea, and it cannot find the whole essence of possession in visible facts. It is so now-a-days. We see a man in the street carrying an umbrella; we cannot at once tell whether or no he possesses it. Is he its owner, is he a thief, is he a borrower, a hirer, is he the owner's servant? . . .Before we attribute possession to a man, we must apparently know something about the intentions that he has in regard to the thing.'[53] At a time when possession had become the chief criterion for ownership, the clerics of Carolingian Francia attempted to overturn claims based on possession by the assertion of counterclaims based on ideology.

---

[49] H. Brunner, *Deutsche Rechtsgeschichte*, vol. 2, pp. 338–9.

[50] J. Semmler, 'Benedictus II, Una Regula–Una Consuetudo,' in W. Lourdaux and D. Verhelst (eds.), *Benedictine Culture 750–1050*, and his earlier studies cited there. (It was later to be a central text for the tenth-century reformers in England, and was translated into Anglo-Saxon.)

[51] *MGH Conc.*, vol. 2, p. 623, echoing Ansegisis I, ch. 77 (*MGH Capit.*, vol. 1, p. 405).

[52] J. Devisse, 'L'influence de Julien Pomère sur les clercs carolingiens', *Revue d'Histoire de l'Église de France*, 61 (1970). The text was also quoted in the 819 capitulary, *MGH Capit.*, vol. 1, pp. 275ff, by Jonas of Orléans, *Patrologia Latina*, vol. 106, cols. 277–8, by Agobard of Lyons, *MGH Ep.*, vol. 5, p. 174, and elsewhere.

[53] F. Pollock and F. W. Maitland, *History of English Law*, vol. 2, pp. 34–5.

In December 828 Wala, the abbot of Corbie, urged that Louis 'let Christ have the property of the church, as though it were another *respublica*, entrusted to His faithful followers for the needs of the poor and of those serving Him. The monarch was to entrust Christ's *respublica* to faithful and wise administrators'. The *schedula* which transmitted Wala's ideas may have been prepared for discussion at the 829 Council of Paris, which was concerned with the problem of safeguarding ecclesiastical benefices, and ensuring that they were used for the clergy, church buildings, the poor and the needs of bishops and abbots. Wala's vocabulary recurs at the Council of Meaux-Paris in 845.[54]

The reform legislation of 816–29 achieved the synthesis of patristic discussions of shared property, set in the context of establishing an exemplary Christian society in all of its orders. Within half a century Carolingian clerics had supplied a revision of that discussion, again in a far more extensive context. The ideals of shared property were incorporated into a new vision of the origins, status and history of church property. The authors of the Pseudo-Isidorian complex of forgeries defended the sacred destination of church property and the illegitimacy of all *precariae* except those voluntarily granted by bishops.[55] Benedictus Levita composed a capitulary ordaining that anyone who had held ecclesiastical property by royal grant needed to procure the property from the bishop or the provost of the church to which it belonged if he wanted to continue to hold it.[56] The king was no longer able to grant church property. Benedict also affirmed that all ecclesiastical landholders must repair their church and pay ninths and tenths, and this capitulary was quoted with approval by Hincmar.[57] In the ecclesiastical decretals of Pseudo-Isidore these claims are set into a vision of history.

In the letters ascribed to Pope Clement it is suggested that the papacy had followed the practice of the apostolic church in securing a life lived in common with shared property. This is regarded

---

[54] *Epitaphium Arsenii*, II. 2, ed. E. Dümmler, pp. 62–3. L. Weinrich, *Wala, Graf Mönch und Rebell: Die Biographie eines Karolingers*; D. Ganz, 'The *Epitaphium Arsenii* and opposition to Louis the Pious', in P. Godman and R. Collins (eds.), *Charlemagne's Heir. New Perspectives on the Reign of Louis the Pious*, esp. pp. 545–6.

[55] E. Lesne, *Histoire de la propriété ecclésiastique en France*, vol. 2, pp. 237–43.

[56] *MGH Leges in Folio*, vol. 2, pt 2, p. 119.

[57] *MGH Cap. Spuria*, in *MGH Capit.*, vol. 1, no. 13, p. 47; cf. H. Fuhrmann, *Einfluss und Verbreitung der pseudoisidorischen Fälschungen*, vol. 1, p. 166.

as normative for all Christians, and for Pseudo-Isidore the common life is that of a clerical, not a monastic community.

In a decree ascribed to Pope Urban I entitled 'On the Common Life and the Obligations of the Faithful', the author asserted that this common life was practised by all good Christians until his own day (AD 222–30). From selling their property and laying the proceeds at the feet of the Apostles, as described in Acts, Christians had progressed to handing over the property itself to bishops, who could use the income to support those living the common life 'because, from their present and future revenues more and better things could be supplied to the faithful leading the common life than from their price; they began to give to the mother-churches the properties and fields, which they used to sell and live from their revenues'. Bishops were the successors of the Apostles, and they owned the possessions of the churches, 'and so are up to now and should always be in the future'.[58] The offerings of the faithful may only be used to support those living the common life, or for relief of the poor. To do otherwise is sacrilege, and risks the fate of Ananias and Saphira. Church lands within the bishopric, for Pseudo-Isidore, are all under the control of the bishop.

The work also includes a letter on the Primitive Church and the Synod of Nicaea, attributed in later collections to Pope Militiades, explaining how at the beginning of the birth of the church everyone sold their possessions and the proceeds were shared according to need. The Apostles foresaw the growth of the church among the nations and so accepted little landed property in Judea. After the conversion of Constantine people throughout the Roman Empire were allowed to become Christian, build churches and donate property to them. Constantine himself gave great donations. From that day men have consecrated themselves and their possessions to God, and rulers have allowed this and themselves given gifts, it says. The monks pray for all mankind, and for monks to be free from secular concerns the church must be richly endowed.[59]

Archbishop Hincmar of Rheims quoted Pseudo-Urban in his

---

[58] *Decretales Pseudo-Isidorianae et Capitula Angilramni*, ed. P. Hinschius, pp. 143–6 (= *Patrologia Latina*, vol. 130, cols. 137–8). *MGH Conc.*, vol. 2, pp. 622 and 765 are the explanations of this change given by the councils of Paris (829) and Aachen (836). For a brief summary of Pseudo-Isidorian teaching on the despoliation of the church, cf. Lesne, *Histoire de la propriété ecclésiastique*, vol. 2, pp. 238–43.

[59] *Patrologia Latina*, vol. 130, cols. 243–4.

legislation of 857 and at the 860 Council of Douzy.[60] Donations to the church are made for the salvation of the soul of the donor, he said.[61] They are not to be used to assist clerics to look after their pigs or goats by paying a herdsman.[62] But Hincmar was equally concerned that the parish priest should have a guaranteed and fixed income.[63] As Devisse observes, he used the collection of capitularies made by Ansegisis as the source for his own diocesan legislation.[64] Devisse also noted the legacy of the Hispana, a systematic collection of Spanish canon law. Hispanic councils had tackled questions of public and private control of church property. The second Council of Braga (572) had decreed that at the death of a bishop, lists of his personal and ecclesiastical property were to be established so that the ecclesiastical property would not be alienated, nor the bishop's heirs lose their own inheritances. In 655 the ninth Council of Toledo extended this ruling to clerics. At Merida in 666 it was decreed that offerings were to be divided into three parts, one for the bishop, one for the priests and deacons, one for the subdeacons and everyone else. Along with Pseudo-Isidore, Hincmar drew on an accepted tradition of received canon law to secure the lands of his see as the support for his parishioners and clerics.[65]

In the Le Mans *Life of St Julian*, who had been a follower of St Peter and was sent to Gaul by Pope Clement, the author, purportedly 'a certain Roman named Sergius', explains how the landowners of Maine had made over their property to the new bishopric and lived in apostolic poverty.[66] This Life is one of the 'Le Mans forgeries', texts affirming that the cathedral of Le Mans had title to all land in Maine. To sustain this argument the forger affirmed that monastic foundations in the diocese were assigned lands by the bishops, but these lands were never alienated from the cathedral.[67] 'Diocesan monasteries were a part of the cathedral temporal.' And

[60] *Patrologia Latina*, vol. 126, cols. 122ff.

[61] *MGH Ep.*, vol. 8, p. 150.

[62] Hincmar's diocesan instructions of 877, *Patrologia Latina*, vol. 125, cols. 779–80.

[63] Hincmar, *Collectio De Ecclesiis et Capellis*, ed. M. Stratmann, p. 94.

[64] J. Devisse, *Hincmar, Archévêque de Reims 845–882*, vol. 1, p. 509.

[65] Roger Collins tells me that specific references to Acts 4 do not occur in Visigothic conciliar legislation.

[66] 'Vita Juliani', in *Actus pontificum Cenomannis in urbe degentium*, ed. G. Busson and A. Ledru, *Archives historiques du Maine*, vol. 2, p. 21, with the discussion in W. Goffart, *Le Mans Forgeries*, pp. 50–61, 195–6.

[67] Goffart, *Le Mans Forgeries*, pp. 227–31.

the founders of monasteries held their estates as *precariae* from the cathedral. The claim was most directly made to the estates of the monastery of St Calais, and in 863 Charles the Bald and Pope Nicholas I rejected these claims and affirmed the rights of the monastery.[68]

Both the Le Mans forgers and the creators of the Pseudo-Isidoran forgeries were concerned to incorporate grandiose claims for bishops in the history of how the ideal of apostolic sharing had been transformed into a system of church property which their contemporaries could recognize. For Pseudo-Isidore, the apostolic common life was the inspiration for the common life of canons in his own day; for the Le Mans forgers the apostolic common life had ensured that the bishop of Le Mans was the lord of all of the lands of Maine. Their concern is a testimony to the power and the importance of the ideological underpinnings of doctrines of property and the power it entailed. Monks, clergy and bishops all sought their share in the legacy of the apostolic common life. The ideal legitimized their practices, even though the effectiveness of such practices depended on a conception of sharing based on the revenues from a system of landholding which was far removed from the ideal of the church at Jerusalem. As Augustine had seen, 'it is much more wonderful not to cling to those things which you possess, than not to possess them at all'.[69]

---

[68] *Annales de S. Bertin*, ed. F. Grat, J. Vieillard, S. Clemencet, *s.a.* 863; for Pope Nicholas, *MGH Ep.*, vol. 6, pp. 624–9, 680–3.
[69] Augustine, 'De Moribus Ecclesiae Catholicae', *Patrologia Latina*, vol. 32, col. 1329.

CHAPTER 2

Teutsind, Witlaic and the history of Merovingian precaria

Ian Wood

The history of the transfer of power from the Merovingians to the Carolingians has been seen in part as a history of the transfer of land. The Merovingians supposedly alienated much of their property, including such favoured villas as Clichy,[1] while the Pippinid ancestors of the Carolingians built a landed power-base from which to expand their authority over the whole of Francia. This power-base was increased dramatically by Charles Martel's seizure of land, largely from the church, and its alienation, whether in grants of property or in *precaria*, that is effectively of usufruct,[2] to his followers.[3]

As a broad sketch of the issues this reconstruction has much to commend it, but it does demand so many caveats that it can only mislead all but the best informed. To begin with the question of the Merovingian alienation of land; certainly this took place. What is not known is the extent to which the losses were counterbalanced by gains. Kings alienated land to secure support, but they also received land from those without heirs and by means of confiscation.[4] Charters, which provide the majority of our evidence on

---

[1] J. M. Wallace-Hadrill, *The Long-Haired Kings*, p. 247.
[2] Du Cange, *Glossarium mediae et infimae Latinitatis*, ed. G. A. L. Henschel, vol. 5, p. 422. On the elision of *precaria* and *ususfructus* in vulgar law, E. Levy, *West Roman Vulgar Law. The Law of Property*, p. 162. On the relation between *precaria*, *beneficium* and *donatio* in vulgar law, E. Levy, *Weströmisches Vulgarrecht: Das Obligationenrecht*, p. 241. For a fuller discussion of the meaning of the term, see below, pp. 43-7.
[3] R. McKitterick, *The Frankish Kingdoms under the Carolingians 751-987*, p. 32. The collection *Karl Martell in seiner Zeit*, ed. J. Jarnut, U. Nonn and M. Richter, which contains a number of contributions bearing on problems discussed here (T. Reuter and H. Wolfram on Charles Martel's land grants, H.-W. Goetz and A. Dierkens on Charles's relations with churches, W. Joch on the Pippinids and the status of Alpaida) appeared after this essay had been completed.
[4] Wallace-Hadrill, *The Long-Haired Kings*, p. 237; I. N. Wood, *The Merovingian Kingdoms 450-751*, pp. 204-5.

royal wealth, only talk about alienation; rarely, if ever, about acquisition. As for the supposed status of the land alienated, who is to say whether a villa like Clichy, favoured by one king, was liked by his descendants?[5]

The Pippinid acquisition of land is less questionable. Yet the precise mechanisms by which the Pippinids acquired their land suggest that something much more complex was at stake than the steady creation of a power-base by one lineage. One problem lies precisely in the notion of a single descent group. The Pippinid family is far too complex for such a reduction. For a start the Pippinid family, as it came to be remembered, is a construct of its Carolingian descendants. Thus there is nothing before the days of Paul the Deacon to suggest that Arnulf was the father of Ansegisel.[6] We do not know with any degree of certainty who Pippin II's paternal grandfather was. Second, although the appellation Pippinid suggests a clear patrilineal descent group, the line of the family did not run directly through any single line, male or female. It passed from Pippin I to his son Grimoald, but with Grimoald the male line ended, and instead the line continued to Pippin's grandson and namesake through a daughter, Begga.[7] After Pippin II it passed not to the descendants of Plectrude, but to those of Alpaida, who may have been Pippin's concubine, or may have been his bigamous wife,[8] but was certainly not his prime companion.

When considered in non-patrilineal terms the Pippinid dynasty becomes very interesting indeed. On the whole one would have to say that Pippinid men married well, because the women seem to have had access to immense estates.[9] In the case of Pippin I this can be hypothesized from what information we have relating to his widow Itta, her daughter Gertrude and their foundation of Nivelles.[10] In the case of Pippin II it can be seen in Echternach, the foundation of Plectrude's mother, Irmina.[11] And there is enough to suggest that Alpaida's family was well established on the lower

[5] Wallace-Hadrill, *The Long-Haired Kings*, pp. 206–7, 241.

[6] Paul, *Gesta episcoporum Mettensium*, ed. G. H. Pertz, *MGH SS*, vol. 2, pp. 264–5.

[7] The evidence for Begga's marriage to Ansegisel is also late: *Annales Mettenses Priores*, ed. B. von Simson, *MGH SRG*, vol. 10, *s.a.* 688, pp. 2–3.

[8] R. A. Gerberding, *The Rise of the Carolingians and the Liber Historiae Francorum*, pp. 117–18.

[9] Gerberding, *The Rise of the Carolingians*, pp. 94–5, 124–5.

[10] Gerberding, *The Rise of the Carolingians*, p. 99.

[11] M. Werner, *Adelsfamilien im Umkreis der frühen Karolinger. Die Verwandschaft Irminas von Oeren und Adelas von Pfalzel*, pp. 35–175.

Meuse.[12] In the case of Irmina, we can see from her will that not only did she belong to a major landed family, but also that she herself was able to dispose of considerable quantities of land.[13] To judge by other wills of the Merovingian period, two of which are also the wills of women, while one is jointly that of an abbot and his mother, Irmina was not unusual.[14] Nor is this concentration on the female side of the family a modern, anachronistic, construct. Pippin II's son Drogo married Adaltrude, the daughter of the Neustrian *maior* Waratto. Their son Hugh, one of the most powerful ecclesiastics of the early eighth century, was regarded, at least at St Wandrille where he was abbot, as the descendant not of Pippin, but of Waratto's widow Ansfled.[15] Considered from the viewpoint of gender the rise of the Pippinids cannot be seen in patrilineal terms, and apparently it was not in the early eighth century.

Marriage seems to dominate the early history of Pippinid landed power. This changes in the days of Charles Martel, with the seizure of church land, and the distribution of benefices, *beneficia* and *precaria*. Again, however, there is a danger of painting too crude a picture of events. First, it is important to recognize how long it took Charles to establish dominance over the Merovingian kingdom. Second, as is well known, it is necessary to note the problems raised by the sources when it comes to considering Charles's seizure of land.

After his victory over Ragamfred and Chilperic II at Amblève in 716 Charles was clearly a force to be reckoned with. The following year he could push the conflict beyond the *Silva Carbonnaria* to Vinchy, where he again defeated his Neustrian opponents. Vinchy allowed him to deal with his stepmother, Plectrude, before moving against a combined Neustrian and Aquitanian force two years later. Chilperic was handed over to him, and it must have seemed as if there was little hope for his opponents thereafter.[16] What is extraordinary, however, is the length of time which passed before Charles interfered fully in the Orléannais and Burgundy, not to

---

[12] Gerberding, *The Rise of the Carolingians*, pp. 117–21.

[13] J. M. Pardessus, *Diplomata, Chartae, Epistolae, Leges ad res Gallo-Francicas spectantia*, no. 449.

[14] Wood, *The Merovingian Kingdoms 450–751*, pp. 206–7.

[15] *Gesta sanctorum patrum Fontanellensis coenobii* (hereafter *GAF*), ed. F. Lohier and R. P. J. Laporte, IV. 1.

[16] *Liber Historiae Francorum*, cc. 52–3, ed. B. Krusch, *MGH SRM*, vol. 2; Fredegar, *Continuationes*, cc. 9–10, ed. B. Krusch, *MGH SRM*, vol. 2; Gerberding, *The Rise of the Carolingians*, pp. 130–45.

mention Aquitaine and Provence.[17] In part he was hamstrung by problems east of the Rhine, though in the end it was the greater dangers affecting Aquitaine from the Muslims in the south-east which gave him his chance. It appears to have been in the aftermath of the victory over Abd ar-Rahman that Charles, under pressure from his supporters, decided to move against Bishop Eucherius of Orléans.[18] Further east Charles still had to bide his time. Ainmar, bishop of Auxerre, who may like Eucherius have been a relative of the noted pluralist Savaric, was not disposed of until after 737.[19]

Turning to the evidence for Charles Martel's supposed seizure of land, this is, for the most part, late. It belongs to the Carolingian period proper, when the reputation and rumoured damnation of Charles was certainly being used as stick to beat Louis the Pious and more particularly Charles the Bald.[20] The Fredegar continuator, however, writing in the mid-eighth century, already talks of general confiscations in the Lyonnais in 733.[21] Further, the will of Abbo of Novalesa also reveals that Charles confiscated land from a number of 'rebels', including Riculf who had fallen in with the Saracens, treasonably (ad infidelitatem).[22] In addition, the eighth-century Vita Eucherii talks of the possibility of a redistribution of offices (honores) in the diocese of Orléans as being an incentive for those who urged Charles to exile Eucherius and his relatives.[23] In view of the parallels between Eucherius and Ainmar it is likely that the later Gesta episcoporum Autissiodorensium is right to talk of substantial secularization of church estates at some time during the dominance of Charles and Pippin III: the estates of the church of Auxerre are said to have been reduced to one hundred mansi in

---

[17] Wood, The Merovingian Kingdoms 450–751, pp. 273–87.

[18] Vita Eucherii, cc. 7–9, ed. W. Levison, MGH SRM, vol. 7.

[19] Gesta episcoporum Autissiodorensium, ch. 27, ed. G. Waitz, MGH SS, vol. 13.

[20] Visio Eucherii: see the Council of Quierzy (858), cap. 7, ed. W. Hartmann, in Die Konzilien der karolingischen Teilreiche 843–859, MGH Conc., vol. 3; U. Nonn, 'Das Bild Karl Martells in den lateinischen Quellen vornehmlich des 8. und 9. Jahrhunderts', Frühmittelalterliche Studien, 4 (1970), at pp. 106–14; W. Hartmann, Die Synoden der Karolingerzeit im Frankenreich und in Italien, p. 207; J. L. Nelson, Charles the Bald, p. 61; I. N. Wood, 'Saint-Wandrille and its hagiography', in I. N. Wood and G. A. Loud (eds.), Church and Chronicle in the Middle Ages, pp. 9, 10.

[21] Fredegar, Continuationes, ch. 14.

[22] Abbo, Testamentum, ch. 56, in P. J. Geary, Aristocracy in Provence. The Rhône Basin at the Dawn of the Carolingian Age, pp. 74–7; see also pp. 129–30.

[23] Vita Eucherii, cc. 7, 9: 'cum omni propinquitate eius', 'cum reliquis propinquis'.

the time of Bishop Aidulf.[24] One other possibly early piece of evidence for Charles's seizure of church property comes in one version of Boniface's letter to Æthelbald, where it is said that 'Charles, *princeps* of the Franks, overthrower of many monasteries and transformer of ecclesiastical wealth to his own use, was overtaken in extended pain and a fearful death.'[25]

The problem with the evidence for the appropriation of church land in the time of Charles Martel is not whether it happened, but what its scale was, and the extent to which Charles, as opposed to his followers, was himself responsible. Nor is the precise chronology entirely clear. We have general statements for the Orléannais and the Lyonnais, and a more specific statement for Auxerre, which may relate to the rule of Pippin III rather than to that of Charles. That the question of the control of land was as live an issue in the days of his sons as in those of Charles himself can also be seen in the canons of the Council of Estinnes (743) where ecclesiastical land granted out as *precaria* is clearly a bone of contention.[26] The problem of distinguishing between developments under Pippin and his father is also present in the one instance where the evidence, albeit ninth-century, is infinitely more detailed: in the account of the abbacies of Teutsind and Witlaic in the *Gesta abbatum Fontanellensium*. Here what is at issue is not the confiscation or seizure of land as such, but simply its grant as *precaria* to laymen. Despite the date of the text, and despite the fact that the monks of St Wandrille did criticize Charles the Bald for his exploitation of monastic lands,[27] there is no reason to think that the *Gesta* misrepresents eighth-century attitudes towards *precaria*. The text drew very heavily on the archives of the abbey, in particular on its charters,[28] and in the crucial passages relating to *precaria* it appears to be summarizing earlier documents. It is worth quoting one passage *in extenso*.

Teutsind, the father of the monastery of St Martin of the church of Tours, was elected as abbot in 734 [*recte* 735/6], in the second indiction, which

---

[24] *Gesta episcoporum Autissiodorensium*, ch. 32; J. M. Wallace-Hadrill, *The Frankish Church*, p. 135.

[25] Boniface, ep. 73, ed. M. Tangl, *MGH Epp. Sel.*, vol. 1, p. 153, n.; Nonn, 'Das Bild Karl Martells in den lateinischen Quellen', pp. 83–9.

[26] Council of Estinnes (743), cap. 2, ed. A. Werminghoff, *MGH Conc.*, vol. 2.

[27] Wood, 'Saint-Wandrille and its hagiography', p. 10.

[28] Wood, 'Saint-Wandrille and its hagiography', p. 9.

was the fifteenth year of the aforesaid King Theuderic [IV]. What sort of lover of God and the saints Teutsind was, what sort of supporter and defender of the Churches, is shown by the works he did in this monastery, and by the gains and losses of monastic property in his day. In the days not of his rule but of his tyranny, this most noble house was ignobly reduced . . . In the days of the aforesaid fathers there were always three hundred monks living here. Under his rule, or rather not his rule but his tyranny, soon all the most noble properties were removed, and this once glorious monastery fell into the greatest poverty. For he took almost a third of its property, and transferred it to the possession of his relatives and king's men. These properties remain out of the possession of this monastery even to this day, as is clear to all those reading the privileges and charters which are held in the writing office of the monastery. It would take an excessive amount of time to relate every case.

But to consider one out of many, I have decided to describe in full the *precarium* which he gave to a certain *comes* Ratharius, so that the removal of those properties from this abbey may be remembered eternally. He gave to this same *comes* Ratharius Osmoy and Varenne,[29] two fiscal properties which are in the *pagus* (rural district) of Béthune, on the rivers Béthune and Arques, together with their appurtenances, that is Cressy, Sideville (?), Magnerotum and the other Magnerotum, as well as Toscaria, and the land on the coast, and the salt-pans and fisheries which were established there; also the vineyards in Giverny, on the River Seine, in the *pagus* of the Vexin, which Abbot Lantbert of holy memory begged from the glorious king Childeric [II], with the backing of his queen Bilichild, and other illustrious men named here: Leodegar, noble bishop and finally martyr, Nivo [Nivard] and Ermonius, Fulcoald, Amalric, Wulfoald, the *maior* of the royal house, Bavo, Waning, Adalbert, Gaerinus, as it is agreed has been written fully in the *gesta* of the aforesaid noble father Lantbert. Similarly with other *patrimonia* in the same *pagi*, that is Sénarpont, Marques, Hodeng-au-Bosc, Bailleul with their appurtenances. Also that half of Envermeu which is Geso, Moriacum, Brachy, which are on the River Saâne, Balançon[30] in the *pagus* of Vimeu, which came from Ambremar and Bertoald, and Boucly, Ruboridum, Rebets, Gamaches,[31] Belleville-en-Caux on the Saâne, Victriacum on the hill, on the river Dun, Ancourt,[32] Gammapiolum, Rumquarias, Muriacum, which is called Chuignolles in the *pagus* of Vimeu, Bouthencourt-sur-l'Yères. That is twenty-eight villas, apart from some of their appurtenances, from two

---

[29] Identification in *GAF*, ed. Lohier and Laporte, p. 48, n. 113; St Saens in F. Lot, *Études critiques sur l'abbaye de Saint-Wandrille*, p. xvi, n. 2.

[30] Identification in *GAF*, ed. Lohier and Laporte, p. 50, n. 119; Beauchamps in Lot, *Études critiques sur l'abbaye de Saint-Wandrille*, p. xvii, n. 4.

[31] Identification in Lot, *Études critiques sur l'abbaye de Saint-Wandrille*, p. 18.

[32] Lot, *Études critiques sur l'abbaye de Saint-Wandrille*, p. 18 reads 'Sitam in monte Aioncurte' as a single place.

pagi, that is Béthune and Vimeu. These *patrimonia* the same *comes* Ratharius received from the aforesaid Teutsind in precarial right, for which he
paid a levy of sixty *solidi* every year at the feast of our father Wandregisel
for the lights of the church. This *precarium* was granted in this monastery
in the year 734 from the incarnation of Our Lord Jesus Christ, on the
fifth of May, that is on Wednesday, which was the twentieth year of the
lordship (*principatus*) of Charles. The levy which the *comes* in question
promised to pay was offered every year to the fathers of the monastery,
without any backsliding up to the days of Abbot Witlaic, from Osmoy
and from Varenne, where the body of St Ricbert lies.[33]

Like a number of other abbots of St Wandrille from this period
Teutsind and Witlaic receive an extremely bad press from the
Gesta.[34] Teutsind's rule is 'tyranny'. We are later told that the Rule
of St Benedict was undermined by Witlaic.[35] To a large extent
the reputation of Teutsind and Witlaic with the community of St
Wandrille is likely to have been determined by their treatment of
the monastery's landed property. Without exception the abbots
favoured by the *Gesta* increased, restored, organized or secured the
protection of the estates of the monastery.[36] Teutsind and Witlaic
did neither. Nevertheless there are good things to be said about
both abbots. Under Teutsind the *praepositus* of St Wandrille was
Ermharius, to whom the author of the *Gesta* attributed the building
of the church of St Michael. Ermharius was also 'a supporter and
lover of the rule and of chaste religion', such that even 'the aforesaid Teutsind [who was also abbot of St Martin's at Tours] was
accustomed to say to the monks of the church of Tours, "Unless
you correct your life and behaviour I will bring my prior Ermharius
from St Wandrille to teach your plough to cut truly" '.[37] As for
Witlaic, despite the disasters of his abbatiate, which included,
apart from his misuse of the monastery's lands, a fire which
destroyed the church of St Peter, he was a benefactor to St Wandrille, and even the *Gesta* lists his gifts. Among them were gospel
covers, a chalice and other liturgical vessels, silk cloths, vestments

---

[33] *GAF*, VI. 1–2.
[34] Wood, 'Saint-Wandrille and its hagiography', p. 11.
[35] *GAF*, XI. 2.
[36] Wandregisel, *GAF*, I. 7; Bainus, *GAF*, II. 1–3; Benignus, *GAF*, III. 4–6; Hugh, *GAF*,
IV. 2; Lando, *GAF*, V. 2; Wando, *GAF*, IX. 2; Austrulf, *GAF*, X. 4; Gervold, *GAF*, XII.
2; Ansegisus, *GAF*, XIII. 8. Compare also *Vita Lantberti abbatis Fontanellensis*, ch. 3, ed.
W. Levison, *MGH SRM*, vol. 5; *Vita Ansberti episcopi Rotomagensis*, ch. 18, ed. W. Levison,
MGH SRM, vol. 5.
[37] *GAF*, VI. 5–6.

and books.[38] The list would be impressive, whether or not it related to a man who had supposedly despoiled the church. That it did little to improve Witlaic's standing in the eyes of his community is an indication of the key role of land in the relationship between an abbot and his monks.

It is therefore worth asking more precise questions about the depredations of Teutsind and Witlaic. Under the two of them there were supposedly great alienations, and the church was almost reduced to beggary. Fortunately, however, the *Gesta* not only makes these allegations, but it also provides a précis of the inventory of the monastery drawn up, as required by the canons on the demise of a bishop,[39] on Witlaic's death.

This is the sum of the possessions of this monastery, which was drawn up on the command of the most unconquered king Charles, by abbot Landeric of Jumièges, and *comes* Richard, in the twentieth year of his reign [787], on the death of the aforesaid father. First, relating to those estates which are seen to belong to the stipends of the brothers, for their own use, 1,313 complete *mansi* are listed, 238 divided *mansi*, 18 *manoperarii* (estates under cultivation by dependants),[40] which together make 1,569, with 158 *absi* (uncultivated estates)[41] and 39 mills. Let out as *beneficia* are 2,120 complete *mansi*, 40 parts, and 235 *manoperarii*, which together come to 2,395, with 156 *absi*. They have 28 mills. The sum of the totality of possessions including whole, half and dependent *mansi* is 4,264 [*recte* 3,964], leaving aside those villas which Witlaic gave to the king's men, or conceded to others in usufruct, which he should not have done at all.[42]

This inventory is remarkable for a number of reasons. First, it shows the massive scale of the estates of St Wandrille. This is something which can also be approached through the numerous references to landed property contained in the hagiography of St Wandrille,[43] and from the few surviving charters.[44] Ferdinand Lot calculated that the abbey held land throughout Neustria, as well as

[38] *GAF*, XI. 2.
[39] Council of Orléans (533), in *Concilia Galliae A511–695*, ed. C. de Clercq, cap. 5.
[40] J. F. Niermeyer, *Mediae Latinitatis Lexicon Minus s.v. manuoperarius*, 'holding worked by spading'.
[41] Niermeyer, *Mediae Latinitatis Lexicon Minus s.v. absus*, 'indicates the state of a tenancy (a farm or a field) not being held by a tenant and therefore usually lying waste'.
[42] *GAF*, XI. 3.
[43] Lot, *Études critiques sur l'abbaye de Saint-Wandrille*, pp. 3–20.
[44] Lot, *Études critiques sur l'abbaye de Saint-Wandrille*, pp. 23–8.

the Angoumois, Saintonge, Provence and Burgundy.[45] Its holdings were clearly enormous, though they are eclipsed by what we know of the property of one bishop of Le Mans, Bertram, most of which was given to his episcopal church at his death.[46]

The holdings of the monastery at the time of Witlaic's death do not suggest that St Wandrille had been reduced to beggary. Certainly, of the 3,964 *mansi* owned by the monastery only 1,313 were still held by the monks for their own use, while 2,395 were held as benefices. What is interesting is that no complaint is made about these benefices. The complaint is about 'those *villae* which Witlaic gave to the king's men, or conceded to others in usufruct'.[47] For these no detail is given, except with regard to those estates granted to Ratharius as *precaria* by Teutsind, for which rent ceased to be paid in Witlaic's day. The same vagueness hits the author when considering the disasters inflicted by Teutsind: apparently one-third of the abbey's estates were alienated, but only 'one out of many' is considered.[48] It would not be unreasonable to conclude that the grant to Ratharius was exceptional.

It is worth exploring the grant to Ratharius in a little more detail. To all intents and purposes the *Gesta* provides a précis of the original charter of donation.[49] The land came originally from the royal fisc, and the grant was made by Childeric II on the advice of his queen Bilichild. The signatories effectively provide a who's who of Childeric's court: the king's chief adviser, Leodegar, bishop of Autun, his brother, *comes* Gaerinus, Nivard, bishop of Rheims, and two of the leading palace officials, the *maior*, Wulfoald, and the *comes*, Waning. Ermonius, Fulcoald and Amalric are less well known, but can be traced in other charters of the period. This was a gift made in the presence of a significant selection of the court.

Nor is the *Gesta* the only text to précis this charter. The *Vita Landiberti abbatis Fontanellensis et episcopi Lugdunensis*, another text of the early ninth century, also describes it in full, adding that the grant was made in the palace of Arlaunum (in the forest of

[45] Lot, *Études critiques sur l'abbaye de Saint-Wandrille*, pp. xii–xxix.

[46] M. Weidemann, *Das Testament des Bischofs Berthramn von Le Mans vom 27. März 616: Untersuchungen zu Besitz und Geschichte einer fränkischen Familie im 6. und 7. Jahrhundert*; Wood, *The Merovingian Kingdoms 450–751*, pp. 207–10.

[47] *GAF*, XI. 3, compare VI. 1.

[48] *GAF*, VI. 1.

[49] *GAF*, VI. 2.

Brotonne) 'in the eleventh year of the aforesaid king in Austrasia, which was his first in Neustria' [673].[50] It was, therefore, a grant which had a very specific political context. Childeric II had just been established in Neustria, in opposition to Ebroin's appointee, Theuderic III; Theuderic had been sent to St Denis, Ebroin to Luxeuil.[51] Childeric, who had hitherto ruled in Austrasia, was apparently seeking, in the first year of his Neustrian reign, to estab- lish a West Frankish power-base, doubtless in opposition to that of Ebroin, which seems to have centred on Soissons.[52] It is, there- fore, little wonder that the charter was signed by the greatest men in the kingdom, and was supported by the queen, who seems to have been a figure of considerable importance in Childeric's reign, perhaps not least because she too was a member of the royal family by birth.[53] The grant was, moreover, a substantial one. Even this, however, does not seem to explain the importance of the estate to the authors of the *Gesta* and the *Vita Landiberti*. Ratharius's *precaria* seem to have had an almost symbolic meaning for the monks of St Wandrille. To understand this it may be helpful to return to the protagonists involved in the precarial grant.

Of Ratharius unfortunately nothing is known beyond what is contained in the *Gesta*. It is only hypothesis that his comital office was based in the Rouen region.[54] Direct information on abbots Teutsind and Witlaic is equally confined to the *Gesta*, but here the narrative is full enough to allow some further exploration. Before becoming abbot of St Wandrille Teutsind was already abbot of St Martin's at Tours,[55] an office that he retained after becoming abbot of St Wandrille, since he was able to place Witlaic over the alms list (*matricula*) of St Martin,[56] and since, as we have seen, he threat- ened the monks of Tours with the austerities of Ermharius.[57] In all probability he was elected to the monastery of St Wandrille soon after his appointment at Tours, since he was appointed to St

[50] *Vita Landiberti*, ch. 3.
[51] Wood, *The Merovingian Kingdoms 450–751*, p. 227.
[52] P. Fouracre, 'Merovingians, mayors of the palace and the notion of a "low-born" Ebroin', *Bulletin of the Institute of Historical Research*, 57 (1984), p. 14.
[53] Wood, *The Merovingian Kingdoms 450–751*, pp. 223, 227, 229, 352.
[54] H. Ebling, *Prosopographie der Amtsträger des Merowingerreiches von Chlothar II (613) bis Karl Martel (741)*, p. 206, offers no justification for the assertion.
[55] *GAF*, VI. 1.
[56] *GAF*, VI. 1.
[57] *GAF*, VI. 6.

Wandrille in 734 or 735, while his predecessor at Tours, Audeland, is said to have taken office in 733.[58] The chronology of Teutsind's preferment, therefore, seems very closely linked to the date of the battle of 'Poitiers', which is now known to have taken place at least a year after its traditional date of 732, at a site rather closer to Tours than to Poitiers.[59] That Teutsind's preferment at Tours and at St Wandrille should be seen in the context of Charles's victory over Abd ar-Rahman may also be implied by the fact that the *Gesta* conclude their account of Teutsind's predecessor at St Wandrille, Lando, with an account of the battle of 'Poitiers', drawn from the *Annales Mettenses Priores*.[60]

One might guess that Teutsind was imposed on St Wandrille. This is nowhere stated, but the Pippinids had for some while shown an interest in the monastery. There is no reason to believe the later Carolingian assertion that Wandregisil, the monastery's founder, was related to Pippin II.[61] Nor should one make too much of the fact that Lando's predecessor, Hugh, was Pippin II's grandson and Charles Martel's nephew. As we have seen Hugh seems to have regarded himself as the grandson of Ansfled, and he certainly took an independent line in all his ecclesiastical dealings.[62] Nevertheless Lando himself had obtained a privilege of immunity from Charles, placing the monastery under the protection of the *princeps*.[63] From the time of Lando, at least, St Wandrille was a Pippinid house, though that does not mean that the monastery accepted the treatment it received from the Carolingians.[64] To judge by the tone of the *Gesta* the monks were only too pleased when Abbot Wido, a relative of Charles, was executed.[65] They also obtained the deposition of Abbot Raginfrid, and the reappointment of Wando, who

---

[58] *GAF*, ed. Lohier and Laporte, p. 46, n. 110.

[59] 'Chronicle of 754', cc. 79, 80, in *Crónica mozárabe de 754: edición crítica y traducción*, ed. E. López Pereira; also trans. K. B. Wolf, *Conquerors and Chroniclers of Early Medieval Spain*; R. J. Collins, *The Arab Conquest of Spain*, pp. 90–1; Wood, *The Merovingian Kingdoms 450–751*, p. 283.

[60] *GAF*, V. 3; *Annales Mettenses Priores*, s.a. 732.

[61] *Vita II Wandregisili, Acta Sanctorum*, July 5, I. 1; *GAF*, I. 2; E. Vacandard, 'Saint Wandrille, était-il apparenté aux rois mérovingiens et carolingiens?', *Revue des questions historiques*, 67 (1900); reviewed in *Analecta Bollandiana*, 19 (1900), p. 235; Wood, 'Saint-Wandrille and its hagiography', p. 10.

[62] *GAF*, IV. 1: Wood, 'Saint-Wandrille and its hagiography', p. 11.

[63] *GAF*, V. 2.

[64] Wood, 'Saint-Wandrille and its hagiography', pp. 10–12.

[65] *GAF*, VII. 1.

had originally been deposed by Charles Martel in *c.*719 as a supporter of the Neustrian *maior* Ragamfred.[66]

Teutsind, then, may well have been a Pippinid appointee. Moreover, it is likely that his career at Tours and St Wandrille was in some way related to Charles's political position at the time of his victory over Abd ar-Rahman. Teutsind can, therefore, be placed very neatly within the traditional picture of Charles Martel's policy towards the church, and indeed his preferment adds some interesting parallels to what the *Vita Eucherii* reveals of Charles's activities in the Loire valley at the time of the defeat of Abd ar-Rahman, for it was only then that Eucherius was deposed from the see of Orléans.[67]

It is, however, Witlaic who may allow us to penetrate further into the complexities of this period. Again it is necessary to return to the *Gesta*.

Witlaic was from the *pagus* of the Hiémois, his father was called Irminus and his mother Witbolda. He was the treasurer (*camerarius*) of the sometime abbot Teutsind, under whose care he was brought up. He controlled the *matricula* of the blessed Martin of Tours, which was given to him by Teutsind as a *beneficium*, and controlled it for somewhile after Teutsind's death. When therefore Austrulf, the abbot of the monastery of Fontanella died, immediately Witlaic decided to go to the palace, carrying numerous gifts of gold and silver with him, and having given them to King Pippin and his hangers-on, he was set up as abbot, as he had hoped, in the second year after Pippin himself had taken the peak of royalty, that is in the year of the incarnation of Our Lord 754, in the sixth indiction.[68]

Witlaic does not look like a simple Pippinid appointee. He came from the Hiémois, a region in which St Wandrille had numerous estates.[69] Unlike Teutsind he seems to have been associated with the monastery from his childhood. He would also have a nephew, Witbold, who hoped to obtain the abbacy.[70] His own acquisition of office, however, points towards the simoniac practices of the early Merovingian period. It would not be difficult to compare him

---

[66] *GAF*, VIII. 1.

[67] *Vita Eucherii*, cc. 7–9.

[68] *GAF*, XI. 1.

[69] *GAF*, III. 5: 'Condatum . . . in pago Osismo, villam quae vocatur Monticellos . . . in pago Osismense'; III. 6: 'Monticellos villam . . . sitam in pago Oximense'; IV. 2: 'villa Dogmaniaco, quae sita est in pago Osismensi.'

[70] *GAF*, XII. 1.

with contenders for episcopal office in the age of Gregory of Tours.[71]
What provides the possibility of an alternative approach to the
precaria of St Wandrille here is not the connection between Witlaic
and the Pippinids, but his position at Tours, where he was in
charge of the *matricula*. The *matricula* of Tours in the mid-eighth
century may be known from one other group of documents, a collection of formulas,[72] for it was to this period that Zeumer dated the
Formulae Turonenses.[73] Indeed there is another possible link between
Teutsind, Witlaic and the *Formulae Turonenses*. Teutsind was abbot
of St Martin: the abbey of St Martin is cited in one of the formulas
for a *donatio* contained in the collection.[74] Zeumer's dating of the
Formulae Turonenses on legal grounds and the chronology of the
careers of Teutsind and Witlaic raise the possibility that one or
other of them may have been involved in the compilation. With
this possibility in mind it is worth turning to the Tours formula
for *precaria*.

To venerable lord 'a', rector of church 'b', and the whole congregation
present there, I 'c'. In response to my request your will granted, and you
ordered that your villa sited in *pagus* 'd', in *condita* 'e', in the place called
'f' be transferred to me, together with all goods pertaining or belonging
to it, under the terms of usufruct. And this you have carried out, on these
terms, that I should not be allowed to sell or give or in any way remove
anything from there, but I am to hold and keep it without prejudice to
you, so that your grant may continue. For this I have agreed to pay 'g'
amount of silver to you every year at the festival of saint 'h', and after
my death the aforesaid estate, whole and entire, with whatever is known
to pertain or belong there, with all its buildings, and whatever has been
left behind at my death, you and the agents of church 'b' are to recall
into their power and possession without any further grant or legal documentation or action by my heirs. And if either I or any of my heirs, or
anyone whosoever, presumes to oppose, challenge or show contempt to
this *precaria*, may he not succeed in what he seeks, may a charge be made
against him, and may he pay 100 *solidi* in compensation. And may this
precaria in no way offer any wrong to you, for the space of however many
years the property is held by me, but may it remain fixed, being renewed

---

[71] Gregory of Tours, *Decem Libri Historiarum*, IV. 35, ed. B. Krusch and W. Levison, *MGH SRM*, vol. 1, pt. 1; Gregory of Tours, *Liber Vitae Patrum*, VI. 3, ed. B. Krusch, *MGH SRM*, vol. 1, pt. 2.

[72] *Formulae Turonenses*, no. 11, in *Formulae Merowingici et Karolini Aevi*, ed. K. Zeumer, *MGH LL in quarto*, sectio 5.

[73] *Formulae Merowingici et Karolini Aevi*, p. 131.

[74] *Formulae Turonenses*, no. 1 (b).

every five years, with this requirement attached, may it remain inviolate for all time.[75]

This formula for a precarial grant may seem unexceptional. It is certainly similar to the grant made to Ratharius, as described in the *Gesta abbatum Fontanellensium*.[76] In fact it differs markedly from other Frankish precarial formulas of the late seventh and eighth centuries. Marculf, for instance, has four formulas relating to *precaria*. One relates to arrangements between a father and his sons.[77] The three others, however, are rather more interesting. Two of them relate to agreements whereby the recipient of the precarial estate promises not only to return that estate, but also to give another to his episcopal benefactor on his death.[78] The remaining, and for our purposes the most important, formula concerns precarial tenure on estates which the beneficiary had previously granted to the bishop.[79] All the Marculf formulas, therefore, conceive of *precaria* within a complex of exchanges, in which the grant of precarial land was only one element in a series of gifts and countergifts. Such extended arrangements must have brought together a church, its benefactors and also the descendants of its benefactors, in obviously continuing relationships.[80]

Two other formularies contain formulas relating to *precaria*. Zeumer dated the formulary of Bourges to the period after 764/5 on the grounds of a dating clause in one of the documents.[81] Its precarial formula again takes a family interest for granted, since it concerns the renewal of a grant made to the beneficiary's father, although it does not reveal whether or not the latter had originally granted the estate to the church.[82] The *Cartae Senonenses*, dated by Zeumer to 768/ 75,[83] contain three precarial documents. All three again relate to estates which had in the first instance been given to the church by the beneficiary.[84] There looks, therefore, to be a presumption in

---

[75] *Formulae Turonenses*, no. 7.
[76] *GAF*, VI. 2.
[77] *Marculfi Formularum Libri Duo*, II. 9, in *Formulae Merowingici et Karolini Aevi*, ed. K. Zeumer.
[78] *Marculfi Form.*, II. 39, 40.
[79] *Marculfi Form.*, II. 5.
[80] Compare B. H. Rosenwein, *To Be the Neighbor of St Peter: The Social Meaning of Cluny's Property, 909–1049*.
[81] *Formulae Bituricenses*, no. 6, in *Formulae Merowingici et Karolini Aevi*, ed. Zeumer; for the date see *ibid.*, p. 166.
[82] *Formulae Bituricenses*, no. 2.
[83] *Formulae Merowingici et Karolini Aevi*, ed. Zeumer, p. 182.
[84] *Cartae Senonicae*, nos. 16, 17, 33, in *Formulae Merowingici et Karolini Aevi*, ed. Zeumer.

Neustrian documents that *precaria* were granted to persons who already had an association with the estate in question, or, at the very least, that the estate was part of a set of exchanges involving the beneficiary's own land. The Tours formula stands in contrast to these. Nowhere in this text is there any implication that a precarial grant was part of a complex of relationships.

Given the distinction between the formula from Tours and those from Bourges and Sens, as well as Marculf's compilation, it is necessary to look briefly at the earlier history of *precaria*.[85] The term *precarium* is defined by the emperor Justinian in his *Digest* of previous legal tradition:

A *precarium* is what is conceded in use to a petitioner in response to prayers for however long, while the grantor agrees. This type of liberality comes *ex iure gentium*,[86] and differs from a *donatio* where who gives, gives in such a way that he does not receive it back: who gives a *precarium* gives in such a way that he will receive it back, when he wishes to take the *precarium* back to himself.[87]

The *Digest* was scarcely known in the early medieval West; moreover Justinian's legislation on *precaria* has been seen as the final gasp of an earlier Roman tradition.[88] Nevertheless Isidore also offers a definition, and although it differs in emphasis, the two definitions are reconcilable:

A *precarium* is when a creditor, having been petitioned with prayer, allows a debtor to take *fructus* from the *possessio* of a *fundus* ceded to him.[89]

In short, for Isidore a *precarium* is a grant of usufruct made in response to the prayer, *preces*, of the beneficiary.[90] Etymologically, of course, the prayer explained the term, and it is worth noting that Justinian also refers to *precibus*. For Isidore, as for Justinian, however, precarial tenure was essentially a temporary right to

---

[85] The history of *precaria* before Justinian is covered by Levy, *Weströmisches Vulgarrecht: Das Obligationenrecht*, esp. at pp. 258–67. Unfortunately Levy did not consider much post-Justinianic Western material, with the exception of Leovigild and Isidore.

[86] i.e. 'natural reason'; cf. C. T. Lewis and C. Short, *A Latin Dictionary*, citing Gaius, *Institutes*, I. 1: 'quod naturalis ratio inter omnes homines constituit, id apud omnes populos peraeque custoditur, vocaturque jus gentium'.

[87] Justinian, *Digest*, XLIII. xxvi. 1, ed. T. Mommsen and P. Krueger, *Corpus Iuris Civilis*, vol. 1; Compare also Justinian, *Novellae*, VII. 120, ed. R. Schöll and W. Kroll, *Corpus Iuris Civilis*, vol. 3.

[88] Levy, *West Roman Vulgar Law*, p. 265: 'The *precarium* . . . was a dying institution'.

[89] Isidore, *Etymologiae*, V. 25, ed. W. M. Lindsay. For Levy's comments on this passage, *Weströmisches Vulgarrecht: Das Obligationenrecht*, p. 164.

[90] Compare Du Cange, *Glossarium mediae et infimae Latinitatis*, vol. 5, p. 422.

usufruct.[91] The Tours formula and the grant to Ratharius would probably not have seemed odd to sixth-century lawyers.

That *precaria* were common enough in Visigothic Spain is apparent not only from Isidore, but also from the laws, where, as in the *Digest*, the temporary nature of a precarial grant is stressed.[92] They are also mentioned in the canons of the sixth and of the seventeenth councils of Toledo.[93] The former is chiefly concerned to ensure the preservation of estates.

In Francia there is also clear evidence for the use of *precaria* from the sixth century onwards. Venantius Fortunatus received precarial estates from Gregory of Tours.[94] Palladius of Auxerre wrote to Desiderius of Cahors about a *praecaturia* held by Chromatia.[95] Another woman, Dunda, is to be found holding the usufruct of an estate by *precaturia* in the will of Bertram of Le Mans.[96] The first unquestionably authentic Merovingian charter to mention *precaria*, a *placitum* of Chlothar III dating to 658, is unfortunately fragmentary.[97] It too involves a woman, this time the wife of Ermelen who opposed her husband's supposed grant of *villae* to St Denis, but was overruled when the *precaria* which she had written was trumped by that in which her husband had granted the estate to Chagliberct. Here, as elsewhere, the term *precaria* clearly refers to the document, rather than the grant or the estate in question.

Although the Visigothic documentation, like the *Digest* of Justinian, implies that a precarial grant was not dependent on close family or social ties, the sixth- and seventh-century Merovingian documentation does suggest that such ties were common factors in Frankish *precaria*. Family connections seem to underlie Chromatia's holding in Cahors, since her brother Deotherius, is explicitly named in Palladius's letter.[98] Family connections are also at stake

---

[91] On the confusion between *precarium* and usufruct, especially in the evidence of the *Lex Romana Burgundionum*, see Levy, *West Roman Vulgar Law*, pp. 162, 198.

[92] *Leges Visigothorum*, X. i. 22, ed. K. Zeumer, *MGH LL in quarto*, sectio 1, vol. 1; see also II. i. 8. Visigothic evidence is discussed by Levy, *West Roman Vulgar Law*, p. 91; Levy, *Weströmisches Vulgarrecht: Das Obligationenrecht*, pp. 164, 264–7.

[93] Council of Toledo VI (638), cap. 5; Council of Toledo XVII, in *Concilios Visigoticos e Hispano-Romanos*, ed. J. Vives et al.

[94] Venantius Fortunatus, carm. VIII. 21, 22, ed. F. Leo, *MGH AA*, vol. 4, pt. 1.

[95] Desiderius, ep. II. 18, ed. W. Arndt, *MGH Epistolae in quarto*, vol. 3.

[96] Weidemann, *Das Testament des Bischofs Berthramn von Le Mans vom 27. März 616*, p. 36, Verfügung 49.

[97] *Diplomata regum Francorum e stirpe Merowingica*, no. 34, ed. K. Pertz.

[98] Desiderius, ep. II. 18.

in the *placitum* involving the wife of Ermelen.[99] Neither, however, is as explicit as the long and splendid document in which Longegisilus grants estates to Hadoind of Le Mans, but retains the usufruct during his lifetime.[100] Unfortunately this document is a forgery. Two Murbach documents, however, may suggest a precarial arrangement closer to that envisaged in the *Formulae Turonenses*, in other words one which was not based on any family connection. In 735 Hildrad was granted the usufruct of an estate given to the monastery by Eberhard, and in return he had to pay an annual rent of 5lb of wax for lights.[101] The following year Hildefrid received a similar grant, this time of two estates which had been given to Murbach by Eberhard, in return for 10lb of wax.[102] There is nothing to indicate that Hildrad and Hildefrid were related to Eberhard, although there might have been some connection.

Taken all together the evidence for *precaria* suggests that already by the early seventh century a wide variety of transactions were included in the term. What was constant was the temporary nature of the grant, which was essentially that of usufruct, dependent entirely on the will of the grantor.[103] The family relationships specified by Marculf and in the Bourges and Sens Formularies – and probably drawn from genuine charters – are likely to represent secondary, albeit early, developments, within the history of *precaria*. They represent the impact of local sensibilities on legal requirements.

Returning to the case of the St Wandrille grant to Ratharius, it is highly unlikely that the *comes* was related to the original donors of the chief estate in question, since the land was fiscal, and had been granted by Childeric II and Bilichild. The fact that the estate had once been part of the royal fisc might, however, have made it an appropriate grant for a *comes*. More likely neither Teutsind nor Witlaic was concerned with any possible traditional proprieties in granting the usufruct of an estate. Certainly, if either of them had been responsible for the Tours formula, or had been aware of it (which is almost certain), then their attitudes towards the concession of an estate in precarial tenure would not have taken the niceties of relationships between the monastery of St Wandrille

[99] *Diplomata*, no. 34, ed. Pertz.
[100] *Diplomata*, no. 238, ed. Pardessus.
[101] *Diplomata*, no. 607, ed. Pardessus.
[102] *Diplomata*, no. 608, ed. Pardessus.
[103] Du Cange, *Glossarium mediae et infimae Latinitatis*, vol. 5, p. 422.

and its beneficiaries into account. It may be that this is at the
heart of the hostility of the author of the eighth-century sections
of the *Gesta* towards Teutsind and Witlaic. As is clear from the
inventory taken at Witlaic's death benefices in general were perfectly acceptable;[104] it was only grants to relatives of Teutsind and
to military followers (*regii homines*) of Charles Martel which were
denounced.[105] It may be significant that there is no mention of
Witlaic's relatives: this need not suggest that he made no such
grants, since it should be remembered that Witlaic and his family
came from a region closely associated with St Wandrille,[106] whereas
Teutsind almost certainly did not. For Witlaic to have granted
estates to his relatives would have been to keep them within the
family of the saint, so to speak.

Taken in the context of Marculf and the Bourges, Sens and Tours
formulas the narrative of the *Gesta* suggests that it was not the transfer of land into the hands of laymen that was at issue, but rather the
transfer of land into the hands of laymen who were not otherwise
associated with the monastery. *Beneficia* and *precaria* were not problematic when they were used to strengthen and reaffirm existing
relationships. In Neustria, however, they could be matters of complaint when no previous relationship existed. One danger in such a
situation was that a beneficiary might fail to pay his dues, and that
an estate might pass out of the control of the abbey. This was ultimately what made the grant to Ratharius so disastrous, and it was
the non-payment in Witlaic's day which rendered the latter most
culpable in the context of estate alienation.[107]

The evidence, as it survives, is not full enough to allow any firm
interpretation of the development of *precaria*. It would be dangerous
to use this evidence to assert that the 730s saw the introduction of
a new type of precarial grant which paid no attention to whether
a beneficiary was already associated with a monastery. Indeed, it
is more likely that the association of precarial grants with close
family or associates was a secondary development, even if there
are indications that such had become the traditional way of viewing
precarial tenure in Neustria. There is every reason for thinking
that the Tours formula was not novel, even though it may well

---

[104] *GAF*, XI. 3.
[105] *GAF*, VI. 2; XI. 3.
[106] *GAF*, XI. 1; XII. 1.
[107] *GAF*, VI. 3.

have been relatively unpopular, and even though Teutsind and Witlaic may have been reviving an unfashionable legal formula. It is possible that *precaria* were being used in new ways by Charles, Pippin and Carloman, but such a change cannot be proved from the St Wandrille, or any other, evidence.

Rather than look at the possible novelty of the practice, it may be safer to return to the question of the promotion of outsiders. Neither Teutsind nor Ratharius appear to have had long-standing connections with the monastery of St Wandrille. Given the power of Savaric it is equally likely that the people who replaced Eucherius and his relatives in the diocese of Orléans were similarly outside the circle of those families which had been associated with that church for two generations or more. The same is likely to have held true for the church of Auxerre. From this point of view the shock caused by Charles Martel was not dependent on any revolution in types of landholding, but rather a response to the unseating of families who had become entrenched over the preceding generations – although it is possible that revived, or even new, forms of *precaria* played their part in this.

There are two other points which are worth noting here. The first concerns those 'king's men', the *regii homines*, who were a bone of contention at St Wandrille, appearing twice in the *Gesta abbatum Fontanellensium*.[108] Those endowed by Teutsind were clearly followers of Charles – despite the anachronistic adjective *regius*, which must indicate that the description does not belong to the early eighth century. They may reasonably be compared to those supporters who benefited from the deposition of Eucherius,[109] and to Charles's military followers (*leudes*) who were given lands in Burgundy.[110] Yet there is nothing to indicate that the reallocation of the estates of St Wandrille was a deliberate policy automatically pursued by Charles himself. Although Teutsind and Witlaic are said to have given land to *regii homines*,[111] neither is known to have been carrying out the orders of Charles or Pippin – and the grant is spoken of in the same breath as the endowment of Teutsind's relatives. The absence of any criticism of Charles over this issue is significant, since the St Wandrille hagiographers were not inclined

---

[108] *GAF*, VI. 1; XI. 3.
[109] *Vita Eucherii*, cc. 7–9.
[110] Fredegar, *Continuationes*, ch. 14.
[111] *GAF*, VI. 1; XI. 3.

to exonerate the Pippinids elsewhere.[112] The evidence for Orléans provides a useful point of comparison. While the *Vita Eucherii* is certainly critical of Charles,[113] the author only claims that it was at the instigation of his supporters (*circumfusi, satellites*) that he exiled Eucherius and his family.[114] Charles's followers seem to have played as significant a role as did the *maior* himself in undermining the established aristocracies. Perhaps as a result *precaria* were not simply, or even primarily, grants to Charles's troops – they went equally to the relatives, possibly female as well as male, of such men as Teutsind.

Second, although the church of Orléans and the monastery of St Wandrille seem to have suffered at the hands of Charles's supporters, they were not actually being punished for treason in the 730s. In so far as any punitive action was meted out against St Wandrille this occurred earlier, with the deposition of Abbot Wando, and even then Wando could himself be seen as having usurped his post from Benignus.[115] Indeed part of the anguish experienced at St Wandrille and Orléans may well have been the shock experienced by centres which were already apparently reconciled to Pippinid rule. Here the case of Neustria after 733 may have been different from that of Burgundy, where Charles put down a rebellion immediately before granting territory in the region to his own followers.[116] The fall of Eucherius, who shows no sign of having been an opponent of Charles, can reasonably be contrasted with that of Ainmar, who was imprisoned after he had failed to prevent the escape of Eudo.[117] Even this may appear to be somewhat harsh justice, as was the deposition of Rigobert of Rheims, who lost his see for remaining studiously neutral, and not opening the gates of his city to Charles during war against Ragamfred.[118] The associates of Maurontus in Provence could more reasonably be portrayed as rebels.[119]

Charles's favour was not to be relied upon. He was certainly not averse to picking off those he distrusted as and when it suited him.

---

[112] Wood, 'Saint-Wandrille and its hagiography', pp. 11–14.
[113] *Vita Eucherii*, ch. 9: 'metu perterritus'.
[114] *Vita Eucherii*, cc. 7, 9.
[115] *GAF*, III. 1.
[116] Fredegar, *Continuationes*, ch. 14.
[117] *Gesta episcoporum Autissiodorensium*, ch. 27.
[118] *Vita Rigoberti*, cc. 9, 12, ed. W. Levison, *MGH SRM*, vol. 7.
[119] Geary, *Aristocracy in Provence*, pp. 129–30.

The treatment of his stepmother Plectrude provides the clearest case in point. Having come to terms with her after Amblève in 716,[120] Charles forced Plectrude to hand over Pippin's treasure once he was better established after Vinchy a year later.[121] Eucherius, Ainmar and Rigobert all experienced similar loss of support at a time when they might well have thought that they had weathered the storm of civil war.

Taking these cases in conjunction with the evidence from Tours and St Wandrille, it is possible to see something of the complexity of the changes which took place in the Frankish kingdom after 714. As Charles expanded his authority from Austrasia into Neustria, Burgundy and ultimately Provence, he had to win over the established aristocracy, secular and ecclesiastical. It seems to have been rare for him to depose an official, whether lay or ecclesiastical, immediately: Wando at St Wandrille was one of the exceptions. Charles apparently looked for opportunities to remove those he distrusted when the time was ripe. Thus he used the rebellions in Burgundy[122] and Provence to act in those regions. Rigobert he picked off for not opening the gates of Rheims to him.[123] Ainmar he deposed for allowing Eudo to escape.[124] Alongside Charles's own opportunistic behaviour, however, was the behaviour of his followers, who urged him to exile Eucherius and his relatives from Orléans. Charles was apparently even less of a prime mover at St Wandrille. There is nothing in the evidence relating to the grant to Ratharius to suggest that Teutsind was acting for Charles. Nor are Charles or Pippin III blamed for other grants made by Teutsind and Witlaic to *regii homines*. Whether or not the Tours formula for *precaria* is indicative of a change in the use of grants, there is no reason to associate Charles with all or even the majority of the instances that precarial tenure was used to challenge entrenched interests. In the next generation, however, the canons of the Council of Estinnes show that Carloman at least found the use of *precaria* to be worth protecting.[125]

[120] *Liber Historiae Francorum*, cc. 52, 53; Fredegar, *Continuationes*, cc. 9, 10; Gerberding, *The Rise of the Carolingians*, pp. 132–42; Wood, *The Merovingian Kingdoms 450–751*, p. 271.
[121] *Liber Historiae Francorum*, ch. 53; Fredegar, *Continuationes*, ch. 10.
[122] Fredegar, *Continuationes*, ch. 14.
[123] *Vita Rigoberti*, cc. 9, 12.
[124] *Gesta episcoporum Autissiodorensium*, ch. 27.
[125] Council of Estinnes (743), cap. 2, *MGH Conc.*, vol. 2.

More generally, there is no early evidence to suggest that abnormally sizable numbers of estates were seized and alienated by Charles. Even Merovingian kings had been known to confiscate the estates of traitors. Nor was the grant of *precaria* or *beneficia* anything new, although the precise nature of precarial grants may have been extended. What was clearly at stake was the fate of entrenched interests, even of those which were not openly in opposition to Charles. At St Wandrille an outsider was granted land, despite the fact that in Neustrian tradition *precaria* seem to have been granted to men or women already associated with the church whose lands were in question. The unpopularity of Teutsind, Witlaic and Ratharius may result as much from alarm that the *status quo* could be questioned as from the scale of any alienations. Despite the supposedly disastrous alienations perpetrated by Teutsind and Witlaic the abbey still had 3,964 properties on the latter's death, and although only 1,569 of these were held for the use of the monks, while 2,395 had been granted out as *beneficia*, the author of the *Gesta* seems not to have been troubled by these other grants.[126] What were at issue were only those grants by Teutsind to 'his relatives and the king's men'[127] and those grants made by Witlaic 'either to the king's men . . . or in usufruct to others'.[128] There is, moreover, nothing other than the vague statement that Teutsind 'took almost a third' of the monastery's property,[129] to show that these estates were numerous. More precisely, although the author insists that it would be tedious to relate all the grants, the only one about which he is specific is that to Ratharius. In the light of all these complications it would clearly be unwise to create an interpretation of the policies of Charles Martel and Pippin III on two passages of the *Gesta abbatum Fontanellensium*. On the other hand these two passages allow some insight into the realities of the impact of Charles and his followers on the social establishment of the early eighth century, as well as the way in which that impact was perceived.

[126] *GAF*, XI. 3.   [127] *GAF*, VI. 1.   [128] *GAF*, XI. 3.   [129] *GAF*, VI. 1.

CHAPTER 3

Eternal light and earthly needs: practical aspects of the development of Frankish immunities

Paul Fouracre

A concern voiced in many of the studies in this volume is the extent to which concepts of immunity are bound up with questions of property and power; hence the need to clear the ground around this subject in an introductory note. As we have seen, discussions about the medieval immunity usually treat the subject as an essentially Frankish phenomenon. In order to say more about the nature and early development of immunities, and to explain more fully some of the issues raised in the introduction to the subject, it is sensible to begin with their origins in seventh-century Francia, and to try to understand both the purposes they originally served and the historical context in which they developed. It is upon this area that the present chapter focusses, and after a few preliminary remarks about current debates in this subject area, it will look at the early history of royal immunities before attempting to assess their historical significance from a new angle.

That Frankish immunities were somehow very important in the development of medieval Europe is a common assumption in outline histories of medieval society.[1] Such overviews tend to be dialectical, that is, they look for the seeds of later developments in a period of history which is seen as transitional. In Francia, this is the Merovingian period (481–751) which 'comes between' antiquity and the middle ages proper, and the seed here is the immunity. One can see why royal immunities might be thus

---

[1] See for instance the remarks about the role of immunities in transforming lord–peasant relations at the end of the early middle ages in W. Rösener, *Peasants in the Middle Ages*, p. 19. Rösener here cites G. Duby, *Early Growth of the European Economy: Warriors and Peasants from the Seventh to the Twelfth Century*, p. 172, but Duby does not actually mention immunities (unlike M. Bloch, *Feudal Society*, vol. 2, ch. 27, pp. 361–2, to whom immunities were crucial in his understanding of the privatization of power, and whom Duby follows in other respects).

regarded: by granting rights of immunity to landowners from the
seventh century onwards, rulers apparently conferred upon them
those judicial rights which gave them complete power over their
property.[2] The concession of jurisdiction over land, that is, over
the inhabitants of the land, is perceived to have been a crucial
element in the territorialization of power in the early middle ages.
The passing of such power from the ruler to favoured subjects is
often said to have been basic to the transformation of lords from
'public officials' to independent rulers in their own right. Although
this development, which amounted to a 'privatization' of power, is
generally said to have gathered pace at the end of the tenth century,
its roots are often traced right back to the mid-seventh century,
when documents granting immunity first appeared.[3]

The history of Frankish immunities is therefore a topical subject
because modern debates about the development of European
society in the early middle ages have tended both to be modelled
on what happened in Francia itself, and to focus on the declining
fortunes of the organized public authority or 'state' as a motor for
change. In recent years the work of E. Magnou-Nortier and of J.
Durliat has reinvigorated this debate by advancing the proposition
that the fiscal system of the later Roman Empire did not collapse
in the early middle ages as scholars have generally believed that
it did.[4] Their challenge to what is a long-established consensus rests
largely on a reinterpretation of the terminology of those Frankish
documents which were concerned with property and with income
from property, and partly it rests upon silence. The term *villa*, for
instance, which conventionally has been understood in terms of
land ownership, has been read by Magnou-Nortier and Durliat as

---

[2] The most succinct statement of this view is M. Kroell, *L'Immunité Franque*, p. 151.

[3] On the privatization of power see for example, P. Bonnassie, *From Slavery to Feudalism in South-Western Europe*, pp. 104–48.; for the roots of that privatization, F. Ganshof, 'L'Immunité dans la monarchie Franque', in *Les liens de vassalité et les immunités, Recueil de la société Jean Bodin*, vol. 1 (1956); K. Fischer-Drew, 'The immunity in Carolingian Italy', *Speculum*, 37 (1962), p. 182.

[4] E. Magnou-Nortier has advanced this thesis in a series of articles, for example, 'Étude sur le privilège d'immunité du IVe au IXe siècle', *Revue Mabillon*, 60 (1984); 'Les "Pagenses", notables et fermiers du fisc durant le haut moyen âge', *Revue Belge de Philologie et d'Histoire*, 65 (1987); 'La gestion publique en Neustrie: Les moyens et les hommes (VIIe–IXe siècles)', in H. Atsma (ed.), *La Neustrie. Les Pays au Nord de la Loire de 650 à 850*, vol. 1. J. Durliat's principal contribution has been his recent work, *Les Finances Publiques de Dioclétien aux Carolingiens (284–888)*.

a purely fiscal term.[5] More generally, silence is taken to imply that direct taxation continued unless the sources categorically tell us that it did not. This argument, as one reviewer of Durliat's work has put it, amounts to saying that the Roman Empire never fell.[6] It claims, in other words, that Europe (or, to be more exact, Francia) in the early middle ages was organized around a government with a strong fiscal base and with a strong set of public institutions, rather than governed by weak states collapsing in the face of advancing private interests. This idea is in one sense truly radical, but it is also put forward within highly conventional polarities which it reverses but does not challenge. It is radical in privileging the public over the private, but conventional in generalizing from Frankish history and in centring its analysis upon the fortunes of the state. In this view the development of immunities remains an important issue, but it is argued that because the documents which granted immunity did not mention direct taxation, when rulers conceded immunities this showed them granting away little of public interest. Modern thinking about immunities has thus been pulled in two opposite directions: they are taken either to show the state giving away the essence of its power, or to show the state maintaining its hold over vital resources.

Although the present study disagrees with the reinterpretation of terminology advanced by Magnou-Nortier and Durliat, it will nevertheless be rather more equivocal about the significance of immunities than is usual. The reason for equivocation is a feeling that the sense of opposition between 'public' and 'private' which is conventional in discussions about Frankish immunities is too strong. It is an opposition rooted in a history dominated by concern with the long-term development of the state, whereas the history of the state is only one strand in the relationship between property and power. From another point of view, that of the early medieval church for instance, the dividing line between the public and the private may have been very blurred: the church drew upon private property to sustain a mission which had a public character. There is, therefore, some advantage to be derived from looking at

---

[5] Magnou-Nortier, 'La gestion publique', pp. 273–85; Durliat, *Les Finances Publiques*, pp. 152–6, 252–6.

[6] C. J. Wickham, 'La Chute de Rome n'aura pas lieu. A propos d'un livre récent', *Le Moyen Âge*, 99 (1993).

immunities from an essentially pragmatic point of view, that is, in terms of what they offered to contemporaries rather than in terms of what they contributed to the history of the European state over the whole early medieval period.

In what follows it will be necessary first of all to examine some of the basic issues raised in conventional discussions about immunities in relation to changes in political structures. This will furnish a basis for contrast and comparison with alternative approaches. The study will then pick up and follow a quite different strand, that is, it will examine the possible significance of the 'movent' clause of the early documents of immunity. This clause stated that the designated purpose in granting the immunity was to provide lighting for the church in question. In most studies the designation is rarely mentioned, let alone discussed, because it is assumed that it is merely formulaic. However, this is an assumption worth testing, on the basis that there is good evidence that the provision of lighting for churches was regarded as important, as well as being expensive, and might, therefore, have been a serious consideration in the granting of an immunity. To some extent, of course, deciding upon the importance of the lighting clause, and then trying to explain that importance, might be regarded as a hypothetical, or even circular exercise, but it is scarcely less so than one which seeks to explain the importance of immunities in relation to the history of the state, for that exercise, as we shall see, also involves speculation about some of the basic features of immunities. It is the essential argument of this chapter that by playing down the importance of immunities in relation to the state, and that by looking at the significance of their lighting clauses we can both see more clearly the cultural context in which immunities developed, and better understand the practical needs which were met by that development. It is to this end that the two strands of discussion will eventually be brought together. First, let us look at the origins and nature of Frankish immunities.

THE ORIGINS OF FRANKISH IMMUNITIES

Maurice Kroell, who in 1910 published what is still the most comprehensive work on the Frankish immunity, estimated that for the period AD 636–840 there were 223 documents issued by kings which either granted or confirmed immunity.[7] As with other kinds of Frankish royal document, the form in which they appeared in the later Merovingian period changed little over the next two centuries. From the charter forms contained in the later seventh-century Formulary of Marculf we can see what was involved when a grant of immunity was made.[8] According to Marculf, when a ruler wished to help a church by bestowing the privilege of immunity upon its head, what the beneficiary received was a document which ordered the exclusion of royal judicial officers from all of the church's lands. These officials and their subordinates were told not to enter the lands to settle disputes (*altercationes audire*), nor to levy the fine known as *fretum* (*fretum exigere*). They were banned from enjoying rights of hospitality (*mansiones*), from the purveyance of foodstuffs (*parata*), and from taking sureties (*fideiussores*).[9] In the form for documents which confirmed existing immunities another, and more general, exclusion was mentioned: officials were banned from collecting other unspecified dues (*redibuciones*) from the lands. The general effect of the immunity is said to have conferred income upon the beneficiary: whatever the 'fisc' had in the past hoped to get from the lands and its inhabitants was now to go to the beneficiary to be used for the lights (*luminaria*) of the church in question.[10] From the evidence of surviving documents, the income could

---

[7] Kroell, *L'Immunité Franque*, pp. 335–53. Kroell believed that the earliest document was one in which King Dagobert I (629–37) granted an immunity to the monastery of Rebais in the year 635, and went on to argue that this grant was the source of later models: *L'Immunité Franque*, pp. 61–5. The opposite is now believed to be true, that is, that the Rebais document was a later forgery based on earlier models. The Rebais forger was, however, probably right in thinking that royal immunities were issued in Dagobert's day. The king's early ninth-century biographer certainly believed that he had issued them: see *Gesta Dagoberti*, ch. 39, ed. B. Krusch, *MGH SRM*, vol. 2, p. 418. Later confirmations refer back to immunities originally granted in the mid-seventh century, and the later seventh-century *Vita Balthildis*, ch. 9, ed. B. Krusch, *MGH SRM*, vol. 2, pp. 493–4, also refers to immunities granted sometime 657–64, but the first surviving document to mention an immunity in the form we see it in Marculf is from the year 688: *Chartae Latinae Antiquiores*, ed. A. Bruckner, M. Marichal, vol. 14 (hereafter *ChLA*, cited by document number), 570.

[8] *Marculfi Formularum Libri Duo*, ed. A. Uddholm, I. 3, pp. 34–6 for concession of immunity, I.4, pp. 38–42 for confirmation of immunity.

[9] *Marculfi Form.*, I. 3; the key concession was: 'ut neque vos neque iuniores neque successores vestri nec nulla publica iudicaria potestas quoque tempore in villas ubicumque in regno Nostro ipsius ecclesiae aut regia aut privatorum largitate conlatas, aut qui inantea fuerint conlaturas, ad audiendas altercationes ingredire aut freta de quaslibet causas exigere nec mansiones aut paratas vel fideiussores tollere non presumatis'.

[10] *Marculfi Form.*, I. 3: 'quicquid exinde aut de ingenuis aut de servientibus ceteris nacionibus, qui sunt infra agros vel finis – seo: super terras – predicte ecclesiae conmanentes, fiscus aut de freta undecumque potuerat sperare, ex Nostra indulgentia

also go towards alms for the poor or towards the feeding of the monks.[11] The key to the privilege remained the exclusion of 'judges' (that is, the count and his *juniores*) from the lands, and the whole privilege could be referred to in abbreviated form as *emunitas absque introitu judicum* ('immunity from the entry of judges').[12] The only significant later addition to these terms was the granting of royal protection (*defensio* or *tuitio*) along with immunity, which became a feature of grants from the time of Charlemagne onwards. By the end of the Carolingian period most of the senior churches and monasteries in the lands under Frankish control had acquired privileges of immunity. As far as we can tell, nobody else had received them.

The origins of immunities in the form that we find them in Marculf are lost to us. It is reasonable to suppose that, like the documents known as *placita* which record cases settled in the royal court, the precise form of document through which immunities were granted was a seventh-century invention.[13] Scattered references in the *Theodosian Code*, principally in Books XI and XVI, show that in the later Roman Empire categories of persons, institutions and imperial lands, and above all churches, were privileged with immunity from a variety of fiscal burdens. These cases of immunity bear little formal resemblance to their later namesake, but where the church is concerned they do specify that one purpose

---

pro futura salutae in luminaribus ipsius ecclesiae per manu agentum/eorum proficiat in perpetuum'.

[11] *ChLA*, vol. 14, 579, an original document of 696 which confirmed an existing immunity, had this form of the clause. *ChLA*, vol. 14, 588, another original confirmation from 716, made the concession for all three: 'for the lamps and allowances and for alms for the poor' ('in lumenarebus vel estipendiis seu et elimoniis pauperum').

[12] Almost nothing can be said about judges in this context. D. Claude reasoned correctly that all counts were judges but that not all judges were counts. From the *Clotharii Edictum*, ch. 19, in *Capitularia Regum Francorum*, ed. A. Boretius, *MGH LL in quarto*, sectio 2 (hereafter *MGH Capit.*), vol. 1, p. 23, he noted that bishops and *potentes* had the right to appoint judges, and this he coupled with a reference to private immunities in *Marculfi Formularum*, I. 14, to arrive at the view that the *Clotharii Edictum* passage pointed to the existence of private judges on the estates of (lay) aristocratic holders of immunity: D. Claude, 'Untersuchungen zum frühfränkischen Comitat', *Zeitschrift der Savigny-Stiftung für Rechtsgeschichte*, 42 (1964), pp. 42–3. There is, however, no other evidence for judges of this type.

[13] P. Fouracre, ' "Placita" and the settlement of disputes in later Merovingian Francia', in W. Davies and P. Fouracre (eds.), *The Settlement of Disputes in Early Medieval Europe*, pp. 23–6. For a counter argument (that *placita* were not so new in the seventh century), D. Ganz and W. Goffart, 'Charters earlier than 800 from French collections', *Speculum*, 65 (1990), pp. 919–20.

of the privilege was to provide extra income for the use of the poor
and for the profit of religion.[14] This rather general wish may find
an echo in later documents, but not so the notion that the clergy
be excused public service in order to free them for devotion to
religion and to protect their holiness. A clause in the Council of
Orléans (511) which refers to immunity for churches, might suggest a continuation of the Roman tradition of exempting church
lands of fiscal origin from limited amounts of tax. It also specifies
that the income from this land should go towards the repair of
churches, alms for the poor and payment for the ransom of cap-
tives.[15] A *Praeceptio* (royal order) issued by Clothar II (584–628)
speaks generally of immunities granted in the time of Clothar I
(511–565) in the context of tax concessions and the banning of tax
collectors from church lands.[16] Finally, Clothar II's *Edict* of 614
guaranteed the rights of those who had obtained immunities from
the king's father and uncles, rights which could thus have been
granted in the later sixth century. Here 'public judges' were
charged with defending the property of the church, priests and the
poor, except where previous kings had granted immunity
to churches, to 'the powerful' or to anyone else.[17] With only this

---

[14] In the *Theodosian Code* the exemptions were mostly from the so-called *sordida munera*, a
variety of dues and services which were specified in XI. xvi, 15: *Theodosian Code*, trans.
C. Pharr, p. 308. See also XI. xvi, 17, 22, p. 309. The position of the church with regard
to direct taxation was less clear cut. *Theodosian Code*, XVI. ii, 10, 15, 24, 25, pp. 442–4,
grant exemptions but also refer to payment in certain circumstances. It is in the same
section of XVI that the *Code* refers to the purpose of the exemptions.

[15] 'Concilium Aurelianense', ch. 5, in C. de Clercq (ed.), *Concilia Galliae A511–695*, p. 6:
'De oblationibus vel agris, quos domnus noster rex ecclesiis suo munere conferre dignatus
est vel adhuc non habentibus Deo sibi inspirante contulerit, ipsorum agrorum vel clerico-
rum inmunitate concessa, id est iustissimum definimus, ut in reparationis ecclesiarum
alimoniis sacerdotum et pauperum vel redemptionibus captivorum, quidquid Deus in
fructibus dare dignatus fuerit, expendatur et clerici ad adiutorium ecclesiastici operis
constringantur'.

[16] *Clotharii Praeceptio*, ch. 11, *MGH Capit.*, vol. 1, p. 19: 'Agraria, pascuaria vel decimas
porcorum ecclesiae pro fidei nostrae devotione concederemus, ita ut actor aut decimator
in rebus ecclesiae nullus accedat'.

[17] *Clotharii Edictum*, ch. 14, p. 22: 'Ecclesiarum res sacerdotum et pauperum qui se defensare
non possunt, a iudicibus publicis usque audentiam per iustitiam defensentur, salva emun-
itate praecidentiae domnorum, quod ecclesiae aut potentum vel cuicumque visi sunt
indulsisse pro pace atque disciplina facienda'. Note that this quotation normalizes a
partly fragmentary text according to the generally accepted reading. A. C. Murray,
'Immunity, nobility and the edict of Paris', *Speculum*, 69 (1994), at pp. 30–4, has expanded
on the last phrase of this passage ('for keeping the peace and imposing public order') in
order to argue that the immunity here was a specialized exemption granted to lay and
ecclesiastical landowners in return for their contribution towards peace-keeping in their
own domains. As Murray goes on to argue, there is no obvious connection between this

information of a general nature to go on, we cannot say much about royal immunities before Marculf, although it is worth noting that between them these three early references to immunity contain the basic ingredients of the later privilege: namely, the banning of officials, relief from fiscal charges and the injunction to spend the savings on church business. As we shall see, much emphasis has been placed on the fact that the guarantee of 614 did not distinguish between lay persons and ecclesiastical institutions. By contrast, all surviving records of actual grants of immunity are concerned with churches and monasteries.

DID THE GRANTING OF IMMUNITIES UNDERMINE PUBLIC AUTHORITY IN FRANCIA?

The feature of immunities which has excited most interest amongst modern scholars has been the banning of royal officials from entry into the lands of the privilege holder. Debate has generally focussed on the nature and quality of the rights effectively transferred to the holder of the privilege by means of this exclusion. Opinion has ranged from the conviction that the rights were full, and alienable with the land, to the view that they amounted to no more than the specific exemptions expressed in the grant, and were tied to the beneficiary named in it.[18] There is, however, general agreement that the beneficiary's gain was the public authority's loss, and that the granting of immunities did mean a significant loss of power for

kind of policing immunity and the sort of exemption designed to benefit churches which appear in documents from the late seventh century onwards, on which subject Murray follows the argument put forward by W. Goffart, cited in n. 18 below. For criticism of Murray's view, see the introduction to this volume, above, p. 13, n. 20.

[18] G. Waitz thought that the rights of immunity lay on all royal land and were transferred with it, even when that land became the 'benefice' of laymen: G. Waitz, *Deutsche Verfassungsgeschichte*, vol. 4, pp. 243–53. This was the line followed by H. Brunner, *Deutsche Rechtsgeschichte*, vol. 2, p. 292. E. Lesne, *Histoire de la propriété ecclésiastique en France*, vol. 1, pp. 266–7, thought that immunity made the beneficiary 'absolute master' of his lands, but also stressed the continuing royal jurisdiction over them. L. Levillain, 'Note sur l'immunité Mérovingienne', *Revue historique de droit français et étranger*, 6 (1927), p. 43, believed that the rights were inalienable from the land itself and could be exercised by whoever held the land, although royal permission was needed before such land could be transferred. That the rights were more limited in scope and disposal was the view of Kroell, *L'Immunité Franque*, pp. 95–6, Ganshof, 'L'Immunité dans la monarchie Franque', pp. 181–4, W. Goffart, 'Old and new in Merovingian taxation', *Past and Present*, 96 (1982), p. 11, and Magnou-Nortier, 'Étude sur le privilège d'immunité', pp. 476–83. T. Sickel in an important early work on the diplomatic of immunity documents was neutral on this question: *Beiträge zur Diplomatik*, vol. 5, pp. 311–28.

the latter. That this process seriously weakened public authority, to the benefit of magnates drawing their social and political power from the control of immunitied land, is an assumption which is often made but never demonstrated. Maurice Kroell's indispensable work, *L'Immunité Franque*, has been highly influential in establishing this view. Although Kroell argued that there was little to link Frankish immunities with anything in the later Roman world, he allowed impressions about the behaviour and attitudes of later Roman *potentes* ('powerful men' or 'magnates') to inform his thinking about the social and political implications of the granting of immunities in the early medieval period. Believing (like many a more recent commentator) that both late Roman and early medieval *potentes* had interests which were not in the long run compatible with the maintenance of a strong and widespread public authority, he imagined that they would quickly have seized upon the opportunities offered by Frankish immunities to further entrench their positions by taking advantage of the privilege to convert their *de facto* power into power *backed by law*.[19] At the heart of Kroell's thinking, and in the minds of other commentators too, lies uncertainty about the meaning of the term *immunitas* itself. For in Latin, as in the modern French, English and German terms *immunité*, *immunity* and *Immunität* which are derived from it, the word can be used to mean a general immunity from the legally constituted power of the state, or it can refer to the kind of specific exemptions we have been discussing. In his understanding of the long-term significance of immunities Kroell seems to have confused the two meanings when he assumed that the granting of specific exemptions must have led to a general weakening of public authority. In his words, when the Merovingian kings granted immunities they had in effect 'introduced into the structure of the Frankish kingdom elements of decay which would act to bring about a slow but continuous weakening of the bonds which united the subjects to the public power'.[20]

To this way of thinking one must make three basic objections (all of which can, in fact, be deduced from Kroell's own observations and from observations made in most other studies

---

[19] Kroell, *L'Immunité Franque*, pp. 71–2. For more recent thinking in this vein, C. J. Wickham, 'The other transition: from the ancient world to feudalism', *Past and Present*, 103 (1984), pp. 15–18.

[20] Kroell, *L'Immunité Franque*, p. 151.

too). Firstly, the term *potentes* is used to mean lay as well as ecclesiastical landowners, with lay lordship being seen as, ultimately, the greater threat to the state. However, there is no specific evidence of grants of immunity to lay persons. Where lay immunity is mentioned, this is only in general terms, either in Formulary examples or in legislation.[21] The general sense that lay persons did receive immunities comes from the guarantee of immunity for *potentes* in the *Edict* of Clothar II, which we looked at earlier; from legislation issued by Charles the Bald in 864; and from two models of documents in the Formulary of Marculf.[22] As we have already seen, the *Edict* of Clothar referred to immunities which had been granted in the later sixth century, but what immunity privileges entailed at that date is uncertain. Clothar's *Edict* may, however, have been the inspiration behind parts of Charles the Bald's 864 legislation: both in effect limited the rights of lords to protect their men when the latter had committed crimes.[23] Let us turn now to the two pieces of formulary evidence for lay immunity. One of Marculf's models is for a private (as opposed to royal) charter in which a layman grants land for the foundation of a monastery. The land is said to have enjoyed immunity, but the term here seems to refer to freedom from the non-royal dues which the donor gives up in order to bestow the land upon the monastery. It may therefore have little to do with the kind of immunities which were granted by the king.[24] The other model, for the confirmation of a grant of fiscal property, does indeed give a confirmation of immunity *absque introitu judicum* to a *secularis vir* (layman) and this is probably the

---

[21] The grants and confirmations of *apprisiones* to laymen in northern Spain from the late eighth century onwards do in some ways resemble the immunities issued to churches, but they were granted in a very different context and for the purpose of defending the frontier against the Moors. See, for example, *Recueil des Actes de Charles II le Chauve*, ed. G. Tessier (hereafter Tessier, *Recueil*), vol. 1, no. 46, pp. 129–32.

[22] *Clotharii Edictum*, ch. 14, p. 22; *Edictum Pistense*, ch. 18, *MGH Capit.*, vol. 2, p. 317; *Marculfi Formularum*, I. 17, pp. 82–4, II. 1, pp. 162–74.

[23] *Clotharii Edictum*, ch. 15, pp. 22–3 refers to the need to deliver up to *agentes publici* any 'homines ecclesiarum aut potentum de causis criminalibus accusati' ('men of churches or of the powerful accused in criminal cases'). *Edictum Pistense*, ch. 18, p. 317, speaks of the need to deliver up malefactors wherever they have taken refuge, be it in, 'fiscum nostrum vel in quamcumque immunitatem aut in alicuius potentis potestatem vel proprietatem' ('on our fisc or in any immunity whatsoever or on the property or in the district of any other kind of powerful man'). This is repeated later in ch. 18 and reference is made to earlier Carolingian legislation on crime committed *infra immunitatem* ('within an immunity'). That earlier legislation which limited the right of asylum did not in fact mention lay immunities (see below n. 28).

[24] *Marculfi Formularum*, II. 1, p. 168.

strongest indication anywhere that laymen could in theory receive from the king the sort of immunity that surviving grants record for the church.[25] Such grants to laymen were made, it is argued, but have not survived: only those given to ecclesiastical bodies would have been preserved. But the gap in evidence here is simply too wide to bridge with this one reference from a formulary. If grants of immunity had been made to laymen in significant numbers, then it would seem extraordinary if there were not at least some trace of them in the countless surviving documents which record the grants made by lay persons to the church in this period. Such documents do, after all, usually include a brief history of whatever land is being granted.

The second objection to seeing immunities as the key to the decline of public authority in Francia rests upon the observation, quite often made, that we know actually very little about the nature and extent of the jurisdiction and other rights enjoyed within them.[26] Although it has sometimes been assumed that the immunist replaced the count as judge of the inhabitants, with the tribunal of the immunity replacing the count's court (the *mallus*), nowhere is this specified. By inference, the immunist would take over from the count and hear disputes and levy the fine known as *fretum*. The only positive evidence of a court actually being held in an immunity comes from contexts of dispute settlement in which the immunity holder provided the court president, but the case was decided by the collective judgement of law-worthy men, as it would have been in any other court.[27] On the other hand, there is some evidence of limitations to the jurisdiction of the immunist. As we have seen, Clothar II's *Edict* of 614 demanded that 'criminal cases' (*causae criminales*) be tried 'in public courts' (*in audientia publica*), and that those who failed to deliver up criminals could be distrained, that is, have their property taken away. Carolingian legislation, in the Capitulary of Pîtres for instance, also demanded that the immunist deliver up those committing 'major crimes' to the

---

[25] *Marculfi Formularum*, I. 17, p. 82.

[26] See, for instance, Kroell, *L'Immunité Franque*, pp. 127–30; Ganshof, 'L'Immunité dans la monarchie Franque', p. 185.

[27] For discussion of a case heard in an immunity (that of St Martin's, Tours), J. L. Nelson, 'Dispute settlement in Carolingian West Francia', in Davies and Fouracre (eds.), *The Settlement of Disputes in Early Medieval Europe*, pp. 56–9.

count, and it was a fairly broad range of crimes which fell into this category.[28] The delivery of criminals to the count became the responsibility of the advocate, the legal representative which each immunity was required to have from the time of Charlemagne onwards. According to the so-called 'Programmatic Capitulary of 802' the local count was to have a say in the choice of advocate, who presided over courts in the immunity.[29] He was required to have hereditary land in the area in which he worked, a stipulation which puts the advocate in the same frame as those judicial officers seen in Merovingian legislation, whose hereditary property in the area in which they functioned guaranteed that they could be subject to distraint to make them answer complaints of injustice.[30] The inhabitants of the immunity thus presumably had some right of appeal against the advocate, and could ultimately call upon royal protection for their property.

There were limits, too, to other rights: late seventh- and early eighth-century charters from the areas around Angers and Le

---

[28] *Capitulare Haristallense*, ch. 9, *MGH Capit.*, vol. 1, p. 48; *Capitulare Legibus Additum 803*, ch. 2, *MGH Capit.*, vol. 1, p. 113; *Capitulare de Latronibus*, ch. 5, *MGH Capit.*, vol. 1, p. 181, all make the same points about the delivery of criminals from immunities, and these points are repeated in *Ansegisi Capitularium*, III. 26. It was to the latter that the *Edictum Pistense*, ch. 18, was probably referring when it mentioned earlier legislation: see *MGH Capit.*, vol. 2, p. 317, n. 46. The 'major crimes' were listed in the year 815 in the *Constitutio de Hispanis in Francorum Regnum Profugis Prima*, ch. 2, *MGH Capit.*, vol. 1, p. 262 as, 'homicidia, raptus, incendia, depraedationes, membrorum amputationes, furta, latrocinia, alienarum rerum invasiones' ('killings, rapes, arson, pillage, maimings, robberies, thefts, unlawful seizures of other property').

[29] *Capitulare Missorum Generale*, ch. 13, *MGH Capit.*, vol. 1, p. 93.

[30] *Clotharii II Edictum*, ch. 12, p. 22. The first clause of this well-known passage has often been quoted out of context to suggest that the Merovingians had surrendered to local people the right to appoint counts, and had thus relaxed their grip on power. The passage as a whole shows that what was actually at stake was the prevention of and compensation for the abuse of judicial power by the count, a quite different constitutional matter: 'nullus iudex de aliis provinciis aut regionibus in alia loca ordinatur, ut si aliquid mali de quibuslibet condicionibus perpetraverit, de suis propriis rebus exinde quod male abstolerit iuxta legis ordinem debeat restaurare' ('no judge from other provinces or regions should be appointed in any other place, so that if he should do any wrong in any circumstances, what he took away wrongly should be restored, according to the law, from his own property'). Murray, 'Immunity, nobility and the edict of Paris', pp. 26–9, thinks that this chapter was modelled on Justinian's *Pragmatic Sanction* of the year 554, with King Clothar making 'a decision to follow Justinian's lead in considering local interests in the appointment of his officials'. Although the drafters of the *Edict* may have been influenced by the text of the *Pragmatic Sanction*, this description of Clothar's decision-making sounds anachronistic. It seems more likely that he was following earlier tradition, and specifically his own father's lead, in insisting on the count's liability for his actions, as expressed, for instance in the 'Edict of Chilperic', ch. 8, in *MGH Capit.*, vol. 1, p. 9.

Mans show the immunist having the right to collect, but not to keep, some of the revenues owed to the fisc. This evidence plays a key part in the argument that direct taxation continued to be levied in Francia, but it is surely not possible to generalize from what was likely to have been a local arrangement. In relation to immunities the point this evidence makes is that they, too, were possibly subject to variations according to local customs.[31] What is more certain is that the Carolingians were generally keen to ensure that those living on immunitied land did not escape the military and labour obligations owed to the king. It may be that rulers were tightening up their control of these obligations from the later eighth century onwards and through their legislation were extending them into new areas, as may be the case in England too in this period.[32] Finally, one wonders how effective the ban on entry of judicial officials was in practice, especially when outlying properties were far distant from the main site occupied by the holder of privilege. The Carolingians were certainly concerned to strengthen protection for immunities, to this end introducing new clauses (the *defensio* and *tuitio*) into the documents themselves and laying down a 600 *solidi* fine to be paid by anyone who infringed the rights of the immunist, which might suggest that these rights were indeed being infringed. Given the essentially weak government of early medieval states, it was more likely that it was the strength of the issuing body which determined the strength of the immunities, than the other way round.

[31] These charters are *Diplomata regum Francorum e stirpe Merowingica*, in *MGH Diplomatum Imperii*, vol. 1, ed. K. Pertz, no. 74, pp. 65–6, and in the same volume, *Spuria*, nos. 67, p. 184; 69, pp. 185–6; 80, p. 195; 85, pp. 199–200; and 93, pp. 206–7. Pertz thought these last five charters to be spurious, but modern opinion is that they derive from genuine originals: W. Goffart, *The Le Mans Forgeries. A Chapter in the History of Church Property in the Ninth Century*, pp. 257–9. For the argument that this material demonstrates a general continuity in taxation, Magnou-Nortier, 'La gestion publique', pp. 300–2, and for the view that it reveals customs of a purely local nature, Ganshof, 'L'Immunité dans la Monarchie Franque', p. 181 and n. 28.

[32] The obligations were included amongst the *sordida munera* from which the church was excused in the *Theodosian Code* (see above n. 14). Carolingian legislation which stipulated that those holding immunities should have to perform these public duties: *Pippini Italiae Regis Capitulare 782–786*, ch. 4, *MGH Capit.*, vol. 1, p. 192; *Capitulare de Functionibus Publicis*, ch. 3, *MGH Capit.*, vol. 1, pp. 294–5; *Capitulare Olonnense Mundanum 825*, ch. 2, *MGH Capit.*, vol. 1, p. 330. On immunities and public burdens in England, see N. P. Brooks, 'The development of military obligations in eighth- and ninth-century England', in P. Clemoes and K. Hughes (eds.), *England before the Conquest. Studies presented to Dorothy Whitelock*, pp. 69–84.

The third objection to the view that immunities carried within them the seed of the kind of independent lordship (*seigneurie banale*) seen in the tenth and eleventh centuries, rests upon the observation that when in the tenth century royal rights did fall into the hands of independent lords, existing immunities were often not the basis of those lordships, nor were the rights exercised within them obviously based on ones traditionally enjoyed within immunities. One might indeed say that 'banal lordship' arose in spite of, not because of, immunities. Given that military power in the hands of lay persons was a key factor in the establishment of independent lordship, it is not surprising that a privilege enjoyed only by ecclesiastical institutions, and reserving high justice and military obligations to a higher authority, was not much at issue. In the tenth century demand for immunities in traditional form west of the Rhine fell as the exclusions they conveyed declined in value, in tandem with the enfeeblement of royal authority. Where immunities did continue to be granted, the traditional form and content, which they had kept since Merovingian times, changed significantly with the addition of the more extensive rights associated with independent lordship. In West Francia the granting of immunities ceased to be a royal prerogative, advocates rose in status as they became military leaders, and the number of confirmations far outstripped new grants. Confirmations seem to have been valued primarily for the notion of protection (*tuitio, defensio*) they invoked, and for the 600 *solidi* fine for invasion, rather than for the exclusion of *iudices publici*, now mostly defunct.[33] In Italy immunities remained little changed until the late tenth century, when they began to convey full jurisdiction over territory, in which cases they were arguably responding to change on the ground rather than provoking it.[34] In Germany the form of immunities began to change rather earlier than elsewhere, for it seems that from the time of Louis the Pious onwards, formularies were no longer used in East Francia. When previous documents were the only available models, the forms of document originally used for grants of immunity came to be used for other sorts of privileges too, like grants of market, mint and

---

[33] Kroell, *L'Immunité Franque*, pp. 297–329.

[34] Fischer-Drew, 'The immunity in Carolingian Italy', pp. 192–3. For cases in Italy in which the holding of a stronghold was the basis from which rights of lordship were extended, see Wickham, below, pp. 227–41.

hunting rights, and conversely such rights began also to be written into immunities. Ottonian immunities thus bear little resemblance to their distant Merovingian ancestors.[35]

In contrast to Kroell's view that immunities caused a weakening of authority, it has been argued that they actually served to preserve it. This argument builds upon the observation that all recorded immunities were granted to the church, and notes that in the early medieval period the church was taking on more and more functions of government. The approach shares with Kroell the conviction that immunities were very important in the distribution of power, but differs in that it sees the state using immunities to by-pass the threat to its position posed by the lay *potentes*.[36] A third line of thinking, in contrast to the other two, plays down the importance of immunities by arguing that relatively little was given away when they were granted. Levillain, for instance, argued that the exclusion of judicial officers from the immunity was aimed merely at freeing the beneficiary from the exactions those officials would have levied.[37] Walter Goffart has developed this line of argument by reminding us that the aim of the grant (like most grants) was to give a gift to the holy. Immunities of Roman type had done this by giving exemptions from various sorts of taxation, but by the mid-seventh century so little taxation remained in Francia that all the Merovingian kings had to give away were the profits of justice and requisitions for royal shelter and sustenance. A new type of immunity was thus developed in order to provide the beneficiary with the profits of justice. In Goffart's words, the privileges of immunity 'mirror the system of public burdens from which they afford full or partial relief'.[38] E. Magnou-Nortier has made similar observations, albeit whilst trying to sustain an argument quite contrary to Goffart's: namely, that since only the profits of justice were granted away, this indicates that other forms of taxation continued to be levied in the Merovingian and Carolingian periods. In her

[35] E. E. Stengel, *Die Immunität in Deutschland bis zum Ende des 11 Jahrhunderts*, pp. 338–41, 590. On how few immunities became the basis of comital jurisdiction in Germany, H. Hoffmann, 'Grafschaften in Bischofshand', *Deutsches Archiv für Erforschung des Mittelalters*, 46 (1990), pp. 460–1.

[36] For a recent restatement of this view, R. Kaiser, 'Royauté et pouvoir épiscopale au Nord de la Gaule VIIe – IXe siècles', in Atsma (ed.), *La Neustrie*, vol. 1, p. 147 and n. 125.

[37] Levillain, 'Note sur l'immunité', p. 63.

[38] Goffart, 'Old and new in Merovingian taxation', p. 6.

view, therefore, the privilege reflects a small part only of the income which was available to the state.[39] The essential weakness in Magnou-Nortier's thinking is that it discusses taxation in isolation from other economic relationships in Frankish society. However, the nature and state of the economy in general must be taken into account if we are to understand the fiscal basis of government, and, more to the point, if we are to estimate the practical benefits that having an immunity brought. So although these scholars have challenged the view that the granting of immunities weakened public authority, little has been said about the more immediate economic and religious needs contemporaries expected immunities to meet. It is to these practical aspects that we now turn by investigating the significance of the lighting clauses.

THE CONTEXT AND IMPORTANCE OF LIGHTING CLAUSES IN IMMUNITY DOCUMENTS

The injunction that 'whatever our fisc had been able to hope for [from the land in question] should now in perpetuity go towards the lights of the church', a term basic to early grants of immunity, has been ignored, because, as was suggested earlier, it is regarded as purely formulaic.[40] But even if it were simply formulaic, it is still important to know why grants of this nature should have employed this particular formula, for formulas were developed precisely because they related to practical needs. In the seventh century, the context in which the profits of immunity came to be dedicated to lighting was that the provision of lighting was actually a gift of some liturgical significance and economic importance. Apart from the simple need to illuminate buildings which were often in use in the hours of darkness, the idea that lamps (*luminaria*) should be kept burning in churches had its origin in the early books of the Old Testament. In the Book of Leviticus Moses was told by God to burn lamps of purest olive oil before the Tabernacle in a ritual that should be handed down the generations for all time. Terrible punishment was threatened against those who let the light go out, and this was a threat which was quoted in ninth-century

---

[39] Magnou-Nortier, 'Étude sur le privilège d'immunité', pp. 474–84. In her view the main advantage of holding an immunity was the right to collect, but not to keep, taxes. This becomes the simple definition of the privilege in Durliat, *Les Finances Publiques*, p. 164.

[40] Above, n. 10.

conciliar legislation.[41] Merovingian church councils did not mention perpetual light, but saints' Lives from the Merovingian period make it clear that oil lamps really were burned throughout the night in churches, and that keeping them filled was a religious duty.[42] Carolingian legislation repeatedly demanded that churches have lamps, and that the bishops should make sure that they were working.[43] Bishops were also responsible for providing the chrism for baptism, and whatever the lamps burned was to be paid for from the income from church property.[44]

Oil was a precious commodity in early medieval Europe north of the Alps and Pyrenees. According to Gregory of Tours, in the later sixth century Marseilles was where one went to get oil, and as we shall see, late seventh-century royal documents also referred to Marseilles in this context.[45] This oil was probably imported from

---

[41] Leviticus 24: 1–4. It was Leviticus 6: 12–13 which was quoted in 'Concilium Aquisgranense a 836', ch. 28, ed. A. Werminghoff, *Concilia aevi Karolini*, vol. 2, *MGH LL in quarto*, sectio 3, vol. 2, p. 739, with the effect of warning that if anyone let the lamps go out they would suffer a terrible fate. Lamps are also the subject of Exodus 27: 17–24, Exodus 40: 4 and 24–5, and Numbers 4: 16 and 8: 1–5. I am grateful to D. Ganz for drawing my attention to these references.

[42] See, for example, *Passio Praejecti*, ch. 38, ed. B. Krusch, *MGH SRM*, vol. 5, pp. 247–8, in which a little oil taken for a night vigil becomes sufficient to light twenty or thirty holy places; or *Visio Baronti*, ch. 11, ed. B. Krusch, *MGH SRM*, vol. 5, pp. 385–6, in which the monk Barontus was asked in a vision why his church was short of lighting and did not burn lamps at all hours.

[43] In *MGH Capit.*, vol. 1: *Capitularia Ecclesiastica ad Salz data 803–4*, p. 119; *Capitula Missorum in Theodonis villa datum primum mere ecclesiasticum*, ch. 8, p. 121; *Capitula de Diversis Causis, 807*, ch. 4, p. 136; *Capitula Missorum vel Synodalia*, p. 182; *Pippini Capitulare Italicum, 801–10*, ch. 7, p. 210; *Admonitio ad Omni Regni Ordines 823–825*, ch. 5, p. 304; *Capitula Italica*, ch. 8, p. 336, in *MGH Capit.*, vol. 2; *Episcopum ad Hludowico Imperatorem Relatio, 829*, ch. 11, p. 33; *Capitulare Missorum Suessionense*, ch. 1, p. 267.

[44] On chrism, *Karoli Magni Capitulare Primum, 769*, ch. 8, *MGH Capit.*, vol. 1, p. 45, which also stipulated that the old chrism be burned in the lamps at the end of the year. On the provision of lighting, 'Concilium Cabillonense 813', ch. 16, ed. A. Werminghoff, *Concilia aevi Karolini*, vol. 2, p. 277: 'Episcopi. . .itaque de ecclesiae facultatibus balsamum emant et luminaria singuli in ecclesiis suis concinnanda provideant' ('Bishops should buy balsam [for chrism] from church wealth and provide for lamps to be set up in each of their churches'). Here the onus was on the bishop to pay so that the priests of each church would not have to bear the charge of providing chrism and lighting, but the arrangement also had the effect of increasing episcopal control over subordinate churches.

[45] Gregory of Tours, *Decem Libri Historiarum*, IV. 43, V. 5, ed. B. Krusch and W. Levison, *MGH SRM*, vol. 1, pt 1, pp. 177, 200. For a survey of the oil trade and Marseilles' role in it in the Merovingian period, D. Claude, 'Der Handel im westlichen Mittelmeer während des Frühmittelalters', in K. Düwel, H. Jankuhn, H. Siems and D. Timpe (eds.), *Untersuchungen zu Handel und Verkehr der vor- und frühgeschichtlichen Zeit im Mittel- und Nordeuropa*, pp. 74–6. Claude did not consider the hagiographical material discussed below and so missed the evidence for oil production in Provence and the role of Bordeaux in the trade.

North Africa and from Spain, but these were not the only sources of oil. The Life of St Ansbert, a work written in the early eighth century, tells of a grant from King Theuderic III (673–90) to the monastery of St Wandrille of an estate in Provence which was to provide oil for its lamps.[46] The mid-eighth-century *Life of St Philibert* has a story in which the monks of Jumièges were running out of oil when Philibert prophesied that they would soon have a year's supply. Miraculously, the next day a ship from Bordeaux arrived in the Seine bearing forty measures (*modii*) of oil. Another time the monks were reduced to putting fat in the lamps until a whale washed up on shore, and from its carcass they obtained thirty *modii* of oil.[47] From this anecdotal evidence it can be seen that olive oil was plainly the preferred choice for lighting fuel, but that being expensive and hard to come by, substitutes could be used.[48]

As an import, the purchase of oil is likely to have required cash, and it is worth remarking that by allowing the beneficiary to collect fines and to keep other charges once due to the fisc, the privilege of immunity was a source of cash. Where provision for lights is mentioned in documents other than immunities, there is also an association with cash, either in relation to exemptions from toll, or as one original charter of 695 stated, where there had been an annual grant of 300 *solidi* to the monastery of St Denis for lighting.[49] That grants for lighting really were intended to fund the beneficiaries' purchase of oil is suggested by a charter model, probably early eighth century, attached as a supplement to the Formulary of Marculf. Though entitled *Immunitas* it is really a toll exemption in favour of a bishop, and it excuses from tolls a certain number of his carts on their yearly run to Marseilles, or to other ports, to buy provision for lighting, or get any other

---

[46] *Vita Ansberti episcopi Rotomagensis*, ch. 9, ed. B. Krusch, *MGH SRM*, vol. 5, p. 625.

[47] *Vita Philiberti*, cc. 37–8, ed. B. Krusch, *MGH SRM*, vol. 5, p. 602.

[48] The difficulties in finding and paying for lighting materials is a surprising omission in D. Hägermann's otherwise very useful survey of the practical needs of the early medieval monastery: D. Hägermann, 'Der Abt als Grundherr. Kloster und Wirtschaft im frühen Mittelalter', in F. Prinz (ed.), *Herrschaft und Kirche*, pp. 345–85.

[49] *ChLA*, vol. 14, 577 records an unusual arrangement in which the king gave land from the fisc to St Denis, in return for which the monastery ceased to receive 200 *solidi* from the fisc and 100 *solidi* from the revenues of Marseilles, which had previously been designated for lighting.

necessity.[50] The document closes with the stipulation that the bishop is to use the profits from these exemptions for the lighting of his church. That it should be taken as normal that the bishop would send to Marseilles for this provision, makes it very likely that the purchase of oil was envisaged.

It is clear that Marseilles maintained both its political and economic links with the north into the eighth century. In 692 King Clovis III exempted St Denis from tolls and confirmed the monastery's right to receive 100 *solidi* yearly from the royal depot in Marseilles, the money to be spent on what was available in the port.[51] This privilege was confirmed again in 716.[52] In the same year the monastery of Corbie also had a *tractoria* confirmed. By this privilege the monastery's agents would receive provisions from toll stations on the route to Marseilles, eight of which were named in the Marculf supplement just quoted. It was also granted substantial amounts of goods in kind from the royal depot at Fosses, near Marseilles. Amongst the goods Corbie was to receive from Fosses were 10,000 pounds of oil and, as usual, the grant was made for the *luminaria* of the monks.[53] In support of the impression of continuing north–south contact that these confirmations give, is the fact that coins bearing the name of the Merovingian kings were minted in Marseilles until the reign of Childebert III (695–710), longer than anywhere else south of the Loire, and that the rulers of Provence appeared at the royal court in Neustria in Childebert's reign.[54]

---

[50] *Marculfi Form.*, Supplementum 1, p. 332: 'ut de annis singulis de carra tanta, quod a luminaria conparandum ad Massilia vel per relicos portos infra regno Nostro, ubicumque missi sui marcare videntur – vel pro reliqua necessitate discurrentis – nullo telloneo nec qualibet reddibucione exinde ad parte fisci Nostri sui discurrentes dissolvere non dibeant'. It is curious that on the facing page Uddholm's translation of the 'a luminaria conparanda' reads, 'pour les besoins des moines'.

[51] *ChLA*, vol. 14, 574. It was this right to receive 100 *solidi* from Marseilles which would be given up three years later in *ChLA*, vol. 14, 577. The *Gesta Dagoberti*, ch. 18, pp. 406–7 may refer to the original of this privilege, in which the money was to be spent 'according to the docking of the ships' ('secundum ordo cataboli'), that is, to buy what was available.

[52] *ChLA*, vol. 14, 589, which shows, incidentally, that in 716 St Denis was again in receipt of the 100 *solidi* from Marseilles, and, presumably, still held the land for which they had earlier been given up in part exchange.

[53] L. Levillain, *Examen critique des chartes Mérovingiennes et Carolingiennes de l'abbaye de Corbie*, document no. 15, pp. 236–7, discussion, pp. 68–72.

[54] On the continuing political contacts between North and South in the reign of Childebert III, P. Fouracre, 'Observations on the outgrowth of Pippinid influence in the 'regnum Francorum' after the battle of Tertry (687–715)', *Medieval Prosopography*, 5 (1984), pp. 9, 11–12, and for the kinship network which underpinned such contacts in the early eighth

These are, therefore, indications that Marseilles remained an important port, and although it was not the only source of oil, it is tempting to think that oil was prominent amongst the commodities which kept it supplied with customers, and that the cash collected in immunities formed a significant part of those customers' disposable income. Cash from this source may, of course, have formed only a small part of the total income which the great ecclesiastical land holders received from rents and other dues, but its significance lay in the fact that it was in effect earmarked for this particular purpose by the kings who had granted the institution immunity, and this purpose was reaffirmed when the grant was confirmed.

From around the second quarter of the eighth century, Provence was beset by warfare and invasion, and Marseilles fell into decline. In 779 when Charlemagne confirmed his father's privilege of toll exemption for the monastery of St Germain des Prés, the monks were given licence to go wherever they wished to buy provision for lighting, but Marseilles was not amongst the places mentioned. This omission may relate to the port's decline, and it may also suggest that to some extent wax candles, which could be obtained in northern and eastern Francia, were replacing oil lamps.[55] There is good evidence for the use of wax in the ninth century, but oil lighting remained important, as we saw earlier from the evidence of Carolingian legislation. Oil lamps may have been preferred because they would give a continuous light throughout the night, and they may generally have been regarded as superior in religious settings.[56] In the mid-ninth century, for instance, it was said that the cathedral church of Le Mans kept thirty lamps and five candles burning on ordinary Sundays, and at least ninety lamps and ten candles were lit on feast days.[57]

---

century, P. J. Geary, *Aristocracy in Provence. The Rhône Basin at the Dawn of the Carolingian Age*, pp. 101–25.

[55] *MGH Diplomata Karolinorum*, vol. 1, ed. E. Mühlbacher, no. 122, pp. 170–1. Interestingly the *Vita Corbiniani ab auctore Arbeone*, ch. 39, ed. B. Krusch, *MGH SRM*, vol. 6, p. 590, a work from Bavaria, written in the second half of the eighth century (but about a bishop of the later Merovingian period), relates a lighting miracle in which candles rather than lamps were burned in the night. This might suggest that in Bavaria the use of oil was generally less common, and it is worth noting in this context that Bavarian law made reference to wax production.

[56] That oil lamps were to be used was sometimes specified, as in Tessier, *Recueil*, vol. 2, no. 333, pp. 236–8, when Charles the Bald asked that, 'three oil lamps be constantly burned'. Tessier, *Recueil*, vol. 2, no. 315, pp. 197–8, provides another example.

[57] 'Gesta domini Aldrici Cenomannicae urbis episcopi', ch. 46, quoted in *Polyptique de St Germain des Prés*, vol. 1, ed. A. Longnon, p. 54, n. 3.

What did change from the mid-eighth century onwards was that a broader range of documents made grants for the provision of lighting. Some immunities and toll exemptions continued to do so, but once royal *defensio* or *tuitio* became a regular feature of immunities, and one of their declared purposes was to enable the beneficiary to live without disturbance of property rights (*in quieto ordine*), then the lighting clause was often dropped from the document. As Goffart has pointed out, the great advantage of having the king's guarantee of *defensio* over land was that it enabled the landowner to enjoy the prerogative of using a sworn inquest to establish his or her rights.[58] This privilege would have become increasingly valuable as churches let out more and more of their land in precarial tenure and wished to re-establish ownership when each precarial agreement came to an end. At the same time, the token rent or *census* which the precarial tenant paid the church in recognition of its ownership, provided a cash income which was sometimes dedicated to lighting. An example of this is in fact provided by the St Wandrille *precaria* discussed by Ian Wood in this volume.[59] So, the same context which made royal protection a necessary stipulation in grants and, especially, in confirmations of immunity privileges, also had the effect of making the provision of lighting a less significant aspect as alternative sources of cash were dedicated to this purpose. Dedicating the *census* to lighting had the effect of conserving the moral purpose of property ownership by the church, even though its property was in the possession of others. By the same token, reserving income for a liturgical purpose was a way of affirming that the property was indeed owned by the church.[60] From this time onwards provisions for lighting would also be made by granting the beneficiary land or income, rather than the right to collect fines or exemption from tolls. The pope provided an example, and possibly set a precedent, in granting land in this

---

[58] Goffart, *The Le Mans Forgeries*, p. 16.

[59] See above, pp. 35–7. A clear example of the connection between *census* payment and lighting is provided by a confirmation charter of the year 849 in which one Adalmann continued to hold land from the monastery of St Martin's Tours, 'unde censuit in festivitate sanctae Crucis . . . annis singulis se daturum ad illum sepulchrum tres solidos argenti ad luminariam concinnandam' ('for which he paid rent on the festival of the holy cross [agreeing] that each year he would at that tomb pay three *solidi* of silver for lamps to be set up'). Note that in this charter the payment for the *luminaria* was in cash, whereas the other dues mentioned in it were to be paid in kind: Tessier, *Recueil*, vol. 1, no. 114, pp. 304–5.

[60] On the moral economy of ecclesiastical property ownership, Ganz, above, pp. 22–5.

fashion.[61] In 783, for instance, Charlemagne granted a villa in the wine-rich Moselle region to St Arnulf's at Metz for lamps to be burned incessantly for the soul of his late wife Hildegarde. That a readily disposable income was involved is the implication of this grant: what was left over from the cost of lighting was to pay for masses to be said and psalms to be sung daily for Hildegarde's soul.[62] The number of these kinds of grants of income from land increases markedly in the course of the ninth century, and may relate to increasing amounts of cash in the countryside. Grants for lighting from Charles the Bald (840–877), which tend to be more detailed than those found in earlier documents, make this connection between land and income very clear.[63] Grants often specified the number and location of the *mansi* which were to pay for the lights and other needs of the beneficiary. That units of production particularly associated with cash were granted, may be indicated from the frequency with which mills, fisheries and places in trading centres were granted. That income from the grant was in the form of silver was on occasion spelled out.[64]

A remarkable feature of grants which dedicated a proportion of income to lighting is that they were nearly all made by kings. The provision of lighting in private charters was unknown in the seventh century, extremely rare in the eighth century, and in the ninth century when private grants did appear, they tended to dedicate people, rather than property, to this purpose. The exclusively royal tenor of early grants begs the question of whether lighting for religious purposes was originally in some way a fiscal

---

[61] 'Concilium Romanum a 761', ed. A. Werminghoff, in *Concilia aevi Karolini*, vol. 2, p. 67, which referred to Pope Paul I granting to his own foundation: 'massas, fundos, casales, colonias, vineas, etiam atque ortua et oliveta seu domos et hospicia, salinas, et aquimola vel piscarias' ('holdings, farms, estates, *colonus* holdings, vineyards, and also crops and olive groves, as well as dwelling houses, salt works, water mills and fishing rights'), in the context of lighting provision and other support for the monks. For Frankish examples, see *Diplomata Karolinorum*, vol. 1, no. 21, p. 30, no. 80, pp. 114–5, no. 83, pp. 119–20, no. 92, p. 133. .

[62] *Diplomata Karolinorum*, vol. 1, no. 149, p. 203. In order to ensure that this gift remained dedicated to its original purpose, the recipient was forbidden ever to give it away as a *benefice* or to lease it out to a lay person *per precarium*.

[63] For examples, Tessier, *Recueil*, vol. 1, no. 60, pp. 171–3, no. 68, p. 196, no. 114, pp. 304–5, no. 134, pp. 335–6, no. 160, pp. 424–6, no. 185, pp. 489–91, no. 215, p. 544, and *Recueil*, vol. 2, no. 230, pp. 13–14, no. 246, pp. 54–6, no. 273, pp. 113–14, no. 315, pp. 197–8, no. 333, pp. 237–8, no. 383, pp. 360–1, no. 435, pp. 473–5.

[64] Tessier, *Recueil*, vol. 1, no. 114, see above, n. 59. Silver was similarly specified in Tessier, *Recueil*, vol. 2, no. 435, p. 474.

responsibility or duty. If it had been, then this might explain why it featured in early immunities. There is, however, no hint of any such responsibility in either the *Theodosian Code* or in early Merovingian legislation where we do find antecedents for other elements of immunities. One explanation for this silence could be that the incorporation of perpetual lighting into ecclesiastical ritual actually post-dated most Roman legislation on church matters. Lighting may have acquired a quasi-fiscal basis by the Carolingian period. Carolingian kings at least legislated to ensure that it was provided, and demanded that where income from *mansi* was earmarked for this purpose, it really did get spent on lighting.[65] Keeping the lamps burning was thus the concern of the ruler, even if the cost was not met by a general charge upon subjects, as seems to have been the case in England in the tenth and eleventh centuries.[66]

Evidence from surveys of church estates (known as 'polyptychs') in northern Francia from the early ninth century onwards, might show how the cash for lighting was raised from certain *mansi*. It indicates that there was a class of people whose duty was to provide lighting for the church. These so-called *luminarii*, or (less often) *cerarii*, were of relatively low social status and are to be distinguished from those who voluntarily donated property or pledged themselves to provide lighting. The *luminarii*, few in number overall, were free hereditary tribute payers. Their annual payment to the church was in coin or wax, and from the more detailed information in the polyptych of St Bertin it can be estimated that the payment amounted on average to about four *denarii* each.[67] Again, we see here a definite link between lighting provision and cash

---

[65] In the *Admonitio ad Omni Regni Ordines 823–825*, ch. 5, p. 304, bishops were admonished to set an example by not appropriating income assigned to lighting: 'ne de mansis ad ecclesiae luminaria datis aliquid accipiant, sic et vos et vestri archidiaconi de eisdem mansis nihil accipiendo aliis exemplum prebeatis, sed potius ad id quod dati sunt servire concedantur' ('they should not take anything from the holdings (*mansi*) which have been given for the lamps of the church, so that by not taking anything from these holdings, you and your archdeacons may set a good example to others, in that what has been given for this purpose should indeed be allowed to be used for it').

[66] Some Carolingian legislation did stipulate that tithes should cover the cost of lighting, for example, *Pippini Capitulare Italicum 801–810*, ch. 7, p. 210, and 'Concilium Meldense-Parisiense 845–6', ch. 78, pp. 419–20. In practice, however, the cost was met from a variety of sources. In England it seems to have been met by a general levy known as 'light-dues' which was extra to the tithe: *Councils and Synods and other documents relating to the English Church*, vol. 1, pt. 1, ed. D. Whitelock, pp. 308, 332.

[67] *Polyptique de St Germain des Près*, vol. 1, pp. 32, 54, 136; F. Ganshof, *Le Polyptique de St Bertin (844–859). Édition Critique et Commentaire*, pp. 29, 83–4.

payment, in contrast to the payments in kind and labour services owed by other inhabitants of the same estate. In Goffart's view, many of the dues which the polyptychs recorded were rooted in late Roman taxation, that is, they had a fiscal basis, but as he also admits, there is no evidence for the raising of such dues from the Merovingian period.[68] We cannot tell, therefore, whether these *luminarii* were of ancient or recent origin, whether, in other words, they were already there contributing to lighting funds when the seventh-century privileges of immunity were granted. It is conceivable that they were somehow called into existence by the privileges themselves, which might have been the case if, for instance, they had been people hitherto contributing to the unspecified dues (*redibuciones*) which are sometimes referred to in the grants.

From the middle of the tenth century onwards, hereditary tribute payers, often called *censuales*, *cerarii* or *tributarii*, begin to appear in grants to the church rather than in estate surveys. From the late eleventh century their appearance is frequent, especially in southern Germany. These people, like the *luminarii* on Carolingian estates, had to pay a yearly due in money or wax, but unlike their Carolingian predecessors they were generally unfree, although some free people did still sometimes voluntarily subject themselves to this kind of service to a patron saint. The unfree appeared in documents because they were the subjects of gifts from landowners to the church: when landowners wished to contribute towards lighting, one way of doing this was to dedicate their *mancipia* to the church to become hereditary tribute payers, that is, to transfer their rent to the church.[69] The human intermediaries of such gifts possibly reflect a deterioration in the legal position of the rent-paying peasantry, in that they may now have been more than ever subject to the lord's arbitrary action. The gifts also show how giving had become targeted upon specific people, rents and services, as opposed to the wholesale alienation of land one sees in early medieval contexts. Both elements are part of the general pattern in which immunities in their traditional form had become

---

[68] W. Goffart, 'From Roman taxation to medieval seigneurie: three notes', *Speculum*, 47 (1972), pp. 388–9.

[69] Ch. Perrin, *Recherches sur la Seigneurie Rurale en Lorraine d'après les plus anciennes Censiers (IXe–XIIe siècles)*, pp. 147–53, and for example of how such people were given, p. 698 ('Traditiones Romaricenses', no. 9). For a late eleventh-century document illustrating the hereditary status of people tied to the church in this way: *Die Traditionen des Hochstifts Regensburg und des Klosters S. Emmeram*, ed. J. Widemann, no. 672, p. 326.

less attractive, as changed social and economic conditions made redundant their original purpose and the privilege they conferred.

The history of lighting in general deserves a proper study. As we have seen, it has a bearing upon a history much wider than that of the liturgy. The following very brief observations on what is a vast and largely unexplored subject are intended only to round off the preceding discussion by placing the question of the significance of the lighting clauses in immunities in a wider context. Provision of lighting seems to have been of particular concern in the early middle ages because of the scarcity and expense of oil. The valuable nature of oil is indicated, for instance, in those many miracle stories in which an oil lamp burns for an exceptional length of time without being refilled. Even when wax was used, this too was expensive.[70] Later in the middle ages, when lighting was by candles, and societies were a lot richer, it still remained relatively expensive, and fraternities were formed to meet the cost.[71] Although early grants of provision are said simply to have been 'for the lamps' (*ad luminaria*) which could mean the general illumination of the church, it is clear from later documents that what donors often wanted was a light to burn incessantly for the soul of a named person. Light had (and has) a symbolic meaning, and an association with eternity, but it was always liable to be turned into a commodity because it was so expensive to provide.[72] We cannot

---

[70] Cf. H. Mayr-Harting's comments on the lighting bill of the church of Magdeburg in relation to the great amount of silver donated to it by the emperor Otto I: 'The church of Magdeburg: its trade and its town in the tenth and eleventh centuries', in D. Abulafia, M. Franklin and M. Rubin (eds.), *Church and City 1000–1500, Essays in Honour of Christopher Brooke*, p. 143.

[71] The *Zeche* of Augsburg, documented from the later thirteenth century onwards, are of particular interest here: not only did the gathering and control of money for lights allow them to develop a degree of social control and some political power, allowing lay people to control supplies for basic liturgical functions was also one way in which the Catholic church would eventually lose control of ritual. See R. Kiessling, *Bürgerliche Gesellschaft und Kirche in Augsburg im Spätmittelalter*, pp. 102–20. I am grateful to P. Broadhead for drawing my attention to this work.

[72] Play was sometimes made on the term 'light' in order to emphasize the link between the material gift and the spiritual benefit or counter-gift. See, for instance, *MGH Diplomata regum et imperatorum Germaniae*, vol. 1, ed. T. Sickel, no. 29, p. 27, a grant of toll income by Konrad I in which it is stated in the *arenga* that, 'si ecclesias dei aliqua semper utilitate fulcire studuerimus, non solum regium morem exercemus, sed etiam aliquod lumen nostrae animae inde promereri speramus' ('if we strive always to provide God's churches with useful support, then not only do we perform a royal duty, we also hope thereby to deserve some light for our soul'). This anticipates the dispositive formula that the grant be made, 'ad concinnanda luminaria iure perpetuo in proprium' ('to set up lamps by right eternal, for ourselves').

say that the privilege of immunity was developed in the seventh century simply, or even primarily, in order to fill church lamps with oil. As we have seen, the content of the privilege shows both that it did have antecedents in Roman and early Merovingian legislation and that it had fiscal, judicial and social as well as liturgical aspects. But the importance of the dedication to lighting was that it brought all of these aspects together by mediating between commodity and eternity. There were, of course, other ways of converting property to spiritual use, such as payment for prayer or the giving of alms for the poor, but it is the universal requirement for an expensive and sometimes scarce commodity which also had a special symbolic importance which makes the provision of lighting stand out. That from this point of observation we can look at the subject of immunities from new angles, is an important part of the conclusion which now follows.

CONCLUSIONS

In this discussion we have followed two different strands of thought about the significance and development of Frankish immunities. One line, unavoidably negative in tone, considered the possible effects immunities had upon the strength of public authority in the longer term. The other looked at them more positively in terms of contemporary needs. The two strands are not entirely separate, and to focus upon the points at which they converge will help to draw together what has of necessity been a somewhat cursory examination of a massive area. A general theme, common to both strands of thought, has been the economic context in which immunities developed. Put crudely, we have seen that immunities became less important as churches (and, later, lords) were increasingly able to get what they needed without recourse to a privilege dispensed by an often distant ruler. It is pertinent here to remember the pivotal role of the church in the economy at large. Churches and monasteries were already very rich landowners by the later seventh century, and the acquisition of immunities must have helped to enhance their wealth by providing them with extra cash, some of which they redistributed in alms and purchases.[73] Movable

---

[73] According to hagiographic tradition, alms were distributed in coin, as, for example, in *Passio Praejecti*, ch. 6, p. 229.

wealth was essential, even for those whose wealth lay largely in land, for it enabled the holder to participate in a wider range of activities than mere possession of land could do. Cash, wax, oil and wine were all movables which were particularly associated with the church, and already in the seventh century we can see the monastery of St Denis holding large stocks of three of these commodities.[74] Immunities must have served to increase a surplus like this, and it was by making use of such advantages that the church not only invested in but also led the development of the economy in Francia.[75] So it could be said that, albeit in a rather indirect way, and amidst a host of other factors, immunities did contribute to the breakdown of public authority over a widespread area in as much as that breakdown was partly the product of increasing wealth in the countryside. By the same token, it was increasing wealth which meant that lighting and other needs could be met from a wider range of sources.

It would, of course, be simplistic to look at immunities purely in economistic terms, or for that matter, to consider them only as providers for liturgical needs. Nor do they simply reveal the legal means by which property was turned into power, which is the most common interpretation of their significance. Nor are they just 'mirrors' of what the state could take from the land. If, on the other hand, all these aspects are considered together rather than separately, then thinking about immunities might begin to capture some of the complexity of the ways in which power and property were related in practice. At the simplest level, through grants of immunity donors ensured that the church received more income from its property and so increased its economic power. But by meeting some of the church's expenditure for liturgical purposes and by almsgiving, the donor also increased his (or in just one case, that of Queen Balthild, her) chances of present well being

---

[74] *ChLA*, vol. 14, 578: St Denis paid a 600 *solidi* fine on behalf of one Ibbo, who in return pledged land to the monastery. *ChLA*, vol. 14, 573: St Denis was pledged to receive 1,500 pounds of oil and 100 measures of 'good wine', possibly again in return for the payment of some kind of fine on someone else's behalf.

[75] For the role of ecclesiastical estate management in stimulating the growth of a cash economy in this period, W. Bleiber, *Naturalwirtschaft und Ware-Geld-Beziehungen zwischen Somme und Loire während des 7. Jahrhunderts*, and for its place in the development of the 'political economy' of Carolingian Francia, see J.-P. Devroey, 'Réflexions sur l'économie des premiers temps Carolingiens (768–877): grands domaines et action politique entre Seine et Rhin', *Francia*, 13 (1985).

and future salvation. In this sense, the grant of immunity was a means of exchanging earthly property for supernatural power. At the same time, by taking on the functions of the count and his subordinates, those holding immunities must have increased their influence over the lives of others, and thus enhanced their social power. Nevertheless, this increase in power over property and clients was a far cry from a weakening of public authority, if for no other reason than that those who received the privilege were amongst the most enthusiastic supporters of that authority, which they called upon to protect their property precisely via requests for confirmation of their privileges of immunity. It is in this kind of situation that our conventional distinctions between the 'public' and the 'private' in the organization of power break down.

If playing down the importance of immunities in relation to the long-term decline of public authority, and if insisting that we think about the significance of the lighting clauses in them, has had the effect of complicating an issue hitherto regarded as relatively straightforward, this would be the strongest recommendation of the approach adopted here. It at least serves to underline the complexity of the relationship between immunities, property and power, and it emphasizes within that relationship a cultural aspect of belief and perception which historians usually ignore. In the seventh century Frankish immunities reached a form which was perceived to be useful and mutually beneficial for both donor and recipient, satisfying material, spiritual and political needs of both parties. The granting of immunities did not compromise the power of the Frankish state, for that state was actually based upon compromise, its authority being in practice always weak. That the Merovingian and Carolingian kings could maintain hold over a massive territory for so long, nearly half a millennium in fact, is a phenomenon of cultural as much as of constitutional history. Immunities lay at the heart of that culture, and their significance lies in the way in which they helped to conserve it. Eventually, as we have seen, immunities in traditional form would become redundant as a process of acculturation and economic growth both multiplied the focal points of authority and moved them from kings to a wider range of lords. For the church, this same process of diversification amounted to a consolidation of its leading cultural position as a wider net of people was drawn into bearing responsibility for its well being and into guaranteeing that its needs would be met. The history of lighting is an element of cultural continuity which stretches beyond the period in which immunities were important, and it allows us to see how the church met its needs at different times and in very different social and economic contexts. In this way, focussing upon lighting helps us to put immunities into a wider cultural perspective. Formulaic or not, the lighting clauses have much to tell us about immunities and about the contexts in which they developed and decayed.

CHAPTER 4

The wary widow

Janet L. Nelson

Over thirty years ago David Herlihy claimed that women between
the Carolingian period and the twelfth century played 'an extraordinary role in the management of family property'.[1] Where Herlihy wrote, cautiously, of women's 'importance' and 'social prominence', the words often encountered in the more recent
historiography are 'power' and 'empowerment'.[2] It may be timely
to re-examine women's power over property in a broad context,
and also in a narrower one. The present book considers property
and power in general. This chapter focusses, first on widows as a
particular kind of women, then on a single instance of an aristocratic widow claiming certain powers over property within the
specific social context of ninth-century Francia. Gender is a useful
category for historians not least because it is a relational term:
its use requires, not that we isolate women, but that we analyse
complementarity between women and men.[3] For women, when
they can be seen, darkly, through the surviving documentary evidence, even when they seem to be acting autonomously, are never
acting alone. They appear, above all, in relation to men: biologi-
cally, alongside, or against, male kin; sociologically, supported by
genuine, or *soi-disants*, ecclesiastical protectors. Women are

My indebtedness to the rest of the Bucknell group goes without saying; but I should also
like to thank Patricia Skinner and Pauline Stafford for helpful comment.

[1] D. Herlihy, 'Land, family and women in continental Europe, 701–1200', *Traditio*, 17
(1961), reprinted in S. M. Stuard (ed.), *Women in Medieval Society*.
[2] See for example J. A. McNamara and S. Wemple, 'The power of women through the
family in medieval Europe', in M. Erler and M. Kowaleski (eds.), *Women and Power in
the Middle Ages*; also the editors' Introduction, and a number of other contributions to
the same volume.
[3] J. W. Scott, 'Gender: a useful category of historical analysis', *American Historical Review*,
91 (1986).

deployed as the agents, allies, pawns, of lay kin, and/or of male ecclesiastical communities.

The church looms large in the source material. In the historiography, its role is disputed. Herlihy saw it as protecting and promoting the legal rights of women. Jack Goody has suggested that it deliberately promoted women's capacity to control landed property, so as to benefit, itself, from female generosity.[4] If Goody were entirely right, then discoverers of women's 'empowerment' might betray a touch of anachronism, the historian's cardinal sin here given a special twist by feminist wishful thinking.[5] But 'the church' did not operate as an external force: religious beliefs were internalized as motivations by early medieval women as well as men. Religious practices and institutions, and churchmen themselves, were enmeshed in the social relations of a world dominated by powerful landed aristocracies. The evidence I shall present belies neat models, yet suggests that an early medieval aristocratic widow could wield power of a sort – could have some room for manoeuvre in shaping the future for herself, her property and other persons in her own social network. To ignore gender – to omit it from, for instance, a discussion of early medieval individuals' rights to bequeath property, as if just the same conditions and constraints applied to men and women alike – is to miss an important dimension of difference in the lives we seek to reconstruct. To include that dimension opens up one approach among others (I claim no more) to early medieval property and power.

The rights, and alleged empowerment, of early medieval women are documented in our sources in reference to property. If women's rights differed from men's, if gender made a difference, it might be that some aspects of the nature of power become clear precisely on that boundary. We might hope, too, to pin down the specificity of earlier medieval ideas about persons – persons as distinct from the collectivities that enfolded (and sometimes stifled) them. Men as well as women are sometimes represented in these documents as individuals, with minds of their own. Such apparent autonomy is not, I think, mere illusion.

[4] J. Goody, *The Development of the Family and Marriage in Europe*, pp. 95, 209, 261.
[5] For antidotes, see B. Gottlieb, 'The problem of feminism in the fifteenth century', in J. Kirshner and S. Wemple (eds.), *Women of the Medieval World*; and J. Bennett, '"History that stands still": women's work in the European past', *Feminist Studies*, 14 (1988).

This paper deals with a sub-group.[6] To claim widows' at least partial empowerment is not the same thing as to claim women empowered as such. Widows and women are distinct, if overlapping, categories. Yet, at the same time, the category 'widow' is gender-specific. There were, of course, widowers in early medieval societies, but they were not treated, in legal or religious terms, as different from other men, nor were they treated in the same way as widows, for good and ill. Widows' remarriage was discouraged, for instance, by Carolingian churchmen, whereas the widower's state was assigned no special religious value and his remarriage was expected.

Information about early medieval widows is relatively abundant, for two reasons. First, demographic conditions among the aristocracy of the earlier medieval world – high male mortality rates ensuing from the engagement of men in institutionalized violence – meant that the number of widows was notably large.[7] Second, the church, since patristic times, had a special place of honour for widows. Some churchmen took this evaluation a logical step further and prohibited widow remarriage: this was an area of debate, with orthodoxy eventually permitting remarriage while simultaneously punishing it by imposing penance.[8] Frankish bishops since the sixth century had forbidden widows to claim the title of deaconess. Yet widows were recognized as a distinct, and honourable, group, acquiring status through continence. Such ecclesiastical attitudes conflicted with the values of the secular aristocracy. The role of women as transmitters of status and property, and mediators of alliance, among the elite depended on their being given in marriage, and the *parentes* of an aristocratic widow would urge

---

[6] Valuable for the later middle ages are the contributions to L. Mirrer (ed.), *Upon My Husband's Death. Widows in the Literature and Histories of Medieval Europe;* and there is much relevant material, some of it early medieval, in E. Amt, *Women's Lives in Medieval Europe.*

[7] K. Leyser, *Rule and Conflict in an Early Medieval Society. Ottonian Saxony*, pp. 51–62.

[8] Jerome, 'Adversus Jovinianum' I. 14, *Patrologia Latina (PL)*, vol. 23, col. 244: '[Paulus] concedit viduis secunda matrimonia. Melius est enim licet alterum et tertium, unum virum nosse, quam plurimos: id est, tolerabilius est uni homini prostitutam esse, quam multis' ('Paul permitted second marriages to widows. Although a second and third [husband] is allowed, it is better that a single husband be carnally 'known' than several: that is, it is more tolerable that she be prostituted to one man than to many'), quoted by B. Jussen, 'On church organisation and the definition of an estate. The idea of widowhood in late antique and early medieval Christianity', *Tel Aviver Jahrbuch für deutsche Geschichte*, 22 (1993), p. 27, and cf. *idem*, 'Der 'Name' der Witwe. Zur 'Konstruktion' eines Standes in Spätantike und Frühmittelalter', in M. Parisse (ed.), *Veuves et veuvage dans le haut moyen age.* See also P. Brown, *The Body and Society*, pp. 147–50.

remarriage 'for temporal glory'.[9] Churchmen's priorities, on the other hand, entailed insistence on chastity, on non-marriage, for these same women. There was a further contradiction *within* ecclesiastical attitudes because of the cross-cutting of gender with class: churchmen needed aristocratic women's material support, yet denied all women religious office. A kind of compromise was reached when aristocratic widows were permitted to vow themselves to chastity, to assume a distinctive dress, and to live 'chastely at home'.[10]

In the Carolingian period, a Frankish noblewoman acquired property in three main ways. The first was through inheritance, in which daughters could share alongside, as well as in default of, sons. The second was through gifts at marriage, when a bride received a gift from her parents (Goody sees this as a kind of advance inheritance) and a gift from her husband.[11] Both these types of gift, which modern commentators often differentiate as dowry and dower, could be termed *dos* in medieval Latin. The function of both was to provide for the woman. There is no clear information on the relative value of these gifts, but in the ninth century descriptive as well as prescriptive sources lay overwhelming emphasis on the husband's *dos*, or *dotalicium*, to his bride. The awkward mid-ninth century case of Count Stephen, who threatened a realm with discord when he attempted to break his betrothal to Count Raymund's daughter, was settled when Stephen agreed to leave the girl's *dos* in Raymund's hands.[12] Legal formulas indicate that the husband's *dos* to his bride was expected to consist in part of movables (bedding, clothes, jewels, utensils; also

---

[9] *Vita Segolenae viduae, Acta Sanctorum*, 5 July, p. 632. (This text dates from the later seventh century: see W. Levison, 'Sigolena', *Neues Archiv*, 35 (1910).) *Parentes* very commonly has the sense of 'kinsmen' in medieval texts: hence the choice of the unambiguous *genitores* when the sense of 'parents' was required; see below, p. 106.

[10] 'Council of St Jean-de-Losne 673/5', ch. 13, ed. C. de Clercq, *Concilia Galliae*, p. 316. Interestingly, they are to be 'under the protection of the ruler' (*sub tuitione principis*). Cf. also *Pactus Legis Salicae*, ch. 100, ed. K. A. Eckhardt, *MGH LL in quarto*, sectio 1, vol. 4, pt. 1, p. 256.

[11] Goody, *Development of the Family*, pp. 206–7, 258–9. Goody distinguishes between direct dowry (paternal payment), and indirect dowry (payment from the groom at marriage or at bereavement). The latter is better (and usually) termed dower. For useful perspectives from a later period, see J. S. Loengard, '"Of the gift of her husband": English dower and its consequences in the year 1200', in Kirshner and Wemple, *Women*, and R. J. Archer, 'Rich old ladies: the problem of late medieval dowagers', in T. Pollard, *Property and Politics: Essays in Later Medieval English History*.

[12] See J. L. Nelson, *Charles the Bald*, pp. 196–7.

livestock[13]) as well as of land. Social and economic standing, which
the formularies may assume but do not specify, would in practice
have determined the total value of those components, and their
value relative to each other: it may well be that for persons lower
down the social scale, movables were relatively more valuable than
land.[14] In the case of noblewomen, land was surely *l'essentiel*.[15]
There is no clear evidence for how large a proportion of the husband's resources should be earmarked. Louis the German, in 862,
provided seventy-six *hubae* (peasant holdings) for his son to *dotare*
his bride. Charles the Bald seems to have given his wife Ermentrude a single large estate as *dos*, and his cousin Conrad also gave
his wife an estate.[16] Count Gerold gave to his wife a *dothalicium*
consisting of lands at two places.[17] According to a legal formula,
the management of the *dos* was to be by 'both equally' during the
husband's lifetime. It has been surmised that 'this often meant, by
the husband himself'.[18] In the mid-ninth century, Count Conrad
apparently acted alone in exchanging with the monks of St
Germain, Auxerre, his wife's *dos* for another villa.[19] In the ninth

---

[13] *Cartae Senonicae*, no. 25, in *Formulae Merowingici et Karolini Aevi*, ed. K. Zeumer, *MGH LL in quarto*, sectio 5 (hereafter *MGH Form.*), p. 197. R. Le Jan-Hennebicque, 'Aux origines du douaire médiéval', in Parisse, *Veuves*, p. 113, n. 48, sees these items as analogous to the morning-gift of earlier times. She argues, against D. O. Hughes, 'From brideprice to dowry', *Journal of Family History*, 3 (1978), that by the Carolingian period other forms of endowment of the bride by her husband, such as morning-gift, had been replaced (or subsumed) by the dower. See also C. Lauranson-Rosaz, 'Douaire et sponsalicium', in Parisse, *Veuves*. Neither considers the argument that a distinction was still being made in Ottonian, and even Salian, Germany between *Morgengabe* which the bride's surviving heirs could inherit, and dower, which reverted to the husband or his heirs: see R. Schröder, *Geschichte des ehelichen Güterrechts*, vol. 2, pp. 242–50, followed now by J. W. Bernhardt, *Itinerant Kingship and Royal Monasteries in Early Medieval Germany, c. 936–1075*, pp. 229, 232. Even allowing for possible differences between Germany and regions west of the Rhine, and for the special character of queens' endowment, I think that Le Jan-Hennebicque has a strong case generally, and that disputes over *dos* arose from persisting uncertainties over reversionary rights. The subject needs further research. Meanwhile, see below, n. 34.

[14] Cf. Hughes, 'Brideprice', pp. 281–4.

[15] Le Jan-Hennebicque, 'Origines', p. 115.

[16] *MGH Diplomata regum Germaniae ex stirpe Karolinorum*, vol. 1, ed. P. Kehr, no. 108, p. 156; G. Tessier, *Recueil des Actes de Charles II le Chauve*, nos. 13bis (842), and 261 (863), vol. 2, pp. 515 and p. 91. It is not clear in either of the two latter cases, however, that this was the total *dotalicium*.

[17] See Le Jan-Hennebicque, 'Origines', p. 118. (The reference here should be to C. Wam-pach (ed.), *Geschichte der Grundherrschaft Echternach*, vol. 1, no. 142.)

[18] So, Le Jan-Hennebicque, 'Origines', p. 116, commenting on *Formulae Andecavenses*, no. 54, *MGH Form.*, p. 23, and apparently inferring that such arrangements prevailed 'dans la plupart des cas'. This formulary dates from the seventh century.

[19] Tessier, *Recueil*, vol. 2, no. 261.

century, some Frankish legal formulas (echoing late Roman law[20]) assigned to the wife full control of her *dos*. According to one formula, the wife's control (*potestas*) was to be *libera et firmissima* with the transfer of the property into her *ius et dominatio*.[21] Another formula, a *testamentum dotis* quaintly termed an *osculum*, provides for a husband's transfer to his 'most beloved spouse' of lands with 'the fullest power of giving, selling, exchanging, and doing freely with them whatever you choose'.[22]

The third form of acquisition likely to come a woman's way was her endowment in widowhood. Variety, and possibly evolution, of custom can be traced. The seventh-century *Lex Ribuaria* prescribes that a Frankish widow should receive a 'third share' (*tertia*) of the joint acquisitions after the marriage;[23] according to a ninth-century Italian formula, a man living under Salic Frankish law should dower his wife with a third share of all his present goods as well.[24] In 821, Louis the Pious ordered *missi* in Flanders to ensure that widows of benefice-holders in that region would receive 'the third part of the shared acquisitions which they have received while together in possession of the benefice'.[25] Louis was evidently trying to ensure that the customary legal provision for widows from inheritance or acquisition would apply also to benefices as a special kind of property. These widows of benefice-holders were not *potentes feminae*, and the emperor's intervention implies that their rights, at

---

[20] See E. Levy, *West Roman Vulgar Law. The Law of Property*, p. 40.

[21] *Cartae Senonicae*, no. 25, *MGH Form.*, p. 196.

[22] *Formulae extravagantes*, I. 11, *MGH Form.*, p. 540: 'plenissima potestas dandi, vendendi, commutandi, et faciendi exinde libere quicquid elegeris.' Cf. no. 9: 'ut facias exinde quicquid volueris, nemine contradicente' ('that you may do therewith whatever you want, without anyone gainsaying you').

[23] *Lex Ribuaria*, 41, 2, ed. F. Beyerle and R. Buchner, *MGH LL in quarto*, sectio 1, vol. 3, pt. 2, p. 95: 'si mulier virum supervixerit, quinquaginta solidos in dude [sc. dote] recipiat, et tertiam de omne re, quod simul conlaboraverint, sibi studeat evindicari' ('If the wife outlives her husband, let her receive 50 *solidi* as her *dos*, and let her strive to claim for herself a third of all the property which they acquired together'). The text implies that while the 50s. (or its value) was to be paid to the widow by the heirs, she herself was to set about securing her *tertia* ('quod simul conlaboraverint': Le Jan-Hennebicque, 'Origines', p. 115, translates 'le tiers des biens du ménage'). Cf. also *Marculfi Formularum Libri Duo*, II. 17, *MGH Form.*, p. 87. For the third share in eleventh-century Catalonia, see M. Aurell i Cardona, 'Ermessinde, Comtesse de Barcelona', in Parisse, *Veuves*.

[24] A. Lemaire, 'Les origines de la communauté de biens entre époux dans le droit coutumier français', *Revue historique de droit français et étranger*, 7 (1928), pp. 588–9.

[25] *Capitularia Regum Francorum*, ed. A. Boretius, *MGH LL in quarto*, sectio 2 (hereafter *MGH Capit.*), vol. 1, p. 301, no. 148: 'Volumus ut uxores defunctorum post obitum maritorum tertiam partem conlaborationis quam simul in beneficio conlaboraverunt accipiant.' The echo of *Lex Ribuaria* is clear: see above, n. 22.

least in benefices, needed to be affirmed and protected. It must be acknowledged that Louis's 821 capitulary is an extremely rare ninth-century reference to the widow's third share; and it is quite possible that the widow customarily received much less. Rather earlier formulary evidence shows that the widow had legally only the right of usufruct to the lands she acquired on bereavement: after her death, the land reverted to the heirs.[26] Life interest might be affected in practice by further variables. An adult son or sons might well assert effective day-to-day control over the mother's *dos*. The widow's alienation of all or part of her *dos* through a gift to the church might be challenged or reversed by her sons: that was why churchmen benefiting from such a gift carefully obtained sons' assent to their mother's act. Remarriage would tend to put the woman's original *dos* under her second husband's control. A widow's own kin had interests in her future as well. Early in Louis the Pious's reign, a Frankish assembly determined that 'whoever wanted to receive a widow in marriage must do so with the consent and agreement of her *parentes*'.[27]

At bereavement, she would acquire her widow's share: at the same time, especially if she were childless, or had children not yet of age, the widow no longer resided under a man's direct authority. But whatever lands she was entitled to by inheritance, by gift of her husband, or by her widow's endowment, an aristocratic woman too might find difficulty in realizing her claims, against the attentions of kin – her own and her husband's – and friends, lay and ecclesiastical (not to mention other predators). For the widow, in other words, the usual social networks of early medieval persons – kin, friends and faithful ones[28] – offered ambivalent support.

While normative legal sources distinguish sharply between full powers over the *dos* and mere life interest in the widow's share, the distinction is less clear in practice. The relatively plentiful charter material from the Carolingian period shows very few cases in which a woman disposed of her *dos*.[29] In 835/6 the widow Irmentrude

---

[26] *Marculfi Formularum Libri Duo*, II. 15, *MGH Form.*, p. 85.

[27] *Capitula Legi Salicae Addita*: 'qui viduam in coniugium accipere vult, iudicaverunt omnes ut... cum parentorum consensu et voluntate... in coniugium sibi eam sumat', *MGH Capit.*, vol. 1, p. 293.

[28] See G. Althoff, *Verwandte, Freunde und Getreue. Zum politischen Stellenwert der Gruppenbindungen im frühen Mittelalter*.

[29] Queen Ermentrude obtained her husband's confirmation of the gift of her *dos* (or part of it) to Corbie, Tessier, *Recueil*, vol. 1, no. 189, p. 494. But it may be dangerous to generalize from queens to other women.

gave her *dothalicium* to Echternach. But her husband Gerold had endowed her with lands he had 'inherited' from his own mother: rather than extract *dos* out of a patrimony seen as an inalienable family possession, Gerold had instead used his maternal inheritance, which was perhaps 'lent' to the incoming bride(s) in each generation.[30] Some prescriptive evidence implies that the *dos* of a childless widow would revert to her family. I know of no case where that occurred. The husband's collateral kin would seek to avert any loss to their patrimony. The woman's 'free control' (*libera potestas*) over her *dos*, whether she was wife or widow, would confront the reality of virilocal marriage, the institutionalized authority of husbands and the powerful interests of agnatic kin. Nevertheless, the claim that there was a generalized 'Carolingian' shift in the ninth century from *dos* to inalienable dower is unconvincing: the handful of formulas showing *dos* itself treated as inalienable are all from Alemannia, not Francia.[31] More research is needed: meanwhile, we can observe custom under pressure in a period of intense competition for landed property. If a husband's agnatic kin pushed for the inalienability of *dos*, individuals, men as well as women, might urge its conversion into religious capital. Classic medieval dower subsuming bridegift, *dos*, and widow's share, was not simply the outcome of the church's imposition of new rules of monogamy.[32] Equally, it cannot be represented simply as the triumph of the patrilineal family. The case histories of widows show more complex intersections of custom and interest, of collective and institutional weight and individual desires.[33]

The three-fold categorization of women's property sketched above is legalistic. A more realistic account would concentrate on two points in the woman's life-cycle. At marriage, she would receive *dos* from her husband, and perhaps at the same time her advance share in her parental inheritance; at this same time, she would move into her husband's house, and under his lordship. Her

---

[30] Cf. above n. 17. For Anglo-Saxon evidence relating to Rutland as queens' dower, see C. Phythian-Adams, 'Rutland reconsidered', in A. Dornier (ed.), *Mercian Studies*; and more generally, P. Stafford, *Queens, Concubines, and Dowagers. The King's Wife in the Early Middle Ages*, pp. 103–4.

[31] S. Wemple, *Women in Frankish Society. Marriage and the Cloister 500–900*, p.113, and n. 58 (p. 261). Cf. Le Jan-Hennebicque, 'Origines', p. 117.

[32] Compare Wemple, *Women*, pp. 112–13, and Le Jan-Hennebicque, 'Origines', p. 113.

[33] Here, as in other respects, a characteristic of women's rights over property seems to have been their malleability and openness to challenge. For some implications, see J. L. Nelson, 'Kommentar', in W. Affeldt (ed.), *Frauen in Spätantike und Frühmittelalter*.

husband's death opened a new phase in a woman's life. Immediately, it signalled a moment of choice. It is on this moment that I now want to focus. The widow could choose to remain *unmarried*: she could become instead a *deo sacrata* (or *deo devota*, or *ancilla Dei*) consecrated to God.[34] Carolingian reformers, while they welcomed the piety of such women, wished to impose claustration, and episcopal control on them. Bishops would acknowledge that *potentes feminae*, women whose social potency derived from high rank and economic resources, as wives in secular life had potential as evangelizers, with particular responsibility for the religious management of their households.[35] As widows, such women could not be coerced. In 829, in a welter of reforming activity in which Louis the Pious sought to pre-empt his critics, and in which gender supplied an apt discourse wherein to represent misrule, bishops were asked to consider what should be done about women who had 'unreasonably assumed the veil for themselves'. The remedy was a hefty reimposition of episcopal control:

From now on, widows are not to veil themselves indiscreetly (*indiscrete*[36]), but they are to wait for 30 days; and then choose what they ought to do, with the advice of the bishop.[37]

After the thirty-day period:

they may [re]marry, or if they decide instead to devote themselves to God, they are to be admonished and instructed that they should not do so in their own homes, but should submit themselves as maidservants to God under the direction of a spiritual mother in a convent.

Later in 829, the reforming hard core of bishops insisted that consecrated widows 'should take thought for their own salvation, lest living indiscreetly, and using a noxious liberty of their own, and

---

[34] For important observations on the contexts (and limits) of choice, see J. Martindale, 'The nun Immena and the foundation of the abbey of Beaulieu: a woman's prospects in the Carolingian Church', *Studies in Church History*, 27 (1990), and D. Baltrusch-Schneider, 'Klosterleben als alternative Lebensform zur Ehe?', in H.-W. Goetz (ed.), *Weibliche Lebensgestaltung im Mittelalter*.

[35] J. L. Nelson, 'Les femmes et l'évangélisation dans le haut moyen âge', *Revue du Nord*, 68 (1986).

[36] This word is more heavily pejorative in medieval Latin than it looks.

[37] *MGH LL in quarto*, sectio 3, *Concilia aevi Karolini*, ed. A. Werminghoff (hereafter *MGH Conc.*), vol. 2, pt. 2, no. 50, ch. 44, pp. 638–9; cf. *Capitulare Ecclesiasticum (817/818)*, ch. 21, *MGH Capit.*, vol. 1, no. 138, p. 278; and 'Council of Paris (829)', ch. 15, *MGH Capit.*, vol. 2, no. 196, p. 42: 'quaedam feminae sine consensu sacerdotum velum sibi incaute inponant'.

wandering about in various places, they incur the peril of their own souls'.[38]

The Council of Paris had envisaged a period of 'instruction' during which the newly widowed who sought the life of consecrated widowhood 'should be diligently admonished that they should be consecrated in such a way that their consecration may be preserved in chastity and humility'. One aim of this 'novitiate' was to deter widows from entering a non-monastic life and to encourage them, instead, to enter a convent under episcopal supervision.[39] The period of 'instruction' was an episcopal rationalization and bid for control of the period of ritual mourning and commemoration for the defunct husband.[40] It is fairly clear that this legislation was ineffective: house-convents did not give way to claustration in the ninth century. On the contrary, the veiled widow retained the option of remaining in her own home.[41]

Prescription needs, as ever, to be checked against practice. Moreover, widows' religious preferences need to be linked with their position in secular life (to treat these aspects in separate compartments has been a shortcoming of some recent historiography). The wording of the Council of Paris of 829 drew heavily on an earlier reforming council of Louis the Pious in 818, whose legislation on consecrated widows got into the collection of Ansegis and ⊦ nce achieved wide circulation. The 818 decree required widows to seek, as well as 'the advice of the bishop', '[the advice] of their own closer and more distant kin (*parentes et amici*)'.[42] Bishops were well aware of the need to accommodate the interests of the family

---

[38] *MGH Capit.*, vol. 2, no. 196, p. 42: 'statuimus quatinus suae saluti consulant nec sic indiscrete vivendo et propria noxiaque libertate utendo et per diversa vagando periculum animarum suarum incurrant'. Cf. *MGH Capit.*, vol. 2, no. 252, p. 227 (Tribur 895).

[39] See D. Hochstetler, *A Conflict of Traditions. Women in Religion in the Early Middle Ages 500–840*, p. 73.

[40] See H. Herold, 'Der Dreissigste und die rechtsgeschichtliche Bedeutung des Totengedächtnisses', *Zeitschrift für Schweizerisches Recht*, 57 (1937), showing that the origins of the thirty-day mourning period are biblical (Num. 20, 29, and Deut. 34, 8), but that it first entered medieval legislation in 818/819 (and survived in several regions down to the twentieth century). See further on the mourning period, A. Angenendt, 'Theologie und Liturgie der mittelalterlichen Toten-Memoria', in K. Schmid and J. Wollasch (eds.), *Memoria. Der geschichtliche Zeugniswert des liturgischen Gedenkens im Mittelalter*, pp. 172–3, 186–7.

[41] 'Council of Mainz (888)', ch. 26, J.-D. Mansi, *Sacrorum Conciliorum Nova et Amplissima Collectio*, vol. 18, pp. 71–2. See further A. Hodgson, 'The Frankish Church and Women', unpublished Ph.D. thesis, University of London, 1992, pp. 228–30, 242–58.

[42] *Capitulare Ecclesiasticum (817/818)*, ch. 21, *MGH Capit.*, vol. 1, no. 138, p. 278.

and to make provision for the woman's property. 'Indiscreet veiling' threatened familial as well as episcopal control. Legislators overtly concerned in particular with the religious status of the veiled widow could not ignore the broader ambiance of the noblewoman's situation.[43] The bishops reported that:

Certain women, under the pretext of taking the veil, without the consent of bishops, are veiling themselves so that they can become the female guardians (*excubatrices*) and female managers (*administratrices*) of churches.[44]

Here the dimension of class is as evident as that of gender. The feminine forms of the nouns *excubator* and *administrator* were oxymorons which, for a ninth-century audience, vividly evoked disorder,[45] and with specific reference to power over property. These widows were *nobiles feminae*, and they had children and landed property (*res*). Louis's bishops denounced such women in the timehonoured tones of misogyny: 'they wallow in their own wealth and luxuries. . . and according to the apostle are dead though alive'.[46] 'Noxious liberty' was the sort that resulted in control over property being exercised, and transmitted, by widows without reference to episcopal authority.

Bishops could be authoritatively protective. A stream of conciliar legislation forbade the abduction of widows: a widow, 'whether she was willing or unwilling', must not be abducted during the thirtyday period, though only if she had been unwilling was subsequent legalization by marriage forbidden.[47] Public penance was imposed on the abductor of a widow (or virgin) 'even if he had subsequently married the widow, with the agreement of her kin (*parentes*), and handed over the equivalent of a dower (*dotalicium*)'.[48] Though power over the widow's property is not mentioned in these conciliar texts, that issue surely must underlie the problem which the bishops had repeatedly to address, namely, the frequency of abductions. The stream of episcopal condemnations became a flood

---

[43] According to Hincmar of Rheims, *De Divortio*, ed. L. Böhringer, *MGH Conc.*, vol. 4, Supplementum, vol. 1, p. 129, the *adulescentula vidua* posed special problems: 'they receive the sacred veil in order more licentiously to abuse a number of men'(!)

[44] 'Council of Paris', ch. 42, *MGH Conc.*, vol. 2, pt. 2, no. 50, p. 638.

[45] Especially repugnant to the bishops, perhaps, was such women's property-interest in *churches*.

[46] *MGH Conc.*, vol. 2, pt. 2, no. 50, ch. 44, pp. 638–9. The Pauline reference is to I Timothy 5, 6.

[47] *MGH Capit.*, vol. 1, no. 138 (818/819), ch. 21, p. 278.

[48] 'Council of Meaux-Paris (845–6)', *MGH Conc.*, vol. 3, no. 11, ch. 65, p. 115.

in the decade or so after 840, when aristocratic pressure on resources grew, especially in the West Frankish and Middle Kingdoms, and when a Carolingian king's claim to protect widows may have become an increasingly valuable instrument of royal patronage.[49]

That house-convents continued to exist says something about the power to choose of at least some aristocratic widows. The choice to become *deo sacrata* has indeed been interpreted as a 'legal subterfuge', used by the woman herself to secure lifelong control over her widow's share.[50] Motives were surely complex: some women took very seriously their responsibility for the liturgical commemoration of their husbands and husbands' ancestors and kin.[51] Husbands intended that they should: a *dos* charter in a St Gall formulary included the request that, 'should I predecease [my wife], whether or not sons are born to us, she should possess the property above-mentioned, and from [renders or income from] it she should make annual commemoration for me on the anniversary day of my burial'.[52] Such a task might best be performed by a *deo sacrata*. But the choice to become one was taken under pressure. The thirty-day delay, which had functioned in classical times as a period of mourning during which black garb had traditionally been worn, might function too, in Carolingian times, as a liminal period in another ɾ ᴐase – in which competing interests, episcopal and familial, could be mobilized, and traded off. A widow anxious not to be remarried might have to act quickly. There were implications for her continuing control of property if the widow remained in her own home as *deo sacrata*: surrounded by her own household, she could retain a life interest in her property and perhaps involve herself in its management. If the widow was childless, her control over that property would not be challenged, or shared, within a few years, by now-adult offspring. But the widow would need protection. The bishop would be anxious to supply this. So too might be the

---

[49] Paris (829), ch. 64; Aachen (836), ch. 23, *MGH Conc.*, vol. 2, pp. 638, 723; Meaux-Paris (845–6), ch. 64, *MGH Conc.*, vol. 3, p. 115; Servais (853), ch. 2, *MGH Capit.*, vol. 2, no. 260, p. 272; Quierzy (857), ch. 2, *MGH Conc.*, vol. 3, p. 398.

[50] Goody, *Development*, p. 256, apropos Lombard practice.

[51] Dhuoda, *Manuel pour mon fils*, VIII. 14, urged her own son to 'pray for the *parentes* of your father who have left to him their property in lawful inheritance', with a list of names at X. 5, ed. and trans. P. Riché, pp. 318–23, 354–5. For other examples, see Leyser, *Rule and Conflict*, pp. 72–3.

[52] *Carta dotis, Collectio Sangallensis*, no. 18, *MGH Form.*, p. 406.

widow's natal or affinal kin, the latter with interests in her *dos* and 'third share' which might originally have formed part of *their hereditas*. We could imagine a widow looking to other forms of ecclesiastical association beyond the institutional authority of bishops – to churches, especially monasteries, with which particular bonds might already have been formed, or could now be formed, by personal gift. A determined widow might also look to a lord on whose protection she had some prior claim, and preferably a lord with access, for instance via comital position, to the courts where local notables were mobilized and local opinion formed. In a world where official and unofficial, public and privatized forms of association and obligation, coexisted and intermeshed, the wary widow had some room for manoeuvre. She could 'divide' her favours, and though she could hardly 'rule', she might opt to retain some power over her property, and over her own life.

Wills, or *testamenta*, were until recently a relatively neglected corpus of evidence for the Carolingian period. The fine study of Brigitte Kasten has remedied that neglect.[53] Several of these documents were demonstrably not death-bed dispositions of property, but give the impression, instead, of tactics aimed at the future security of the testator him- or herself. As with comparable materials from the Merovingian period, and from Anglo-Saxon England, roughly a quarter of the Carolingian dossier assembled by Kasten are women's wills.[54] The Anglo-Saxon examples have generally been read as evidence for the security of Anglo-Saxon women's property rights; but the opposite inference can be made, namely, that women needed to muster all the support they could in order to strengthen the likelihood that their wishes would be carried out.[55]

---

[53] B. Kasten, 'Erbrechtliche Verfügungen des 8. und 9. Jhdts', *Zeitschrift für Rechtsgeschichte*, 107 (1990).

[54] For Merovingian wills, see U. Nonn, 'Merowingische Testamente', *Archiv für Diplomatik*, 18 (1972), and *idem*, 'Erminethrud – eine vornehme neustrische Dame um 700', *Historisches Jahrbuch*, 102 (1982). For Anglo-Saxon wills, see D. Whitelock, *Anglo-Saxon Wills*, and *idem* (ed.), *The Will of Æthelgifu. A Tenth-Century Anglo-Saxon Manuscript*; also Amt, *Women's Lives*, pp. 130–6.

[55] See P. Stafford, 'Women and the Norman Conquest', *Transactions of the Royal Historical Society*, 4 (1994), forthcoming. The will of Æthelgifu is a particularly good example of the mobilizing of support: 2,000 men from three shires. For south Italian evidence, see P. Skinner, 'Women, wills and wealth in medieval southern Italy', *Early Medieval Europe*, 2 (1993).

Despite an enormous proliferation of written documents from the Carolingian period, the number of surviving wills is small.[56] A similar phenomenon in post-Conquest England had been explained by way of the new prevalence of lordship, hence of dependent tenure rather than ownership. Against this, it has recently been pointed out that there were plenty of post-obit gifts after the Conquest and these presupposed notions of ownership and freedom to alienate.[57] Similar considerations apply to the Frankish world of the eighth and ninth centuries – a world in which noble Franks used their landed wealth to assert their status and identity through the commemoration of their dead. Testaments were one available strategy. Kasten points out that the great variety in the formal traits of testaments reflects the *erbrechtliche Experimentierfreudigkeit* ('delight in experimentation in reference to legal inheritance') of the eighth and ninth century. The phrase is a happy one (especially in German); but we should remember that the 'delight in experimentation' was on the part of the draftsman, not the testator. Further, in Kasten's otherwise illuminating discussion of the documents, the issue of gender is ignored. Yet if women had specific responsibilities where liturgical commemoration was concerned, they also had specific reason to fear for the security of their own commemorative dispositions and, more broadly, the property rights that underpinned them. Women as such, even those of high social status, were among those who were traditionally classed as, and in some cases demonstrably felt themselves, in need of protection.

The focus in the rest of this paper will be on one widow's powers and responsibilities, needs and uncertainties. I shall argue that her case, curiously neglected in the historiography until very recently, reveals the constraints within which she acted and, at the same time, her perception of those constraints and adoption of appropriately wary strategies. Thus one widow's situation will point to

---

[56] The thirteen examples discussed by Kasten, 'Erbrechtliche Verfügungen', represent an amended version of the list of G. Spreckelmeyer, 'Zur rechtlichen Funktion frühmittelalterlicher Testamente', in P. Classen (ed.), *Recht und Schrift im Mittelalter, Vorträge und Forschungen*, vol. 23 (1977), pp. 109–10. For definitional problems, see below, p. 98. Other ninth-century documents could be classed as wills: Cristina La Rocca is preparing a study on a number of north Italian examples.

[57] J. C. Holt, 'Feudal society and the family in medieval England, I', *Transactions of the Royal Historical Society*, 32 (1982), pp. 197–8; for a different view, S. Reynolds, 'Bookland, folkland and fiefs', *Anglo-Norman Studies*, 14 (1992), p. 225.

some of the complexities of power over property in the early Middle Ages.

The widow was named Erkanfrida, and this is her testament:[58]

Memorandum of how and in whose presence Erkanfrida made arrangements about her property and provided for its transfer into the hands of distinguished men to be dealt with after her death.

[1] Thus, when noble men had gathered together, I Erkanfrida came before that assembly at a place called Steinsel,[59] and commended to [the care of] the venerable[60] count Adalard, lay-abbot and count, and also to Waldo, Folcuin and Beretland, and the two Huodilberts, whatever I have been seen to possess by way of inheritance in the county of Trier in the county of Bedagau in the place called Peffingen; and in the county of Ardennes in the place called Wampach; and in a third place called Mersch on the banks of the Alzette that demesne-manse (*mansus dominicus*) and the whole estate (*fiscus*) pertaining to it, except for the church of St Michael with all that pertains to it, which my lord Nithad gave me as my *dos,* and which I have handed over to St Maximin and I have had a *testamentum* drawn up and it has been written, in an accurate and reasonable way, at that same place.

[2] I have freely transferred those properties into the hands of those above-mentioned on the following conditions, that if I should desire that the properties revert to me through the hands of those men or even of one of them, I shall [be able to] do it; but if I do not so desire, I have decided, likewise through their hands, according to what was arranged by my lord above-mentioned, that if his nephews [and nieces], that is, the six male children of his sister Irminburg, plus the son of his brother Rimigarit who is called Reginbold, and Reginbold's sister Thiodrat, plus the son of his second sister Thetbirga, should wish to acquire them, 100 lb. in gold and silver should be paid over on the fortieth day after my death by those nine persons among them, and the total sum [divided] between the following 20 monasteries thus, one by one, in memory of me and of my kin (*parentes*) and of my husband Nithad:

---

[58] My translation is from the edition of C. Wampach, *Urkunden- und Quellenbuch zur Geschichte der altluxemburgischen Territorien,* vol. 1, pp. 87–90 (reproduced in the appendix to the present paper, below, pp. 111–13). His edition, with full notes and bibliographical references, superseded those of G. Waitz, *Forschungen zur deutschen Geschichte,* 18 (1878); and H. Omont, 'Testament d'Erkanfrida, veuve du comte Nithadus de Trèves', *Bibliothèque de l'École des Chartes,* 52 (1891). (Omont apparently did not know of Waitz's edition.) For a photograph of the manuscript, see Wampach's Plate III at p. 192. Wampach divided the text into sections, and I retain these.

[59] In modern Luxemburg, in the Alzette valley. See Map 1.

[60] The adjective *venerabilis* signifies a lay-abbot, according to Wampach, *Urkunden- und Quellenbuch,* p. 87, n. 10. But cf. below, p. 107.

(i)	St Maximin [Trier]	100s.
(ii)	St Peter [the cathedral church of Trier]	100s.
(iii)	Oeren [dioc. Trier]	100s.
(iv)	Pfalzel [dioc. Trier]	100s.
(v)	Mettlach [dioc. Trier]	100s.
(vi)	Tholey [dioc. Trier]	100s.
(vii)	between St Euchar [Trier] and St Paulin [Trier] and St Quiriacus, Taben [nr. Saalburg, dioc. Trier]	100s.
(viii)	Hornbach [dioc. Metz]	100s.
(ix)	Malmedy [dioc. Cologne]	100s.
(x)	Stavelot [dioc. Liège]	100s.
(xi)	Inden [dioc. Cologne]	100s.
(xii)	St Hubert [dioc. Liège]	100s.
(xiii)	between St Goar and Münsterappel [dioc. Trier]	100s.
(xiv)	between St Castor and St Alexander and St Eventius [dioc. Trier]	100s.
(xv)	St Cyriacus [Neuhausen, dioc. Worms]	100s.
(xvi)	Worms [cathedral]	100s.
(xvii)	St Nazarius [Lorsch, dioc. Worms]	100s.
(xviii)	[SS Peter and Paul] Weissenburg	100s.
(xix)	Speyer [cathedral]	100s.
(xx)	St Leo [dioc. Speyer]	100s.

And those properties are in no way to be handed over to them until they have paid, on the day above-mentioned, the price laid down, and [then] they can divide this *villa* between them by a fair [*aequa* – ?equal] arrangement.

[3] If the price of the above-mentioned properties is not paid, I have likewise decreed that the above-mentioned venerable witnesses should hand over and bestow those lands to the places of the saints as alms for us (*in elemosinam nostram*, i.e. to commemorate us).

[4] But I have earmarked, outside their [i.e. the nephews' and niece's] power to grant or agree, for St Maximin at Trier, the church of St Michael for the endowment of that church, since I myself have assigned it, [to pass] after my death to [one of] the places of the saints, namely to St Maximin, in memory of my husband and myself.

[5] Concerning what I had in Peffingen, I have decided on the following conditions: that if Bernard pays 30 lb. as a price for it after my death, it shall be handed over to him, and that price shall be paid to the monastery of Prüm, so that for as long as that money (*pecunia*) shall last, our anniversary day shall be commemorated. But if [Bernard] does not pay the price, nothing at all of that property is to be given to him, but it is to be given

instead in our memory to [one of] the places of the saints, namely Prüm.

[6] Concerning what my lord had at Wampach, he decided that it should be given to the sons of Bernard, except for that church and those properties which Burgirid gave to my lord in the *villa* called Skizzana.[61] That church and those lands, which the above-named Burgirid gave him, [my lord] ordered should be given to the monastery of Prüm.

For the rest, I beg you earnestly for God's sake, and I bear witness before God and Christ Jesus who is to judge both the quick and the dead, that the above-mentioned inheritance with the slaves and the movables above-described, that is, those above-mentioned, you are to divide and distribute between the places listed, as you wish to render account for them [to Him] in whose name I have been trustful concerning your love and have confided and commended myself to your good faith.

The document terms itself a *commemoratorium*: a formal notice of a public, legal act made as permanent evidence. I shall call it a will, accepting Kasten's definition of a type of early medieval legal document whose provisions centred on liturgical commemoration and were to come into force after the death of the testator.[62] Uncertainty about its exact legal status parallels doubt over its diplomatic. The document's form, a long strip of parchment, would suggest an original, that is, one drawn up on the same occasion as, or immediately after, the arrangements recorded. But the absence of witnesses' names, name of scribe, and date, at the end of the document,[63] has been thought, on the other hand, to indicate a copy written two or three generations after the event, and well after the death of the 'testatrix' herself.

The document needs to be seen as one of a series. In particular,

---

[61] Wampach, *Urkunden- und Quellenbuch*, p. 85, identifies this as Schimpach, just east of Wampach (see Map 1). He also suggests, *ibid.*, an identification of Burgarit with 'the prefect of the royal huntsmen' mentioned in ch. 58 of the Astronomer's *Life of Louis the Pious*, ed G. Pertz, *MGH Scriptores*, vol. 2.

[62] Kasten, 'Erbrechtliche Verfügungen', pp. 240–4, modifying earlier attempts at definition, and supplying further references.

[63] Wampach, *Urkunden- und Quellenbuch*, p. 86, does not consider the possibility that the manuscript is incomplete, but otherwise fairly summarizes the two arguments, Omont's for the document being an original, Waitz's for it being an early tenth-century copy. Wampach does not mention a significant observation of Omont, 'Testament d'Erkanfrida', p. 574, n. 2: 'a little strip of parchment on which the last 7 lines of the text have been written has been added'. This feature, clear in the photograph (Wampach's Plate III), could support Omont's case. The script of the document is a book hand.

it follows, and so can be dated by reference to, another, dated, document: Erkanfrida's grant to St Maximin, Trier, on 1 April 853.[64] Here Erkanfrida transfers:

> my property (*res*) which belongs to me by gift of my lord Nythald[65] in the place called Mersch, the church of St Michael, the house and the court-yard (*casa et curtile*), with its demesne lands, meadows and pastures;[66]
> a wood at Beningen, Hunsdorf and Businesberch;
> a mill;[67]
> 12 manses with these *mancipia* [96 names of bondsmen and bondswomen follow] of whom I now free seven [all of them additional to the 96 named].

Erkanfrida 'hands over' (*trado et transfundo*) all these to the community of St Maximin on the following terms: that every year on the feast of St Martin (11 November) a lavish meal (*opulenta refectio*) should be provided for the brethren from the property just trans-ferred, 'so that they, at that time of the year, should more willingly commemorate us in vigils and masses'. This is, in other words, a perfect example of that privatized liturgical commemoration which was such a strong feature of Carolingian lay piety, and of the 'pious gastric alchemy'[68] whereby this-worldly lay generosity was converted, via monastic consumption, into divine favour and next-worldly benefit. But notice that Erkanfrida's reference in her will (section 4) to the church of St Michael reveals what the grant of 1 April 853 does not: that the church with its appurtenances is to pass to St Maximin only 'after my death'. In other words, Erkan-frida retains a life interest in it: something we should never have suspected from the seemingly categorical and immediate 'hand-over' declared in the April 853 grant itself.[69]

---

[64] Wampach, *Urkunden- und Quellenbuch*, no. 88, pp. 80–2: from a thirteenth-century cartulary copy.

[65] The quite different spelling of the name as compared with that in the will, probably reflects the choice of the thirteenth-century cartulary scribe.

[66] The church of St Michael had constituted Erkanfrida's *dos*. Erkanfrida's will, while making this explicit, above p. 96, at the same time treats separately the other property at Mersch. For further discussion see below, p. 105. I therefore amend Wampach's punctuation by substituting a semi-colon for a comma here. The edition of H. Beyer, *Urkundenbuch zur Geschichte der Mittelrheinischen Territorien*, p. 89, indicates a series of *punctus* in the cartulary copy.

[67] I substitute a semi-colon here too.

[68] So, M. Rouche, 'Les repas de fête à l'époque carolingienne', in D. Menjot (ed.), *Manger et boire au moyen âge, Actes du Colloque de Nice (15–17 octobre 1982)*, p. 276.

[69] Kasten, 'Erbrechtliche Verfügungen', pp. 263, 284, noting that the survival of the two mutually illuminating documents is a lucky accident.

In what circumstances is Erkanfrida making this 853 grant? She does not say in so many words that her husband is dead: she makes the grant 'to rescue the soul of my lord Nythald and my own soul'. Nevertheless, it is fairly clear that she is a widow. She alone makes and subscribes the grant. Further, she identifies herself, and is likewise identified in the text, as *deo sacrata*. She foresees as possible future challengers to her act, herself, or 'someone of the heirs or kin of my lord'. She provides that if in the future 'lords (*seniores*) or their local agents (*magistri*)' misuse or alienate property intended for 'the common benefit of the brethren [of St Maximin]', then 'the heirs of my lord, to whom it pertains by hereditary right, shall have the power (*potestas*) of retrieving and possessing the whole [property] and vindicate it for their own use, unless it is restored again to the monks above-mentioned'.

Erkanfrida refers back to this document in the will:[70] it thus supplies a *terminus post quem* for the will itself. How closely linked in time are the two documents? The reference in the will to Count Adalard as *venerabilis* indicates that he was a lay-abbot. He was lay-abbot of Echternach from 849 to 856.[71] This would give a dating-'fork' of 853–6 for the will. But I think we can infer from its internal evidence a tight sequence for Nithad's death, Erkanfrida's becoming *deo sacrata*, the grant of Mersch, and lastly the will.

Two other documents are relevant. One is a letter-cum-charter from Abbot Ansbald (860–86) and the community of Prüm to Erkanfrida, their 'lovable and most sweet sister in Christ'.[72] The abbot and brethren recall that 'your husband Nithad, once very dear to us' had left the estate of Hannapes[73] to Prüm; also that

---

[70] Above, section 1. She terms it a *testamentum*, using the word in its more general sense of 'document'.

[71] Wampach, *Urkunden- und Quellenbuch*, p. 87, notes, with evident surprise, that Echternach is not on the lengthy list of Erkanfrida's monastic 'legatees'.

[72] This has survived in the tenth-century *Liber aureus* of Prüm, and is edited in Wampach, *Urkunden- und Quellenbuch*, no. 93, pp. 92–4, where it is dated 'not long after Ansbald's assumption of office, because Erkanfrida was already a widow in 853': not a very compelling argument, for she may have been widowed young.

[73] This was granted by Charles the Bald in 845, Tessier, *Recueil*, vol. 1, no. 69, pp. 197–8 (also preserved in the Prüm *Liber aureus*), to Nithad who had previously held the land as a benefice. It was then left by Nithad to Prüm, Beyer, *Urkundenbuch*, no. 72, p. 80. On Nithad, and his possible relationship to Nithard the historian, see J. L. Nelson, *Politics and Ritual in Early Medieval Europe*, pp. 232–3, which draws on R. Hennebicque, 'Structures familiales et politiques au IXe siècle: un groupe familial de l'aristocratie franque', *Revue historique*, 265 (1981), pp. 298–9, 309–10.

'since then, you have strenuously and nobly (*strenue et nobiliter*) marked the anniversary of his death in the service of our brethren'. While Ansbald and his brethren are sure that Erkanfrida will ensure the continuance of these arrangements as long as she lives, 'you have no successor of your line (*nullus styrpis tue successor*) nor any relative in whom you dare put confidence that, after your death, they would maintain, from the above-mentioned property given us, the *memoria*, year by year, with due preparations, of you and of your late husband Nithad, who was dear to us'. Erkanfrida, says the abbot, has therefore requested that he and community themselves take responsibility for the annual commemorative meal and liturgical celebrations 'for both of you'. Ansbald formally records how these arrangements are to be effected: 'the bailiff (*provisor*) of Hannapes will most diligently supply to our brethren all the produce necessary, each year, for the *optima refectio* on 30 April'. From this document, it seems clear that Erkanfrida had retained a life interest in Hannapes: only after her death (and there is nothing here to indicate that that was thought to be imminent) would the community of Prüm have to assume direct responsibility for the *memoria*. The bailiff sounds like hers – hence Ansbald's concern to pin down the man's duties in supplying 'our brethren'.

The last document dates from 960, when Archbishop Henry of Trier confirmed to St Maximin Erkanfrida's grant of the church of Mersch and its dependencies 'which, in the interim, had largely passed out of control of St Maximin'.[74] Presumably Erkanfrida's arrangements for her and Nithad's *memoria* had lapsed. She herself had foreseen that her grant might be challenged by her husband's kin or diverted by *seniores* and their *magistri*.

Erkanfrida's 'will' attracted some interest in the later nineteenth century:[75] this was no coincidence, as the property rights of married women were then matters of topical interest.[76] There was interest, too, indeed rather fierce debate, over the precise canonical implications of Erkanfrida's being a *deo sacrata*.[77]

[74] Wampach, *Urkunden- und Quellenbuch*, no. 169 (also Beyer, *Urkundenbuch*, no. 89); note that Henry (or the scribe) assumed that Erkanfrida had been a countess.

[75] Cf. above n. 7.

[76] The nineteenth-century flowering of historiography on Anglo-Saxon women's property rights offers a good parallel: see Stafford, 'Women and the Norman Conquest'.

[77] See J. Marx, 'Das Testament der lotharingischen Gräfin Erkanfrida', *Trierer theologische Zeitschrift Pastor bonus*, 6 (1894), p. 141, and H. V. Sauerland, 'Das 'Testament' der

Otherwise, local historical scholarship was mainly concerned with the identification of the places mentioned in the document. Recently, Brigitte Kasten has clarified its legal status as a post-obit gift ('Treuhandschenkung auf den Todesfall'), hence to be categorized as a will, while Regine Le Jan-Hennebicque has incisively discussed its evidence for the evolution of dower rights.[78] In the context of the present book, interest centres on Erkanfrida's powers (the plural is important) over the property she deals with here, and, further, with the constraints on the exercise of those powers, with varieties, ambiguities and inconsistencies, not only in their nature, but in their envisaged change over time. Conditionality and provisionality are crucial dimensions. We shall have to consider how far they are gender-specific.

The first thing that complicates the issue is Erkanfrida's retention of a life interest. Secondly, she does not bequeath, but rather 'commends' property, at three geographically quite distinct places (see map 1), to Adalard and five other laymen who are to act, seemingly, as trustees.[79] Thirdly, it becomes clear that the widow 'has [property rights]' in different ways at each of the three places; and that this accounts for the varying terms and qualifications detailed in the text for the future disposition of the various properties. Erkanfrida's situation was already complex enough. Her (or the scribe's) ordering of the material in this text at first sight seems perverse, even arbitrary. But closer attention shows that the document has a logic – or rather that Erkanfrida knew what she was doing when she listed properties at Peffingen, Wampach and Mersch, then set out detailed provisions for Mersch, Peffingen and Wampach.[80] My discussion follows her initial listing.

lotharingischen Gräfin Erkanfrida', *Jahrbücher der Gesellschaft für lotharingische Geschichte und Altertumskunde*, 7 (1894); J. Marx, 'Das "Testament" Erkanfridas', *Jahrbücher der Gesellschaft, für lotharingische Geschichte und Altertumskunde*, 7 (1895); Sauerland, 'Das "Testament" Erkanfridas', *Jahrbücher der Gesellschaft, für lotharingische Geschichte und Altertumskunde*, 8 (1896).

[78] Kasten, 'Erbrechtliche Verfügungen', pp. 261–4; Le Jan-Hennebicque, 'Origines', pp. 118–19.

[79] This would be the natural translation of Kasten's term 'Treuhänder'. But see below, pp. 108–9.

[80] The pattern is thus: mention of properties at Peffingen, at Wampach, at Mersch (section 1), followed by detailed provisions for Mersch (sections 2–4), for Peffingen (section 5), for Wampach (section 6).

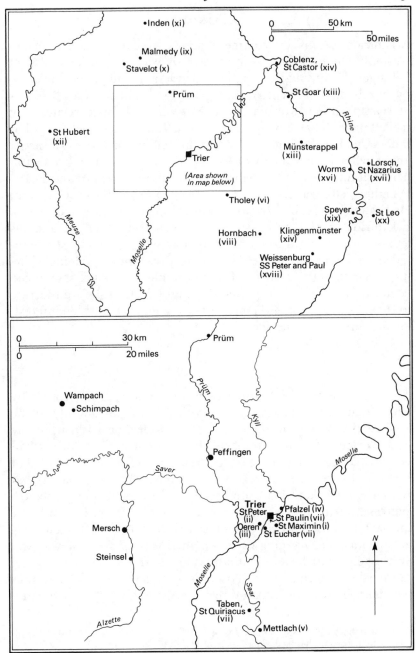

Map. 1. Places mentioned in Erkanfrida's testament

PEFFINGEN

Erkanfrida begins by commending to Adalard and his fellow-trustees 'whatever I am seen to have by way of inheritance . . . at Peffingen'.[81] Although no explicit distinction is made, for instance by supplying a different verb (or phrase) for Erkanfrida's holdings at Wampach and Mersch, the term *hereditas*, I think, relates only to Peffingen. That is why in section 5, Erkanfrida refers to 'what I have held in Peffingen', and she herself can make a *convenientia* about what is to happen to her Peffingen lands after her death. This is a three-way arrangement: between her, Bernard and Prüm. Whether Peffingen passes to Bernard or to Prüm, the crucial point, for Erkanfrida, is that *memoria nostra* will be taken care of at Prüm. Erkanfrida is able to provide for this herself. Adalard and his fellow-trustees are not mentioned again in section 5. In commending Peffingen to them, then, is Erkanfrida retaining a life interest in (and the usufruct of) her own inherited lands, mobilizing Adalard and the rest to protect her rights? Or is she transferring to them now control of the property, in effect her own life interest, for the duration of her life?

WAMPACH

The brief mention of Wampach in section 1 does not clarify by what right Erkanfrida is dealing with this property. Only in the final section 6 does it emerge that she is dealing with 'what my lord [Nithad] had at Wampach'. Her statement that Nithad had wished this property to pass 'to Bernard's offspring' implies that Bernard himself was a relative of Nithad. The suggestion that Bernard was Erkanfrida's son[82] seems to be excluded by Ansbald's express statement 'you have no successor of your line', and by the fact that Bernard's consent is not required for Erkanfrida's arrangements concerning her *hereditas*. It is possible, however, and even likely, that he was Nithad's son by another woman; hence 'Bernard's offspring' were Nithad's grandchildren. The further details mentioned in section 6 relate to Nithad's rights – evidently

---

[81] Le Jan-Hennebicque, 'Origines', p. 119, takes Peffingen to have been inherited by Erkanfrida from her late husband. This seems likely, given the claims of Bernard. See also below, p. 107.

[82] Sauerland, 'Das "Testament" der lotharingischen Gräfin Erkanfrida', p. 293.

two distinct sets of rights – at Wampach. In addition to his own (presumably inherited) land here, he had been given a church and other property, and these latter he ordered to be given to Prüm. Here, then, Erkanfrida merely rehearses arrangements already made. Again, Adalard and the other trustees are unmentioned: implicitly, though, they are witnessing, and underwriting, Erkanfrida's confirmation of her deceased husband's bequests. She has no other stake in the Wampach properties: by implication, Nithad's death is a very recent event.

MERSCH

The will's entire central section, sections 2–4, must be read as referring *only* to Mersch. The arrangements here were complicated. The property at Mersch comprised distinct elements. Erkanfrida disposed separately of parts of this multiple estate because she had them by distinct types of right. The church of St Michael and its appurtenances had come into her possession as her *dos* from her husband. Erkanfrida had already 'sequestrated' this and given it (appropriately) as '*dos*' to St Maximin,[83] in a separate legal transaction, perhaps at St Maximin itself.[84] But as noted above, she asserted, here in the will, her own life interest. 'The *mansus dominicus* and all the estate (*fiscus*) belonging to it' at Mersch, were now transferred by Erkanfrida 'freely' (*liberaliter*) into the hands of Adalard and his fellow-trustees: not unconditionally, however. Erkanfrida specified 'that if I should desire that those properties should revert to me through the hands of those men or of only one of them, I should [be able to] do it'. There was another time limit too, which was to come into effect after Erkanfrida's death, should she *not* have decided, meanwhile, to recover the properties: on the fortieth day after her death, her husband's nephews and niece should have the right 'in accordance with my husband's wish', to acquire them – but here Erkanfrida specified yet another condition, this time for the *nepotes*: they must lay out 100 lb. of bullion in arranging for the commemoration of Erkanfrida and her parents (*genitores*), as well as of her husband Nithad, by a total of 20

---

[83] The extended sense of the word *dos* to cover endowments of churches must have resonated with its other, gendered, sense.

[84] This could but need not be the implication of the fact that the document was drawn up there.

religious communities. Erkanfrida's concern was to secure liturgical commemoration for herself, her parents[85] and her husband. Only if they guaranteed this, by payments to the listed monasteries, would Erkanfrida permit the eight nephews and one niece to get their hands on Mersch. Clearly, those intended to ensure her wishes on this point were carried out were Adalard and his co-trustees. Their reward was the having of the main Mersch estate for as long as Erkanfrida lived, unless or until she should 'desire' its return.

The *dos* was clearly a gender-specific type of property-holding. How 'strong' a form was it? Just after her husband's death, Erkanfrida made the grant to St Maximin in terms that betokened the fullest possible rights of ownership: 'I hand over my property and I wish the transfer to be permanent' (*trado traditumque in perpetuum esse volo. . . res meas*). (And later: *trado adque transfundo.*) So, *dos* was a 'strong' form of property right in the sense that Erkanfrida could alienate it (and indeed retain her own life interest in it) without anyone else's express consent. At the time she made her will, however, Erkanfrida had also acquired the remainder of the 'whole estate at Mersch'. Le Jan-Hennebicque plausibly argues that this acquiring had occurred following Nithad's death; and she suggests, further, that the rest of the Mersch estate, plus the lands at Peffingen and Wampach, together amounted to one-third of Nithad's inheritance.[86] There seems to be no way of confirming or denying this suggestion; Erkanfrida's terming of Peffingen her 'hereditas' could work either way. In the will Erkanfrida planned that the Mersch property (excluding the church) would be used to make liturgical provision for *her own parents* as well as her husband and herself; and meanwhile, she 'transferred' this property to trustees in such a way that she retained (so she claimed) complete freedom to revoke the concession whenever she wanted. Liturgical commemoration – of her parents, and her husband, alongside herself – by communities of her choice was how Erkanfrida conceived of and expressed her personal identity, her

[85] *Genitores* rather than *parentes* is surely used to make the meaning absolutely clear. Cf. Dhuoda's commemoration of a number of her husband's kin, plus, it seems, her own mother and father: above, n. 50.

[86] Le Jan-Hennebicque, 'Origines', p. 119.

woman's version of *strenuitas* and *nobilitas*. Finally, she could 'decree' that the Mersch lands themselves were to be divided among the twenty named churches, should the 'price' not be handed over by Nithad's kin.

Erkanfrida's powers over the rest of the property she acquired as a widow seem, however, less strong than those she had at Mersch. She claimed no reversionary rights except at Mersch; and there alone she 'decreed' the destination of the lands after her death. Yet she called Peffingen her *hereditas*, and her powers there involved more than a life interest, since she herself stipulated the terms on which Bernard could acquire them. At Wampach, by contrast, she just carried out her husband's wishes.

It is an obvious inference from the information Erkanfrida herself supplied (in the 853 grant, as well as in the will), and it is indeed explicitly stated by Abbot Ansbald in his letter-charter, that she and Nithad had no children. She mentioned neither siblings nor collateral kin of her own.[87] On her death, she foresaw that Nithad's collateral kin would have strong claims, and she acknowledged these both in the 853 grant, and in the will. There was also, perhaps, a stepson – Bernard. Even during her lifetime, Erkanfrida's rights were vulnerable, as she well knew: in the same breath as she asserted the primacy of her wishes (*si ego desiderarem*) she 'commended' her lands to the protection of a group of powerful men. What did such commendation mean? A parallel has been seen in contemporary monasteries commending themselves to kings. Erkanfrida was more vulnerable than those institutions, and her 'venerable witnesses' were closer to home. One was her late husband's lord. As for the rest, the plural *venerabiles* has seemed puzzling, for only Adalard could have qualified, as a lay-abbot, for this title. The will's editor termed the other five men 'prominent fellow-inhabitants of the region' (*Gaugenossen*).[88] That they may have been, but the scribe, perhaps echoing Erkanfrida herself, extended the epithet 'venerable' to the whole group, not in virtue

---

[87] Though Erkanfrida is likely to have had *some* kin of her own, however distant. Apparently there were no arrangements like those found in Scandinavia for women's reverse inheritance: B. Sawyer, *Property and Inheritance in Viking Scandinavia: The Runic Evidence*, esp. pp. 32–4.

[88] Wampach, *Urkunden- und Quellenbuch*, p. 87, n. 9.

of their all being abbots (or lay-abbots) themselves,[89] but because of their association with Adalard. One of the five, Huodilbertus, was very probably the man who a few years earlier had acted as witness to a similar transaction of trusteeship – though this time the 'trustee', a royal *vassus*[90] named Folrad, was termed *fideiussor* (surety) – involving Adalard's brother Gerard, again with Prüm as beneficiary.[91] Waldo and the rest were, I would guess, as Nithad had been, faithful men (*fideles*) of Adalard, helping him rebuild a career and a power-base in the Moselle valley region from 844 onwards.[92] When Erkanfrida 'commended' her property, she got the favour and support of a great lord and his local clients to ensure her and her husband's well-being in the after-life, at the same time relying on that lord to take care of her interests as well as his own. The lord owed such care to the relict of his *fidelis*: at the same time, the request, and his acceptance of the assignment, enhanced his prestige. The peers and comrades of the dead man shared that: they gained respect (as *venerabiles* by association), and their role in protecting Nithad's widow reinforced their group solidarity as Adalard's men. But their collective role was not that of trustees in the modern sense, disinterested stake-holders. Adalard and his men stood to benefit from the commended lands, perhaps by managing them, but I suspect, though the will does not spell this out, also by taking the usufruct for as long as Erkanfrida lived: otherwise what would have been the significance of her assertion at this moment of the right to 'reverse' the transfer?

[89] Waldo can perhaps be identified with the Abbot Waldo who came west with Adalard in 861: *Annales Fuldenses*, s.a. 861, ed. F. Kurze, *MGH SRG*, p. 55; see T. Reuter (trans.), *The Annals of Fulda*, p. 47, n. 4. For the possibility that Waldo was abbot of St Maximin, Trier, see the forged charter (but perhaps using some accurate material) of Lothar II, *MGH Diplomata Karolinorum*, vol. 3, *Die Urkunden Lothars I und Lothars II*, ed. T. Schieffer, *Lothar II*, no. 39, pp. 451–2. See further E. Wisplinghoff, *Untersuchungen zur frühen Geschichte der Abtei S. Maximin bei Trier*, p. 25.

[90] This term here means a man who acted as the king's agent in a particular locality, in this case, evidently a man of some standing. See now S. Reynolds, *Fiefs and Vassals. The Medieval Evidence Reinterpreted*, pp. 84–105.

[91] Wampach, *Urkunden- und Quellenbuch*, no. 83, p. 78 (where Folrad's name also appears as Folcrad). Cf. *MGH Diplomata Karolinorum*, vol. 3, *Lothar I*, nos. 68, 84, pp. 181, 206. See W. Kienast, *Die fränkische Vassallität*, pp. 214, 219 (though his general views about vassals need revision in the light of Reynolds, *Fiefs and Vassals*).

[92] Interestingly, Erkanfrida did not turn to Archbishop Theutgaud of Trier (847–63), though his church was among the beneficiaries of her will. Her husband, of course, had had long-standing prior links with Adalard: see Nelson, *Politics and Ritual*, p. 232, n. 158.

The widow's power over these properties, though she reaffirmed it in principle, turned out to be shadowy, and ephemeral, in terms of earthly benefits. On the other hand, she had put her chosen trustees under an obligation, and done so in the full glare of a public occasion 'when noble men had gathered together':[93] Adalard's credibility as lord, the others' as *fideles* and good men, would rest on their carrying out of the widow's wishes for the gaining of next-worldly benefits.[94] To legitimize his power in the region, Adalard must appear a convincing protector, and be one too. Everyone knew what widows suffered at the hands of bad men. Care of widows was an acid test of good lordship.[95]

During her widowhood, Erkanfrida became a *deo sacrata*. This did not mean a total renunciation of earthly goods. While it seems scarcely likely that she could ever in fact have resumed control of the main Mersch lands, Erkanfrida retained a life interest in the church of St Michael 'with all that pertains to it' – which, as noted above, included a diversified estate, one part of which was large enough to have a labour force of over 100. Furthermore, the letter-charter of Ansbald seems to show that she continued to play a part in the management of the estate, Hannapes, which her husband had given to Prüm, implying that she retained a life interest here as well.[96] Erkanfrida was not a *potens femina*, nor had her husband been a count; but nor had he been a mere benefice-holder. Erkanfrida, like

---

[93] The opening words of the will indicate this, though there is no witness list (perhaps because the document as it survives is incomplete?). For widowhood as a time of more public activity for women, see J. Bennett, 'Widows in the medieval English countryside', in L. Mirrer (ed.), *Upon My Husband's Death. Widows in the Literature and Histories of Medieval Europe*, p. 103. In this respect, what was true of peasant widows was also true of noble ones.

[94] The implications of the link between power and reputation, and the role of 'community reassessment' of the standing of 'big men' in the context of dispute settlement, are notably well brought out, in ways that illuminate other earlier medieval societies, by W. I. Miller, *Bloodtaking and Peacemaking. Feud, Law and Society in Saga Iceland*, pp. 245–7.

[95] A classic illustration comes in the *Epitaphium Arsenii*, I. 26, ed. E. Dümmler, p. 55. For the antitype, a local tyrant who exploited widows' vulnerability but apparently 'imposed on one widow too many', see C. J. Wickham, 'Land-disputes and their social framework in Lombard–Carolingian Italy', in W. Davies and P. Fouracre (eds.), *The Settlement of Disputes in Early Medieval Europe*, p. 121. The good king as the protector of widows and orphans was a biblical, and medieval, stereotype.

[96] Le Jan-Hennebicque, 'Origines', though she does not mention the Ansbald letter, comments (p. 119) on the Hannapes estate: 'Erkanfrida n'avait cependant rien hérité des biens laonnois que Charles le Chauve avait concédés à Nythad en toute propriété en 845'.

Nithad, belonged to the lesser nobility, clients of a great magnate (Adalard), but possessed of quite substantial wealth, inherited and acquired. Such persons thus had their share of social power. Yet once widowed, Erkanfrida became, in a sense, one of the *pauperes* – the powerless, dependent on the power of others, socially beyond and above her. Gender made a difference.

A widow with children had some security as far as her property was concerned. But that security could well prove transient. A widow with adult sons, or stepsons, was thus in quite a different position from that of a widower, precisely because of the durability of paternal authority. A widow's own kin might offer protection; but they could also impose pressures to remarry. A widow without sons of her own had a certain independence, even power. But *seniores* and *magistri* lurked, potential subverters of the best-laid schemes; so too did her husband's nephews. For all the *strenuitas* and *nobilitas* she might possess, a widow was vulnerable. The part played by gender in that vulnerability becomes clear if we compare Erkanfrida's position with that of another contemporary testator, Eccard.[97] Both these persons lacked sons of their own, and predatory nephews prowled around both. In neither case does the will seem to have been made on a death-bed: both testators also wanted to provide for their own earthly sustenance in years to come.[98] Both sought special ties with saints and their ecclesiastical 'cultivators' to ensure the well-being of their souls after death – hence the wills: and both used trustees to ensure that the terms of the wills were carried out. Here, though, a striking difference appears. Eccard was a great magnate, with personal access to the king, and his twelve trustees were his own men (*homines*), long-standing followers, clients, and recipients of Eccard's largesse.[99] Erkanfrida's main trustee was himself a great magnate and the co-trustees were his men, not hers. Thus the relationship between

---

[97] See Kasten, 'Erbrechtliche Verfügungen', pp. 268–338; also for comments on Eccard from another angle, J. L. Nelson, 'Dispute settlement in Carolingian West Francia', in Davies and Fouracre (eds.), *The Settlement of Disputes in Early Medieval Europe*, pp. 53–5.

[98] This is clear in Erkanfrida's case, and convincingly argued for Eccard's by Kasten, 'Erbrechtliche Verfügungen', p. 336.

[99] Kasten, 'Erbrechtliche Verfügungen', p. 334, translating *homines* as 'Vassallen', provides evidence for this relationship. In his will, Eccard left the king (Charles the Bald) a pair of falcons and a pair of hunting-dogs: M. Prou and A. Vidier (eds.), *Recueil des chartes de l'abbaye de St-Benoît-sur-Loire*, no. 25, p. 66.

testator and trustees was fundamentally different in the two cases: partly through class but also through gender, Erkanfrida's position was that of a dependant, a suppliant, whereas Eccard was master of his own affairs. He could expect that, after his death, his men would observe the obligations of fidelity. She professed herself confident of her trustees' love (*caritas*), but hers was the hope placed by the weak in the strong. Erkanfrida, the *deo sacrata*, placed ultimate trust in the saints and their power. She mustered an impressive number of saintly supporters, and attempted to construct a friendship network spanning heaven and earth. Echternach's puzzling absence from the list might reflect a certain ambiguity in Erkanfrida's feelings towards Adalard, Echternach's lay-abbot, and a desire to keep open alternative options which were also alternative sanctions – the only ones she could hope might be effective. Since the pressures of the world weighed heavy on a woman, and not least on a widow, Erkanfrida needed to be wary. In the end – and here indeed was the power of the weak – she could remind Adalard and the others that they themselves would have to render account one day to the heavenly reckoner.

APPENDIX I: THE LATIN TEXT OF ERKANFRIDA'S WILL

From C. Wampach, *Urkunden- und Quellenbuch zur Geschichte der altluxemburgischen Territorien*, pp. 87–90. The letters in square brackets represent Wampach's reconstruction of the text where there are lacunae in the parchment original.
Note: Places mentioned in the will are marked on Map 1, with the exceptions of the convent of St Eventius (dioc. Trier), and St Cyriacus (dioc. Worms), whose locations I have been unable to identify.

[Com]memoratorium qualiter et quibus presentibus [Erkanfr]ida res suas disposuit atque in manus inlustrium virorum disponendas contradidit post suum discessum.
[1] Convenientib[us] itaque in unum nobilibus viris, ego Erkanfrida in eodem conventu adveniens, in loco nuncupante Steinseli, commendavi Adalardo venerabili comiti, necnon et Waldoni, Folcuino atque Beretlando, duobusque Huodilbertis, quicquid habere visa sum hereditatis in comitatu Treverensi, in pago Bedinse, in loco qui vocatur Peffinga, et in comitatu Ardinense, in loco nuncupante Wanbahc, et in tercio loco qui appellatur Mariscus super ripam Alsuntiae, illum mansum dominicum et omnem illum fiscum ad eum pertinentem,

ex[ce]pta illa ecclesia sancti Michaelis cum om[ni in]tegritate quae [a]d eam pertinet, quod mihi senior meus Nithadus in dot[em dedi]t, quam tradidi ad sanctum Maximinum, et feci consc[ribere testa]-mentum quod ibidem scriptum veraciter et rationabi[liter habe]tur. [2] Ea videlicet racione liberaliter in manus [illorum supra]dictas res transposui, ut si ego desiderarem illas [per illo]rum manus vel saltim unius illorum ad me rever[ti, faciam; s]i vero non, similiter per illorum manus statui secun[dum d]isposicionem supradicti senioris mei, ut si nepotes sui, filii scilicet sororis sue Irminburge mares VI., et filius fratris sui Rimigarit nomine Reginboldis, et soror eius nomine Thiodrat, et filius secunde sororis sue Thetbirge adquirere vellent, inter hos novem C. libras inter aurum et argentum post discessum meum die quadragesimo persolverent et precium inter XX. monasteria, id est: ad sanctum Maximinum C. solidos, ad sanctum Petrum similiter, ad Horreum similiter, ad Palatium similiter, ad Mediolacum similiter, ad Toleiam similiter, et inter sanctum Eucharium et sanctum Paulinum et sanctum Quiriacum ad Attavanum solidos C., ad Hornbahc similiter, ad Malmundarias similiter, ad Stabulaus similiter, ad Indam similiter, ad sanctum Hucbertum similiter, et inter sanctum Goarem et Appola monasterium solidos C., et inter Castorem et sanctum Alexandrum et sanctum Eventium C. solidos, ad sanctum Cyriacum solidos C., ad domum Wormaciae similiter, ad sanctum Nazarium similiter, ad Wiz-enburc similiter, ad domum Spire similiter, ad sanctum Leonem simil-iter solidos C., singillatim in memoriam mei et genitorum meorum vel coniugalis mei Nithadi dividerent, et ipse res nullatenus illis ante traderentur, quousque precium statutum sub die memorato persolvant et hanc villam inter se aequa disposicione[100] dividerent. [3] Quod si precium supradictarum rerum persolutum non fuerit, similiter decrevi ut supra memorati venerabiles testes in elemosinam nostram ipsas res ad loca sanctorum traderent atque transfunderent. [4] Sequestravi autem ad sanctum Maximinum Treverensem ecclesiam sancti Michaelis ad dotem ecclesie ab eorum tradicione vel conventione, quoniam ego ipsa in memoriam coniugalis mei et meam ipsam post discessum meum locis sanctorum delegavi, id est ad sanctum Maximinum. [5] De hoc vero quod in Peffingis habui, statui sub tali convenientia ut si Bernardus XXX. libras precii ex hoc persolverit post meum discessum, illi tradatur, et illud precium Prumie monasterio deferatur, ut inde agantur dies anniversarii nostri quamdiu haec pecunia subsisterit. Quod si et precium non dederit, nec illi quicquam de his rebus detur, sed locis sanctorum, id est Prumie condonetur in memoriam nostram. [6] Quod vero ad Wanbahc habuit senior meus, disposuit dari filiis Bernardi, preter illam ecclesiam et illas res quas Burgiridus eidem seniori meo in villa nuncupante Skizzane dedit. Hanc aecclesiam vel illas res,

---

[100] *Sic*, correctly, from photograph in Wampach. His edition wrongly gives 'dispocione'.

quas memoratus Burgiridus ei dedit, iussit ad monasterium Prumie dari. De reliquo obsecro vos propter Deum obnixe et testificor coram Deo et Christo Jhesu, qui iudicaturus est vivos et mortuos, ut supradictam hereditatem[101] cum mancipia et peccunia suprataxata, id est suprascripta, sic dividatis et ordinetis per loca denominata qualiter racionem vultis reddere, pro cuius nomine ego de vestra caritate fisa me ipsam vestrae fidei credidi commendatam.

[101] *Sic*, correctly, from photograph in Wampach. His edition wrongly gives 'heredidatem'.

CHAPTER 5

Lordship and justice in the early English kingdom: Oswaldslow revisited

Patrick Wormald

One of Domesday Book's most celebrated pronouncements is that on the bishop of Worcester's liberty for the triple-hundred of Oswaldslow.

The Church of St Mary of Worcester has a Hundred, called 'Oswaldslow', in which belong 300 hides. From these the bishop of that church has, by an arrangement of ancient times, all render from jurisdiction and all customary dues there belonging to his demesne sustenance, both the king's service and his own, so that no sheriff can have any claim there, either in any plea or in any other case whatever. The whole shire testifies to this. ('Ecclesia Sanctae Mariae de Wirecestre habet unum hundret quod vocatur Oswaldeslaw, in quo iacent ccc hidae. De quibus episcopus ipsius ecclesiae a constitutione antiquorum temporum habet omnes redditiones socharum et omnes consuetudines inibi pertinentes ad dominicum victum et regis servitium et suum ita ut nullus vicecomes ullam ibi habere possit querelam nec in aliquo placito nec in alia qualibet causa. Hoc attestatur totus comitatus.')[1]

The hide was the standard unit of assessment for taxation and other forms of service in eleventh-century England. The commissioners who surveyed William the Conqueror's new realm in 1086 are here declaring that, on the evidence of the county community, profits of justice, dues and sundry obligations that might

[1] *DB* i 172a, *Worcestershire* 2:1. Domesday Book is normally cited by folio number from Farley's edition, and by subsection in the county-by-county series, general ed. J. Morris; translations are usually those of the Alecto edition. Legal texts are cited from *Die Gesetze der Angelsachsen*, ed. F. Liebermann, using the title he gives them (usually a king's name). A (more or less) *viva voce* statement of this paper's case is included in N. P. Brooks and K. Cubitt (eds.), *St Oswald of Worcester: Life and Influence*. I am very grateful to Professor Brooks (and to the editors of this volume) for the opportunity to make a more considered statement here. I am also of course indebted to the other members of this forum for characteristically shrewd and sensistive criticism, and to one member in particular, Dr Jenny Wormald, for no less characteristic encouragement and support.

otherwise have been owed to the king from a set of estates assessed at three hundred hides, and notionally consolidated into one of the eight 'hundreds' that formed the administrative subdivisions of the county, were paid instead to the bishop of Worcester; that the king's officers were excluded from exercising their normal judicial functions as regards the area involved; and that this had long been the position.

Part of the passage's fame derives from the importance naturally attached to it by the church of Worcester itself. The cartulary assembled by the Worcester monk Hemming at the end of the eleventh century reproduced it no less than three times: once inserted into the originally early eleventh-century cartulary that made up Hemming's 'Part I', and twice more in the part that was his own responsibility. The second of these three rehearsals was followed by a detailed account of how this testimony was sworn by 'the whole shire with the encouragement and assistance of the most holy and wise father, the lord Bishop Wulfstan, before Bishop Remigius of Lincoln, Earl Walter Giffard, Henry de Ferrers and Adam brother of Eudo the king's steward', those of the king's 'leading men' who surveyed that area; and of how a 'copy' of the testimony was 'kept in the royal treasury with the *descriptiones* of the whole of England'.[2] Domesday historians have cherished this text as one of their precious external records of the making of the great survey, and the only one that actually names a team of commissioners.

But it has been of crucial importance, too, to historians concerned with the question of 'private justice' in Anglo-Saxon England. For Maitland, it established that the 'seigneurial' or 'feudal' justice that his continental compeers had found in early medieval Europe was developing in pre-conquest England too. On the view that his unmatched authority made classical, Worcester's privileges were by no means unique. Pre-conquest kings, in particular Edward the Confessor (1042–66), had been granting away the machinery and perquisites of royal justice 'with reckless

---

[2] *Hemingi Chartularium Ecclesiae Wigorniensis*, ed. T. Hearne, vol. 1, pp. 287–8. The entry in 'Part I' is at vol. 1, p. 72, and the other 'Part II' entry (which in effect repeats that in 'Part I') is at vol. 1, pp. 298–9. For the structure of Hemming's Cartulary, see N. R. Ker, 'Hemming's Cartulary', in R. W. Hunt, W. A. Pantin and R. W. Southern (eds.), *Studies in Medieval History Presented to Frederick Maurice Powicke*.

liberality', and with potentially grave effects on both royal revenue and enforcement of the royal will.[3] Maitland's case was designed to rebut the proposition put by Henry Adams in the first thorough discussion of the subject. In Adams's view, all that kings had alienated before the reign of Edward the Confessor were the *profits* of justice: landlords received the fines hitherto payable to the king's officials, in Domesday parlance 'the render from jurisdiction', but those officials continued to direct proceedings; only under the 'Norman-hearted Edward' did the courts themselves begin to pass into the hands of private lords.[4] Maitland pointed out that the alienating formula familiar in Edward's writs can already be found in earlier authentic documents: Cnut in 1020 granted Archbishop Æthelnoth 'sake and soke, and . . . [the pleas of] *griðbryces 7 hamsocne 7 forestealles 7 infangenes þeofes 7 flymena fyrmðe* over his own men within borough and without . . . and over as many thegns as I have granted him to have'. Furthermore, these pleas are listed in Cnut's laws, together with *fyrdwite*, as 'rights which the king possesses over all men in Wessex [and in effect Mercia and the Danelaw too], unless he wishes to honour anyone further'.[5] Maitland not unreasonably took this to signify that these pleas were the major elements of royal jurisdiction, and accordingly read laws and writs to mean that Cnut and his successors had no hesitation in granting them away.

In addition, Maitland discovered that among exceptions to the increasingly standard exemptions from royal service in eighth- and ninth-century charters might be not only military duties and work on forts and bridges, but also *angild* (compensation or redress due to the victim of an offence) whereas the *wite* (fine) was to be retained by the grant's beneficiary. A beneficiary's perquisites might further include *furis comprehensio*, which Maitland plausibly understood as summary justice over those caught in the act of theft, and equated with the

---

[3] F. W. Maitland, *Domesday Book and Beyond*, pp. 307–45.

[4] H. Adams, 'The Anglo-Saxon courts of law', in H. Adams (ed.), *Essays in Anglo-Saxon Law*, pp. 27–54.

[5] P. H. Sawyer, *Anglo-Saxon Charters: An annotated List and Bibliography* (hereafter S, cited by no.), 986; *Gesetze*, ed. Liebermann, II Cnut 12, 14, 15. For the meaning of all the technical terms in the text, see below, p. 119; the symbol '7' signifies the word 'and'.

infangenepeof of later writs.[6] Applying the robust common sense
that was his forte, he demanded whether anyone but the beneficiary in question could be expected to collect these profits:
'no one in the middle ages does justice for nothing'.[7] It would
follow that a right to hold the courts in question was implicit
in grants of the financial penalties they levied. The point about
the Oswaldslow privileges is that they proved that such rights
were ancient: 'surely the whole county would not have spoken
thus of some newfangled device of the half-Norman Edward'.
In sum, 'we cannot see either in the history of England or in
the history of the Frankish Empire any reason why we should
shrink from [the conclusion that] a royal grant of land in the
ninth and tenth centuries generally included, and this as a
matter of "common form", a grant of jurisdiction . . . jurisdiction
of the most exalted kind . . . The well endowed immunist of St
Edward's day' (as Maitland found it 'convenient' to call him)
'has jurisdiction as high as that which any palatine earl of after
ages enjoyed.' A dominant theme in Maitland's interpretation
of the development of English law in the central middle ages
was the struggle of kings from Henry II (1154–89) onwards to
assert their monopoly control of judicial proceedings. As he saw
it, the 'franchises', or substantially independent jurisdictions,
that the Plantagenets were to struggle so hard to uproot, were
deeply embedded.

It will at once be evident to readers of other chapters in this
volume that Maitland was here extrapolating from the experience
of the Frankish Empire as understood by the legal historians of
his own time. The Old English monarchy was firmly set on the
same slope down which Frankish royal power had slithered so
remorselessly. The reassessment of the continental immunity that
those chapters involve could thus have had serious implications
for the case Maitland made. As it is, however, rethinking had
begun much longer ago among students of the English scene,
and had already assumed some of the same lines as those now

---

[6] The relevant charters are (in chronological order) S 58, 154, 106, 171, 185, 183, 186,
188, 278, 292, 314, 322, 199, 206, 1277, 218, 220, plus S 1301, an Oswald lease apparently
to the same effect. Not all these texts are of acceptable credibility: see next note.

[7] Maitland also thought that court-holding could actually be read into a few of these
charters, but their language is anything but pellucid, and they are among the more
diplomatically suspect of the series: S 183, 278.

being taken for the continent. For even Maitland, who liked 'to cheer myself by saying that I have given others a lot to contradict', might have been shaken by the sight of the wreckage in which almost all of his thesis has come to lie.[8] The assault was led by one of his few peers among twentieth-century historians of English law. In essence, Julius Goebel reasserted Henry Adams's position. He fully accepted the evidence that the perquisites of justice were alienated from the eighth century onwards.[9] What he denied, as Adams had, was that this entailed court-holding rights such as would alone have added up to really independent jurisdiction. Like Adams, he stressed that the laws which allot duties and receipts to landlords are absolutely silent about the courts of lords. This is in marked contrast to Henry I's 1108 writ on the shire and hundred courts, which is quite explicit about the 'lord's court'.[10] Above all, Goebel found no trace in laws or charters of clauses providing for the sort of exclusion of sheriffs or other royal officials claimed by Wulfstan for Oswaldslow, and a central feature of formulas for continental immunities from the earliest days. 'Although' he wrote 'individuals are occasionally put in possession of a whole hundred, the landlord seems to have worked no metamorphosis in the hundred court comparable to the conversion of the Frankish *mallus publicus* into a feudal court in France'; and 'since actual lord-over-man control has not yet reached the strength and magnitude which it has in tenth-century France, one cannot be too cautious in

---

[8] Maitland's wholly characteristic remark should suffice to answer those (including some reviewers of the previous volume in this series) who see any challenge to his views as mere presumption. Another of his aphorisms was that 'the lawyer must be orthodox, otherwise he is no lawyer; an orthodox history seems to me a contradiction in terms'. That significant new lines of argument on the history of English law in the earlier middle ages can hardly be essayed without pitching lists against Maitland is the true mark of his stature as a historian.

[9] J. Goebel, *Felony and Misdemeanor*, pp. 339–78 (note that he made assumptions about the continental situation which are challenged elsewhere in the present volume). It is unnecessary to go along with Goebel's critique of Maitland's case on the *angild* charters (which he may possibly in any case misrepresent), *ibid.*, pp. 348–58: whether, as he insists, the word means 'restitution' (of stolen goods) or merely 'compensation', as he took Maitland to think, the point is in either case that a beneficiary's right to collect the *wite* for an offence should not prejudice an injured party's right to redress. But Goebel made a very good case that early references to *furis comprehensio* (e.g. S 180, 1861) were grants of the king's prerogative of ransom on the flagrant thief, as reflected in early Kentish and probably West Saxon law: *Gesetze*, ed. Liebermann, Wihtred 26; Ine 12.

[10] *Gesetze*, ed. Liebermann, Hn. com. (Henry I on shire and hundred courts), 3:1.

inferring a court where the Anglo-Saxon laws speak of rights in fiscal terms'.

Naomi Hurnard's masterly paper on 'The Anglo-Norman franchises' chose a different and ultimately even more destructive line of attack. She was able to show conclusively that the pleas apparently 'reserved' by Cnut's law, yet in fact alienated by his and the Confessor's writs, were not the major pleas, as Maitland had thought, but on the contrary, amendable offences, hence of relatively minor importance. It is quite clear from Cnut's own code, to say nothing of early-twelfth-century evidence like the *Leges Henrici Primi*, that a whole number of serious crimes were amendable only at the king's discretion, and these were not in Cnut's list of those usually reserved but sometimes alienable.[11] *Griðbryce* was not breach of the king's peace as such but (more or less literally) 'disturbance of the peace', a lord's peace included. *Forstal* is little more than 'common assault'. *Hamsocn* is simply assault in a house. By the later twelfth century, these offences had ceased even to count as pleas of the crown, and were being dealt with by sheriffs rather than king's justices. Of pleas that featured in eleventh-century writs but not Cnut's laws, *infangenetheof* was a capital plea, yet justice on the flagrant thief was essentially routine. As for *sac 7 soc*, there is no reason to think that they covered anything more important.[12] It was in fact precisely because these were minor or 'borderline' pleas to which lords might by that token be entitled, that it was necessary for the king to say that their entitlement was not a matter of course. If, then, 'the most common type of grant did not convey higher criminal jurisdiction, it follows that franchises of this kind were extremely rare'. We thus arrive at the fall-back position provisionally adopted by Hurnard, and subsequently defended by Florence Harmer and Helen Cam. These scholars, while conceding that private jurisdictions could never have extended beyond hundred level, went along with Maitland's argument that, when hundreds as jurisdictional districts coincided with

---

[11] N. D. Hurnard, 'The Anglo-Norman franchises', *English Historical Review*, 64 (1949). II Cnut 13, 15a–16 (in almost the same 'breath' as the clauses Maitland discussed), 64; *Gesetze*, ed. Liebermann, *Leges Henrici Primi* 10:1–4.

[12] Hurnard tellingly quotes F. Pollock and F. W. Maitland, *History of English Law*, vol. 2, p. 453: 'this [i.e. Cnut's] catalogue of pleas of the Crown may at first sight look comprehensive; in reality, it covers but little ground'. (For the fundamental meaning of *sac 7 soc* see p. 129 below.)

territory held by a lord, he was 'almost of necessity the lord of the court as well as the lord of the land'. One of Cam's papers consists essentially of a list of hundreds where this appears to have been the case.[13] Hence, the 'sake and soke' and the rest alienated in eleventh-century charters were the minor pleas which alone could be heard at this level, while more serious cases invariably went to shire courts that were never privatized. All that then remains of Maitland's thesis is a *likelihood* (my emphasis) that wholly-owned hundreds where lords were entitled to collect fines for offences that could be discharged by monetary payments would have passed so totally under their control that they became *de facto* lords of the hundred's court. But any degree of assurance that court-holding was indeed involved once again rests squarely on Oswaldslow's recorded privilege: Cam found this evidence 'unequivocal'.

The state of scholarly play is thus as follows. It is no longer clear that continental immunities had any more serious effects on justice than the transfer of judicial profits into ecclesiastical hands for religious uses. There is no demonstrable link between the creation of immunities and the rise of 'seigneurial' justice. The 'privatization' of Frankish justice was a complex process in which the collapse of royal power was only one element. In England, the documentary evidence concentrates much more heavily on the purely fiscal aspects of judicial privilege. There seems to be no question of private control of anything above the lowest hundredal level of jurisdiction. What remains at issue is whether the evidence from Oswaldslow entitles one to believe that alienation of judicial revenues encompassed exclusion of royal officials; whether there is any other reason to believe that landlords controlled hundred courts; and at a more general level, what signs there are that royal direction of justice was atrophying in such a way as itself to promote the growth of private jurisdiction.[14]

---

[13] *Anglo-Saxon Writs*, ed. and trans. F. Harmer, pp. 73–85, 123–31, etc.; H. Cam, 'The evolution of the medieval English franchise', and 'The private hundred in England before the Norman Conquest', both reprinted in *Law-finders and Law-makers in Medieval England*, pp. 22–43, 59–70. Cf. Cam's review of Goebel's *Felony and Misdemeanor*, *American Historical Review*, 43 (1938), pp. 585–6, and Hurnard, 'Franchises', p. 292, n. 1, for their distancing of themselves from Goebel's more extreme position.

[14] The ramifications of these issues are still too vast and various to receive more than summary treatment here. For fuller discussion of the general themes raised by the particu-

The first point is that, whatever the Domesday commissioners were told, the bishop's perception of his rights over Oswaldslow had not been shared by all shire landholders thus potentially affected. Throughout the decade before 1086, Worcester had been embroiled in an intractable dispute with its most prominent neighbour and rival, the abbey of Evesham. This is one of the three best-known pleas of the Conqueror's reign; unlike the other two, it has not been closely studied since the early twentieth century.[15] We derive most of our knowledge of it from the sort of extended narrative of proceedings that is relatively unusual in pre-conquest England, but was becoming a well-established genre in Normandy. Like the accounts of Lanfranc's plea at Penenden Heath and Ely's at Kentford, this text is both *ex post facto* and *parti pris* (on Worcester's behalf).[16] Fortunately, another feature of post-conquest disputes is that they are illuminated by more than one record. In this instance, we also have the king's writ initiating proceedings, and another royal writ confirming Wulfstan's victory. A third writ of the presiding judge, Bishop Geoffrey of Coutances, reports Wulfstan's success to 'Bishop Remigius, Walter Giffard, Henry de Ferrers, Adam and other barons of the king'; the reason for it emerges from a fifth and final document recording an agreement between Wulfstan and Walter, and again 'witnessed by . . . Bishop Remigius, Henry de Ferrers, Walter Giffard and Adam, who had come to survey the land in that county'. This is of course the team of Domesday commissioners said by Hemming to have heard the county's oath about Oswaldslow. The case was not, then, settled by the original judgement, and resolution came only in 1086 itself.

The story of the plea in outline is that Bishop Wulfstan claimed from Abbot Walter of Evesham 'sake and soke, burial, church-scot and the exactions and all the customs which are due to the church

---

lar case of Oswaldslow, see ch. 10 (part iii) of my forthcoming *The Making of English Law: King Alfred to the Norman Conquest*.

[15] J. H. Round, 'Introduction to the Worcestershire Domesday', *Victoria County History of Worcestershire*, vol. 1, pp. 252–6. A full dossier of the documents of the case is supplied (in each case with translation) by F. and C. Thorn in *Domesday Book, 14: Worcestershire*, Appendix V, H, and by R. C. van Caenegem in *English Lawsuits from William I to Richard I*, no. 15 (the version used here).

[16] van Caenegem, *Lawsuits*, nos. 5, 18. A seminal discussion of all these suits and their documentation is D. Bates, 'The land pleas of William I's reign: Penenden Heath revisited', *Bulletin of the Institute of Historical Research*, 51 (1978).

of Worcester in the hundred of Oswaldslow', in particular 'the
king's geld and service and military expeditions on land and sea
for the fifteen hides in Hampton and the four hides in Bengeworth,
which the abbot had to hold from the bishop, as the other tenants
of the church freely hold for all due service to the king and the
bishop'. The case was heard by Bishop Geoffrey and 'a great gathering of neighbouring counties and barons'. Wulfstan had a strong
team of 'lawful witnesses', where Walter had to make do with the
body of St Ecgwine. On the advice of his 'friends', Walter gave in
and 'agreed to conclude a concord with the bishop'. Eventually,
an agreement was worked out.[17] Two points about the suit need
particular attention. In the first place, Bengeworth and Hampton
were in effect different disputes: they raised different issues which
were differently resolved. The four hides of Bengeworth were
claimed by both Worcester and Evesham, for reasons set out by
Hemming and by the Evesham *Chronicon* respectively. Each claim
was supported by a neat little crop of fabricated or interpolated
documents. A possible reconstruction of the background is that
Bengeworth had indeed been Worcester property, and that Abbot
Æthelwig of Evesham (d.1077) had gained control of it by virtue
of his position as the king's viceroy in the West Midland shires,
and his expert manipulation of the mechanisms of property taxation.[18] But whatever the rights and wrongs, Wulfstan effectively

---

[17] It should be noted that the position described in the survey itself (DB i 174a, 175d; 2:72,
74–5; 10:11–12) seems to reflect the *pre-agreement* position: Evesham's four Bengeworth
hides are listed among Worcester's holdings, but in fact surveyed in Evesham's own fief
(the Bengeworth hides surveyed in Worcester's being those of Sheriff Urso); while of
Hampton, the Worcester section says (pointedly?) that 'before 1066 the bishop of Worcester had from them only the geld for his hundred; the rest was fully discharged at the
church of Evesham'. This is thus another instance where a dispute was resolved before
the commissioners without actually affecting Domesday's text: P. Wormald, 'Domesday
lawsuits: a provisional list and preliminary comment', in C. Hicks (ed.), *England in the
Eleventh Century*.

[18] For the Evesham account, see *Chronicon Abbatiæ de Evesham*, ed. W. D. Macray, pp. 94–5
with pp. 89–90; for the geld mechanism and the way in which it could be exploited, see
Hemingi Chartularium, vol. 1, pp. 277–80, with M. K. Lawson, 'The collection of Danegeld
and Heregeld in the reigns of Æthelred II and Cnut', *English Historical Review*, 99 (1984),
p. 735; and Wormald, 'Domesday lawsuits', p. 75. For Worcester's earlier tenure of
Bengeworth, see S 1341, apparently an authentic lease by Bishop Oswald of 980, and S
1282, an alleged lease of 907 by Bishop Waerferth to Abbot Cynelm of *Evesham* that is
certainly a forgery. S 991 is a purported writ of Cnut's from the Evesham cartulary,
granting one Brihtwine a lifetime interest in Bengeworth with reversion to Evesham; this
may be a basically genuine document, whose original beneficiary was St Mary's *Worcester*,
and which was doctored when land and title passed into Æthelwig's hands.

surrendered his territorial claims in the 1086 agreement. 'The bishop . . . claimed all that land as his demesne, but since the abbot humbly acknowledged this, the bishop . . . granted the land to the abbot . . . on condition that the abbot should do honourable recognition for it and service, in such a way and for so long as the bishop might require.' By contrast, Worcester did not make a claim to land at Hampton, and no Worcester documents, forged or otherwise, back one up. The relevant texts are both from the Evesham cartulary; one suspiciously claims an earlier bishop's witness that King Edward had allowed Evesham 'sake and soke', so that the abbot 'should answer to no man over any matter in respect of that land except the king and his followers'.[19] It was on that point that Wulfstan stuck, and here that he triumphed in the final compromise: 'the abbot recognized . . . that those fifteen hides [i.e. Hampton] justly belong to the bishop's hundred at Oswaldslow, and must pay the king's geld with the bishop and all other services that belong to the king, and depend on it for their pleas (*et inde idem requirere ad placitandum*); and similarly as far as the aforesaid four hides in Bengeworth are concerned'. That was also the point covered by the Worcester forgery that did relate to Hampton as well as Bengeworth.[20] Real estate seems to have mattered less to Wulfstan than lordship of Oswaldslow, which thus emerges as the burden of his original suit. The particular importance of the hearing of pleas was stressed by Bishop Geoffrey's report of proceedings (*ibi debent placitare*). The dispute thus underlines the urgency with which Wulfstan pressed his case for the Oswaldslow jurisdiction in 1086, at the same time as showing that his claims were far from uncontroversial, and that he (or his aides) were not above manipulating the evidence in their support.

The other point shows that he was well-placed to do so. The 'trustworthy persons' (*probabiles personae*) ready to offer sworn evidence in Worcester's support were listed as follows: 'Edric, the

---

[19] S 1398; the more plausible text is S 1223.

[20] S 118, a supposed grant by Offa of Mercia (757–96) of the manor of Cropthorne with Hampton and Bengeworth as appendages, wherein twenty-five hides (the Hampton–Bengeworth total) were allowed to be detached for the benefit of the bishop's kin on condition that the tenants maintained full service to the bishop and his successors. (There need be no question but that the Hampton at stake was the one near Evesham, and not Hampton Lovett, to which Worcester did have a claim, but which had been lost in entirely different circumstances: Wormald, 'Anglo-Saxon lawsuits', no. 103; still less Hampton Lucy, Warwicks, which was secure in Worcester's possession: *DB* i 238c, 3:1.)

steersman of the bishop's ship in the time of King Edward and leader of that bishop's army in the king's service, and on the day he offered to swear he was a man of Bishop Robert of Hereford and held nothing from Bishop Wulfstan. Kineward, who was sheriff of Worcestershire and who had seen this, was also present . . . Also present were Siward, a rich man from Shropshire, Osbern fitz Richard, and Turkil of Warwickshire, and many other senior and noble men'. What made these men *probabiles* was not their standing in society, but their expert knowledge. Standing in society was just what Edric and Kineward now lacked: the former had lost the land that went with responsibility for the bishop's military service, while the latter was no longer sheriff. Siward may have been wealthy but his local holding (if any) was just five hides. No one, on the other hand, was better placed than an ex-steersman of the bishop's ship and an ex-sheriff to know about Oswaldslow's pre-conquest obligations. Of the others, Osbern son of Richard was an addressee of the Conqueror's writ on the case, and 'Turkil of Warwickshire' is surely the 'Thorkel of Arden' who has entered student folklore as one of two Englishmen who survived as tenants-in-chief in 1086. A modern lawyer (or historian) wishing to assemble convincing evidence on Oswaldslow's liabilities would pick just that sort of team. Yet this point has a twist. The evidence of these figures may have been expert, but it was scarcely impartial. Edric had been a Worcester tenant, even if he 'held nothing' by the time the case was heard. Kineward was also an ex-tenant of the bishop's in respect of all his main Worcestershire estates, and it has been shown that he was probably from the family of (Archbishop) Wulfstan I of Worcester, which had long-established links with the see. Siward, Osbern and Thorkel were (or had been) Worcester tenants too.[21] It is more than mere cynicism to wonder whether such men would have given a detached report of any weaknesses the bishop's claim had.

Now, if Worcester was able to manipulate the spoken as well as the written evidence in its dispute with Evesham, this may have a very important bearing on the testimony about Oswaldslow sworn to the 1086 commissioners. We have already seen that it was the

---

[21] Edric: *DB* i 173c, 2:52; Kineward: *DB* i 172d, 173a, 174a, 2:13, 19, 73; Siward: *DB* i 173b, 2:33; Osbern: *DB* i 172d, 2:14; Thorkel: *DB* i 173c, 2:56. A. Williams, 'Introduction', in A. Williams (ed.), *The Worcestershire Domesday*, pp. 24–6.

commissioners who presided over the dispute's final settlement. When we examine those who witnessed it, we find exactly the same sort of tenants and contacts of the bishop as had secured Wulfstan's original victory: Edric 'of Hindlip' is the lawsuit's 'steersman'; Godric of Perry was probably Archbishop Wulfstan's great-nephew and another long-standing tenant; Archdeacon Ailric, Ordric 'the Black' and Ælfwine son of Brihtmær had similar links.[22] In other words, men who probably represented the Worcester interest already had the commissioners' ear on the subject of Oswaldslow. Whether or not the bishop actually briefed them what to say about his rights, they are more than likely to have expressed his views. We have no way of knowing that these views were balanced by those of parties, for example Evesham, who saw things differently. The bishop of Worcester's massive local endowment gave him a strong hold over 'county opinion'. Just because that opinion was enshrined in Domesday Book that is no guarantee of its veracity.

If we now turn to the documentation supposedly supporting Worcester's Oswaldslow claims, it becomes rather less surprising that they had been disputed. Hemming makes it quite clear what he thought this supporting documentation was. The same scribe gives the same (capitalized) title in the same red ink to Bishop Oswald's letter of *c*.964 informing King Edgar of the terms on which Oswaldslow's tenants could expect to hold and serve as to the account of Domesday's verdict just a few folios before: INDICULUM LIBERTATIS DE OSWALDES LAWES HUNDRED. But a title to 'liberty' is scarcely what this was. In fact the chief reason for believing it substantially authentic is that, in a context where Hemming shows that evidence for Oswaldslow's liberty was at a premium, the *Indiculum* gives no support whatsoever for its jurisdictional privileges. The one possible reference to judicial rights simply penalized those who defaulted on their obligations to their landlord: 'but if any of the aforesaid dues shall be withheld by virtue of the offence of default (?) (*delicti prevaricantis causa*), the default shall be made good in accordance with the bishop's right (*jus*), or [the tenant] shall lose the gift and land he had before'.[23] This was not immunity as it would have been

[22] *DB* i 173c, 2:52; *DB* i 173d–174a, 2:61, 73; *DB* i 173a, 173c, 2:20, 24, 57 (cf. *Vita Wulfstani*, ed. R. R. Darlington, III.15, p. 55); *DB* i 173bc, 2:32, 55–6; *DB* i 172d, 2:10; Williams, 'Introduction', pp. 25–6, 31.
[23] S 1368; *Hemingi Chartularium*, vol. 1, pp. 292–6.

understood at the abbey of Fleury, where Oswald had recently been a monk.[24] By the very same token, however, any document that does appear to uphold the Oswaldslow privileges, but was somehow unavailable to its exponents in 1086, must instantly fall under the darkest suspicion. Such is the notorious *Altitonantis* charter, apparently a grant by Edgar to Oswald, which Hemming (or Wulfstan) would have found a great deal better suited as an *Indiculum Libertatis* properly so-called:

[I grant] the rights and powers of these possessions *cum* [with] *tolle et teame* [in effect justice over the market] *et saca et socne et infangenepeof*, and the fine for offending against their own privileges, and the penalty for the crime which in English is called contumacy (?) (*ofersewnesse*) and *gyltwite*, nor shall any of my reeves or bailiffs or servants or officials diminish or infringe this liberty of my munificence in anything . . . [I grant] the three hundreds . . . at the place which it was agreed to call Oswaldslow in his honour, where lawsuits are decided according to the custom of the country and the rights of laws, and the bishop himself . . . has the fines for offences in the church's right, and the penalty for the crimes called *ofersegenesse et gyltwite*, and whatsoever the king has in his hundreds.[25]

The point that sceptics about this charter have rightly stressed, and that has been crucially missed by the long and valiant campaign in defence of its authentic basis, is not merely that it is omitted by both Worcester's eleventh-century cartularies, but that it is not reproduced by Hemming when it is evident from everything else he says that it would have been of the utmost value to him.[26]

There is no reason to doubt that Edgar did something special for Oswaldslow. It was, as *Altitonantis* itself says, renamed after Oswald (having perhaps been called *Oslafeshlau* before), and Worcester made no such claims for its other 1086 holdings. Quite possibly, as *Altitonantis* also implies, a triple-hundred *was* created in Edgar's time, and was one of a series geared to naval organization.[27] The bishop of Worcester could well have been granted the

---

[24] See for example *Recueil des Actes de Lothaire et de Louis IV, rois de France (954–87)*, ed. L. Halphen and F. Lot, no. 27, pp. 67–8.

[25] S 735.

[26] *Cartulary of Worcester Cathedral Priory*, ed. R. R. Darlington, pp. xiii–xix; P. H. Sawyer, 'Charters of the reform movement: the Worcester archive' in D. Parsons (ed.), *Tenth-Century Studies*, pp. 85–7; E. John, *Land Tenure in Early England*, pp. 81–167; E. John, 'War and society in the tenth century: the Maldon campaign', *Transactions of the Royal Historical Society*, 27 (1977), pp. 192–3.

[27] See the interesting possibilities raised by P. Taylor, 'The endowment and military obligations of the see of London: a reassessment of three sources', *Anglo-Norman Studies*, 14 (1992), pp. 299–303; and for 'Oslafeshlau' see S 1436.

profits of its judicial administration at that stage. But none of this is sensibly believed on the say-so of *Altitonantis* alone. A recent statement has made the strongest case yet that it is an outright forgery, datable to the time when a charter of Stephen was also forged to confirm it.[28] Least of all can we believe its judicial clauses. *Ofersew[ge]nesse* and *gyltwite*, twice included among the penalties reserved to the bishop and monks, are not in fact part of tenth-century forensic vocabulary. On the contrary, it must be a further suspicious circumstance that the first of these terms is otherwise found only in the writings of a twelfth-century lawyer who made something of a speciality of seignorial justice – and whose work was available in at least one Worcester manuscript.[29]

The claims registered in 1086 for the freedom of Oswaldslow from the attentions of the king's officials are therefore without pre-conquest documentary foundation. The earliest acceptable text saying anything to that effect is, significantly, a writ of the Conqueror to Prior Ælfstan that is presumably to be dated some time in the course of the Worcester–Evesham dispute. Its provision that 'I am unwilling that anyone intrudes himself in the affairs of the monks except through the prior of the church' contrasts strikingly with the Confessor's writ to Prior Wulfstan himself, which says no such thing.[30] Not only, indeed, does Worcester's privilege lack authentic documentary support. It can also be shown to have become the subject of doctored evidence parallel to what has already been suspected for the testimony supplied to the Domesday commissioners. In so far as Oswaldslow has provided

---

[28] J. Barrow, 'How the twelfth-century monks of Worcester perceived their past', in P. Magdalino (ed.), *The Perception of the Past in Twelfth-Century Europe*, pp. 69–71; Darlington, *Cartulary of Worcester*, pp. lxvii–lxix.

[29] *Gyltwite* appears to be otherwise unrecorded in any context and could well be a scribal coinage. *Ofersew[ge]nesse* occurs elsewhere only in *Quadripartitus*, a Latin translation of Anglo-Saxon laws from the early twelfth century, and *Leges Henrici Primi*, a later work by the same author: *Gesetze*, ed. Liebermann, II Æthelstan 20:1 (MS 'K'); II Cnut 29:1; *Leges Henrici Primi* 34:3; 35; 41; 42:1; 48:1a; 50:3; 51:7; 53:1–1b; 60:1a; 61:1; 61:8a; 65:2; 80:9a; 81:2–3; 87:5. Judging from these passages, the author equated it with *oferhiernes*, the Anglo-Saxon disobedience fine of 120 shillings. A semantic shift of *oferseon* from 'oversee', towards 'overlook', i.e. 'neglect', already occurs in Archbishop Wulfstan (1002–23): *Wulfstan, Sammlung der ihm zugeschriebenen Homilien*, ed. A. Napier, no. 50, p. 270; under its influence, a twelfth-century writer who was no Old English speaker adapted the sense of 'defiance [of law]' into 'neglect', while also making it a perquisite of private judicial lordship. For *Quadripartitus* MSS, see now P. Wormald, " *'Quadripartitus'* ", in G. Garnett and J. Hudson (eds.), *Law and Government in Medieval England and Normandy: Studies Presented to J. C. Holt*.

[30] *Regesta Regum Anglo-Normannorum*, vol. 1, ed. H. W. C. Davis (hereafter *Reg.*, cited by no.) 252, *Cartulary of Worcester*, p. 7; S 116. *Reg.*, vol. 1, 106, a comparable writ for Æthelwig and Evesham, is most unlikely to be authentic; cf. nn. 32–6 below.

the 'unequivocal' instance of immune jurisdiction before 1066, the case for 'privatized' justice in Anglo-Saxon England is seriously weakened.[31]

It is further undermined when we switch attention from Oswaldslow itself to other purported cases of pre-conquest judicial immunity. A point of considerable moment is that Anglo-Saxon charters with provisions like those of *Altitonantis* are, almost without exception, as dubious as *Altitonantis* itself. Goebel was justly suspicious of documents making such claims for Ely, Peterborough, Abingdon and Chertsey; Maitland had failed to note that where the Latin text of Ely's privilege expatiated on its jurisdictional rights, the Old English version (probably early eleventh-century) spoke only of *eallum þa socne* (which need only mean judicial profits).[32] Texts where Goebel was prepared to admit the 'first tentative employment' of an exclusion clause were all seen by Harmer as spurious or interpolated.[33] The diplomas that spell out the privileges of medieval England's greatest liberties, Glastonbury, Ramsey, Ely again, and Bury St Edmunds are all, likewise, largely or wholly bogus.[34] The one formula in an authentic preconquest record that approaches the terms of William I's writ for

---

[31] Questionable too, therefore, is the Anglo-Saxon variant on traditional interpretations of the Ottonian *Reichskirche* (for which see now T. Reuter, 'The "imperial church system" of the Ottonian and Salian rulers: a reconsideration', *Journal of Ecclesiastical History* 33 (1982), pp. 358–64): that Oswaldslow was set up by Edgar as a loyal, because reformed, counter to anti-reform local particularism embodied in Ealdorman Ælfhere of Mercia. Ælfhere was very much a member of the West Saxon ruling elite and related to the royal family: A. Williams, '*Princeps Merciorum Gentis*: the family, career and connections of Ælfhere, ealdorman of Mercia', *Anglo-Saxon England*, 10 (1981). He was also a patron of Glastonbury, and D. J. V. Fisher long ago showed that his *later* enmity to Oswald's Mercian houses arose from political rivalry over the succession to Edgar between him and Oswald's patron, Ealdorman Æthelwine: 'The anti-monastic reaction in the reign of Edward the Martyr', *Cambridge Historical Journal*, 10 (1952), pp. 266–70.

[32] S 779 (cf. J. Pope, 'Ælfric and the Old English version of the Ely privilege', in P. Clemoes and K. Hughes (eds.), *England Before the Conquest. Studies in Primary Sources presented to D. Whitelock*), 787, 1066, 1095. If, as Napier and Stevenson were (uncharacteristically) prepared to admit, S 912 (Æthelred for St Alban's) is broadly acceptable, it remains suspicious that its provisions on judicial liberty are almost identical with the certainly forged charter of Offa for the abbey, S 136. And if S 1128 is also not wholly unacceptable, it could well have been tampered with, given Westminster's record. But Goebel's suspicions should probably not have extended to S 321, 1450, 880.

[33] S 1066, 1089, 1051, and 'weaker forms', S 1102, 1477, 1094, 1065; S 1102 may be acceptable, but its purport is probably misunderstood by the Hereford cartularist and/or by Goebel himself.

[34] S 499, 966, with the infamous S 250; S 798, 1030; S 1051; in Bury's S 980, Cnut says nothing about exclusions, though Henry I, in referring to it (*Reg.*, vol. 2, 644), does – he may have been influenced by the unquestionably fraudulent S 995, in Harthacnut's name.

Prior Ælfstan comes from a Christ Church Canterbury writ, where Cnut forbids that 'anyone take anything therefrom except [the archbishop] himself and his officers'. Even this might mean no more than that judicial (and other) revenues are to be collected only by the church's agents.[35] A particularly instructive case is Abingdon's supposed private hundred of Hormer. A writ of Henry I in reference to it contains an exclusionary clause. So does a writ of the Confessor. But if the latter were authentic, it is odd that neither the writs of the Conqueror and Rufus nor Henry's first two writs on the subject make any such stipulation. The Confessor's writ seems very likely to be a forgery.[36] It is not just that those who postulate extensive pre-conquest immunities must depend on dubious texts. The very prevalence of such fabrications may say something about the urgency that the issue was assuming in the post-conquest world.

In assessing whether entitlement to the revenues of courts did, as a matter of fact, extend to holding (in the sense of summoning and directing) court sessions, the question of whether or not royal officials were forbidden from entering the courts in question is obviously important. But the revised view of continental immunities presented in this volume suggests that it may not have been as crucial as Maitland and Goebel both thought. So what other evidence is there that Anglo-Saxon landlords might be court-holders? One red herring needs to be removed from the track at once. This concerns the ambiguity of the word 'soke'. The primary meaning of *socn* is beyond doubt 'suit of court', just as *sacu* has a basic sense of 'dispute'. For the author of *Leges Henrici Primi*, *socna* could certainly denote a lord's right to hold his own court.[37] The word is ubiquitous in Domesday Book, and there is reason to think that those who were 'sokemen', or within a lord's soke, had once upon a time owed him suit of court by virtue of their tenure. This being so, Domesday's sokes might be understood as representing jurisdictional rights that extended to the holding of courts. Yet not a single entry in the whole immense survey

---

[35] S 986; but Harmer had very little respect for most other writs where the formula appears, S 1086, 1088, 1089, 989 (three for Christ Church, one for St Augustine's); and if S 1153, for the Old Minster, is more plausible, this writ has certainly been tampered with, and the particular phrase might well be considered suspect.

[36] *Reg.*, vol. 2, 1477; vol. 1, 49, 289; vol. 2, 728, 1111; S 1066.

[37] E.g. *Leges Henrici Primi*, 25ff.

seems to say as much. The term was used to describe a lord's receipt of 'customs' of any kind.[38] They included judicial forfeitures, but not only these, and not only in respect of either privileged endowment or ancient jurisdictional structure. The most one can say is that there may be a relationship between socage and the lord's jurisdiction over what would later be called his 'manorial' court.[39] But 'manorial' jurisdiction is no more to be confused with franchisal rights than is 'seigneurial' with 'feudal' lordship. The one arises from the relationship between lords and tenants, the other from the relationship between lords and royal or princely authority. Franchisal, unlike manorial, jurisdiction, must surely entail control of courts which had once, in some sense, been 'public'.

Nonetheless, Cam's list of private hundreds depends heavily on Domesday evidence. Of her total of 129 (or, in effect, 105, since thirty-one subsist in one of six multiple groups), seventy-three are known only from a Domesday record – intermittently supported by a pre-conquest charter – of lordship of a territorial area that coincided with a hundred. Five more are deduced from the far from conclusive basis that they were originally granted as 100 hides. The remainder consist of hundreds which are actually said by Domesday to have rendered profits of justice to their lords, and/or which are the subject of pre-conquest writs and charters referring to judicial rights (no authentic writ grants a hundred in as many words).[40] Very occasionally, the great survey is quite forthcoming about these rights.[41] Usually, it is reticent, even taciturn. Not once

---

[38] This is argued by a leading modern Domesday expert, David Roffe, in 'Brought to book: lordship and land in Anglo-Saxon England' (an as yet unpublished paper which he was kind enough to show me).

[39] This institution is, I think, entirely unrecorded in pre-conquest sources. *Rectitudines singularum personarum*, the fullest statement of legal arrangements on an Anglo-Saxon manor, says only that *se ðe scire healde* ('he who holds the shire', i.e. sheriff?) should be familiar with estate arrangements and district custom, 4: 6 (in *Gesetze*, ed. Liebermann): a provision most naturally taken to indicate that justice at the manor level came into the remit of the shire court.

[40] Cam, 'Private hundred', pp. 67–70; the figures can be worked out from her numerical code.

[41] Most famously, the bishop of Winchester's rights at Taunton, *DB* i 87c, 2:1; the bishop's apparent control of the borough court might recall Otto I's grants of his 'ban' over towns like Magdeburg and Corvey to the local church: *Diplomata Ottonis I*, ed. T. Sickel, *MGH Diplomata Regum et Imperatorum*, vol. 1, no. 27, p. 300. But, where these charters alienate *aliqua iudiciaria potestas*, or *ullam . . . districtionis aut disciplinae sententiam*, it is unclear that the bishop of Winchester had even assumed control of the monthly hundred court, as Hurnard observed, 'Franchises', p. 447.

(except at Oswaldslow) is there any implicit or explicit indication of court-holding. For all that Cam had rejected Goebel's case against pre-conquest court-holding when reviewing his book in 1938, all that she felt sure of by 1957 was 'that certain rights to revenue that normally went to the kings had been ceded by them to the holders of the hundreds, and that such concessions, whether sanctioned by written record or by long custom, were accepted by post-conquest kings as good titles to administrative and judicial functions unknown to the original donors'.[42] This is a position not at all unlike Goebel's own.

What the formal legislation of Anglo-Saxon kings has to say about lordship in its judicial capacity falls into two categories. From the seventh century onwards, and more especially from the early tenth, lords were made responsible for the good behaviour of those who were commended to them. Provided they discharged these responsibilities properly, they could expect to profit from what became due from their men's misbehaviour, but entitlement was prejudiced by incompetence or, of course, collaboration.[43] Commendatory lordship, like soke, is widespread in Domesday Book; the new aristocracy was very prone to confuse it with soke, and with whatever else might arise from lordship of property.[44] But Maitland himself recognized a 'great gulf' between the lord's duty to produce men in a public court or satisfy claims against them, and his holding of an actual court; and though Goebel allowed that a policy of 'deliberately working *hlafords* into the main structure of law enforcement . . . left ample room for . . . extortions which could ripen into positive custom', neither he nor others found any sign that ripen they did.[45] The other category of laws comprises decrees about the sharing out of property forfeited to courts. These begin with an order of Æthelstan (924–39) that they be divided between

---

[42] 'Private hundred', p. 67. In his paper cited at n. 38, Roffe concludes from Domesday evidence that 'simple sake and soke never conferred hundred jurisdiction on its own, and . . . its corollary of bookland merely entitled its holder to a share of farm, fines and forfeitures in a . . . royal court'; he also cites ch. 5 of his Leicester Ph.D. thesis, 'Nottinghamshire and the North: a Domesday study' (1987), to the effect that 'suit was regularly paid to the hundred and wapentake [courts] from estates held with sake and soke'.

[43] *Gesetze*, ed. Liebermann, Ine 50, II Æthelstan 2, V Æthelstan 1, IV Æthelstan 4–5, III Edmund 3, I Æthelred 1:5, 7–13, III Æthelred 4 – 4:2, II Cnut 28:1, 30:1, 3b, 30:6–31a:2, 36, 42 etc.

[44] For this, see P. H. Sawyer, '1066–86: a tenurial revolution?', in P. H. Sawyer (ed.), *Domesday Book. A Reassessment*, pp. 79–83.

[45] Maitland, *Domesday Book*, pp. 333–6; Goebel, *Felony and Misdemeanor*, pp. 359–60.

the king and those who 'ride against' the contumacious. Later in the reign, the king is replaced by a *landhlaford* if the latter's property is bookland, while the riders are called a 'fellowship'. Later still, the hundred receives the 'fellowship's' share.[46] This scarcely amounts to an extension of the landlord's rights. We have already seen that eighth- and ninth-century charters gave lords an expectation of receiving fines paid from their privileged property in full. They now have to share their perquisites with the public body that helps to bring the delinquent in question to order. So far from affording evidence that royal justice was passing into private hands, the whole drift of pre-conquest legislation tends to integrate lordship into its administration. The sort of references that Carolingian capitularies make to immunities have absolutely no English counterparts.

We may finally return to litigation. By the reign of Henry I, it is not difficult to find cases heard in lord's courts. The evidence is not even confined, as we might expect it to be, to the operations of the great churches.[47] But it is exceedingly difficult to find anything comparable in the pre-conquest records. The very same type of source that proves the most fruitful after 1066, cartulary chronicles like that of Abingdon, is barren in the Anglo-Saxon period. Wulfstan of Dalham and Ealdorman Æthelwine are even found hearing pleas in or near the precincts of Ely abbey itself, something that would have been inconceivable by the reign of Richard I.[48] What has been interpreted as a case heard in Ealdorman Byrhtnoth's court was nonetheless heard again at Cambridge, presumably before the shire. The only other possible instances relate to forfeitures collected by the abbot of Peterborough, so to a sort of jurisdiction that is uncontroversial.[49] Equally pertinent in this connection is a point made by David Bates in discussing the Penenden Heath

---

[46] *Gesetze*, ed. Liebermann, II Æthelstan 20:4, VI Æthelstan 1, Hundred 2:1, II Edgar 3:1, III Edgar 7:1, II Cnut 25:1. Laws arranging for safeguarding of stolen or disputed stock by *landhlaford* or *landrica* (I Edward 1, II Æthelstan 10, I Æthelred 3, cf. IV Edgar 3–11), sometimes invoked in this connection, are beside the point.

[47] van Caenegem, *Lawsuits*, nos. 162, 164–5, 174, 182, 187, 198–9, 208–9, 214, 219 etc.

[48] P. Wormald, 'A handlist of Anglo-Saxon lawsuits', *Anglo-Saxon England*, 17 (1988), nos. 116, 120. See the perceptive comments of E. Miller, *The Abbey and Bishopric of Ely*, pp. 28–34; yet even he is prepared to envisage that abbatial rights encountered only after 1066 had imperceptibly developed before.

[49] Wormald, 'Handlist of Anglo-Saxon lawsuits', nos. 128, 50–1.

plea. The records, he says, 'seem to have caught the Canterbury liberty at different moments in the process of its definition. They seem to offer two related versions of the franchise which the evidence suggests was only gradually organized in the last decades of the eleventh century'. To be precise, the later versions are a good deal more specific (and ambitious) than the earlier.[50] This is a very salutary illustration of the development of claims for judicial privilege at, but not before, the time when Bishop Wulfstan stood up before the Domesday commissioners.

The general tenor of the evidence is such, then, as to suggest that if the bishop of Worcester really had the jurisdictional rights that Domesday recorded, they were without parallel in England before 1066. We have already seen that their documentary basis is as open to grave suspicion as those of every comparable claimant, and that they were in any event vigorously controverted. Consequently, there is a strong likelihood that the testimony attributed to the shire in 1086 was indeed as much of a distortion of the facts as we have seen that Wulfstan had every chance of making it. How, if so, should his triumphant *démarche* be understood? What would have induced the pious bishop to shake off the drowsiness that normally overcame him whenever mundane business was transacted in the shire court, and deploy the holy guile that came naturally to so many other saints? What would that imply for a more general assessment of the nature of franchisal jurisdiction in England during and after the eleventh century? And how should all of this affect the view we take of the power of central government under the last Anglo-Saxon kings and their successors?

The first point is that Wulfstan evidently needed some sort of privileged reinforcement of his church's position. Before 1066, he was well-equipped to dictate the sheriff's movements by less formal means. However, this comfortable arrangement must have been shattered by the unique trauma of 1066 itself. Æthelwig of Evesham was now even better placed to influence the course of justice in his church's interests than its Worcester rival had been accustomed to. The new sheriff, Urso, was a Norman predator *par excellence*, whose name was the subject of a famous epigram by Wulfstan's predecessor, Archbishop Ealdred, 'Hattest u Urs,

---

[50] Bates, 'Penenden Heath', pp. 6–10; van Caenegem, *Lawsuits*, no. 5 (A–B, K).

have þu Godes kurs'.[51] Exclusion of the scions of the new regime
in favour of a formalization of the bishop's traditional mastery was
a logical move, not least as it reflected what Wulfstan's fellow
churchmen seem to have been increasingly seeking.

That there should have been a general quest for entrenched
control in the aftermath of the Conquest could have one of two
rationales. Helen Cam argued that franchises as understood in
the high middle ages were indeed more extensive than those of
Anglo-Saxon times, because they were themselves a response to
the growing power of the 'state', and this power had not yet fully
evolved in the tenth century, still less before.[52] This 'evolutionary'
model might be given more 'catastrophic' shape by supposing that
the Conquest introduced a marked rise in central government
pressures on landlords. The sins of sheriffs are certainly highlighted
by church chroniclers in the century after 1066 as they were not
before.[53] Wulfstan would then have been adjusting to changed
times. Still, the impoverished pre-conquest evidence allows a few
glimpses of royal judicial officers who were as overbearing as their
Norman successors, and called forth the same vigilance from the
saintly guardians of ecclesiastical privilege.[54] A different model may
therefore be advanced tentatively: judicial liberties flourished after
the Conquest as they had not earlier, because they reflected expectations long acquired by the great churches of Francia, and
imported by the new ruling class from their original home.[55] In
that case, Wulfstan would have been taking a leaf from his neighbours' book. Either way, the difficulties which Maitland conceived
his founders of the Common Law to have had with franchises are
unlikely to have owed anything to a flawed inheritance from their
Anglo-Saxon predecessors. That legacy may even have contributed
to the ultimate victory with which he credited them.

If, contrary to the claims of the one member of the establishment
who was still in a position to know, the pre-conquest lords that
collected fines and forfeitures were not thereby entitled to elude
the purview of royal justice like their post-conquest heirs, this

---

[51] William of Malmesbury, *De Gestis Pontificum Anglorum*, ed. N. E. S. A. Hamilton, p. 253
(roughly translated, this means 'if you are called Urse, and you have God's curse').
[52] Cam, 'Evolution', pp. 38–43.
[53] Picot of Cambridgeshire gave Ely much the same vexation as Urso did Worcester: *Liber
Eliensis*, ed. E. O. Blake, pp. 210–13.
[54] Wormald, 'Lawsuits', nos. 154–6, 167, 171.
[55] Cf. D. Bates, *Normandy Before 1066*, pp. 204–6.

would not in itself exclude the possibility of their managing the courts which levied them. On the continent, as is argued elsewhere in this book, immunity from public officials and private jurisdiction could be two different things. The right to keep out sheriffs need not have meant a right to hold courts. Such a right could have developed regardless. All the same, *inability* to keep out sheriffs ought to have aborted any trend in that direction. Kings who continued to intrude their judicial agents seem *less likely* to have countenanced control of their courts by landlords, and more likely to have been able to prevent it. And, as a matter of fact, the evidence for private court-holding in Anglo-Saxon England is as exiguous as for the exclusion of the king's justices. Advocates, essential to the operations of Carolingian and Ottonian immmunities which did possess a judicial aspect, are quite unknown in England, for example. Maitland's belief that the immunity had taken a firm hold on the framework of royal jurisdiction before the Conquest has had a significant effect on diagnoses of the Anglo-Saxon body politic in general.[56] No reader of this book is any longer going to be satisfied with a simple equation of governmental health and lack of immunities. But even if immunities were still to be seen as germs of decline in the king's capacity to fulfil his judicial responsibilities, the Anglo-Saxon picture would give us no grounds for finding a further key to the collapse of 1066 in the debilitation of royal justice. Its profits may have been alienated, but the signs are that its servants were intrusive and its arenas monopolized.

Landed property (other than the king's) was not in its own right a basis for the exercise of judicial power in early England. To the average litigant, it may not have made much difference that his case was stitched up because the sheriff was in the bishop's pocket, rather than because the bishop had the formal right to shut him out. But it mattered a great deal to his posterity in centuries to come that the ordinary 'free' man was by definition entitled to be heard by the king's court as well as a lord's. It also matters to the historian whether Wulfstan exerted his ascendancy by

---

[56] For Maitland's influence on (e.g.) the formative views of Robert Fossier, see J. Campbell, 'Was it infancy in England? Some questions of comparison', in M. Jones and M. Vale (eds.), *England and her Neighbours, 1066–1453. Essays in Honour of Pierre Chaplais*, p. 2. Cf. J. Strayer, *On the Medieval Origins of the Modern State*, pp. 14–15; I have taken issue with Strayer's assessment of early English 'statehood' in '*Engla Lond*: the making of an allegiance', *Journal of Historical Sociology*, 7 (1994).

manipulation of political patronage as opposed to the assertion of jurisdictional rights, because it matters whether we think that relations between property and power in eleventh-century England had more in common with what early modern historians study than with patterns in the Carolingian Empire's twilight. It affects our view of more history than England's alone to know that the lords of Oswaldslow guarded their legal interests not by means of mechanisms to be expected of a 'feudal' epoch but by virtue of the sort of power-brokerage associated with the functioning of states in much more recent times.

CHAPTER 6

Adding insult to injury:
power, property and immunities in early
medieval Wales

Wendy Davies

There is little to indicate, for much of the early medieval period in
Wales, that ownership of land involved anything more than the
power to collect rent, produce and profits from that land – whether
production was organized through a direct labour force or through
tenancies. Most charter texts are surprisingly vague about the
powers conveyed when property changed hands, and the proprietary terms that are so characteristic of English and continental
charters are strikingly absent. It looks as if landowners' interests
were primarily economic, although to the extent that they controlled a dependent workforce they inevitably acquired power over
people too. This vagueness is especially marked in the earliest texts,
of all types, that is of sixth- to eighth-century material, and is often
so for the ninth- and tenth-century period.

By the eleventh century, however, power over property could
clearly bring the landowner more than rents and produce and it
looks as if the tenth century was a turning point in attitudes and
practice. In what follows, I shall investigate the incidence of compensation to landowners for offences committed on their lands;
explain the Welsh concepts of *nawdd* (protection), *sarhaed* (insult)
and *braint* (privilege), and show how they provide the mental
framework for such compensations; detail the establishment of the
earliest territorial immunities which excuse the holder from royal
demands, and the development (and historical context) of more
elaborate immunities held by institutions; and, finally, isolate the
essential processes that led to this development. In the end, the
individual's right to protect turned into the institution's right to
exemption from political dues and demands.

COMPENSATION TO PROPRIETORS FOR BREACH
OF THEIR PROTECTION

By the eleventh century some landowners in Wales expected compensation when offences were committed on their properties. Our best evidence of this relates to ecclesiastical landowners; whether or not lay proprietors could expect the same is a debatable issue.[1] Llandaff charter texts detail a range of circumstances which provoked compensatory payments to the bishop of Llandaff: when Asser ap Marchudd murdered Gulagguin, round about 940, the families of the two men reached an agreement in relation to their own damages; but then Asser and his father gave land to the local bishop.[2] When Cadwallon ap Gwriad quarrelled with Rhydderch ap Beli in Bishop Joseph's court, round about 1040, they came to blows, Cadwallon eventually drawing blood from his adversary. The bishop thereupon imprisoned him, until he acknowledged his wrongdoing. Later, Cadwallon's father and cousin came to the bishop, Cadwallon apologized for the deed, and together the family gave the bishop their church of St Brides, with adjoining land.[3] When Caradog ap Rhiwallon, a member of King Meurig's retinue, abducted another man's wife – at the church door – both he and his lord ended up by making grants of property to Bishop Joseph, as well as returning the woman to her husband.[4]

[1] See further below, pp. 160–1.
[2] *The Text of the Book of Llan Dâv*, ed. J. G. Evans with J. Rhys, 223 – hereafter cited as LL; cf. other examples, LL 212, 214, 244, 245, 255; various dates from *c.*862–*c.*1035. K. L. Maund, in *Ireland, Wales, and England in the Eleventh Century*, maintains that the narrations of the Llandaff charters are largely fictitious. This is an interesting approach, which is marred by (i) the absence of any diplomatic analysis, (ii) the assumption that there must have been a single sequence of kings, which must therefore determine the dating of all texts, (iii) the *a priori* assumption that the texts must have been invented in the twelfth century. The argument is therefore unconvincing. For detailed assessment of these texts, see W. Davies, *The Llandaff Charters*, pp. 21–3, and individual charters thereafter; note also L. K. Little, 'Spiritual sanctions in Wales', in R. Blumenfeld-Kosinski (ed.), *Images of Sainthood in Medieval Europe*, pp. 74–6, on the well-evidenced occurrence of liturgical *clamor* (a special liturgy for use in times of difficulty, involving prayers, curses and – at times – the humiliation of relics) in the tenth and eleventh centuries.
[3] LL 263. This offence is not, of course, peculiar to Wales in the early middle ages – fighting in someone's house, for example, was an offence requiring compensation to the householder in early and late Anglo-Saxon England, for the same reason – breach of protection; e.g. Laws of Aethelbert, 8, 13, 15; Laws of Alfred, 3, 5, in *Die Gesetze der Angelsachsen*, ed. F. Liebermann, vol. 1, pp. 3–4, 50–2.
[4] LL 261, 259.

These cases are perfectly clear. Although formulas inserted into the texts at a later date tend to describe the grants to the bishop as penitential grants, the ecclesiastical landowner in practice derived income when offences were committed on his property.[5] Murder, assault, bloodshed and abduction, of lay people, all brought him additional income. Owning land brought more than rents and produce.

Some of these offences are referred to as 'violation of "sanctuary" ', *refugio uiolato*. Such was Caradog's abduction of Seisyll's wife, which happened at the church door; whether or not the grants subsequently made to Bishop Joseph had a penitential overtone, primarily they were grants made as compensation to the bishop for the violation of his *refugium*. When King Nowy assaulted Argoed in the ecclesiastical settlement (*podum*) of Tryleg, round about 960, the offence was again described as 'violation of sanctuary' – Argoed was probably the son of the church's *lector*; compensation for the violation again took the form of a land grant to the church.[6] Other attacks on religious personnel in the tenth and eleventh centuries – the attacks on the deacon, Eli, at St Arvans, and on Bishop Herewald's nephew Berthutis at Llandaff, as well as fighting with the bishop's household, and raping a nun at Llandaff – were similarly classified and provoked similar responses.[7] Although the attacks could have been treated – in other cultures – as

---

[5] The Llandaff charter texts are, in their twelfth-century forms, composite texts deriving from several phases of accretion and editing. The work of different editors can be identified, so that – in most cases – the text of the original charters can be established and the formulas added later can be differentiated. A group of formulas, emphasizing the power of synods and the misery of the penitent, was added to many of the narrations in the twelfth century. For detailed discussion, see Davies, *Llandaff Charters, passim*.

[6] LL 217; Arcoit filius Dissaith: cf. 'Dissaith lector', first after the bishop in the witness list of the charter. Cf. 'Dissaith lector, Aircoit doctor' in LL 222.

[7] LL 218, 267, 271, 249b; cf. LL 239 (LL 222, 176b and 127a on the surface look similar but I do not think these passages belong to the original texts). See also the Llancarfan charters, published as cc. 57 and 67 of 'Vita Sancti Cadoci', in A. W. Wade-Evans, *Vitae Sanctorum Britanniae et Genealogiae*, where the church of Llancarfan was compensated for intra-family killings – two nephews and a brother respectively; in the former case the murderer was given 14 years of penance, after he made the grants. These charters derive from seventh-/eighth-century texts, but the manuscript tradition is long and doubtless corrupt, and I would not wish to depend on them as purely eighth-century examples; see W. Davies, 'The Latin charter-tradition in western Britain, Brittany and Ireland in the early mediaeval period', in D. Whitelock, R. McKitterick and D. Dumville (eds.), *Ireland in Early Mediaeval Europe*, p. 260.

problems of lordship, here they were seen as offences against the bishop's powers of protection.[8]

These cases involve more than 'sanctuary' in the customary western European sense (ecclesiastical places of refuge for criminals and other fugitives, where they could be safe from pursuit and assault – usually for a specified limited term). They are about ecclesiastical privilege. They have little connection with fugitives; they relate to a special category of legal offence; they include offences committed on a range of religious properties, and offences committed by people with no previous criminal association; they are offences against the church, as well as offences against the individual damaged and his or her family. This is an expanded notion of sanctuary.

Round about the time that many of these charters were recorded, the same principles were expressed in hagiographic texts. The most extended treatment occurs in the 'Life of Saint Cadog', written by Lifris from materials in the Llancarfan archive in the second half of the eleventh century.[9] Llancarfan is in the Vale of Glamorgan and was the site of a powerful monastery from at least the seventh century until the church and its appurtenances were given to St Peter's Gloucester round about 1100. Lifris was archdeacon of Glamorgan, *magister* of the monastery, and son of Bishop Herewald of Llandaff, ten miles to the east; he witnessed charters in the 1070s.

Chapter 22 of the 'Life' is a long tale about a conflict involving King Arthur and the saint's intervention to bring a resolution. Despite considerable circumstantial detail, the story hangs on the issue of violated sanctuary – *refugium*. A man called Ligessog had killed three of Arthur's men. Ligessog fled to Saint Cadog for protection and spent seven years safely in Cadog's region (*pagus*). Arthur eventually caught up with him and the case came to judgment; Arthur was awarded a number of cows as compensation

---

[8] There are similarities with Peace of God texts here, of the late tenth and eleventh centuries, with their emphasis on protection of the (unarmed) clergy; however, the penalties in these Welsh cases, and the nature of the offence, are quite different; see T. Head and R. Landes (eds.), *The Peace of God: Social Violence and Religious Response in France around the Year 1000*, pp. 4, 327.

[9] 'Vita Sancti Cadoci', in Wade-Evans, *Vitae Sanctorum Britanniae et Genealogiae*, pp. 24–140. For critical discussion see H. D. Emanuel, 'An analysis of the composition of the "Vita Cadoci"', *National Library of Wales Journal*, 7 (1951–2); C. N. L. Brooke, 'St Peter of Gloucester and St Cadoc of Llancarfan', in N. K. Chadwick et al., *Celt and Saxon*, pp. 283–322; W. Davies, 'Property rights and property claims in Welsh "Vitae" of the eleventh century', in E. Patlagean and P. Riché (eds.), *Hagiographie. Cultures et Sociétés*.

for the killings. However, Cadog's powers of protection had been violated by Arthur's intrusion and divine retribution therefore intervened to turn the cattle into ferns. Thereafter, Arthur confirmed the *refugium*, the monastery's powers of protection over the *pagus*, and extended the term of the protection to seven years, seven months and seven days.

Thus told, the Ligessog story could be read as a classic sanctuary story: Ligessog was a criminal who sought refuge with the saint. But the 'sanctuary' encompasses the whole of Cadog's region; and the notion of Cadog's *refugium* is elaborated in the following chapters, 23–5, and returns again in the final chapters of the published 'Life', 69–70 (this latter material was possibly included by Lifris but may still have been 'free-floating' in the eleventh century). That Cadog's refuge applied to more than criminal sanctuary is made clear by specifying a range of different offences that constituted violation. Abduction and arson within the zone of protection are punished by divine blinding, until the blinded kings seek pardon, make grants and confirm Llancarfan's powers of protection; and theft is punished by imprisonment, until confirmation. The confirmations come from the famous King Maelgwn of Gwynedd and his son Rhun, and from King Rhain of Brycheiniog – kingdoms of north-west and mid-Wales respectively, lying outside the south-eastern kingdom of Glywysing/Morgannwg (see Map 2).[10]

These stories are not, of course, accurate accounts of the doings of real people: they are stories told to legitimate Llancarfan's claims. Famous kings are invoked to add their confirmations, thereby supplying different quasi-historical contexts and an apparently long tradition. What is significant is not the particular detail of each tale, but the strength and consistency of the principle of protection. The *refugium* has both a temporal and a spatial dimension here: 'Cadog's *pagus*' recurs in the text – the geographical space of the abbot's power.[11] The temporal aspect is spelled out: anyone who came to the abbot for protection would remain

---

[10] 'Vita Cadoci', cc. 22, 69; ch. 24; cc. 25, 70.

[11] The precise territory intended is not always clear: the *regio* of Gwynllŵg is implied as the area of the *pagus* in cc. 23 and 25, and is explicitly identified in ch. 69; but the *regio* of Penychen (in which Llancarfan lay) is implied in ch. 24 (because thieves camp in Gwrynydd to the west and cross the river Thaw). Gwynllŵg lay to the east of Penychen, and Gwrynydd to the west (see Map 3). Cf. ch. 69 – no tax was due in Gwynllŵg, although Llancarfan would pay it on lands outside that area (see below, pp. 149, 153).

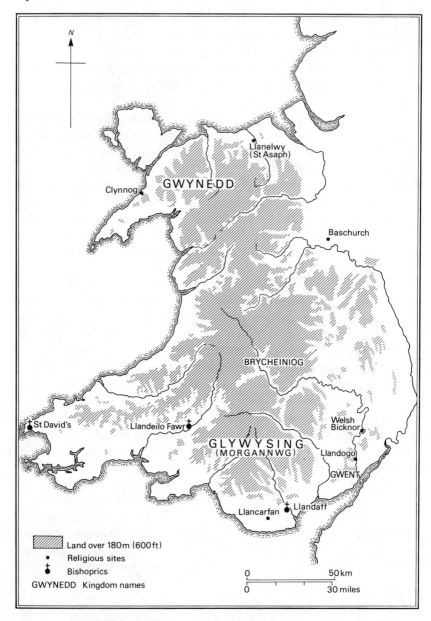

Map 2. Early medieval Wales

protected for seven years, seven months and seven days – wherever he went subsequently. Whether spatially or temporally determined, the saint's power of protection is a right proclaimed and jealously guarded by Llancarfan.

Chapter 69 of this 'Life' refers in passing to the *refugium* of Saint David in West Wales, and other Welsh 'Lives' make comparable claims for the saints that they celebrate: when clerical vestments and a chalice were stolen from Saint Gwynllyw's church (Newport), Ednywain 'violated the privilege[12] of the saint and the church';[13] King Maelgwn violated the privilege of Llanelwy (St Asaph, north-east Wales) when he pursued a man who had injured his son across the bounds and limits of the monastery's protected zone (*immunitas*);[14] and a late medieval confirmation of privileges to Clynnog Fawr (north-west Wales) includes the monastery's right to protect those seeking refuge from royal taxes, strong men and burdensome pledges.[15] The notion is neither exclusive to Llandaff nor particular to the preoccupations of clerics of the southeast. Though better evidenced in the south-east, because considerably more pre-Conquest written material survives, it occurs in other parts of Wales – as it also occurs in later legal, and other, texts from the north and the west.[16]

You do not have to believe every detail of this material to notice that these 'Lives' and hagiographic dossiers are witness to the vitality of a powerful notion in eleventh-century Wales: major churches had powers of protection; intrusions on to protected land brought special punishments, because of violation of the protection; and offences committed on protected land or in protected time carried extra penalties.

---

[12] See below, pp. 146–7, for discussion of the legal idea of 'privilege'.

[13] 'Vita Sancti Gundleii', ch. 14, in Wade-Evans, *Vitae Sanctorum Britanniae*.

[14] 'Mete et limites terrae immunitatis sanctae ciuitatis Llanelwy existunt (there follows a perambulation) . . .Et si quis uiolauerit predictam immunitatem. . .excommunicatus est'; these are early charter fragments within miscellanea found by Bishop Einion in 1256, later copied into the fifteenth-century St Asaph text, Alter Liber Pergameneus; see Davies, 'Latin charter-tradition', p. 271.

[15] *Registrum vulgariter nuncupatum 'The Record of Caernarvon'*, ed. H. Ellis, p. 258; this text draws on earlier texts – see further Davies, 'Latin charter-tradition', p. 271.

[16] *Llyfr Iorwerth*, ed. A. R. Wiliam, 71, pp. 43–4; *Llyfr Colan*, ed. D. Jenkins, 293, p. 17. See H. Pryce, 'Ecclesiastical sanctuary in thirteenth-century Welsh law', *Journal of Legal History*, 5 (1984), p. 5. See also M. Miller, *The Saints of Gwynedd*, pp. 114–15, for some later examples of saintly *refugia*.

NAWDD, SARHAED AND BRAINT: PROTECTION, INSULT AND PRIVILEGE

The Welsh word for a body's power of protection is *nawdd*; *nawdd* is commonly translated into Latin as *refugium* in legal and other texts.[17] 'Protection' is a well-defined concept in Welsh law and is in the first instance temporal: a freeman could offer protection for a known, limited period. The concept has close parallels in early Irish law (*snádud*) and in Germanic law (*mund*); the Irish case has a special significance in conferring protection from legal distraint. Welsh texts not only give legal substance to the idea of 'protection'; they also territorialize it: the *noddfa* (*nawdd* + *ma*, 'place'), the area within which *nawdd* is exercised, was the practical outcome. The *refugium* that was violated in the Llandaff texts with which I began is not merely a notional sphere; it is the physical space of the church's protection. This might extend beyond the church building itself – witness the abduction outside the door, the fighting in the bishop's court, the intrusion into the *podum* – and by the eleventh century was likely to be a clearly defined, publicly known zone. There are parallels in the *termonn* land surrounding monastic properties in Ireland and in the English 'chartered sanctuaries' of the north.[18] In southern Scotland, albeit at a much later date, we find the *gryth/gyrth* of the church of Luss – a surrounding three-mile zone, which was an especial 'liberty' with rights especially protected and powers of jurisdiction over criminals therein;[19] and in Cornwall, again at a later date, we find the 'privileged sanctuary' of Padstow, where land and houses outside the church were included in the sanctuary area.[20] The English and southern Scottish parallels are particularly close: legislation of

---

[17] H. Pryce, *Native Law and the Church in Medieval Wales*, pp. 168–9. This usage of *refugium* is rare outside Celtic Latin. See further below, pp. 158–9.

[18] Pryce, *Native Law*, p. 170, on *terminus* in the eighth-century Irish collection of canon law; D. Hall, 'The sanctuary of St Cuthbert', in G. Bonner, D. Rollason and C. Stancliffe (eds.), *St Cuthbert, his Cult and his Community to AD 1200*, especially pp. 426–7.

[19] *Regesta Regum Scottorum*, vol. 5, *The Acts of Robert I*, ed. A. Duncan, no. 55, p. 340, cf. no. 83, pp. 365–6; though this charter is dated 1315 the concept is precisely parallel. (Cf. *refugium, Regesta Regum Scottorum*, vol. 1, *The Acts of Malcolm IV King of Scots 1153–65*, ed. G. W. S. Barrow, no. 219, p. 246.) *Gyrth* or girth is from Anglo-Saxon *griŏ*, i.e. 'peace', sphere of protection; cf. Laws of VIII Aethelred 5 in *Gesetze*, ed. Liebermann, vol. 1, p. 264, which details compensations for violation of the *griŏ* of churches of different grades.

[20] L. Olson, *Early Monasteries in Cornwall*, p. 72.

the Anglo-Saxon period includes special penalties for breach of a church's peace, a peace that could be expressed in spatial terms.[21]

Although secular respect for these ideas would doubtless have depended on local circumstances and power politics, the Welsh concept is strongly evidenced in the anecdotal material of the eleventh century; it is also there in the tenth, as in the examples cited above. There are no good examples from the very early middle ages, which suggests that the territorialization of *nawdd* is late, rather than early, pre-Conquest practice in Wales. The establishment of *noddfeydd* – like the girths of Scotland – must have been partly influenced by the ecclesiastical law of sanctuary, with its emphasis on protected space, but the native importance of the individual's (or institution's) power of protection survived to make the *noddfa* more than a simple sanctuary.

The concept of *nawdd/refugium* and *noddfa* was sustained into the twelfth and thirteenth centuries and beyond in Wales. Giraldus Cambrensis described it like this in the late twelfth century:

Around them [the churches] the cattle graze so peacefully, not only in the churchyards, but outside, too, within the fences and ditches marked out and set by bishops to fix the sanctuary limits. The more important churches, hallowed by their greater antiquity, offer sanctuary for as far as the cattle go to feed in the morning and can return at evening. If any man has incurred the hatred of his prince and is in danger of death, he may apply to the church for sanctuary and it will be freely granted to him and his family.[22]

Explicit references to the *noddfa* of this or that church also survive in twelfth-century texts.[23]

Twelfth- and thirteenth-century texts explicitly articulate the principle that major ecclesiastical landowners could expect compensation for offences committed in the *noddfa*.[24] Such abuse was an affront to the honour of the saint, and of the church, occasioning compensation over and above any compensation due to the injured parties. Several versions of the Welsh law texts, recorded in the

---

[21] See above nn. 3 and 19; and below, conclusion, pp. 254–6.

[22] Gerald of Wales, *The Description of Wales*, I. 18, trans. Thorpe, p. 254.

[23] Pryce, 'Ecclesiastical sanctuary', pp. 2–3; see further below, n. 66.

[24] Cf. Ireland in the late seventh century, where compensatory penance was required to a church as well as payment to kinsmen for homicide committed in church; T. M. Charles-Edwards, 'The pastoral role of the church in the early Irish laws', in J. Blair and R. Sharpe (eds.), *Pastoral Care before the Parish*, p. 65.

thirteenth century and later, comment on this type of offence; it remained living law:

The *dirwy* and *camlwrw* of court and church, if the wrong is done in the cemetery, are to be double. If the wrong is done outside the cemetery in the sanctuary-place (*noddfa*), £7 will be the amount of the *dirwy*. The abbot, if he is versed in the letters and discipline of the Church, will receive half of the church-*dirwy*. And the learned youths of the church will receive the other half. . .And that revenue is given not as an offering but to the saint in particular.[25]

Compensation was due to the saint because of the insult implicit in the violation. The medieval Welsh word for insult is *sarhaed*, which also means the offence of insult, as well as compensation to the victim as a result of the offence. Compensation varied in accordance with status.[26] A free person suffered insult when his or her honour was besmirched. In the Welsh law texts the term *sarhaed* seems to have replaced an earlier word *wynebwerth*, literally 'price of face', for compensation for insult (although *wynebwerth* was retained as a term relating to compensation for sexual offence within marriage). The parallelism between face and honour is evident.

One text from the Llandaff charter collection puts flesh on this notion. Early in the tenth century, insult (*iniuria*) was done to the bishop; details are not specified in the text but the implication is that the insult consisted of fighting in his court, like several of the later cases which provoked compensation; there is no suggestion of physical injury.[27] It was subsequently judged that King Brochfael, who was responsible for the insult, should make reparations by literally paying to the bishop, in pure gold, 'pretium faciei suae', the 'price of his [the bishop's] face', in length and breadth. Here, in a text of *c*.905, the notion behind *wynebwerth* can still be taken literally – compensation assessed in accordance with the size of the man's face and therefore value of his honour; by the 1020s these things are just 'insult' – important enough to be compensated, but no longer spelled out in a practical way.

Other texts noted above refer to the 'privilege' of a church. The Welsh for 'privilege' is *braint*, a word which refers to a

---

[25] From the Cyfnerth Redaction of the Welsh laws (late twelfth century, southern Welsh), Huw Pryce's translation, *Native Law*, p. 180. *Dirwy* and *camlwrw* are payments.
[26] See D. Jenkins and M. E. Owen (eds.), *The Welsh Law of Women*, pp. 216, 220.
[27] LL 233.

specific Welsh legal concept: the legal privilege due to a person in accordance with his status (often translated *dignitas*[28] in Latin texts). Every free man had his proper privilege, and any insult had to be compensated (*sarhaed*) in accordance with the level of that privilege. (In practice the Welsh legal notion of privilege comes close to that of honour in earlier, Irish texts.[29]) Although the Welsh law texts are suffused with this idea, it is unusual to find a written specification of privilege. However, this certainly happened at Llandaff; there are also eleventh- and twelfth-century references to the privilege of other saints – David and Padarn, for example – and references to written privileges, although no texts survive, of Saints Cadog and Padarn;[30] it is therefore quite conceivable that other such documents were constructed. The Llandaff drafters may have worked within a familiar Welsh tradition.[31]

EARLY IMMUNITIES

Some texts go farther than instancing *nawdd* and *noddfa*. At Llandaff, a short text was formulated some time within the period 950–1090 (at very outside limits), most probably during the episcopate of Bishop Joseph, 1022–45; this text attempted to encapsulate the particularity of the church's special privilege.

[It is] free from king and everyone except Teilo and his church of Llandaff and its bishops. For any disgrace, insult (*sarhayt*), wrong, and injury which the king of Morgannwg and his men and his servants might do to Teilo's bishop and his men and servants, the king of Morgannwg shall come to Teilo's *gundy* (court) at Llandaff to do right and justice and suffer judgment for the wrong that may be done to Teilo's bishop and his men and servants. Its lands shall be without military service, tax, distraint. And every law which the king of Morgannwg may have in his court, Teilo's bishop shall have completely in his court likewise.

---

[28] Cf. T. Reuter, 'The medieval German *Sonderweg*? The Empire and its rulers in the high middle ages', in A. Duggan (ed.), *Kings and Kingship in Medieval Europe*, pp. 182–6, on a Cambrai dispute about rights, described in terms of *dignitates*, and his comments there on the importance of the idea of status.

[29] Cf. the use of the word *dirwy* (originally 'honour price', cf. Irish *dire*, 'honour price') for the fine for insult by violation of a church's *nawdd*, above, p. 146.

[30] See above, pp. 140–3; cf. the *iudicialis liber* of Cadog, 'Vita Cadoci', ch. 37; *lex Paterni* of Padarn, 'Vita Paterni', ch. 26, in Wade-Evans, *Vitae Sanctorum Britanniae*.

[31] See W. Davies, *Wales in the Early Middle Ages*, pp. 62, 137–8; see below, pp. 158–9.

This text is part of a composite text known as 'Braint Teilo', the 'privilege of Teilo'; the longer – and later – part, 'Braint Teilo' Part One, I shall discuss below; this earlier, shorter part is 'Braint Teilo' Part Two (since it follows Part One in the form in which it is preserved).[32] Its primary concern is to protect the episcopal community of Llandaff from interference by the local king, the king of Morgannwg (the principal kingdom of south-east Wales). It goes a stage further than stating the inviolability of the *noddfa* and the need for compensation if offences were committed within it: it claims that the *lands* of the bishopric should be immune from royal demands for military service, tax and distraint; and it claims that the bishop should have the same jurisdiction in his court as the king had in his. The ban on intrusion into the *noddfa* has here been expanded into an exemption – and extended to all episcopal lands. This is a claim that Llandaff lands are an immunity, a rather special immunity as Llandaff was to be exempt from the demands of the king, as well as the demands of royal officers. It is also a claim of private jurisdiction – a territorially-based private jurisdiction. Already in the eleventh century Llandaff was claiming to be an island outside the limits of royal interference, intrusion and control.

This is a very basic and unelaborated statement, but it is a step beyond the hagiographic claims. Its formulation (which is in Welsh) invokes concepts which are distinctive to Welsh law, and which are omitted in the Latin translation which accompanies it. Most striking is *sarhayt*, i.e. *sarhaed*, 'insult'. It is *pre*-Conquest, and it is Welsh; it seems to be a local development, not an import.[33] (In fact, there is no good reason to suppose that this is simply rhetorical – there are tenth- and eleventh-century Irish cases of compensation to churches, and later Welsh cases of compensation to bishops for fighting in church and also of ecclesiastical synods determining penalties for laymen.[34])

Similar attitudes are evidenced in the hagiographic material already discussed, and it is clear that the approach was not

---

[32] LL, pp. 118–19, 120–1; see W. Davies, 'Braint Teilo', *Bulletin of the Board of Celtic Studies*, 26 (1974–6), p. 135. For the date of the text, *ibid.*, p. 132.

[33] See further below, pp. 155–6.

[34] Irish cases of compensation to churches in 986 and 1072, cited by D. Ó Corráin, 'Nationality and kingship in pre-Norman Ireland', in T. W. Moody (ed.), *Nationality and the Pursuit of National Independence*, pp. 22, 24. Welsh cases: Pryce, *Native Law*, pp. 154–62.

confined to the church of Llandaff. The 'Life of Cadog', from nearby Llancarfan, again has relevant material. Both the story of King Maelgwn's confirmation of Cadog's *refugium/nawdd*, and also that about King Rhain, include immunity phrases:[35] land in Gwynllŵg given to Cadog's family (*stirps*) by the king should be free of tax; Cadog himself commended Gwynllŵg to King Meurig, free of tax except for the small quantity of three days and nights military service.[36] Another passage – one that relates Cadog's death and arrangements for his succession – makes a clear point about the immunity of Llancarfan but makes it in a different way: the dying saint commended his community into the hands of his successor Elli, ordering that no king or noble or bishop should ever have any powers of jurisdiction over him, and ordering that any wrong done to the community should be judged by the community itself.[37] This is the same point as that made by 'Braint Teilo' Part Two; and it is also reflected in chapter 16 of Cadog's 'Life': here the saint proclaimed that henceforth twelve ordained clerics could always provide good judgment for his country; and twelve unordained clerics should do so if there were insufficient ordained clerics; and twelve boys if there were none of them.[38] Whether or not we believe the stories, Lifris is claiming a moderate fiscal immunity for Llancarfan in the late eleventh century, and a rather developed judicial immunity. These claims were elaborated in passages added shortly after Lifris wrote, but most of this material was omitted by Caradog (who wrote another 'Life of Cadog') fifty years later. The stories provide a sense of the perspective and expectations of a southern Welsh religious house, whether or not any king or local aristocrat respected them.

---

[35] 'Vita Cadoci', cc. 22, 69, at ch. 69; *ibid.* cc. 25, 70, at ch. 25.

[36] 'Patrocinare meam patriam atque hereditatem Gundliauc, sitque libera ab omni fiscali censu, excepto quod pergant tecum in exercitu ad prelium tribus diebus et noctibus, et si amplius tecum ierint, cibabis eos', 'Vita Cadoci', ch. 25.

[37] 'nullus mundanus potens rex, neque episcopus, nec optimas, de aliqua controuersia seu iniuria super uos umquam diiudicet. Sed, si quispiam uobis quotlibet nefas irrogauerit, siue quilibet uestrum alium iniuriauerit, uel in qualibet alia causa quae quoquomodo super uos dicatur, ex uobismetipsis iudices uestri fiant', 'Vita Cadoci', ch. 37. The terms of this exemption from royal, aristocratic and episcopal judgment are not dissimilar to those of the foundation charter of the monastery of Cluny, of September 910; *Recueil des chartes de l'abbaye de Cluny*, ed A. Bernard and A. Bruel, vol. 1, no. 112, pp. 124–8, at p. 126.

[38] Cf. 'Vita Cadoci', ch. 22.

'BRAINT TEILO' PROPER AND THE EXTENDED IMMUNITY

By the twelfth century Llandaff was by contrast claiming a very extended immunity. The main text of 'Braint Teilo' (i.e. Part One) is lengthy and specific:

Here is the law and privilege of the church of Teilo of Llandaff which these kings and princes of Wales gave to Teilo's church and to all the bishops after him for ever, confirmed by authority of the popes of Rome. All the law shall be available to the church and to its lands, free from every service royal and secular, from *maer* and *canghellor* (royal officers), from public courts within the country and without, from military service, distraint, and keeping watch. Jurisdiction shall be to it completely, over thief and theft, robbery with violence, homicide, secret killing and arson, brawling with and without bloodshed – all the fines to it completely – over breach of protection (*nawdd*) within the enclosure and without, over ambush in the woods and outside, and over public assault in every place on Teilo's land; right and judgment to the people of the church of Teilo's *gundy* (court) at Llandaff and in his court. Water and pasture and woods and meadow equally to Teilo's people; trade and mint at Llandaff, and harbourage on Teilo's land for the ships which may disembark on its land, wherever it may be.[39]

The immunity described here is indeed very detailed. It claims for the episcopal community of Llandaff exemption from regalian rights, from royal and other secular attempts to demand payments or service (including military service and keeping watch), from the commandeering of goods, and from the liability to appear at, give service at or be answerable to public courts. Furthermore, it claims complete powers of jurisdiction for itself over all cases of theft, killing, murder, assault, arson, breach of protection and ambush – powers, that is, both to hear and to fine the cases; the list here is a developed one and is comparable to the evolving list of 'royal' pleas in England. And it claims property rights too: rights to trade and take the profits, set up a mint, and control the berthing of ships; rights also, I think, to 'common' facilities, to woods and grazing outside the arable (*cum omni communione*).

This text was written in the early twelfth century, between 1110 and *c*.1129, and was subsequently copied into the original *Liber Landavensis*.[40] By that time Llandaff was established as a powerful episcopal see, with an energetic and thrusting leader in Bishop

---

[39] Davies, 'Braint Teilo', pp. 134–5.
[40] *Ibid.*, pp. 131–2.

Urban (1107–34), trained at Worcester cathedral.[41] Urban started building a new cathedral church for Llandaff in April 1120, and became deeply involved in property disputes with the bishops of Hereford and St David's, about claims to ownership of episcopal properties and about defining the bounds of his diocese. Many of Urban's claims were confirmed to him in 1128, although the pope referred the decision back to London in the following year, and the earlier judgments were reversed in 1133. The original *Liber Landavensis*, which includes charters, lists of properties and 'Lives' of the founding and other saints, must have been put together in the course of these disputes, most probably in the 1120s.[42] 'Braint Teilo' was included in the collection that was copied into *Liber Landavensis*, as one of many documents then available in the Llandaff scriptorium. Indeed, the gist of the document was repeated in several of the 'Lives' included in the book and phrases from it were added to many of the charters when they were copied into the collection.

'Braint Teilo' appears to have been composed in the context of a very local dispute, that between Bishop Urban and his community at Llandaff and the new Norman lord of Glamorgan, Robert of Gloucester, who held the lordship from 1107 and became earl in 1122. A new borough had been established at Cardiff, two miles to the south of Llandaff; lands and jurisdiction were disputed between Urban and Robert, resulting in a written agreement in 1126. 'Braint Teilo' attempts to define the position of the episcopal community at Llandaff against that of the new borough.[43]

'Braint Teilo' is so-called because of the formulation of its opening line: 'bryein eccluys Teliau o Lanntaf', in Welsh, and 'priuilegium sancti Teliaui . . . et ecclesiae suae Landauiae' in Latin, i.e. the privilege of the church of Teilo of Llandaff (Welsh)/of Saint Teilo and his church of Llandaff (Latin). From 1120 the church at Llandaff was dedicated to saints Dyfrig, Teilo, Euddogwy and Peter, thereby drawing together a complex of earlier episcopal traditions of southern Wales and associating them with an apostolic saint. Saint Teilo, whose own date and personal circumstances

---

[41] Cf. Wormald, above, pp. 123–6.
[42] See W. Davies, '*Liber Landavensis*: its construction and credibility', *English Historical Review*, 88 (1973).
[43] See below, pp. 156–7. See also Wickham, below pp. 227–9, for some comparable developments in Italy.

are poorly evidenced and exceptionally unclear, had previously been associated with the episcopal church of Llandeilo Fawr ('the great church of Teilo'), which had dependencies and properties in mid-south Wales (see Map 2). In the early ninth century the *episcopus Teiliav*, Teilo's bishop, had witnessed transactions at or near Llandeilo Fawr, but by the early tenth century the community and its archive seem to have been dispersed – for reasons that we do not know. By the early eleventh century, Llandaff (already the site of a monastery for several centuries) had inherited the traditions of Teilo: priests of Llandaff became *presbiteri Sancti Teliaui*, priests of Saint Teilo, and the documents associated with Saint Teilo became fixed in the Llandaff archive. We do not know precisely how or why this transfer was effected, but somehow the traditions of Llandeilo Fawr became attached to Llandaff. *Gref Teliau* and *cirografo [Teiliaui]*, Teilo's charter (in Welsh and Latin), are alluded to in forged and genuine eleventh-century Llandaff texts; by the time of Urban in the early twelfth century, the tradition of Teilo had the pre-eminent status at Llandaff and it was the *cyrografum sancti patroni nostri Teiliaui*, the charter of our holy patron Teilo, which Urban adduced as his ancient authority when he wrote to Pope Calixtus in or before 1119. The 'Braint' text was probably intended to represent that ancient *cyrografum*.[44]

HISTORICAL CONTEXTS

What lies behind these 'immunities', of their several types ? Do they arise out of ancient Welsh tradition, or recent historical circumstances ? Many of the Llandaff charters have interpolated formulas signifying that their properties were free of any fiscal burden – 'sine ullo censu terreno nisi ecclesiae'. These phrases were added in the 1120s, at the time of writing the original *Liber Landavensis*, and are not evidence of any early type of immunity.[45] However, a tiny number of the charters does have fiscal exemption formulas which are integral to the original texts: 'liberam/liberatum ab omni tributo/fiscali tributo' only occurs in

---

[44] It patently obviously is not an ancient *cyrografum*. For all this, see W. Davies, *An Early Welsh Microcosm*, pp. 139–59, esp. pp. 139–41, 145, 153–5. NB also D. Jenkins and M. E. Owen, 'The Welsh marginalia in the Lichfield Gospels, Part I', *Cambridge Medieval Celtic Studies*, 5 (1983), pp. 48–55.

[45] W. Davies, *Llandaff charters*, pp. 9–17, 23–5.

mid-eighth- and mid-ninth-century texts, and is almost entirely confined to Ergyng (south-west Herefordshire);[46] 'liberam ab omni debito' occurs once, 'quietam ab omni re' twice, and 'liberum ab omni re' once, in the same period and area.[47] The fact that these phrases occur rarely, and in a single small zone, for a limited period, suggests that they reflect a distinctive regional approach and that – as early as the mid-eighth century – local kings might abandon any claims to demand a return from religious properties (or, at least, that it was locally conceivable that they might.) At this earlier period the kings were kings of Glywysing (south-east Wales) and the beneficiaries were churches other than Llandaff (the recording source(s) may well have been Welsh Bicknor and/or Llandogo – both on the River Wye, the former five miles north east of Monmouth, the latter ten miles north of Chepstow).[48] It looks as if the clerics of the mid-Welsh border had a rudimentary sense of immunity. In fact, three grants of property were made together with the *census* (payment) that was due from them: these are grants made at Monmouth, *c.*733, the king consenting; somewhere in the same neighbourhood, *c.*745; and of land near Tintern (lower down the Wye) in 955, following episodes at St Arvans and Caerwent (see Map 3).[49] This is again the same limited region.[50] The 955 occasion follows the much-discussed incident of breach of *refugium/nawdd*, and the grant is part of the settlement agreed on account of that breach; it was a royal grant; and the text spells out the fiscal exemption – 'all the land of the kin of Guoruot [Penterry, near Tintern], with fields and streams, woods and hawking rights, and all the payment previously made to the king'.[51]

On the grounds of these few charters, it is reasonable to suppose that ecclesiastical communities on the borders of England and

---

[46] LL 161, 170, 174a, 184, 191, 209b, 228.

[47] *Ibid.* 169b, 185, 170.

[48] Davies, *Microcosm*, pp. 151–7.

[49] LL 175/186b, 198a, 218. Cf. the *autourgon logisimon* of the Byzantine Empire, below, p. 205.

[50] Four of the Llancarfan charters, 'Vita Cadoci', cc. 55, 62, 64, 68, also refer to fiscal immunities. They relate to the Vale of Glamorgan and southern Gwent. These must derive from seventh- or eighth-century texts (see above n. 7); however, since our present texts are late additions to the 'Life' by Lifris we cannot be certain that the fiscal phrases are original and I would not therefore wish to hang an argument on them. I doubt, in fact, that many Welsh kings had regular institutionalized fiscal powers at these early dates; see W. Davies, *Patterns of Power in Early Wales*, pp. 82–3, 86.

[51] LL 218: 'totus ager generationis Guoruot cum campo & fontibus cum siluis et ancipitribus cum omni censu qui antea dabatur regi'.

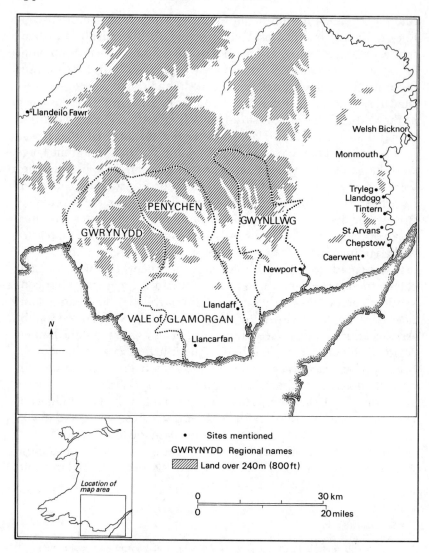

Map 3. Sites in south-east Wales

Wales were thinking in terms of fiscal exemption as early as the eighth century – of the kind that it was believed patristic writers like Ambrose and Augustine had recommended.[52] To that extent there are very early forerunners of immunities in the River Wye zone. However, they are certainly not extensive immunities of the 'Braint Teilo' type and there is no hint of associated judicial privilege, nor of military exemption.[53] Given the location of these cases on the English border, it is conceivable that attitudes were influenced by English clerics (although there is no hint of exemption from the fortress work that characterizes midland English charters of the eighth century).[54] However, these texts relate to a very small area and to a border region: it must be extremely unlikely that immunities were characteristic of Welsh society as a whole at these early dates.

Part Two of 'Braint Teilo' comes from a period of political and ecclesiastical consolidation, in the late tenth and early eleventh centuries. Everything suggests that Morgan, a king of the mid-tenth century who gave his name to Morgannwg, was thought to be an effective ruler. He appeared at the court of the English king; and he seems to have worked from the south-east as a single consolidated kingdom. By the third decade of the eleventh century cracks are evident in the structure of that single kingdom and several rival aristocratic families contended for kingship within the area.[55] Meanwhile, the monastery at Llandaff had absorbed the episcopal traditions of Llandeilo Fawr, adopted Teilo as its patron saint and – by about 1020 – become the seat of a bishopric itself. Under the episcopacy of Joseph, there was considerable activity – involving the English king in consent to consecration, organizing the archive, securing new endowments, gaining ceremonial confirmation of possessions, appointing canons.[56] It is therefore easy to see why the church of Llandaff may have taken steps to establish the immunity of its possessions in the early eleventh century. New leaders began to establish new kingships; the power of local rulers seemed to increase; and the new episcopal establishment needed

---

[52] See above, p. 149.
[53] See above, introduction, p. 14.
[54] See below, p. 162.
[55] Davies, *Microcosm*, pp. 95–6.
[56] *Ibid.*, p. 155; W. Davies, 'The consecration of bishops of Llandaff in the tenth and eleventh centuries', *Bulletin of the Board of Celtic Studies*, 26 (1974–6), pp. 66–70.

to establish traditions and create a protective network for itself. The territorial immunity was their mode of protection.

The later, Part One, of 'Braint Teilo', as I have said, belongs to a very specific period of local dispute and very particular historical circumstances. The Norman Conquest of Wales began round about 1070 and by the turn of the century Norman lords controlled a wide strip west of the border and much of southern Wales. This was known as the 'March' of Wales, and the Norman lords as the marcher lords, and this March ultimately occupied a high proportion of the land of Wales.[57] Marcher lords displaced local rulers, and often put Welsh monasteries in the hands of English and continental foundations. The lords of the March had extensive political power – by right of conquest – and exercised military, fiscal and judicial powers in their own right; in effect, they behaved like small-scale kings.[58] Robert of Gloucester became lord of the marcher lordship of Glamorgan in 1107; kings of Morgannwg had already disappeared in the 1080s, Cadwgan ap Meurig of the old line apparently being dead by 1072 and Caradog ap Gruffudd (ap Rhydderch) dying at Mynydd Carn in 1081. Cadwgan, king of Morgannwg, was last heard of granting property to Bishop Herewald in the neighbourhood of Llandaff round about 1070, and Caradog, also king, did so in Gwent a few years later.[59] Robert of Gloucester had rights of holding courts, creating boroughs and markets, issuing coin and taking tolls. These were largely new political powers,[60] for boroughs, markets, coin and tolls were unknown in Wales prior to the Conquest. In claiming comparable rights for Llandaff, Urban sought to put the powers of the bishopric on a par with the (new) powers of the local lord. For the detail of his claim he drew on what was going on around him, not on ancient local precedent.

[57] For full consideration of this process, see R. R. Davies, *Conquest, Coexistence and Change: Wales 1063–1415*, pp. 24–107.

[58] There is an extensive literature on this subject. J. G. Edwards argued that their powers were inherited from the powers of the Welsh princes that they replaced; Rees Davies has demonstrated convincingly that this was not so and that their powers derived from the act of conquest. J. G. Edwards, 'The Normans and the Welsh March', *Proceedings of the British Academy*, 42 (1956); R. R. Davies, 'Kings, lords and liberties in the March of Wales, 1066–1272', *Transactions of the Royal Historical Society*, 29 (1979).

[59] LL 267, 272; cf. Iestyn ap Gwrgan, LL 271.

[60] Comital powers in twelfth-century Germany may be analogous: Benjamin Arnold has argued that *domini terrae* had new 'allodial' jurisdictions over newly claimed land; cf., for example, B. Arnold, *Princes and Territories in Medieval Germany*, pp. 63–8.

Hence, many parts of 'Braint Teilo' Part One reflect local customs of very recent origin. Exemption from the obligation to keep watch seems to refer to the castle guard which was one of the two obligations of holding by knight service in the lordship of Glamorgan; the power to hold a market and issue coin seem to have been very recent introductions. There is nothing here that does not have an English and/or continental parallel; there is nothing that is distinctively or exclusively Welsh.[61] The immunity that Llandaff claimed at this period was therefore as much an immunity against the incursions of local lords as it was an immunity against the king; the powers that Urban claimed for Llandaff were as much marcher lordly powers as they were royal. Indeed, it was essential to Urban's strategy to make a strong claim for powers as well as for exemptions.

Part One of 'Braint Teilo' reflects so developed an immunity that it could well be termed a *seigneurie*; it seeks to establish a zone of exclusive political control for the bishop, a zone in which he had many, specified political rights; as such it reflects the organization of power of the new local lords.[62] Part One is markedly different from the *earlier* Part Two of 'Braint Teilo', with its much less detailed specification of exemptions and with its preoccupation with exemption from the power of the king of Morgannwg. The difference between the texts, and the reasons for the change, can be explained by the nature and circumstances of political change in Wales in the later eleventh and early twelfth centuries. New rulers came in; a new relationship developed with the English state to the east; some of the new men brought in continental contacts and ideas; and the very fact of conquest was itself a stimulus to the development of new institutions, as it also created a need to redefine relationships.

DISCUSSION

The eleventh-century Llandaff immunity is framed explicitly and repetitively against the power of the king of Morgannwg. It is concerned with compensation for insult, and with the necessity of bringing the king to the bishop's court when he defaulted, in other

---

[61] See Davies, 'Braint Teilo', for detailed consideration of all the terms.
[62] Cf. the comments of R. R. Davies, *Conquest, Coexistence and Change*, p. 95.

words with royal infringement of the church's *nawdd*. It is also concerned with exemption from 'burdens', basic royal demands of tax and military service; and with (somewhat vaguely determined) powers of jurisdiction for Llandaff's judicial court. This is expressed in spatial terms and is a clear expression of an immunity. It is both a *nawdd/refugium* text and an immunity text.

This early eleventh-century situation certainly holds for the south-east. Was it peculiar to that part of Wales ? This is difficult to answer, because of the predominance of south-eastern material in the written record. It is not inherently improbable that fiscal immunities had developed in Welsh Wales by the eleventh century,[63] and – more certainly – the *noddfa* and the special ecclesiastical privilege that went with it, is unlikely to have been peculiar to the southeast. One of the poems of the collection known as *Canu Llywarch Hen*, no earlier than the ninth century and quite possibly of the tenth or eleventh, refers to the *braint* of 'eglwys Basa', Basa's church, generally thought to be Baschurch in Shropshire; whether or not the identification is correct, the poetic cycle is of mid-, rather than southern-, Welsh origin.[64] From north-east Wales, the Llanelwy material cited above, with its emphasis on the penalties and consequences of a king crossing the bounds and limits of the church zone, is likely to have a pre-Conquest origin; and from the northwest the Clynnog material is similarly suggestive of pre-Conquest origins.[65] From the west ecclesiastical privilege is implicit, as *refugium* is explicit, in the 'Life of St David'.[66] It is also quite clear that the concepts continued outside the southeast in the

---

[63] It is possible that the monastery of Clynnog, in north-west Wales, had a relatively early fiscal immunity; such is certainly recorded in King Edward's confirmation charter (including earlier material), but its origin is impossible to date (Davies, 'Latin charter-tradition', p. 271); ninth-century Breton, and eleventh-century Scottish and Irish charters and charter fragments also include fiscal immunities; 'Vie de Saint Paul de Léon', ed. Ch. Cuissard, *Revue Celtique*, 5 (1881–3), cc. 18, 19; St Andrews Cartulary, in A. C. Lawrie (ed.), *Early Scottish Charters*, no. 14, p. 11; St Andrews 'foundation' charter, in W. F. Skene (ed.), *Chronicles of the Picts, Chronicles of the Scots*, pp. 186–7; Kells charters, *Notitiae as Leabhar Cheanannais 1033–1161*, ed. G. MacNiocaill. (Already in the late seventh century, Irish canonists had proclaimed the fiscal exemptions and fiscal powers of Irish abbots; see further W. Davies, 'Clerics as rulers: some implications of the terminology of ecclesiastical authority in early medieval Ireland', in N. P. Brooks (ed.), *Latin and the Vernacular Languages in Early Medieval Britain*, pp. 86–7.)

[64] *Canu Llywarch Hen*, ed. I. Williams, pp. 38–9; see J. Rowland, *Early Welsh Saga Poetry: A Study and Edition of the Englynion*, pp. 147, 435–6, 591 ('eglwysseu bassa', literally 'Basa's churches', in the plural; but the place-name is treated as if it were singular).

[65] See above, p. 143.

[66] *Rhigyfarch's Life of St David*, ed. J. W. James, ch. 57, pp. 24–5; this chapter is only found in the Vespasian text of Rhigyfarch and could conceivably be of south-eastern origin.

twelfth and thirteenth centuries: the (later) legal texts are especially full on north Wales; there is a charter recording royal confirmation of *refugium* to St Michael's church, Trefeglwys, in mid-Wales; and, in the annals, we find a *noddfa* at Llanddewi Brefi in the west.[67]

Nawdd and *noddfa* are 'Welsh', and not merely south-eastern. Are they quintessentially Welsh, operative throughout historic time, until the Norman Conquest introduced different ways of doing things? For how long had the eleventh-century *noddfeydd* been in place? It is exceptionally difficult to assess this, because of the paucity of early written texts, but neither the territories nor the institutionalization of legal compensations look ancient. The sixth-to ninth-century charters, for example, are devoid of indication of anything other than straightforward economic powers over property: they indicate, and sometimes detail, rent or profits; they do not speak of protection or refuge. Especially noteworthy, from the ninth century, are the charters of the Lichfield marginalia, from central southern Wales, which detail renders and little else.[68]

However, the concept of *nawdd* itself is undoubtedly ancient (cf. Irish *snádud*). The Old Testament notion of *civitates refugii*, safe havens for those who had killed, was evidently influencing ecclesiastical thinking in Ireland from the late seventh century,[69] and this knowledge must have encouraged the territorialization of the native concepts. The canonical material in which the Irish ideas are expressed was certainly known in pre-Conquest Wales. We do not know precisely when texts were transmitted, but some time in or after the eighth century and before the tenth is not an unreasonable suggestion. By the tenth century ecclesiastical language and practice was clearly diverging in Celtic areas.[70] It is also reasonable to suppose that the ecclesiastical law of sanctuary, as manifest in

---

[67] *Brut y Tywysogion, Red Book of Hergest version*, ed. T. Jones, s.a. 1109, 1147, pp. 60, 126; H. Pryce, 'The church of Trefeglwys and the end of the "Celtic" charter-tradition in twelfth-century Wales', *Cambridge Medieval Celtic Studies*, 25 (1993); cf. Pryce, *Native Law*, p. 172.

[68] LL pp. xliii–xlvii; Jenkins and Owen, 'Welsh marginalia, Part I', pp. 50–6.

[69] Pryce, *Native Law*, p. 169.

[70] W. Davies, 'The myth of the Celtic church', in N. Edwards and A. Lane (eds.), *The Early Church in Wales and the West*, pp. 18–20: there was in many respects a shared Latin culture for several centuries in Wales, Cornwall, Ireland, to some extent Brittany, and possibly Cornwall. Clerics used the same (ancient) biblical texts and the same distinctive terminology; they worked in a tradition strongly influenced by the late classical grammatical tradition and by the Old Testament/Mosaic law. This is evident by the eighth century, while differences were becoming marked by the tenth.

western Europe, perhaps especially in its fifth- and sixth-century forms, had some influence, given its focus on the notion of sacred, safe space.[71] We might then postulate a slow development towards the establishment of the *noddfa* over the eighth to tenth centuries, with a corresponding development of legal institutions over the ninth to eleventh centuries. Exemption from secular demands, and the establishment of immunities in the continental sense, is not well evidenced at the earlier dates and seems to be a later process in Wales.[72]

The critical issues – which are difficult to resolve – are whether protection was confined to the *noddfa* or extended to all properties owned; and whether or not this merely applies to ecclesiastical landowners or applies to all (major) landowners, secular as well. There are certainly earlier and later church claims of privilege extending beyond the *noddfa*;[73] and 'Braint Teilo' itself specifies the offence of *nawdd*-breach, both within the enclosure and without. Whether or not these claims were regularly respected is open to question, but it looks as if some clerics were claiming special powers beyond the *noddfa* by the central middle ages. All our evidence of the *noddfa* is ecclesiastical, although the root concept of *nawdd* is not. Huw Pryce is certainly of the opinion that the *noddfa* had *become* ecclesiastical by the twelfth century.[74] The weight of the present evidence suggests that the territorialization of *nawdd*, and all that followed from that, was a distinctively ecclesiastical

---

[71] Fifth- and sixth-century church councils were quite explicit on the point that the asylum offered by churches to fugitives might extend beyond the church itself – to include ecclesiastical dwellings in the precinct and/or an area 30–5 paces beyond the walls or doors of the church; see J. C. Cox, *The Sanctuaries and Sanctuary Seekers of Medieval England*, pp. 3–6. The idea did not die and was strongly revived in the late tenth and eleventh centuries, especially in the context of the Peace of God movement; see, for example, P. Bonnassie on Catalan *sagreres* (> *sacraria*), in *From Slavery to Feudalism in South-Western Europe*, pp. 252–4, and H.-W. Goetz, 'Protection of the church', in Head and Landes (eds.), *The Peace of God*, pp. 264–5. Although this can be easily allied to the concept of the *noddfa*, it is worth remembering that it is conceptually different: it is essentially to do with defining a space where fugitives may be safe, whereas the *noddfa* is essentially to do with defining the space appropriate to an individual's powers of protection.

[72] Although the establishment of fiscal exemptions is entirely *conceivable* before this, on the basis of the influence of the same late seventh-century canonical material (see above n. 62), there is no evidence of it outside the borders. Note R. Chapman Stacey on immunities in Irish and Welsh law, 'Ties that bind: immunities in Irish and Welsh law', *Cambridge Medieval Celtic Studies*, 20 (1990): these are immunities in a different sense, i.e. transactions without sureties but 'immune' from claims.

[73] Pryce, *Native Law*, p. 172.

[74] Pryce, *Native Law*, p. 174.

process: it was to do with protecting ecclesiastical property and the special needs of churches.[75] In the absence of secular evidence we cannot be sure that this was a peculiarly ecclesiastical institution, but it certainly looks like that.

Why, then, the development? Should we look for an internal or an external explanation? What processes can explain the ultimate establishment of complex landlord immunities? There are three prominent possibilities: English influence, the needs of the Christian church, and rulership. Let me take them one by one.

First, rulership: the judicial aspect of these immunities – the claim to hold a court and be exempt from royal courts – has little significance if kings were not claiming such powers. There is no hint of judicial privileges in early charter material. It looks as if the establishment of judicial immunities was a reaction against *developing* royal power: as kings began to intrude, landowners reacted. Moreover, by the late tenth century, more and more kings seem to have been claiming fiscal powers; and, if tax-taking was frequently, or characteristically, *collected*, by the king or his agent, it is easy to see the significance of physical exclusion from a property and to see why it became a concern in the tenth century. And it is easy to see why this was a matter of honour: to maintain honour (in Welsh terms, to enjoy the privilege appropriate to your status), a freeman needs to maintain a degree of independence of action – the higher your status, the greater the degree of independence that you need. Limitation of your independence of action – by demanding military service or tax, for example – is an assault against due and proper privilege, a besmirching of honour, an insult. Expressing the limits of your independence in territorial terms – literally defining its bounds – goes hand in hand with the territorialization of *nawdd*. It only became necessary when rulers started to make demands – for tax or military service or to try cases – and started to impinge upon that independence. Thereby, quickly, the offence of insult turns into the offence of intrusion. There is a mass of evidence to show that rulers were becoming more energetic and more demanding in the tenth and eleventh

---

[75] Southern Welsh law texts suggest that every landowner was a judge. This seems to mean that southern landowners, *qua* landowners, took part in the business of legal courts, as members of the court; see Jenkins and Owen, 'Welsh marginalia, Part II', *Cambridge Medieval Celtic Studies*, 7 (1984), pp. 99–100. I know of nothing that suggests that this refers to the *noddfa*.

centuries. This must in itself have been a major stimulus to the development of counter-powers.

Secondly, the Christian church: ecclesiastical institutions undoubtedly had a level of practical organization superior to the secular and they were also concerned to have full control of their personnel and properties. A desire for special protection, coupled with a superior ability to effect what they wanted, are sufficient reasons in themselves for the establishment of immunities and *seigneuries*.[76] We know that in Ireland, in the early post-conversion period, clerics saw themselves as rulers; they had political power just as every noble had political power; words of rule were used of clerics as they were of secular leaders. In a few cases it looks as if the fact of clerical rule was deemed – *de facto* – to exclude kings; hence land given to St Patrick's church was 'liberated' from the king. Already in the seventh century these are quasi-immunities, islands of exemption, although they do not appear to have developed into the full-blown immunities of the continent.[77] The early stages of Irish development are better evidenced than the Welsh, but there is every reason to believe that comparable processes were at work.

The third possibility is the English interaction. It is well known that there was a close interaction between Welsh and English rulers from the late ninth century, and that this introduced some major political changes into Wales.[78] Welsh rulers spent time at the English court, especially in the first half of the tenth century, and some English ideas began to filter through to Wales – particularly in the context of inflated ideas of rulership. To the extent that Welsh rulers were encouraged by the example of the English ruler, it is reasonable to argue for some English influence here; and it is also the case that an English version of the *noddfa* developed in the chartered sanctuaries of at least the north and west.[79] But England does not provide any models for the developed Welsh immunity of the eleventh and twelfth centuries. Indeed, it might be argued that its late pre-Conquest development was leading in the opposite direction, away from exemptions.[80]

---

[76] Cf. the actions of the abbot of Redon, in south-eastern Brittany; W. Davies, *Small Worlds. The Village Community in Early Medieval Brittany*, pp. 188–200.

[77] Davies, 'Clerics as rulers'.

[78] Cf. Davies, *Patterns of Power*, pp. 61–79.

[79] See above, nn. 18–20, and also n. 3.

[80] See above, Wormald, pp. 131–2.

Can I attempt a possible chronology? Ecclesiastical power became evident in places in Wales in the eighth century, at which time there were also some signs of kings acquiring some powers over subject populations in the south. Rulers had little success in institutionalizing their powers in the succeeding centuries, but it is certainly the case that they became more physically active, and more evident across the whole Welsh stage. The image of the (devastating) arrival of the northern king is recurrent in the southern hagiography: Arthur comes, Maelgwn comes, Rhain comes, as Anarawd certainly had come from Gwynedd in the late ninth century. It is entirely conceivable that churches reacted to the sharper profile of kings, and the increased chance of them appearing and seizing, by putting up barriers and by taking guard. It makes sense to suppose that territorialized immunities developed in Wales as a response to increased threats of ruler intervention, building on an established ideology of special protection for the church (itself an intensification and particular application of the local institution of *nawdd*). Tenth-century Wales was in fact strikingly devoid of institutions for the maintenance of royal political power. But people with power abounded – and expressed their power in darting, sometimes long-ranging, predatory raids.[81] It was against this – these open manifestations of crude power – that churches developed their (differently based) institutions, through writing and record keeping and ritual. Thus, they armed themselves.

Ruler ranging and ruler raiding began to become evident in the late ninth century;[82] it intensified to an extreme degree during the tenth. The critical period for the development of the Welsh immunity must be the first half of the tenth century. By the end of the century some kings were making military as well as fiscal demands on landowners. By the early eleventh century *nawdd* had been well and truly territorialized, and immunity texts focussed on exemption from royal interference. By the early twelfth, in response to the particular institutions and political developments of the locality, at Llandaff that exemption had become considerably elaborated.

There are three principal strands in this development: an ancient notion that a freeman could legally offer protection to another, for

---

[81] See Davies, *Patterns of Power*, especially pp. 80–91.
[82] Discounting the different phase of the seventh century.

a limited term; a need for the growing ecclesiastical establishment to acquire control, and therefore political power, over its lands and dependants; and an increasing manifestation of ruler power, perhaps boosted by knowledge of English ideas. They have quite different, and unconnected, origins, but it is the interplay of the three which is responsible for the development of this particular form of territorial immunity. By the mid-eleventh century this concurrence had taken place.

CHAPTER 7

Property transactions and social relations between rulers, bishops and nobles in early eleventh-century Saxony: the evidence of the Vita Meinwerci

Timothy Reuter

At some time in the late 1020s a scribe who probably belonged to the Paderborn cathedral chapter made two formless records of a property transaction on a small sheet of parchment:[1]

When the lord bishop Maeginuuerc directed his journey to Rome, he gave to Athulf and Hicila for the inheritance of Hatheburg fifteen talents [pounds] and four *mansi* [landholdings] with twenty *mancipia* [slaves or serfs]. Each of them should pay five shekels [shillings] of silver.

When Bishop Meinuuerc came back from Rome, he then again gave to the aforementioned in reconciliation one sable fur coat and ten shillings in coin.[2]

Meinwerk, bishop of Paderborn from 1009 to 1036, was a well-placed and wealthy aristocrat, related to several important families in north-western Westfalia and lower Lotharingia as well as to Emperor Henry II; before his appointment he had served in the royal chapel under Otto III and Henry II.[3] He owed his

---

[1] As there are often two versions of these transactions, references in the following notes will normally cite them simply by the number given in the appendix, which gives full details of transmission. The following abbreviations will be used: *VM* = *Vita Meinwerci episcopi Patherbrunnensis*, ed. F. Tenckhoff, *MGH SRG*, vol. 59; *RHW* = H. Erhard, *Regesta Historiae Westfaliae, accedit Codex diplomaticus*; references are to the items in the *Codex* by number. In addition, royal diplomata are cited in the conventional manner as D(D) followed by the ruler's initial and ordinal number and the number(s) of the diploma(ta) in the MGH editions: D O I = *Die Urkunden Konrad I., Heinrich I., und Otto I.*, ed T. Sickel, and so on (see list of abbreviations, pp. xiii–xiv, for full details).

[2] Nos. 98 and 99 (*RHW* version). The dating element is provided by the reference to Meinwerk's journey to Rome. He is known to have taken part in the imperial expeditions of 1014–15 and 1026–7: H. Bannasch, *Das Bistum Paderborn unter den Bischöfen Rethar und Meinwerk (983–1036)*, pp. 169, 198–200. Tenckhoff, the editor of *VM*, thought (p. 62 n. 7) that the reference must be to the second expedition, and this would fit in with the tendency for grants to Paderborn to be challenged in the early years of Conrad II's reign (see below at n. 62).

[3] The main source for all this is *VM*, cc. 3, 5, 11, 219, pp. 6, 7–9, 17–19, 131–3. For Meinwerk's family connections see also Bannasch, *Bistum Paderborn*, pp. 150–8.

appointment not only to this service but also to his wealth: allegedly, his response to being offered the bishopric was to say that he
could erect a better one from his own resources, and he was evidently expected by Henry II to use his patrimony to endow his
new bishopric, as were a number of his contemporaries.[4] He was
favourably remembered in Paderborn on a number of counts: for
his own endowment of the church with buildings and church orna-
ments, especially for the rebuilding of the cathedral church, dedicated in 1015 following the disastrous fire of 1000; for his monastic
foundations, Abdinghof and Busdorf; for his endowment of the
bishopric with much of his own *hereditas* and his success in
attracting donations from clerics and lay persons within the diocese; and for his skilled exploitation of royal service to secure benefits for his bishopric. His 'Life' (the *Vita Meinwerci*, henceforth *VM*)
was written between 1155 and 1165 by Conrad, abbot of
Abdinghof, the most important of the monasteries founded by
Meinwerk.[5] Conrad, writing rather later than most biographers of
Meinwerk's contemporaries, provided a picture not so much of the
virtuous bishop in the monastic mould as of a prelate active on
behalf of his bishopric.[6] He shaped his work rather like a

---

[4] *VM*, ch. 11, pp. 17–18. For the parallel cases of Thietmar of Merseburg and Unwan of
Bremen see H. Hoffmann, *Mönchskönig und rex idiota. Studien zur Kirchenpolitik Heinrichs II.
und Konrads II.*, pp. 64–70. Bernward of Hildesheim is known to have endowed his foundation St Michael with his own *hereditas* while retaining it under his own control as long
as possible; see H. J. Schuffels, 'Bernward Bischof von Hildesheim. Eine biographische
Skizze', in M. Brandt and A. Eggebrecht (eds.), *Bernward von Hildesheim und das Zeitalter
der Ottonen*, vol. 1, pp. 37–8, 41 and D. Hellfaier, 'Früher Besitz des Klosters St Michael
zu Hildesheim im 11. Jahrhundert', *ibid.*, vol. 2. As this mirrors very closely Meinwerk's
own behaviour in respect of his *hereditas* and his foundation of Abdinghof (see Bannasch,
Bistum Paderborn, pp. 150–7, 229–37, 250–60 for details), it seems plausible that it was
also expected of Bernward in 993 that he would endow Hildesheim with his inheritance.
[5] K. Honselmann, 'Der Autor der Vita Meinwerci vermutlich Abt Konrad von Abdinghof',
Westfälische Zeitschrift, 114, pt. 2 (1964); his arguments on authorship, on which see also
H. Bannasch, 'Fälscher aus Frömmigkeit: Der Meinwerkbiograph – ein mittelalterlicher
Fälscher und sein Selbstverständnis', *Archiv für Diplomatik*, 23 (1977), pp. 226–9, do not
change the date of composition of *VM*, established by Tenckhoff in his edition, pp. vi–vii.
[6] On the changes in the ideal of prelacy found in *vitae* see O. Engels, 'Der Reichsbischof in
ottonischer und frühsalischer Zeit', in I. Crusius (ed.), *Beiträge zu Geschichte und Struktur der
mittelalterlichen Germania Sacra*. But Engels underestimates the specific context of individual
vitae – on which see also S. Coué, 'Acht Bischofsviten aus der Salierzeit – neu interpretiert',
in S. Weinfurter (ed.), *Die Salier und das Reich*, vol. 3, *Gesellschaftlicher und ideengeschichtlicher
Wandel im Reich der Salier* – and exaggerates the dominance of the monastic ideal of prelacy
before *c.*1050; there were other role-models. See my *'Filii matris nostrae pugnant adversum nos*:
bonds and tensions between prelates and their *milites* in the German high middle ages', in
G. Picasso (ed.), *Chiesa e mondo feudale nei secoli X–XII*, and also the literature cited below,
n. 26.

'cartulary-chronicle': the narrative of *VM* is interspersed with *pièces justificatives* in the form of excerpts from or paraphrases of papal and imperial diplomata, and contains a central block of well over a hundred notices (with a few more scattered elsewhere in the narrative) of various kinds of transaction between the bishop and members of his diocese involving lands and movable property. Among these is a record of the above transaction with some divergences from that of the contemporary notice and some additional detail:

A certain other woman, Hatheburg by name, conferred all her inheritance on the church [of Paderborn]; which Atholf, a *miles* [military follower] of the archbishop of Cologne, together with his wife, Hicila by name, strove to infringe and make invalid, and were given by the bishop, on his way to Rome for his own affairs, fifteen talents and four *mansi* with twenty *mancipia*, each of whom paid five shekels of silver.

After the bishop had returned from Rome he gave the aforesaid persons sable furs in reconciliation and in this way ensured that the gift which had been made should be fully and legally confirmed.[7]

These brief accounts and their discrepancies encapsulate many of the problems presented by the sources for tenth- and eleventh-century property ownership. The records of such transactions were normally informal notices. In East Francia they were no longer intended to be produced in legal proceedings, unlike their precursor the *carta*.[8] At most they could have identified the witnesses to the original transaction, and in practice the evidence discussed here does not in any case suggest that disputes were adjudicated in formal proceedings involving the production of evidence.[9]

---

[7] Nos. 98, 99 (*VM* version).

[8] For the importance of *ostensio cartae* – production of a charter as proof of right in court proceedings – in Italy at this time and earlier see C. J. Wickham, 'Land disputes and their social framework in Lombard–Carolingian Italy', in W. Davies and P. Fouracre (eds.), *The Settlement of Disputes in Early Medieval Europe*, pp. 114–18. R. McKitterick, *The Carolingians and the Written Word*, pp. 65–75, discusses the use of charters in legal proceedings in the Frankish kingdoms and argues that the provisions of the Salic and Ribuarian laws were indeed followed in practice, but the evidence she adduces is largely west Frankish; in her discussion of the St Gallen and Fulda material, *ibid.*, pp. 76–129, there seems to be no reference to the use of these charters in subsequent court proceedings. The provisions of the law codes and capitularies apply in any case to charters produced by a public charter-writer (*cancellarius*), an institution which had died out in east Francia by the late ninth century and scarcely penetrated Saxony. For these developments see P. Johanek, 'Zur rechtlichen Funktion von Traditionsnotiz, Traditionsbuch und früher Siegelurkunde', in P. Classen (ed.), *Recht und Schrift im Mittelalter, Vorträge und Forschungen*, vol. 23 (1977), esp. pp. 140–5.

[9] On the settlement of later challenges to donations see below at nn. 6ff., 91.

Arguably, the context of such notices was at least as much that of liturgy and the preservation of *memoria* as that of litigation. Peter Johanek has put this very clearly: their function was not to bind the donors, but rather to provide them with a reinforcement of the 'obligation of the ecclesiastical community to preserve their donation to the saint . . . and protect it against an alienation which would have endangered the purpose of the gift and hence the value of the preservation of their *memoria*'.[10] It is no accident that the surviving cache of Paderborn 'originals' looks very like another contemporary cache of superficially quite different documents, the eleventh-century monastic professions from St Michael's, Hildesheim, which are also written in bookhand on small parchment rectangles.[11] Both belong to the sphere of the church's internal, institutional memory, though this could be pragmatic as well as spiritual, as when one original was endorsed in a contemporary hand: 'the bishop still owes 24 *solidi* [shillings]'.[12] Even in the twelfth century, when notices had given way to sealed charters, these too were often used in the German kingdom (*Reich*) to record internal administrative arrangements.[13]

Since notices had little or no set form, they included whatever their scribe felt like recording in whatever way he felt like recording it, though there were, of course, models and traditions to follow.[14] We do not always know the criteria behind their selection of information; a great deal is taken for granted which is not accessible to us, and this often makes the notices ambiguous or unclear, far more often than the smooth prose of modern scholars might suggest. In the transaction cited, to take a trivial example, was it Athulf and

---

[10] Johanek, 'Rechtlichen Funktion', p. 145; for further reasons why the donors might have wished to ensure that alienation did not take place see the arguments presented by Jahn and Hartung (below at nn. 21f.).

[11] See M. Brandt and A. Eggebrecht (eds.), *Bernward von Hildesheim und das Zeitalter der Ottonen*, vol. 2, pp. 594–7, no. IX–2, for illustrations and discussion.

[12] No. 35 (*RHW* version).

[13] P. Johanek, 'Die Corveyer Traditionen als Gedenküberlieferung', and T. Reuter, 'Gedenküberlieferung und -praxis im Briefbuch Wibalds von Stablo', both in K. Schmid and J. Wollasch (eds.), *Der Liber Vitae der Abtei Corvey*, pp. 128–9 and 175 respectively.

[14] K. Honselmann, *Von der Carta zur Siegelurkunde. Beiträge zum Urkundenwesen im Bistum Paderborn, 862–1178*, pp. 46–50, sorts out the work of the eight scribes who can be identified, and discusses (pp. 50–67) the diplomatic of the notices; he notes (p. 50) that each group of notices written by a single scribe also has its own peculiarities of phrasing against those found in other groups, and a computer-assisted analysis of the vocabulary and phraseology of the notices which I have carried out confirms this. The inference is that the scribes composed the notices themselves, and had some freedom in how they did it.

Hicila or the *mancipia* who each had to pay five shekels; and if the latter, once only, annually or more frequently?[15] More important is the question whether the counter-gifts of food to the donors of land often recorded in the transactions are once-off affairs or annual payments, as they are sometimes explicitly said to be. In one case a man called Ecelin gets in return for 'whatever he holds by hereditary right in Haaren with eight *mancipia* and all that pertains to it' an annual rent of corn, pork and sheep, while his consenting son and heir Meinhard gets a horse, a linen cloth, corn and pork: once off or annually?[16] Selectivity also means that we cannot easily draw inferences from what is *not* mentioned. For example, many of the notices of property transactions from Meinwerk's pontificate include a 'reversionary clause'; should the bishop or his successors violate the conditions of the gift or renege on their counter-gifts, the donors may take back their own without further ado. In so far as the notices can be dated, these clauses seem to have been most common in the notices recording transactions from early in the pontificate; but it would be rash to assume that this reflects a change of 'policy' on Meinwerk's part rather than mere notarial preferences and practices.[17]

What appear to be legal records thus turn out to be more like fragmentary (and often contextless) narratives. They are also not necessarily contemporary with the events they purport to record. Apart from a few hoards of originals (e.g. from Cluny or St Gallen) records of this kind survive from northern Europe mostly as later copies (e.g. in cartularies). These were subject not only to rewriting with nefarious intent but to other forms of reworking: systematic

---

[15] The *VM* version of no. 98 is quite clear: 'cum XX mancipiis, quorum unusquisque V siclos argenti solvebat'. The *RHW* version might be thought more ambiguous: 'cum XX mancipiis. Unusquisque eorum solvere debet V siclos argenti', and Tenckhoff (*VM*, p. 62 n. 6) thought that the reference was to Athulf and Hicila.

[16] No. 37; note also no. 32, which specifically says that a gift of consumables is made 'in that year alone'. On the annual rents see F. Irsigler, '*Divites* und *pauperes* in der Vita Meinwerci. Untersuchungen zur wirtschaftlichen und sozialen Differenzierung der Bevölkerung Westfalens im Hochmittelalter', *Vierteljahresschrift für Sozial- und Wirtschaftsgeschichte*, 57 (1970), pp. 472–7.

[17] Honselmann, *Carta*, pp. 53–4, 72, notes the decline in the use of the 'unusual' clause; Bannasch, *Bistum Paderborn*, p. 256, even supposes that the provision helped to make donors more willing to donate (without explaining why then it was apparently used less often in Meinwerk's later years). In fact it is a characteristic feature of such notices all over the east Frankish/German kingdom, as Honselmann himself notes (p. 66), and can even be found in royal diplomata (e.g. D O I 202 for Salzburg and 203 for St Emmeram, Regensburg).

abbreviation, and glossing in the light of local knowledge and guesswork. This places a further layer of perception between us and the original transaction besides that imposed by the arbitrary practices of contemporary scribes. In the example just seen, the main differences between 'original' and twelfth-century text are the explanation of the conflict as one over inheritance; the identification of Athulf as a follower of the archbishop of Cologne; the statement that Meinwerk was going to Rome on his own affairs; and the omission of the ten shillings paid as part of the final reconciliation. Of these, the first, third and fourth might simply be gloss or carelessness; Athulf's status is given some credibility by the fact that Heribert of Cologne gave support to Adela, Meinwerk's mother, and her second husband Balderich (also a Cologne *miles*).[18] Such alterations are not necessarily the norm, but we must always reckon with the possibility of changes on this scale. The commonest kinds of change are the abbreviation of witness lists, and alterations in the titles given to persons and and in technical terms which reflect the conditions of a later period. Common also is the reworking of formless notices to make them look like more formal charters (the preferred instrument of the high middle ages).[19] All these changes can be found in the *VM* material.

The records are frozen moments in the course of a narrative; and while we may know something more about the human participants, these frozen moments are normally all we know about property. We learn about it, in other words, mostly when it changes hands; we know far more about ownership than about the use made of ownership (except to give it up). Even that would not be so serious if it were always clear that these property transactions actually took place, but only in very rich archives can we expect direct confirmation that the church seemingly favoured by the original transaction later actually controlled the property. Early medieval records of a transfer of property are frequently isolated, often with no further references for centuries: only from the thirteenth century onwards do we have densely clustered information about the lands

---

[18] *VM*, cc. 139–40, pp. 71–2, and Bannasch, *Bistum Paderborn*, p. 179; the context is Adela's and Balderich's feud with Wichmann, murdered in 1016, and Adela's dispute with Meinwerk about the disposal of the family inheritance.

[19] An early example of such a transformation is no. 79 (cf. below, n. 130). See Honselmann, *Carta*, esp. pp. 125–8; P. Johanek, *Die Frühzeit der Siegelurkunde im Bistum Würzburg*; and for repeated and extended updating of earlier material over several generations, W. Davies, *The Llandaff Charters*.

held by the bishop and chapter of Paderborn, for example, which means that we do not know whether Meinwerk's settlement with Athulf and Hicila actually stuck.[20]

Beyond the absence of corroborating evidence lie more fundamental difficulties. When members of a kindred are found repeatedly donating what is apparently the same piece of land to Cluny, or exercising what look very like proprietary rights over lands which their ancestors had on the face of it already made over unconditionally and completely to St Gallen, Fulda and other East Frankish monasteries, it is clear that such transactions, whatever they may have been, were not clean-break transfers of rights.[21] In some cases they were probably largely fictive. The late Joachim Jahn and Wolfgang Hartung, expanding on hints dropped by earlier scholars, recently argued that many donations were not so much donations as a means of protecting a kindred's lands against the effects of partible inheritance. This applies especially to those which restrict the circle of persons to whom the church could give the property out in benefice. Hartung cites a particularly striking donation to St Gallen by Eidwart and his son Iltibold, 'in this manner, that as long as we are alive we may hold the above property [for an annual rent of two *denarii*] ... and our children may do so similarly after our deaths and all the posterity which they may generate in all eternity (*usque in sempiternum*) may do so'.[22] In effect, St Gallen is not here really receiving a grant at all. Rather, it is offering its privileged status as a church, which does not die and whose property is therefore not subject to partible inheritance, to provide an entail (a restriction keeping the property undivided in the male line of descent) for Eidwart and Iltibold in return for

---

[20] M. Balzer, *Untersuchungen zur Geschichte des Grundbesitzes in der Paderborner Feldmark*, gives an exhaustive account of property ownership in the immediate surroundings of Paderborn in the later middle ages; only rarely can he relate the property recorded in the late medieval evidence to the transactions we are here concerned with.

[21] For Cluny see B. H. Rosenwein, *To Be the Neighbor of St Peter: The Social Meaning of Cluny's Property, 909–1049*, pp. 49–77 (though here the later 'donations' are presented as quitclaims, so that it is often unclear who held the usufruct in between donations). For east Frankish traditions to monasteries see J. Jahn, 'Tradere ad Sanctum: Politische und gesellschaftliche Aspekte der Traditionspraxis im agilolfingischen Bayern', and W. Hartung, 'Adel, Erbrecht, Schenkung: Die strukturellen Ursachen der frühmittelalterlichen Besitzübertragungen an die Kirche', both in F. Seibt (ed.), *Gesellschaftsgeschichte. Festschrift für Karl Bosl zum 80. Geburtstag*, vol. 1.

[22] Hartung, 'Adel, Erbrecht, Schenkung', p. 429.

two pence per year and the vague expectation of a reversion should the line die out. To give land to a church or monastery and receive it back precarially could thus have similar effects to those produced by 'booking' land in Anglo-Saxon England or entailing it in late medieval England.[23] Scribal freedom to choose what to record means that such arrangements may also lie behind transactions even when such a reservation is not made explicit.

Considerations like these have led to a partial dissolution of straightforward notions of property in some important recent discussions. Property is here presented not merely as a straightforward something which is held, acquired or accumulated by an individual or an institution with an eye to the more or less autistic exercise of power derived from its ownership. It becomes a rather different something as well: a medium through which relations of friendship, kinship and enmity, as well as of patronage and deference, can find public and often highly ritualized expression precisely at those points at which rights in it are being granted away or modified. Chris Wickham has argued in a Tuscan context that both giving and failing to give to a monastery might express alignment with local factions, at least until the institution became so wealthy that it was itself a force to be reckoned with.[24] Barbara Rosenwein and Stephen White, looking at Cluny and at a range of monasteries in western France respectively, have shown how such donations created a permanent relationship between institution and donor, one which might be renewed and reaffirmed in subsequent generations even, paradoxically, in what look like challenges by the original donors' kin to their ancestors' gifts.[25] The emphasis here – owing much to sociological and social anthropological modes of analysis – is on the transactional: the point made earlier, that property is by and large only perceptible when

---

[23] For the way in which 'booking' land changed the way in which property could be disposed of see P. Wormald, *How do we Know so Much about Anglo-Saxon Deerhurst?*, pp. 4–7; and for similar effects caused by royal gifts of land *in proprietate* see K. Leyser, 'The crisis of medieval Germany', in *idem*, *Communications and Power in Medieval Europe: The Gregorian Revolution and Beyond*, pp. 35–41.

[24] C. J. Wickham, *The Mountains and the City: The Tuscan Appennines in the Early Middle Ages*, pp. 262–5; see also the more general discussion in ch. 7, 'The distribution of land-ownership and the cycles of gift-giving', especially pp. 191–7, 210–15.

[25] Rosenwein, *To Be the Neighbor of St Peter*, esp. pp. 47–8, 202–7; S. D. White, *Custom, Kinship and Gifts to Saints*, pp. 151–76; see also *idem*, '*Pactum . . . legem vincit, et amor iudicium*: the settlement of disputes by compromise in eleventh-century western France', *American Journal of Legal History*, 22 (1978), pp. 302–3.

its status changes, is turned to the historian's advantage by a kind of intellectual ju-jitsu.

Yet there are some difficulties in simply transferring such an analysis to the donations Meinwerk secured for Paderborn. The networks built up by monasteries in Tuscany, Burgundy and western France – and no doubt elsewhere – have a simple explanation: monasteries were weak in public, institutionalized power, but strong in the charisma provided by prayer and relics and in the service offered by commemoration of the dead. The social and political networks they established by reiterated and reciprocal property transactions helped to protect monastic wealth; their weakness in conventional political terms was a positive advantage. Bishoprics, by contrast, certainly had more of the charisma provided by prayer and relics in most of pre-Gregorian Europe than we might *a priori* suppose, but they were hardly unthreatening in the way that monasteries were. Bishops were public figures, with a role-model which had traditions going back at least to the sixth century: spiritual leader, judge, centre of a territorially defined community.[26] And in the Ottonian and Salian *Reich* many bishops acquired public powers going even beyond this late antique tradition. Meinwerk was prominent among them. In the course of his pontificate he acquired the comital rights of four counts over several counties for his bishopric.[27] Besides these he also received other rights and grants of

---

[26] E. Magnou-Nortier, 'Les Évêques et la paix dans l'espace franc (VIe–XIe siècles)', in *L'Évêque dans l'histoire de l'église*; E. A. James, '*Beati pacifici*: bishops and the law in sixth-century Gaul', in J. Bossy (ed.), *Disputes and Settlements*; W. Hartmann, 'Der Bischof als Richter. Zum geistlichen Gericht über kriminelle Vergehen von Laien im früheren Mittelalter', *Römische Historische Mitteilungen*, 28 (1986); K.-F. Werner, 'Observations sur le rôle des évêques dans le mouvement de paix aux Xe et XIe siècles', in *Medievalia Christiana XIe–XIIe siècles. Hommage à Raymonde Foreville*. Several of the articles in T. Head and R. Landes (eds.), *The Peace of God: Social Violence and Religious Response in France around the Year 1000*, also bear on the topic.

[27] To the comital rights of uncertain nature and extent which Paderborn is known to have held in the tenth century (confirmed in D O III 387 [1001] and D H II 45 [1002]), Meinwerk added the following: Hahold's comital rights in various places, granted by D H II 225 (1011), confirmed in D H II 344 (1016); Dodico's *comitatus* in the Hessigau, the Nethegau and the Niddergau, granted by D H II 439 (1020), regranted to the archbishop of Mainz following Conrad II's accession and restored in 1033 (D C II 198); Liudolf's comital rights south of Paderborn (Henry II's diploma is known only from a summary in *VM*, ch. 172; the income from the grant was to be used to maintain the church of Paderborn, rather in the way that the Merovingian and Carolingian grants of immunity discussed by Paul Fouracre above, pp. 68–76, were to fund lighting); Hermann's *comitatus* in the Augau, Nethegau and Hessengau (D C II 178). For further details see Bannasch, *Bistum Paderborn*, pp. 306–20; F. Irsigler, 'Bischof Meinwerk, Graf Dodiko und Warburg: Herrschaft, Wirtschaft und Gesellschaft des hohen Mittelalters im

land.[28] True, there was a blip in his relations with rulers during
the last years of Henry II's reign and the early years of Conrad
II's. Henry II's authority appears, perhaps as a result of his
illness, to have declined somewhat from about 1021–2 (though
this may in part be an optical illusion caused by the end of
Thietmar of Merseburg's *Chronicon* in 1018); certainly grants to
Meinwerk ran thin in these years. Conrad II's accession in 1024
had something of the flavour of a general election which the
opposition unexpectedly won, and Meinwerk was unusual not
so much in falling from favour as in being able to recover it
fairly quickly.[29]

Notwithstanding such fluctuations, Meinwerk was a king's
man, someone who could be trusted not only to hold a bishopric
but also to build it up. At the time of the appointment both
Meinwerk and Henry II agreed to put substantial resources into
the bishopric, which, though not a rich one, still occupied a key
position on the important transit corridor between the royal
core-land of east Saxony and that around the Meuse and lower
Rhine.[30] As the ruler of a bishopric which was a powerful force
in its own right in eastern Westfalia, he might be supposed to
have threatened precisely that circle of potential donors from
which, as we shall see shortly, he profited, and to have done
so in two different ways. The first of these lies in the set of
phenomena known to historians as the 'Ottonian–Salian imperial
church (system)'. This implies the use by rulers of prelates as
instruments of 'central' government. Grants of royal rights to

---

östlichen Westfalen', *Westfälische Zeitschrift*, pp. 126–7 (1976–7); H. Hoffmann, 'Grafschaften in Bischofshand', *Deutsches Archiv für Erforschung des Mittelalters*, 46 (1990), pp. 426–30.

[28] Bannasch, *Bistum Paderborn*, pp. 334–5, summarizes the 21 grants of land (in some
cases Henry II and Conrad II were merely giving necessary royal sanction to private
donations). D C II 178 (see n. 27) granted not only comital rights but also royal
expectations of reversions and confiscations, on which see K. Leyser, 'Crisis',
pp. 35–41.

[29] For the loss and restoration of favour see Bannasch, *Bistum Paderborn*, pp. 192–202 and
the narrative in D C II 198 of 1033 restoring Dodico's county to Paderborn after its
temporary alienation to Mainz (drawn on by *VM*, ch. 198): 'mutato regno mutatis etiam,
ut solet, amicis et consiliariis [with the change in rule being accompanied, as usual, by
a change in the ruler's friends and counsellors]'. I intend to discuss Conrad II's election
at greater length elsewhere.

[30] For the terminology of 'core-lands' and 'transit zones' and the modern view of the functioning of the royal *iter* which lies behind them, see now the valuable summary in J. W.
Bernhardt, *Itinerant Kingship and Royal Monasteries in Early Medieval Germany, c. 936–1075*,
pp. 3–84.

prelates of the kind just seen were made with greater security precisely because prelates were appointed by the ruler and their position was not heritable. They were – so runs the theory – established as a kind of counter-weight to local lay aristocratic power, and local aristocrats might be expected to have resented them accordingly.[31] The second potential threat Meinwerk posed to his local lay magnates lay in 'territorialization' (or at least a 'territorial policy', *Territorialpolitik*). Beginning in the late tenth and early eleventh century German magnates – not only bishops but others – began to turn the sum of their wealth and powers into a lordship which was greater than its component parts and extended over lands they did not themselves own.[32] These two potential sources of tension between bishops and lay magnates, though conceptually separable, are clearly interlinked: grants by rulers of 'public' powers to prelates could and did form an important component of nascent ecclesiastical territories, while eleventh-century rulers apparently tried to discourage lay territorial concentrations of power either by placing various kinds of obstacle in the way or by promoting magnates to offices elsewhere in the *Reich* and thus shifting the focus of their interests.[33]

The question whether the donations to Paderborn really ran counter to such *a priori* expectations about the relations between Meinwerk and local magnates can be resolved only by a closer look at the transactors and the transactions. The transactors come from a wide social range, though it is not always easy to pinpoint them socially or to assign them to family groupings, and the editing of the notices inserted in *VM*, where this can be identified, also suggests caution.[34] There were very prominent nobles among the donors, though it would appear that many of the most important families of the region are not represented.[35] Clerics, nuns and noble

---

[31] The traditional view is set out and criticized in T. Reuter, 'The "imperial church system" of the Ottonian and Salian rulers: a reconsideration', *Journal of Ecclesiastical History*, 33 (1982), pp. 360–4; for the subsequent controversy see Bernhardt, *Itinerant Kingship*, pp. 26–35, and the forthcoming paper by Rudolf Schieffer in the proceedings of the Düsseldorf Academy.

[32] T. Mayer, *Fürsten und Staat*, is the classic statement; for a fine English-language survey of the problematic and its historiography, see B. Arnold, *Princes and Territories in Medieval Germany*, pp. 61–73.

[33] S. Weinfurter, 'Die Zentralisierung der Herrschaftsgewalt im Reich durch Kaiser Heinrich II.', *Historisches Jahrbuch*, 106 (1986), pp. 271–85.

[34] See Appendix 2, pp. 194–5.

[35] See Bannasch, *Bistum Paderborn*, pp. 269, 326–7, and below at n. 100.

women acted through an advocate, since they were not legally competent to act for themselves;[36] nobles, free men and *pauperes* could act on their own behalf. The great majority of the notices dealing with gifts also refer to the consent of an heir or heirs, normally termed 'most rightful', occasionally 'legitimate', 'sole' or 'basic'.[37] Fewer than 30 per cent of the heirs are not qualified by one of these adjectives, and the 'originals' do not suggest that there was any twelfth-century reworking in this respect. Where it is not explicitly said that X is Y's heir then the text usually states the relationship to the donor of those who consent, which implicitly identifies them as heirs. Many of the notices recording the consent or agreement of the heir or heirs, and a few which do not, also refer to the consent of the donor's wife.[38] The circle of relatives who appear as heirs is a small one. Apart from males or females described simply as heirs, we find sons, daughters, sisters, brothers, and also mothers; there are also one niece, one father and, most remarkably, one wife.[39] Only a minority of the transactions record the consent of more than one heir, and of these again only a minority record heirs who are related to the donors in different ways.[40]

The great majority of notices purport to record straightforward gifts of various combinations of lands, rights and people to the church of Paderborn. These range in size from the huge gifts of counties with associated large-scale estates by Hahold, Dodico

---

[36] E.g. nos. 5 (cleric Folcmar), 11 (nun Haburg), 83 and 84 (widow Fretherun). Where advocates are not mentioned for such people, their named heirs presumably acted for them.

[37] The standard formula, found in about 70 per cent of the notices mentioning heirs, is *iustissimus heres*, appropriately inflected; *legitimus* occurs in nos. 23 and 55, *primitiva* in no. 19, and *unica* in no. 80.

[38] The wife consents with other heirs in nos. 2, 20, 25, 26, 34, 41, 42, 45, 65, 67, 68, 73, and alone in nos. 27, 33, 50, 62, 69, 77 (a reconciliation).

[39] Mother: nos. 19, 45, 53, 56, 65, 82, 95, 96; niece: no. 29; father: no. 24. The wife appears in no. 67: 'cum consilio et uoluntate iustę heredis suimet uxoris' in the *RHW* version, which *VM* smooths to 'cum consilio et voluntate uxoris suę et heredum suorum'. A wife who was also an heir ought probably to have been within the prohibited degrees of relationship, but the *RHW* text is clear and unmistakable, and there is no strong reason to accept the clarification offered by *VM*.

[40] Multiple heirs in nos. 3, 4, 6, 16, 19, 23, 34, 42, 46, 48, 49, 51, 58, 67, 73, 85, 87, 88, 95 and 96. Generally the heirs are either of unspecified relationship or all of the same specified grade, but in no. 19 we find a mother and a brother, in no. 46 a brother and a son, in no. 95 a mother and a related advocate and in no. 96 a mother and two sons. The list of heirs not of the same grade might be extended by including advocates (see above, n. 36).

and Sigebodo, all members of the Hahold clan, down to gifts of a few parcels of land or *mancipia*.[41] Normally the notices specify more or less precisely what the donors gave and where it lay, and name witnesses to the transaction.[42] A number of them state that the gift is made from pious motives, usually for the salvation of the donors' souls and those of their relatives.[43] Very occasionally the gifts contain additional clauses which explicitly exclude named lands or people from the gift which might otherwise have fallen under the notice's more general formulation.[44] The gifts are mostly made outright, but in a few cases the donors retain an interest of a life or lives in the property given.[45] The notices also usually list what was given in return by the bishop, and often seem concerned to use vocabulary which implies that there is no necessary or automatic connection between the gift and the counter-gift: the bishop gives the counter-gift 'for a reward' or 'moved by pity'.[46] The counter-gifts normally go to the donors, but sometimes to other consenting parties.[47] The counter-gifts are also very varied: they include money, horses, arms, furs and other valuable items of clothing, cloth and food.[48] Slightly less common, though still frequent, are counter-gifts of people, of rights from land and churches, of lands and estates – usually made as benefice or *precaria* for a life or lives.[49] Only very occasionally are such

---

[41] For the Haholding gifts see Bannasch, *Bistum Paderborn*, pp. 52–69, 260–5, and Irsigler, 'Bischof Meinwerk, Graf Dodiko und Warburg'. As examples of small gifts take no. 60 (2 *pueri*) or no. 62 (*unum agrum*).

[42] The 'originals' all have witnesses; where they are absent in *VM* this is presumably the result of twelfth-century abbreviation.

[43] Seven for the souls of the giver(s) alone; twelve for their souls and those of their relatives; three, nos. 29, 36, 83 (though not no. 84) for specified relatives. Six donations mention the sins of the donors.

[44] Nos. 19 and 24 except named serfs or ministerials; nos. 43 and 85 except lands (no. 43 for life only).

[45] Nos. 19, 42, 43, 51, 62, 79; the details are not always clear.

[46] *Misericordia motus*: nos. 2, 3, 13, 18, 24, 34, 44, 50, 64, 79, 87; *pro mercede*: nos. 3, 7, 37, 50, 52, 64, 85, 87, 94.

[47] To wives: nos. 2, 31, 45, 57, 65; to heirs: nos. 3, 7, 12, 14, 15, 56, 88 (here to them alone).

[48] For details see Irsigler, '*Divites* und *pauperes*', pp. 463–74. Note also what was said above at n. 16 about the possibility that apparently one-off gifts may in reality have been annual rents.

[49] Gifts of people: nos. 3, 5, 10, 24, 40, 47, 76, 77, 81, 83, 84 (*familias*, i.e. family units); nos. 60, 78 (individuals, including a cleric!). Gifts of churches: nos. 8, 9. Gifts of lands and rights: nos. 1, 3, 5, 7–9, 11–13, 16, 40, 42, 44, 46, 47, 51, 55 etc. There is no sharp line visible between grants of income from land (presumably earmarked through the episcopal treasury) and grants of estates with control – the confusion is most evident

things as anniversaries, prayers or confraternity with the church
of Paderborn mentioned.[50]

   Much of this is the common currency of any collection of similar
material in Western Europe between the ninth and the twelfth
centuries (when land transactions start to be described using more
juristically precise and differentiated vocabulary), though there are
a few deviations from what is usual elsewhere. The main difficulties
lie not in interpreting the technical meaning of the transactions,
but in determining their social meaning. This is easiest for the
specialized transactions. Leaving aside the pure witness lists,[51] we
have at one end of the spectrum a few public records of cash payments and some straight sales, to be distinguished from the far
more numerous transactions which might be interpreted as sales,
to be discussed shortly.[52] These are, seemingly, pure cash affairs.
At the other end of the scale there is a strong welfare element
visible. In four transactions poverty is explicitly mentioned as a
reason for the transfer, though all are presented as gifts to which
wife and/or heir(s) consent.[53] Several others appear to have had
the primary or secondary purpose of providing pensions for wives,
concubines and mothers.[54] Women in particular made donations
in return for life rents of varying sizes, ranging from a huge one in

---

in the lack of clarity about whether it is ploughlands (*aratra*) or the tithes (secular or
ecclesiastical?) due from ploughlands (*aratra decimationis* or *aratra decimationum*) which are
being given. Except for no. 65, all such grants were made for a life or lives; there seems
to have been a distinction made between precarial tenure and beneficial tenure (cf. no.
1 in the *RHW* version: 'non in precariam sed in beneficium'), but this has been blurred
by the twelfth-century editing, which has eliminated almost all references to precarial
tenure. The distinction may have lain in the obligations attached: a *precaria* was perhaps
a mere temporary alienation, while a *beneficium* carried services with it (cf. nos. 15, 42,
92, and also no. 24: 'beneficium . . . sine servitio').

[50] Nos. 1, 5, 7, 19, 20, 24, 108.

[51] Nos. 108, 113–15.

[52] No. 100 says of two *predia* 'gravi pecunia . . . acquisivit'; no. 101 uses 'comparavit' for a
transaction in which two 'families' are bought for seven ounces of gold and three pounds
of pennies. 'Comparando' is also mentioned as one method in the multiple summary, no.
102. Other transactions may simply look like sales because of editing or terseness, e.g.
no. 90, which begins 'De Embriki domnę Ibican dedit episcopus X malder
decimationum. . .'. Nos. 2, 35, 59–60, 77, 81, 86, 88 deal with public gifts of money to
an intermediary to make payment on behalf of the bishop to the ultimate recipient,
though we are not necessarily always dealing with sales here.

[53] Nos. 67–70.

[54] Nos. 9, 53, 54, 83/84 provide for annual rents for a mother, a mother, a concubine and
a daughter respectively; note also nos. 47 and 70, with annual rents for a man and his
daughter and a man and his son respectively. No. 56, which grants a man a life-rent,
explicitly excludes his consenting mother; did close or consenting relatives perhaps normally expect to have such pensions continued during their lifetimes, if the donor pre-
deceased them?

return for a huge gift of three estates made by the widow Fretherun down to much more modest arrangements.[55] Evidently we are dealing here with the economic and legal protection which Meinwerk could provide, particularly visible in an exchange where a woman is granted among other things a house in Paderborn and lands to go with it in return for the gift of an estate.[56]

Four of the transactions represent in effect payments of fines.[57] Thietmar Billung, brother of Duke Bernard II, was fined thirty shillings for his plundering of the treasury of Herford, and paid by giving an estate; one Sigibodo offended 'by chance more than was just' against the church and also compounded for his offence with an estate; Meinwerk paid homicide-fines for three men who gave themselves and their property to Paderborn in return; and he used the opportunity of a charge of sacrilege to reclaim a benefice which had become hereditary. Interestingly, three of these payments were presented as gifts, with the usual accompanying consent of wife and/or heirs; in the case of the reclaimed benefice there was even an additional donation matched by a counter-gift.[58] The bishop's spiritual jurisdiction is revealed here as in effect an important source of revenue and means of social control, though it had to be made socially acceptable by disguising the element of coercion involved.[59] A rather larger number of notices deal with occasions on which property transactions were challenged by the kin of the original donors.[60] Occasionally it is simply said that they resigned their claims. More usually the sweetener is mentioned which induced them to do so. Such payments were usually on a smaller scale than those made in connection with original grants, but they could be very large indeed: Bern, who challenged the donations made by his relatives, the Haholding counts Dodico and Sigebodo, was given eighty-three pounds for a 'full reconciliation'.[61] A

---

[55] Nos. 83 and 84 (two versions of the same transaction, one presumably superseding the other) record Fretherun's gift in 1018 of three estates, countered by gifts of two estates (no. 83) or of an enormous annual food-rent supplemented by tithes, serfs and ploughlands (no. 84); no. 53 deals with much smaller life-rents for a Tiedi and his mother Wilburga in return for a gift of 70 fields and two farmhouses.

[56] No. 96.

[57] Compare the examples discussed by Wendy Davies, above, pp. 139–41.

[58] Nos. 71 (Thietmar Billung), 72 (homicides), 73 (Sigebodo) and 74 (the reclaimed benefice with additional gift and counter-gift).

[59] See below at nn. 102–6 for lay resentment of spiritual jurisdiction.

[60] For a list see n. 91.

[61] Nos. 106, 107. The 83 pounds consisted of 20 ounces of gold, 46 pounds of silver, a *pallium* (strictly, a bishop's stole; here a cloak, or perhaps a tapestry) worth 4 pounds,

noticeably higher proportion of these quitclaims is datable than of the original grants, and it is striking how many fall between about 1022 and about 1028, the period when, as we have seen, Meinwerk for various reasons lacked backing at court.[62]

The bulk of the transactions, however, are not so easily categorized and interpreted. There are virtually no hints about the point in the life-cycle at which the donors made their gifts, for example, even when the counter-gift includes an element of social security provision.[63] Some may have been intended to bind lands to a particular branch of a kindred; some may simply have sought to increase the donors' landed wealth during their own lifetimes.[64] The very lack of detail means, however, that we should not assume that these homogeneous-looking transactions all had homogeneous backgrounds. Yet the collection considered as a whole rather than as isolated transactions leaves a very strong impression: that we are here in very many cases dealing with what are in effect sales, however varied the stories which may lie behind them. When a counter-gift consists not just of one fur but of several, not just of one horse but of several, when items of value are also given a cash equivalent, or when the list of items is summed to a total in pounds, then the natural inference is that we are dealing with something like an equivalent value of the property given, not a mere symbol.[65] Moreover, several of those transactions where the counter-gifts are relatively small amounts of money, food and clothing might look more like sales if the sums mentioned were really meant to be annual rents rather than once-off gifts.[66] We should also take into account the non-material benefits which will have accompanied most such transactions: at least the friendship and goodwill of the

---

and 30 mares, followed by a further payment of 2 pounds of silver and 2 ounces of gold, said to be 'all that was promised except for 2 talents [pounds]'.

[62] No. 23 is datable to 1020–36, no. 81 to the span 1027–36 (probably at the beginning), no. 82 to 1024, no. 98/99 to 1026, nos. 106/7 to 1022–3, no. 108 to 1024, no. 109 to 1024, nos. 110 and 111 to 1030. See above at n. 29 for the background.

[63] Exceptions: no. 38 makes provision for possible future children; no. 20 was made after the death of Count Dodico's only son.

[64] For the first possibility, see above at nn. 21ff.; for the second see e.g. Dodico's donation, no. 20.

[65] E.g. nos. 22, 50 where the value of a *pallium* (see n. 61) is given in pounds; nos. 13, 88 and 94 where a money sum is said to be made up of 'gold and silver and horses [in no. 94]'; and the numerous transactions where the counter-gift consists of a number of items, e.g. nos. 49 (an ermine cloak, 2 horses, 22 shillings), 76 (a long list beginning '2 families [of serfs], 2 horses, 2 oxen, 2 cows, 10 sheep. . .'), 106 (details given above, n. 61).

[66] See above at n. 16.

bishop and the cathedral chapter, even if formal fraternity was rare.[67]

Yet to call the transactions sales and leave it at that would be to miss several points. The most important is that the kind of distinction between gifts and sales which perhaps begins to be possible for economically more advanced areas like northern Italy or juridically more advanced areas like twelfth-century Burgundy is misleading for rural Saxony in the early eleventh century. The distinction between sales and gifts has much exercised historians of the post-Carolingian era, but on the whole they have concentrated on the *legal* aspects – are gift formulas being used to disguise sales (or in some cases vice versa)? – while assuming that the distinction itself presents no conceptual difficulties.[68] Yet in the kind of society we are dealing with here, the anonymity and absence of ongoing relations between the partners implicit in the modern contrast between a sale and a gift is meaningless:[69] you do not sell to your enemies or people whom you do not know any more than you give to them. The contrast between an asymmetrical gift-relationship and a symmetrical sale-relationship is also pretty meaningless here: on the one hand there was no market to set prices, which is why the cautious phrasing 'something like an equivalent value' was used above, while on the other hand the gift in our modern sense of a voluntary and free act which expects no return and creates no obligations did not really exist. Though churchmen might proclaim an ideology of the free gift made for love, they needed to do so precisely because their world expected gifts either to be matched by counter-gifts or to create obligations, 'gift debt', as it were.[70] The gift–counter-gift nexus does not

---

[67] Implicit in some of the transactions conducted by clerics, but for laymen mentioned only in no. 24.

[68] E. Z. Tabuteau, *Transfers of Property in Eleventh-Century Norman Law*, pp. 28–30, with references (pp. 287–8) to the discussions by French legal historians; C. B. Bouchard, *Holy Entrepreneurs. Cistercians, Knights, and Economic Exchange in Twelfth-Century Burgundy*, pp. 56–65.

[69] *Pace* Bouchard, *Holy Entrepreneurs*, p. 64. The two concepts are, of course, ideal types for our own world as well – consider, for example, relationships between large-scale suppliers and their purchasers, inherently long-term rather than one-off, or the offers of 'free gifts' from perfect strangers which pour through our letter-boxes.

[70] Notoriously, the reinterpretation of many such transactions as simoniacal in the generation after Meinwerk's death was to create serious tensions between ecclesiastics and their aristocratic clients.

have to be a free exchange between equals, and may be just as much a means of exploitation as can sales and purchases by a dominant producer or consumer in a modern market economy.[71] On the other hand, the 'price' set in sales is likely to vary with the status of the participants.[72] The contemporary distinction, in other words, is more between transactions with an explicit and those with an implicit return: in a sale, this is stipulated at the time, whereas with a gift the return is left to the recipient, who will operate, however, under rules known to both parties. There is no reason to suppose that Meinwerk's counter-gifts were spontaneous, that donors did not know what they were going to get in return before they made their gifts.[73] But there was a widespread feeling that selling (as opposed to the exchange of gift and counter-gift) was inappropriate behaviour for those who considered themselves to be free or of higher status – in other words for the social stratum which provided the bulk of Meinwerk's donors. Even transactions which were functionally sales – meaning that contemporaries might have interpreted them as sales *and* that we would see in them an exchange of broadly equivalent values – will tend to be presented as gift–counter-gift exchanges under such circumstances: hence the way in which the formulas of the notices appear to lay stress on the absence of any connection between gift and counter-gift.[74]

---

[71] See W. I. Miller, *Humiliation; and Other Essays on Honor, Social Discomfiture, and Violence*, pp. 15–51, 210 n. 5 and 212 n. 47, and R. Samson, 'Economic anthropology and vikings', and 'Fighting with silver: rethinking trading, raiding, and hoarding', in *idem* (ed.), *Social Approaches to Viking Studies*, for an analysis of the role of gifts in exploitation and asymmetrical relationships.

[72] This is the implication of much of the ethnographic literature, applied convincingly and coherently to the evidence for contemporary Iceland by W. I. Miller, *Bloodtaking and Peacemaking. Feud, Law and Society in Saga Iceland*, pp. 77–109. Direct confirmation from the *VM* material is hard to produce, since precise and comparable measurements are not given either for lands or for counter-gifts. In two exchanges involving a farm-house and twenty *agri*, a *pauper* received a house, a pig, a pound, five bushels of corn and two linen cloths (no. 69) whereas a *liber* received a horse, twelve shillings, two linen cloths, two pigs and six bushels (no. 31); the minor discrepancies do not suggest any exploitation of the *pauper*'s weakness. But it would appear that counter-gifts matched to some extent the *status* of the recipients, with gold, furs and horses going to nobles and victuals and clothing to those less well-off.

[73] On the tendency of many medieval rituals to be publicly presented as spontaneous and uncalculated even when their details had been carefully worked out in advance see G. Althoff, 'Demonstration und Inszenierung. Spielregeln der Kommunikation in mittelalterlicher Öffentlichkeit', *Frühmittelalterliche Studien*, 27 (1993).

[74] See above at n. 46.

Whatever lay behind individual land sales – possibilities include the need to pay off debts (perhaps incurred as royal or episcopal fines) or to balance income deficiencies, as well as a simple desire to realize assets either for conspicuous consumption or to deal with temporary cash-flow problems – they were not unproblematic. The rules of inheritance in Saxony at this time – as in much of Europe – seem to have allowed not only claims by very distant relatives but also 'reverse inheritance' by fathers and especially by mothers. This may not have led to inheritance claims by maternal kin, but it could certainly give them a potential interest in the disposal of property. It would have taken the four horsemen of the Apocalypse to render Saxon land-holders so heirless as to be able to dispose of their land without having to take anyone else into account.[75] The purchaser thus had to be in a position not only to provide something like a selling price but also to give the transaction a form which was socially acceptable for heirs – and wives, who, as we have seen, also had interests in the matter.[76] It seems plausible to suppose that this could more easily be done by a person or body whose power and authority were of a different kind from that possessed by the donors.

Could Meinwerk and his church have provided both the selling price and the legitimation for the transaction? Clearly the resources were there. The transactions themselves show how easily Meinwerk could draw on liquid assets and use them to oil social and political relations. Franz Irsigler has given an impressive summary of the movable wealth employed by Meinwerk as recorded in these transactions.[77] The sheer size of episcopal lands and the continuity of episcopal administration – unlike lay landed wealth, not subject to continual disruption by partible inheritance – will have helped to create surplus wealth. Moreover, Paderborn, though hardly a town of the first rank even by North European standards, was the only significant urban centre within the diocese. Irsigler has offered a view of Meinwerk as an up-to-date and economically aware prelate who derived from the now flourishing urban

---

[75] Leyser, 'Crisis', p. 38, discusses the reversion of 'heirless' land to the king; this, however, is not allodial land but land originating as royal grant, to which quite different rules applied.

[76] See above at n. 38.

[77] Irsigler, '*Divites* und *pauperes*', p. 464: 103 lb in pennies, 117 lb of gold and silver, 113 talents (monetary pounds), 32 ounces of gold and 9 marks.

and mercantile centre of Paderborn the furs, swords and other luxury goods with which he enticed the members of the local elites, and there is obviously something in this.[78] Yet Meinwerk the entrepreneur may take second place to Meinwerk the bishop. Many of these luxury goods – the swords and furs in particular – were not consumer goods in the sense that they needed constant replacement. They were long-lived enough to circulate as wealth; but we have good evidence, starting with rulers and reaching some way down the social spectrum, that whatever claims, legitimate or otherwise, heirs might make on immovable wealth they could do little to prevent the old, the pious and the dying from disposing of their movable wealth as they wished.[79] VM itself provides a good illustration of this in the anecdote about a practical joke played by Henry II on Meinwerk which led the bishop to suppose that he would die in five days: he immediately took steps to have all Paderborn's movable wealth distributed among the churches and the poor, and forced Henry to make restitution on a large scale when the deception was exposed.[80] The bishops of Paderborn may thus have received many of the valuables they dispensed among their clientele through testamentary donations rather than from merchants, and could presumably expect some of their gifts to return by the same route in due course.

What is less easy to establish is the relationship between the size of this wealth and that of lay wealth. On the one hand we have the example already adduced of Thietmar Billung, a duke's brother allegedly unable to pay the thirty *solidi* needed for a fine and having to do so by presenting Paderborn with an estate.[81] On the other hand we have Meinwerk himself, the second son of a family less prominent (though correspondingly less widely spread) than the Billungs, who was nevertheless able to endow his bishopric with

[78] *Ibid.*, pp. 464–72.

[79] For the Carolingians see T. Reuter, 'Plunder and tribute in the Carolingian Empire', *Transactions of the Royal Historical Society*, 35 (1985), p. 80; for the wills of Kings Alfred and Eadred and of Bishop Ælfwold of Crediton see P. H. Sawyer, *Anglo-Saxon Charters: An Annotated List and Bibliography*, nos. 1507, 1515, 1492.

[80] *VM*, ch. 187, pp. 107–8.

[81] No. 71. Problems of poverty or cash-flow may have lain behind this, but need not have done. The Billungs might have chosen land rather than cash either because it was less humiliating (the narrative makes it clear that Thietmar was fined, but presents the gift of land as a pious grant) or even because they expected to go on holding the land in benefice.

vast tracts of land.[82] We also have the recipients of Meinwerk's largesse themselves. Bern, who was given eighty-three pounds in cash (a sum so large that apparently even Meinwerk could not find it all at once) was presumably, for a time at least, wealthy; and that sum was handed over by Meinwerk merely to secure a 'reconciliation', not for an original grant, though the grants were very large and important indeed.[83] Yet by implication this was only a part of Meinwerk's income; and a bishopric like Paderborn supported a noble life-style not just for its bishop but for the members of its cathedral chapter. Its resources are probably better compared with those of a major noble kindred; but unlike the wealth of, say, the Billungs or the counts of Werl, it was concentrated and focussed on an institution, rather than being dispersed among many members of a kindred.

If we turn to the legitimation of these transactions, it is evident that monasteries and bishoprics enjoyed a special position as regards gifts of land.[84] There is plenty of evidence from all parts of Europe in the Carolingian and post-Carolingian eras that gifts to churches were challenged by donors' contemporary or later kin, but these challenges were rarely if ever made on a level of fundamental principle. Members of a kindred claimed that they had not been consulted, or that their rights had not been respected; they did not claim that the gift could not or should not under any circumstances have been made. If they wanted to go further and nullify the grant completely they had to resort to what their clerical opponents called usurpation; to enter into legal proceedings, whether formal or informal, was in effect to acknowledge that the gift was legitimate. If they were lucky or powerful or both, they had their claims acknowledged; but the acknowledgements took

---

[82] See above at n. 4. Hoffmann, *Mönchskönig*, p. 69 n. 163, is rightly sceptical about the figure of 1100 *mansi* named by *VM*, ch. 29, p. 33; but the endowment was clearly substantial.

[83] Nos. 106–7.

[84] Cf. also *Lex Saxonum*, cc. 61–2, in *Leges Saxonum und Lex Thuringorum*, ed. C. von Schwerin, p. 32: 'Traditiones et venditiones omnes legitime stabiles permaneant [all donations and sales made lawfully shall stand]' but 'Nulli liceat traditionem hereditatis suae facere praeter ad ecclesiam vel regi ut heredem suum exheredem faciat, nisi forte famis necessitate coactus . . . mancipia liceat illi dare ac vendere [No one is allowed to make a gift of his inheritance, except to the king or to a church, so as to make his heir an ex-heir, unless compelled by hunger . . . but he may give or sell serfs]'. It is a very moot point just how far this represents ninth-century, let alone eleventh-century, Saxon law in detail, but as a general statement of principle it is significant.

forms which did not call the gift as such in question.[85] Of course, there is the danger of optical illusion here: successful challenges using brute force have inevitably left no mark in charters, and hence no charter record of what the challengers said and thought – the occasional stories of cynical or contemptuous remarks made by laymen about such gifts may suggest that not everyone took the church's role as universal heir lying down. Nevertheless, enough donations were apparently never challenged for us to be able to conclude that they could be seen, and frequently were seen, as wholly legitimate.

Even though Meinwerk thus had the material and ideological resources to act as land-broker for local magnates this still does not explain why they were willing to turn to him: why choose a bishopric to give or sell land to when its bishop was wielding increasing amounts of public power and building up a powerful position in the region, especially as there were monasteries available which posed no such threat? Yet it is in fact more difficult to find signs that Meinwerk's public power was a potential threat to local magnates than one might expect. The gifts of comital powers from rulers and of lands from the nobles and free men of the dioceses do not seem to have been welded together to 'territorialize' the now much more extensive possessions of the bishopric.[86] Nothing suggests that Meinwerk used his counter-gifts of precarial and beneficial land rights to get rid of outlying lands and create a more consolidated territory centred on Paderborn itself. Counter-grants (e.g. of 'top-up' estates given on a life interest basis together with the original grant) are frequently located close to the original grant.[87] This is notably true of the transactions which made up Meinwerk's single most spectacular gain, the securing of the Dodico inheritance.[88] Where they are not close to the land granted they are just as likely to be the reverse of consolidatory: gifts of

---

[85] See the references given above, n. 25.

[86] Bannasch, *Bistum Paderborn*, pp. 289–97, discusses the evidence for the reorganization of estate management under Meinwerk. It is very inconclusive, and probably coloured by the twelfth-century conditions familiar to its author.

[87] Cf. especially nos. 13, 24, 45, where the counter-gift is said to lie in 'neighbouring places' (*finitimis locis*). The statement above is necessarily impressionistic, however; a full mapping would be very time-consuming (and in view of the uncertainty about many of the locations difficult to realize).

[88] No. 20; see Irsigler, 'Bischof Meinwerk, Graf Dodiko und Warburg', pp. 189–92 and map 2. Of course, Meinwerk may here have intended that Dodico should carry out the necessary administrative reorganization before all the estates reverted to Paderborn.

outlying lands find a response in counter-gifts of lands close to Paderborn.[89] Hints at territorial conflicts are not wholly absent. *VM* and related contemporary material offer glimpses at the kind of exchanges between bishops and magnates we should expect in demarcation conflicts: prolonged disputes; killings or maimings of dependants carried out in a deliberately insulting manner.[90] Yet given the potential for such conflicts it is probably more surprising how scarce such hints are. There are indeed 'reconciliations' (settlements made after an earlier grant had been challenged), and the smooth stories of 'reconciliation' offered by *VM* are no doubt misleading: it is hard to suppose that Meinwerk's habitual and immediate reaction to challenges was 'Sorry, forgot about you; would a few ounces of gold be all right?'[91] But there does not seem to have been much territorial thinking behind the challenges. Indeed, it is not at all clear that all land rights were of such a kind as to lend themselves to territorial organization: tenth- and early eleventh-century Saxon aristocrats often look more like *rentiers* than landlords, living off income from land and other things rather than from the power which went with controlling the production of that income. This contrasts with their West Frankish contemporaries, many of whom were developing the *seigneurie banale* at about this time.[92]

Most striking of all is the relationship between the grants of comital rights and the *VM* private charter material. Since the latter stretches over the whole of Meinwerk's pontificate one would expect his steady acquisition of comital rights to have left traces in it, but there are none that I can see. Carolingian precedents, if these still had any meaning in early

---

[89] E.g. no. 96, a house in Paderborn itself with 30 *aratra* attached, or no. 5 (though here the recipient is a member of Meinwerk's cathedral chapter).

[90] For Meinwerk's relations with Thietmar Billung see nos. 71, 108; for his property disputes with the prominent Paderborn *miles* Godebold see nos. 78 and 80, the latter showing us the other episcopal *milites* intervening to restore peace. See also below at n. 104.

[91] For the challenges and reconciliations see nos. 23, 77–8, 81, 82, 86, 89, 98 and 99, 106, 108–10.

[92] K. Leyser, 'Henry I and the beginnings of the Saxon Empire', in *idem, Medieval Germany and its Neighbours, 900–1250*, pp. 23–4, 41–2. *VM* records numerous counter-gifts of *decimatio* (possibly tithes, but possibly also secular rents) by Meinwerk, and the term *aratrum decimationis* (tithings on a carucate) is so frequent as to make one wonder whether it is meant even when *VM* only records gifts of *aratra*. For the *seigneurie banale* in West Francia see the discussion by Chris Wickham, below, pp. 221–3, and the Conclusion, below, pp. 246–7, as well as J.-P. Poly and E. Bournazel, *The Feudal Transformation, 900–1200*, pp. 25–38.

eleven-century Saxony, required transactions involving landed property to have been made in the *mallus* of the count in whose *pagus* the lands being granted lay, but this model hardly ever seems to work.[93] There are only three references to a *mallus* in the whole of the *VM* material, and all three are to that of Paderborn's advocate, Amalung.[94] Counts normally witness in twos or threes, often in much greater numbers, though some mere nobles may have been turned into counts by Meinwerk's biographer.[95] Sometimes it is clear that the transaction was carried out and witnessed at a royal assembly.[96] Other witness lists may well represent occasions on which Meinwerk was surrounded by those who actually held his counties – as a bishop he could not act as count in person, and had to appoint someone to do the task.[97] But we are hardly dealing with a comital *mallus* where counts are present in force; much more likely venues are a feast held at the centre of an episcopal estate, or else an episcopal synod (diocesan or provincial).[98] What the charter material does not reveal, in other words, is Meinwerk touring his diocese and visiting his newly acquired counties now being

---

[93] *MGH Capit.*, vol. 1, no. 39, ch. 6, pp. 113–14 (*Capitulare legibus additum, 803*); no. 139, ch. 6, p. 282 (*Capitulare legibus addenda, 818–19*). Neither specifically mention the *mallus*, only the need for *legitimi testes* at such transactions; but since they lay down different modes of proceeding for donations within and without the donors' county, the implication is clear enough.

[94] All in the same transaction, no. 15. There are several other transactions (nos. 44, 45, 74, 85 and, arguably, 64) which are said to have taken place 'in presentia X comitis et aliorum multorum' or some similar formula, but it would be going quite far to deduce a comital *mallus* from these, given the possibility of abbreviation by the author of *VM*.

[95] See below at n. 120.

[96] E.g. no. 26 (witnessed by eight counts at Mühlhausen in 1024); no. 75 (witnessed by fifteen counts in the royal *curtis* at Merseburg); no. 82 (witnessed by ten counts together with the advocate of Hildesheim and, very unusually, a woman, the Lady Sophia, abbess of Quedlinburg).

[97] Hoffmann, 'Grafschaften im Bischofshand', pp. 461–2; A. Erler, 'Ecclesia non sitit sanguinem', in A. Erler (ed.) *Handwörterbuch zur Deutschen Rechtsgeschichte*, vol. 1, *Aachen – Haustür*.

[98] The transactions rarely record either a day or a place; of the few which give a location, nos. 6, 23, 27, 63 and 78 are located on episcopal estates (nos. 23 and 27 at the Warburg, the centre of the lordship acquired from Dodico). Nos. 6 and 78, significantly, are dated on or close to the date of the reconsecration of the cathedral (15 September, cf. *VM*, ch. 29, p. 33), which would have been a major event in Paderborn's calendar. One may envisage regular exchanges of hospitality between Meinwerk and his comital clients which will have left few traces in our sources; but note that the key episode in Meinwerk's difficult relationship with the local saintly hermit, Heimerad, took place at a *convivium* held by Count Dodico (*VM*, ch. 13, p. 21).

run for him as going concerns by local magnates. Comital rights may have brought him cash, but not, apparently, jurisdiction.[99]

This may help to explain the absence of a strong sense of rivalry between Meinwerk and his local nobles. It is true that hardly any members of the really big families in the region around Paderborn can be identified as making gifts to the church.[100] Yet that does not imply rivalry or hostility, for the Billungs, the counts of Werl and Northeim and the rest turn up with great regularity as witnesses in the notices, and that implies that they participated in the annual round of church festivals centred on Paderborn and the greater episcopal estates and centres. If they do not appear as making gifts and/or selling land to Paderborn, it was probably because they had no need to: most of them will have been *milites* of the church already, and so have enjoyed the spiritual and material benefits of association with it, including benefices granted for service rather than as part of a counter-gift, something hardly touched on in the charter material.[101] There were specific points of conflict, as for example in the feud between Thietmar Billung and Meinwerk or in the various challenges made to grants, almost all of which seem to have come from members of the greater nobility. But these did not preclude essentially good relations between lay nobles of the diocese and the bishop.

The kind of jurisdiction most frequently seen exercised by Meinwerk and his contemporary bishops is not secular but spiritual, and it is here that we find the clearest evidence of conflict between bishops and lay nobles. Bishops could use spiritual jurisdiction in the course of conflicts with lay nobles over monasteries and other rights, especially as lay nobles, though they might feud fairly brutally against their own kind without much risk, were open to severe

---

[99] Hoffmann, 'Grafschaften in Bischofshand', concluded that this was the normal result of grants of comital rights to prelates in Germany before the mid-eleventh century.

[100] See above, n. 35.

[101] *VM*, ch. 14, p. 23, relates how Bernard II Billung was granted the duchy of Saxony on Meinwerk's intervention, and became his faithful man, thus providing an *exemplum* to illustrate the ideal form of the relationship. Details are otherwise sparse in the Paderborn evidence: no. 41 mentions a benefice granted for military service; no. 80 shows how the *milites* of Paderborn reconciled Meinwerk with his *miles* Godebold. See on the relationship Reuter, '*Filii matris nostrae*'.

penalties if they tried to treat prelates in this way.[102] It was Thietmar Billung's dispute with Meinwerk over the monastery of Helmarshausen, among other things, which led to his defiant plundering of Herford and subsequent humiliation at a diocesan synod.[103] There was a rash of such disputes between lay magnates and bishops in Saxony in the late 1010s and early 1020s, in some of which Meinwerk was involved.[104] Bishops in the *Reich* also challenged the validity of what they saw as incestuous marriages on a number of occasions in the early eleventh century, and on several of these occasions they were evidently encouraged to do so by the ruler.[105] These aspects of episcopal authority were sufficiently resented to be openly challenged at the diocesan synod held by Godehard of Hildesheim in 1025, immediately after the accession of Conrad II. The lay nobles at the synod, led incidentally by Meinwerk's opponents, Bernard II Billung and his brother Thietmar, were determined not to accept ecclesiastical punishments which touched either their honour or their property: they intended to keep their boots on.[106] Yet though episcopal authority and jurisdiction might in these special contexts be used against local magnates, and might even be used with the ruler's encouragement and backing to further the ruler's own purposes, there is little link visible between this kind of power and the territorial power of the bishop.

One issue remains: why make donations to a bishopric rather than to monasteries? Of course it is not a case of either/or: the kindreds which gave to the royal monastery of Corvey in this period, for example, overlapped with those found in *VM*.[107] But

---

[102] T. Reuter, 'Unruhestiftung, Fehde, Rebellion, Widerstand: Gewalt und Frieden in der Politik der Salierzeit', in S. Weinfurter (ed.), *Die Salier und das Reich*, vol. 3, *Gesellschaftlicher und ideengeschichtlicher Wandel im Reich der Salier*, pp. 308–9.

[103] See no. 71 and the commentary in *VM*, ch. 158, pp. 82–3; for the background see Bannasch, *Bistum Paderborn*, pp. 50, 179, who sees the attack as the product an inheritance dispute between Thietmar and his sister Godesti, abbess of Herford.

[104] Reuter, 'Unruhestiftung', p. 309; Leyser, 'Crisis', pp. 27–8.

[105] See Hoffmann, *Mönchskönig*, pp. 52–5, for some of these cases; he rightly points out that their interpretation as deliberate anti-aristocratic policy is problematic, since more often than not the intervention could not be made to stick.

[106] The account was discovered by Hans-Joachim Schuffels of Göttingen in an early modern copy of a more extensive version of the *Vita prior* of Godehard of Hildesheim than that published in *MGH SS*, vol. 11, pp. 167–95; he has drawn on it in a number of conference papers, but, regrettably, has so far not published it. For bishops' imitation of the royal ritual of *deditio*, in which rebels acknowledged submission by entering the ruler's presence barefoot and in sackcloth and ashes, see Reuter, '*Filii matris nostrae*'.

[107] L. Schütte, *Die alten Mönchslisten und die Traditionen von Corvey*, vol. 2, *Indices und andere Hilfsmittel, passim*.

bishoprics did in fact have certain attractions. Royal control of episcopal elections and the concomitant tendency to appoint bishops from outside the diocese offered potential donors a certain guarantee that Paderborn would not be held permanently by members of a hostile family. Local family monasteries were not attractive as institutions to donate to except to the founding kindred and its clients, while royal monasteries were not only rare in the region but probably could not provide the resources which were so important for Meinwerk's transactions, or at least not on the same scale: the contemporary series of *traditiones* for Corvey consequently show a series of much smaller gifts with a strong welfare element to the transactions in that the gifts in effect provided for the upkeep of a monk, whose entry was purchased in this way by his kin.[108]

VM and its related material provide us – incidentally but convincingly enough – with an ecology of the relationship between royal and episcopal power. From his twelfth-century perspective Conrad of Abdinghof repeatedly stressed how Meinwerk sedulously served rulers and sought their goodwill in order to win favours in return. But the sedulous service lay in feeding and attending the itinerant royal court, and in providing contingents of troops.[109] Neither Meinwerk nor his biographer saw royal service as lying in control of the bishop's own region. This should not surprise us. The model by which a ruler merely establishes a bishop in a particular locality and then expects him to function independently as a reliable official has evident flaws: if the ruler's power is so great that he can do this, why the need of an intermediary? Conversely, if episcopal power is so established that its wielder can act independently as a pillar of royal government, why should he bother to do so?[110] But a model which takes symbiosis on board begins to look more plausible: the ruler can do certain things for his bishops (not least provide the protection which goes with royal goodwill), and vice versa, so that there are pay-offs for both sides. This explains behaviour in terms of self-interest as well as in terms of loyalty or

---

[108] K. Honselmann (ed.), *Die alten Mönchslisten und die Traditionen von Corvey*, pp. 71–82.

[109] For references to Meinwerk's *iuge servitium, sedulum obsequium*, and similar phrases in royal service see *VM*, cc. 12, 144 (by implication), 166, 168, 198, 202, 205, 207, 215–16, 218, pp. 20–1, 76, 91, 94, 114, 117, 119, 120, 127–8, 131. Frequently, Conrad of Abdinghof drew here on the phraseology of contemporary royal diplomata.

[110] P. Johanek, 'Die Erzbischöfe von Hamburg-Bremen in der Salierzeit', in S. Weinfurter (ed.), *Die Salier und das Reich*, vol. 2, *Die Reichskirche in der Salierzeit*, pp. 83–4, 100–3.

policy (drives and impulses not to be neglected, but hardly in themselves enough to sustain structures permanently). It also explains why property grants start to look fragile and reversible precisely at those moments at which symbiosis breaks down. It is when there is no ruler or when the links between prelate and ruler are cut, as in Henry II's final illness-laden years and the opening of Conrad II's reign, that grants to Paderborn are most likely to be challenged.[111] Equally, it is at the beginning of Conrad II's reign – partly because of the political uncertainty produced by a change of ruler, partly perhaps because Conrad II was genuinely less predisposed to favour the episcopate than his predecessor had been – that the authority of bishops *as bishops* is openly and consciously challenged by lay magnates.[112]

This link between aristocratic–episcopal relations and the macro-political climate incidentally confirms that both the property transactions and the challenges to them could be something more than merely symbolic: to pick an unfavourable time for Meinwerk suggests a genuine attempt to make the challenges stick, or at the very least a desire to maximize returns. *VM* and its related material are unusual here in providing us with a narrative context, which may suggest that where – as for example with contemporary Cluny – we have charters alone with little or no surrounding narrative we may be too ready to provide static, functionalist, symbolic interpretations of challenges which better-informed contemporaries might have been able to explain in terms of the ebb and flow of regional politics. As we have seen, however, it would be quite wrong to take the challenges as showing fundamental antagonism between bishop and lay magnates: the relationship between the two was just as symbiotic as that between bishop and ruler. Curiously, rivalry with other bishops, notably those of Mainz and Cologne, is as least as visible in *VM* as that with lay magnates. The inherent territoriality of a diocese is clearly visible here; such competition as existed was with similar structures rather than the much less coherent and diffusely focussed ones of lay lordship.[113]

The Paderborn material is undoubtedly slippery considered as

---

[111] See above at n. 62. For a possible parallel in contemporary Wessex compare the 'reaction' following Edgar's death: P. Stafford, *Unification and Conquest*, pp. 57–9.

[112] For the Billungs' challenge see above at n. 106; for Conrad II's and Henry II's relations with episcopate and lay nobility see Hoffmann, *Mönchskönig*, pp. 137–44.

[113] Bannasch, *Bistum Paderborn*, pp. 22–6, 262–3, 268–9, 315.

records of property ownership. The notices do not appear to vary very much, but behind them may lie very different foregoings and outcomes. Charters, in other words, need examination as narrative sources, even though the narratives they offer are often very fragmentary. This makes them individually unclear, not in the sense that they are incomprehensible, but rather in the sense that the transactions recorded in most of the notices might have been points in one of several quite different narratives. They acquire a much more certain and definite meaning when encountered in bulk: the sum of all these property transactions and their fragmentary contexts shows Meinwerk to have been a powerful magnate. But powerful in what sense? His power is best defined as location at the centre of the network of social exchanges which made up a diocesan community. That means that it was not in the first instance power which could be used to dominate other power holders, either in Meinwerk's own interests or on behalf of the rulers on whom Meinwerk depended. Meinwerk's very large resource-base and his special position as a bishop allowed him rather to dominate (in a different, more metaphorical sense) the network. The resources and the special position allowed conspicuous consumption in the form of church building, monastic foundations, and no doubt elaborate church ceremonial accompanied by ritual *convivia*; in other words, the local exercise of patronage and generosity on a large scale which kept Meinwerk's network of aristocratic clients happy.[114] They also supported the royal service needed to retain royal favour and protection.[115] In other words, the main effect of Meinwerk's resources was to maintain their own existence, but in doing so they also maintained the existence of a bishop and his bishopric as an institution and as a community.

This might not seem much; but pre-Gregorian bishoprics would hardly stand alone as historical examples of institutions whose energies were largely devoted to self-perpetuation. Moreover, if we look beyond the Westfalian horizon, interesting comparisons become possible. Bishops in post-Carolingian Europe have on the whole been less intensively studied than either reformed

---

[114] See above at n. 98, and for the church building (with concomitant feasts and gift-exchange at crucial points, especially the dedication) see also Bannasch, *Bistum Paderborn*, pp. 229–50, 252–6 and G. Mietke, *Die Bautätigkeit Bischof Meinwerks von Paderborn und die frühchristliche und byzantinische Architektur.*

[115] See above at n. 109.

monasteries or their lay patrons; and yet the bishop and his diocese
showed a remarkable degree of homogeneity across the whole of
Europe, far greater than that found in institutions called 'king' or
'count'. Contemporary southern French bishops engaged in the
early Peace of God movements might at first sight look very different from their late Ottonian colleagues in Saxony (or in Wessex)
exercising a not very precisely defined mixture of secular and spiritual jurisdiction over their aristocratically dominated diocesan
communities.[116] But within varying socio-political environments
they were all exploiting the potential of the episcopal role-model
defined above. It was this unique position which enabled bishops
to move between the two sides of the $e = mc^2$ equation, converting
property into a kind of power and back again.

APPENDIX 2: SURVIVING NOTICES OF PROPERTY TRANSACTIONS FROM MEINWERK'S PONTIFICATE

Well over a hundred notices of various kinds of transaction between the
bishop and members of his diocese involving lands and movable property
are included in *VM* as cc. 31–129. About forty of these notices also survive
independently as originals along with a handful of originals not included
in *VM*; these have been separately edited, for the most part in *RHW*.[117]
A few have survived as isolated copies in eleventh-century manuscripts
from Paderborn and Abdinghof or in late medieval and early modern
Paderborn cartularies. 'Originals' is here used as a term of convenience
for notices written in contemporary hands on scraps of parchment, normally one but occasionally more per scrap, sometimes with dorsal notices
or addenda.[118] Since, as explained above, such notices had no primary
legal force, to say that they are 'originals' means only this: that these
scraps of parchment represent the first occasion on which the transaction
was recorded in writing; and that this occasion was roughly contemporary
with the transaction.[119] In *VM* the 'originals' have often been reworked
in various ways: witness lists are sometimes abbreviated;[120] the status
of participants is sometimes deliberately or accidentally changed or

---

[116] See above at nn. 26, 102ff.; and for Wessex, P. Stafford, *Unification and Conquest: A Political and Social History of England in the Tenth and Eleventh Centuries*, pp. 167–8.

[117] See above, p. 165, n.1.

[118] Nos. 31 and 57–60 are all entered on a single sheet of parchment, as are nos. 94 and 96, and nos. 98 and 99. Nos. 77 and 101 have dorsal notices referring to the transactions (see above at n. 12).

[119] That is clear enough from the palaeography of the notices; whether the notices were written down before, at the time of, or following the public transfer of property which defined the transaction itself is not normally clear.

[120] Compare, for example, the two versions of no. 6.

misinterpreted;[121] occasionally we are presented with information not in the 'originals' or with discrepancies between the *VM* version and the 'original' (which of course makes the reliability of those notices found only in *VM* a little problematic).[122]

Most of the notices in *VM* are undatable and could hardly have been dated by Conrad of Abdinghof, who nevertheless offers a chronological framework for them: Meinwerk's endowment of the bishopric with much of his own *hereditas* early in his pontificate and his rebuilding and rededication of the cathedral church in 1015 following a fire are presented as inspiring a series of donations from others.[123] This dating-point has generally been followed by modern historians, but it is not in fact a compelling assumption that no donations were made before 1015; some at least of the notices might well belong to the period 1009–15, or even to the end of the pontificate of Meinwerk's predecessor Rethar, since the bishop is not always named in them.[124] The following list makes no attempt to establish a chronology, simply giving the notices in their order in *VM* (with references where appropriate to the originals as edited in *RHW*), followed by a few stragglers not found in *VM*.

1	*VM*, ch. 31	
2	*VM*, ch. 32	(*RHW*, no. 87,1)
3	*VM*, ch. 33	
4	*VM*, ch. 34	
5	*VM*, ch. 35	
6	*VM*, ch. 36	(*RHW*, no. 87,2)
7	*VM*, ch. 37	(*RHW*, no. 87,3)
8	*VM*, ch. 38	

---

[121] Bannasch, *Bistum Paderborn*, pp. 274–5.

[122] Tenckhoff (*VM*, e.g. pp. 35 n. 7, 52 n. 5, 62 nn. 3 and 6) and Honselmann (*Carta*, p. 57) appear to have thought that at least in some cases there existed as well as the 'original' a fuller but now lost contemporary charter drawn on by *VM*. Yet in spite of some discrepancies not always easily explained there is still no reason to treat these notices as preparations for the production of 'real' charters; they are not to be compared with the *Vorakte* of the St Gallen charters, which are brief notices of a transaction written on the margin of the charter by the *cancellarius*, often in shorthand. See on these *Die Vorakte der älteren St Galler Urkunden*, ed. A. Bruckner, and also D. P. Blok, *De oudste particuliere oorkonden van het klooster Werden*, pp. 89–121, who discusses parallels elsewhere.

[123] *VM*, ch. 29, pp. 33–4, introducing the series of notices of property-transactions, cc. 30–129. Within the series, however, the notices are grouped according to the status of the donors (clerics, women, nobles, others), followed by groups recording particular kinds of transaction: gift-sales enforced by poverty (nos. 67–70), and then a series of transactions many of which include references to later disputes of the gift or to secular or ecclesiastical fines as the occasion for the transfer of property (*VM* 100–28). See Bannasch, *Bistum Paderborn*, pp. 270–3, on the ordering.

[124] A point well made by Bannasch, *Bistum Paderborn*, p. 170 n. 107, and 'Fälscher aus Frömmigkeit', pp. 230–3, though he assumes that the notices ascribed to Meinwerk's pontificate are indeed to be dated to within it.

9	*VM*, ch. 39	(*RHW*, no. 87,4)
10	*VM*, ch. 40	
11	*VM*, ch. 41	
12	*VM*, ch. 42	
13	*VM*, ch. 43	
14	*VM*, ch. 44	
15	*VM*, ch. 45	
16	*VM*, ch. 46	
17	*VM*, ch. 47	
18	*VM*, ch. 48	(*RHW*, no. 87,5)
19	*VM*, ch. 49	(*RHW*, no. 95)
20	*VM*, ch. 50	(*RHW*, no. 96)[125]
21	*VM*, ch. 51	
22	*VM*, ch. 52	
23	*VM*, ch. 53	
24	*VM*, ch. 54	
25	*VM*, ch. 55	
26	*VM*, ch. 56	
27	*VM*, ch. 57	
28	*VM*, ch. 58	
29	*VM*, ch. 59	(*RHW*, no. 87,6)
30	*VM*, ch. 60	
31	*VM*, ch. 61	(*RHW*, no. 87,7a)[126]
32	*VM*, ch. 62	
33	*VM*, ch. 63	(*RHW*, no. 87,8)
34	*VM*, ch. 64(a)	
35	*VM*, ch. 64(b)	(*RHW*, no. 87,9)[127]
36	*VM*, ch. 65	
37	*VM*, ch. 66	(*RHW*, no. 87,10)
38	*VM*, ch. 67	
39	*VM*, ch. 68	
40	*VM*, ch. 69	(*RHW*, no. 87,11)
41	*VM*, ch. 70	
42	*VM*, ch. 71	
43	*VM*, ch. 72	(*RHW*, no. 87,12)
44	*VM*, ch. 73	
45	*VM*, ch. 74	
46	*VM*, ch. 75	(*RHW*, no. 87,13)
47	*VM*, ch. 76	

---

[125] The version in *RHW* also survives only as a copy.

[126] *RHW*, no. 87,7a–e are all entered on the same piece of parchment, though they are quite separate notices. This first one itself concerns three separate transactions.

[127] *VM*, ch. 64 records a sale of land and the subsequent sending of a further sum of money entrusted to a messenger before witnesses; only this second transaction is noticed in *RHW*, 87,9.

48	*VM*, ch. 77	(*RHW*, no. 87,14)
49	*VM*, ch. 78	
50	*VM*, ch. 79	(*RHW*, no. 87,15)
51	*VM*, ch. 80	
52	*VM*, ch. 81	(*RHW*, no. 87,16)
53	*VM*, ch. 82	
54	*VM*, ch. 83	
55	*VM*, ch. 84	(*RHW*, no. 87,17)
56	*VM*, ch. 85	
57	*VM*, ch. 86	(*RHW*, no. 87,7b)
58	*VM*, ch. 87	(*RHW*, no. 87,7c)
59	*VM*, ch. 88	(*RHW*, no. 87,7d)
60	*VM*, ch. 89	(*RHW*, no. 87,7e)
61	*VM*, ch. 90	(Diekamp, *Supplement*, no. 703)[128]
62	*VM*, ch. 91	
63	*VM*, ch. 92	
64	*VM*, ch. 93	(*RHW*, no. 87,18)
65	*VM*, ch. 94	(*RHW*, no. 108)[129]
66	*VM*, ch. 95	
67	*VM*, ch. 96	(*RHW*, no. 87,19)
68	*VM*, ch. 97	
69	*VM*, ch. 98	
70	*VM*, ch. 99	
71	*VM*, ch. 100	(*RHW*, no. 87,20)
72	*VM*, ch. 101[130]	
73	*VM*, ch. 102	
74	*VM*, ch. 103	
75	*VM*, ch. 104	
76	*VM*, ch. 105	
77	*VM*, ch. 106	(*RHW*, no. 87,21)
78	*VM*, ch. 107	
79	*VM*, ch. 108	(*MGH SS*, vol. 11, p. 129, n. 39)[131]
80	*VM*, ch. 109	

[128] The original, printed by Diekamp, is badly damaged and legible only in part.

[129] The version in *RHW* also survives only as a copy.

[130] Three men make themselves over to Paderborn to avoid the consequences of a homicide; Meinwerk lawfully reconciles them with their enemies and pays the blood-price. Honselmann, *Carta*, p. 46, makes this into two notices, but there seems no strong reason to assume this.

[131] A copy in the eleventh-century Abdinghof Evangeliary, which appears to have tried to transform the notice into a charter recording the grant as if made by the Hoda who in the notice appears as challenging the grant made by his mother: it begins like a charter, 'In nomine domini nostri Ihesu Christi Meginwercus Paterbrunnensis sedis Dei gratia presul. Omnibus presentibus et futuris volumus notum fieri, qualiter . . .', and one would expect it to continue in the first person, but it then shifts to the third person 'Episcopus autem Meinwercus ob illam reconciliationem. . .'.

81	*VM*, ch. 110	
82	*VM*, ch. 111	
83	*VM*, ch. 112	
84	*VM*, ch. 113	
85	*VM*, ch. 114	
86	*VM*, ch. 115	
87	*VM*, ch. 116	(*RHW*, no. 87,22)
88	*VM*, ch. 117	
89	*VM*, ch. 118	
90	*VM*, ch. 119	
91	*VM*, ch. 120	(*RHW*, no. 87,23)
92	*VM*, ch. 121	
93	*VM*, ch. 122	(*RHW*, no. 87,24)
94	*VM*, ch. 123	(*RHW*, no. 87,25a)
95	*VM*, ch. 124	(*RHW*, no. 87,26)
96	*VM*, ch. 125(a)	(*RHW*, no. 87,25b)
97	*VM*, ch. 125(b)[132]	
98	*VM*, ch. 126(a)	(*RHW*, no. 113a)[133]
99	*VM*, ch. 126(b)	(*RHW*, no. 113b)
100	*VM*, ch. 127	
101	*VM*, ch. 128	(*RHW*, no. 87,27)
102	*VM*, ch. 129[134]	
103	*VM*, ch. 134 (first part)	
104	*VM*, ch. 136	
105	*VM*, ch. 137	
106	*VM*, ch. 173[135]	
107	*VM*, ch. 174	
108	*VM*, ch. 195	(Honselmann, *Carta*, no. 27)[136]
109	*RHW*, no. 107	(summarized *VM*, ch. 202)
110	*VM*, ch. 203[137]	
111	*VM*, ch. 204[138]	
112	*VM*, ch. 208[139]	

[132] The final sentence of *VM*, ch. 125, does not correspond to anything in *RHW*, 87,25b.

[133] As these two notices, though found on the same piece of parchment, are clearly separated by a space and by a change of ink, they have been numbered separately here.

[134] A list summarizing at least twelve traditions.

[135] This and the following chapter appear to summarize at least one notice of a reconciliation following an attempt to dispute nos. 19 and 20.

[136] A witness list which follows Diekamp, *Supplement*, no. 735, on the same piece of parchment and is entitled 'De testibus adfuerunt ad Uuerla de Helmu(uar)desh(usun)' (but is not the same as no. 113); see Honselmann, *Carta*, p. 58 and n. 56, who argues that it was drawn up at the Saxons' meeting at Werla in 1024 to discuss the succession to Henry II. The account in *VM*, ch. 195, presumably drew on it.

[137] A transaction recorded in D C II 157.

[138] A transaction also involving Conrad II, though no diploma of his has survived for it.

[139] A gift and exchange by one Wittilo; since royal land was involved, the transaction is recorded in a diploma (D C II 171).

113   *RHW*, no. 93a[140]
114   Diekamp, *Supplement*, no. 734[141]
115   *ibid.*, no. 735[142]
116   Honselmann, *Carta*, no. 19[143]
117   *ibid.*, no. 20[144]
118   D C II 198, appendix[145]

[140] A witness list with the note 'De abbatia Helmwwardesh'; to be taken in conjunction with D H II 371. The three originals *RHW*, 87,28–30 are to be dated later than Meinwerk's pontificate.

[141] A contemporary witness list beginning 'Willice O. . . eorum complices. . .'; Münster, Staatsarchiv, Fürstbistum Paderborn, Urkunde 44.

[142] A contemporary and fragmentary witness list; Münster, Staatsarchiv, Fürstbistum Paderborn, Urkunde 43.

[143] There is a puzzle here which I have not been able to resolve. This and the following notice are mentioned by Honselmann, *Carta*, p. 167, in his table of charters from the diocese of Paderborn (nos. 19, 20). He describes them as originals, but refers to a seventeenth-century ms. (Paderborn, Theodorianum, Pa. 77 1, pp. 34 and 35). Though the table gives references to the discussion in his text, there is no mention of these charters on the pages cited, or, so far as I can see, elsewhere in the book.

[144] See n. 142.

[145] Münster, Staatsarchiv, Fürstbistum Paderborn, Urkunde 43, a badly preserved fragment of what appears to be a charter of Meinwerk's; the few surviving words correspond largely to the text of D C II 198, and it may be that the fragment represents a draft of D C II 198 provided for the imperial notaries, though it could also be a charter of Meinwerk's on the same subject, the restoration of a county which had been taken from Paderborn at the beginning of Conrad's reign and given to Mainz.

CHAPTER 8

Monastic exemptions in tenth- and eleventh-century Byzantium

Rosemary Morris

The nature of Byzantine exemptions has long been the subject of debate. In the recently published *Oxford Dictionary of Byzantium*, Mark Bartusis was suitably cautious in his entries on exemption and the word usually used to identify it: *exkousseia*. He identified two areas of controversy. Firstly, whether *exkousseia* should be identified with 'Western concepts of *immunity*', which 'always imply judicial immunity', or should simply be seen as 'a type of *exemption* from certain obligations of the state and from *introitus*, the entry of officials into estates'. As Bartusis put it: 'Some scholars in fact consider the application of the Western medieval concept of immunity to Byzantium as inappropriate and misleading and prefer the more limited concept of exemption'.[1] Secondly, given that *exkousseia* always involved freedom from *fiscal* burdens – so much is agreed – did it imply exemption from the *telos*, the totality of charges in cash and kind for which landowners were liable, or simply from the *epereiai*, a word used from the tenth century onwards to describe extraordinary state requisitions in cash or kind, usually required by state officials (especially the military) sent from Constantinople, but sometimes demanded by local administrators?[2]

The time is ripe for another look at the problem of *exkousseia*, not the least because, as this collection of essays demonstrates, it is not possible to assume that there was a single Western medieval concept of immunity which 'always' implied certain freedoms, but also because the publication of up-to-date editions and commentaries on many of the documents at the heart of the debate, has

---

[1] A. P. Kazhdan et al. (eds.), *Oxford Dictionary of Byzantium*, s.v. 'immunity'.
[2] *Oxford Dictionary of Byzantium*, s.v. '*exkousseia*'. There are various spellings of this word: *exkousseia; exkouseia; exkousia*, etc.

established much more certainty about the reliability of the texts and their dating as well as allowing the addition of more items to the dossier of evidence. In particular, documents from the archives of the monasteries on Mount Athos (particularly those of the Great Lavra and the Georgian Monastery of Iviron) and from that of the monastery of St John the Theologian on Patmos, are now available in much better editions than those commented upon by the earlier participants in the debate.[3] There is another important dimension, too. Efforts have been made, by examining the extent of the exemptions from the provision of goods and services attatched to many monastic documents of the eleventh century, to assess the political and economic effects of the withdrawal of such revenues, commodities and facilities from the control of the Byzantine state. Thus the study of exemptions has formed part of a much wider discussion about the nature and extent of central and regional power in the eleventh century; a debate in which the nuances of the evidence have often been obscured by their deployment in an increasingly theoretical debate.[4]

In examining the evidence, one simple point (often lost sight of) needs to be emphasized. Even in a state as traditionalist as Byzantium, fiscal and judicial arrangements, and the vocabulary used to describe them, themselves evolved. While it is clear that the concepts of both exemption and immunity were long established by the time of the Justinianic legal collections, the circumstances in which they were later applied varied. The nuances of ninth-century exemption terminology in the earliest available documents were not necessarily still relevant in the eleventh century; such terms as, for example, 'complete exemption' (*kathara exkousseia*) have to be traced over time. There is also another difficulty: that of diplomatic. It has been customary to interpret the long lists of exemptions found in eleventh-century documents as a sign of the widening scope of the institution. But this might have had more

---

[3] See *Actes d'Ivirôn*, vols. 1 and 2; *Actes de Lavra*, vol. 1 and *Actes du Prôtaton* for Athonite examples; *Byzantina Engrapha tes Mones Patmou* (hereafter *BEMP*), vols. 1 and 2 for Patmos.

[4] See G. Ostrogorsky, 'Pour l'histoire de l'immunité à Byzance', *Byzantion*, 28 (1958), H. Melovski, 'Einige Probleme der exkusseia', *Jahrbuch der österreichischen Byzantinistik*, 32/2 (1981), L. Maksimović in C. Schmitt et al., *Lexikon des Mittelalters*, vol. 4, pp. 392–3 and, most recently J. F. Haldon, 'The army and the economy: the allocation and redistribution of surplus wealth in the Byzantine state', *Mediterranean Historical Review* 7/2 (1992), pp. 146–51, repeated verbatim in 'Military administration and bureaucracy: state demands and private interests', *Byzantinische Forschungen*, 19 (1993), pp. 53–60.

to do with diplomatic practices than with judicial realities and we should be wary of *assuming* that formulas reflected reality. In the case of lists of exemptions, we surely have to look at each example and locate it both in time and in context.

In Roman law, there were two types of exemption: *excusatio* and *immunitas*. *Excusationes a muneribus* (exemptions from public services) were granted to specific groups, such as women, men under twenty or over seventy years of age, the fathers of three or more children and certain professional groups, teachers, physicians, veterans and *decuriones*. What they were freed from were *munera personalia*: the performance of personal services, such as serving in the army. Other kinds of *excusatio* included the *excusatio a tutela*, the exemption from the duty of guardianship which could be allowed in, for example, cases of poverty, illness or the possession of other tutorships.[5] The section in the *Digest* dealing with these matters, *De vacatione et excusatione munerum*, made it clear that exemption from *munera* was not permanent and had to be applied for each time a request was made for their performance. Two types of exemptions from *munera* were identified: 'full', if the exemption included release from military service, or 'partial' when dispensation from other *munera* was involved. In addition, no dispensations could be allowed from burdens which were imposed on property, such as 'a levy for making up a road', or the provision of *angarii* (billeting of soldiers) 'except for those to whom it has been granted by the emperor'.[6]

Excusatio, then, was a temporary exemption from a variety of public duties (taxation, military service, the perfomance of *corvées*, provision of goods and services, performance of personal duties) granted to certain groups or individuals by the emperor. The principles of *excusatio* enunciated in the *Digest* were repeated word for word in the late ninth-century Byzantine legal compilation of the *Basilika* and thus were well known in the period with which we are concerned.[7] But while the Byzantine Greek word *exkousseia* was obviously derived from the Latin *excusatio*, what it actually implied was much more akin to the exemptions described in Roman law under the heading of *immunitas*. For by *immunitas* was meant a

---

[5] A. Berger, *Encyclopedic Dictionary of Roman Law*, p. 461. See also Fouracre above, pp. 58–9.
[6] *Digest*, L.5.
[7] *Basilicorum libri lx, series A, Textus*, ed. H. J. Scheltema, D. Holwerda and N. van der Wal, LIV.5. For the contemporary use of the *Basilika*, see N. van der Wal and J. H. A. Lokin, *Historiae iuris graeco-romani delineatio*, pp. 81–7.

general exemption from specified taxes or public charges granted as a personal privilege to individuals, families or specific social groups, the most important of which, in the present context, was the immunity from the performance of *munera personalia* granted by Constantine the Great to the clergy, which also applied to monks. The *Digest*, in its section *De iure immunitatis*, declared that *immunitas*, though permanent when granted to individuals, was not automatically to be transmitted to their heirs; the exemption, to be passed on, had to have been specifically granted to the family or heirs and, even then, was not preserved in the female line. If, however, the *immunitas had* been generally granted, then 'it should last forever for successive generations'.[8] The differences between *excusatio* and *immunitas* need to be emphasized because they help to clarify the problem of defining the nature of *exkousseia*. Was the grant petitioned for or given on the imperial initiative? Was it permanent or temporary? Could it be passed on to heirs? The answers to all these questions can be of assistance in elucidating both the intention and the consequences of the grant.

With these caveats in mind, evidence about the process of exemption in the Middle Byzantine period (when the forms of taxation familiar from Late Rome – land tax, renders in cash or kind, extraodinary requisitions and services – could still be found) can now be discussed. It is necessary to focus on *monastic* exemption and *exkousseia* for two reasons. Firstly, because the majority of exemption lists have been preserved in monastic documents which, as is well known, have survived far better than those of Byzantine lay archives. Secondly, because it has been suggested that exemption by the imperial power from fiscal and judicial dues and jurisdictions was used particularly in the monastic context as a way of promoting and patronizing favoured religious houses, and this view needs to be debated. Here it is necessary to make clear that we are not dealing with the various *temporary* exemptions from taxation, particularly on land, which were a feature of the Byzantine fiscal system.[9] What is at issue here are permanent exemptions –

---

[8] *Digest*, L.6; see Berger, *Encyclopedic Dictionary*, p. 492.
[9] Land which had been abandoned, for example, was first of all granted a *sympatheia* or lessening of tax and then, after thirty years had elapsed, was declared to be *klasma* and was resold, at a low price by the state, see N. Oikonomides, 'Das Verfalland im 10. und 11. Jahrhundert: Verkauf und Besteuerung', *Fontes Minores*, vol. 7 (1986) and M. Kaplan, *Les hommes et la terre à Byzance du VIe au XIe siècle*, pp. 399–408. *Sympatheia* and *klasma* were routinely established by provincial tax officials after every fiscal survey and were

including *exkousseia* and *ateleia* (the word used in the *Basilika* to translate *immunitas*) – which could only be granted by the imperial power.

By the tenth century, complete exemption from taxes (the Roman *munera canonica*) had probably long been established as a method of patronizing churches and monasteries, which, in Byzantine law, were held to have legal *personae*. The process was akin to the Roman grant of *immunitas*. The so-called *Fiscal Treatise*, composed in the first half of the tenth century, explained the process of *logisima* by which lands might be completely or partially freed from taxes and all record of them struck out, erased or even literally torn out of the cadasters. This practice was long-standing: 'They [the *logisima*] came into existence in former times at the hands of long-deceased emperors and up to the reign of the wise Lord Leo [VI], as he is called.'[10]. Leo VI (886–912) instituted an inspection of all the *logisima* of the Empire and ordered them to be checked and noted in the documents of the government offices concerned. The *logisima* were of two main varieties: the *prokatespasmena logisima*, exemptions from paying taxes to the *demosion* (fisc) granted to specific institutions or individuals (an early and isolated example may have been the grant in 688 by Justinian II of salt-pans near Thessalonika to the church of St Demetrios in the city, free from all future taxation); and *solemnia logisima*, revenues from lands not owned by the individuals or establishments concerned which were diverted to them by the *demosion*. The author of the *Fiscal Treatise* indicated that they could replace the direct cash subsidies – the *solemnia*:

A *solemnion logisimon* is when the emperor, instead of a *solemnion* given to such-and-such a holy establishment, having been invited by the heads or the functionaries or monks in the holy establishment, [allows that] the same totality of the public revenue of village lands not subject to the same pious house is assigned and exempted, so that the exempted money is supplied by the villagers to that holy house instead of the tax collector by right of the foregoing *solemnion*.[11]

---

particularly to be found in areas which had suffered from barbarian attack, such as Macedonia at the end of the tenth century.

[10] For the *Fiscal Treatise* (also known as the *Marcian Treatise* from the sole manuscript's present location in the Marcian Library in Venice), see F. Dölger, *Beiträge zur Geschichte der byzantinischen Finanzverwaltung*, pp. 113–23 (Greek) and C. M. Brand, 'Two Byzantine treatises on taxation', *Traditio*, 25 (1967), pp. 48–57 (Eng. trans.), esp. pp. 117–18 (Dölger), 50–2 (Brand).

[11] *Fiscal Treatise*, pp. 117 (Dölger), 51 (Brand). See H. Grégoire, 'Un édit de l'empereur Justinien II', *Byzantion*, 17 (1944–5).

A third device was that of the *autourgon logisimon* (sometimes short-ened to *tourgon logisimon*), by which a monastery, though not for-mally exempted from taxation, was allowed to collect and keep its own taxes.[12]

Although the evidence of the *Fiscal Treatise* indicates that *logisima* were particularly intended to aid ecclesiastical institutions, the *Treat-ise* does mention *solemnia logisima* being granted to 'such and such a hostel or old people's home [two of the so-called *euages oikoi*] or mon-astery or church *or someone else*', clearly implying that these exemp-tions could be granted to the laity.[13] There are certainly eleventh-century examples where this was the case. An official copy in the archives of Iviron of an extract from a fiscal register dated to a little after December 1098, declared that the Emperor Alexios I Komn-enos (1081–1118) had assigned the tax payment of the whole of the village of Radolibos in Macedonia to one of its landowners, the widow Kale Pakouriane.[14] A similar case had occurred in 1086, when Alexios Komnenos assigned the fiscal revenues of the village of Chos-tiane, again in Macedonia, to the general Leo Kephalas.[15]

The *logisima* were thus devices for exempting favoured individ-uals and institutions from the payment of taxes or for diverting fiscal revenues in directions to which imperial largesse would almost certainly already have been forthcoming. They could be associated with an *exkousseia* from specific dues and services (as in the case of the Kephalas grant) but were clearly distinct from it. We should perhaps see them as the organization of imperial gifts of money by other, perhaps more convenient, means, since the diverting or remitting of tax revenues avoided the necessity of transporting quantities of gold over long distances, always a haz-ardous business. Although the process might be initiated by the beneficiaries, it was firmly in the hands of the emperor (as the *immunitas* had been in Roman times) and should be seen as one of the varied expressions of his *philanthropia*, an important aspect of the articulation of imperial power in the provinces.

---

[12] *Fiscal Treatise*, pp. 118 (Dölger), 52 (Brand).
[13] *Fiscal Treatise*, pp. 117 (Dölger), 50 (Brand).
[14] *Ivirôn*, vol. 2, no. 48 (after Dec. 1098). This was done according to the process known as *ekphonoumenon logisimon* – described in the *Fiscal Treatise*, pp. 117 (Dölger), 51 (Brand) – whereby the imperial official noted above the relevant entry in the *kathesis* (open register) of the logothete of the *genikon* (the bureau in charge of the cadasters and the collection of the land tax) that the tax on the property had been assigned to a named individual.
[15] *Lavra*, vol. 1, no. 48 (1086).

We should be wary, however, of too precise a characterization of the type of grant we are dealing with. In the early monastic archival material, it is often unclear from the context precisely what kind of exemption is at issue. For often the earliest surviving examples of monastic exemptions were phrased in general terms, and this raises the important question of whether they were all embracing or narrowly specific. The archives of Athos provide some interesting examples. The earliest extant document in the archives of the Protaton (the central organization of Athos), a *chrysoboullon sigillion* of Basil I dated to June 883, declares that no official or layman down to the humblest miller should 'vex' (μὴ ἐπηρεάσῃ) the monks of Athos and those of the nearby monastery of John Kolobos at Hierissos. What does this term mean? That they were freed from the extraordinary state requisitions and fiscal surcharges, such as fortress building, transport provisions, *corvées* (all *munera* in the Roman sense) or, as Denise Papachryssanthou the editor of the *Actes du Prôtaton* has maintained, that they were completely exempted from tax? Or, since the document also deals with squabbles over pasture rights on Athos with their lay neighbours, should we understand it to mean that the imperial officials 'from *strategoi* (provincial military governors) to the most humble office holder' were being urged to assist the monks to resist *these* particular 'vexations'?[16] It is not at all clear. A similar doubt must hang over an act of Leo VI of February 908, which again dealt with encroachments and, at the end, decreed that the monks of Athos should remain 'unharmed' (ἀπαρενοχλήτους) from any kind of *epereia*.[17] It is not until August 934, with a chrysobull of Romanos Lekapenos, that it looks as though *epereia* is definitely being used in a technical sense. A place called the *kathedra ton geronton* (lit. 'old mens' seats'), just beyond the boundary of Athos, was to be free from *epereia*, *angareia* and *zemia* (which we could now translate as 'fiscal charges', 'public *corvées*' and 'exactions') which might be imposed by civil or ecclesiastical authorities. The document implies that this had been the situation in the past by using the phrase 'free. . .as it has been until today', but, if this was the case, it had not been made explicitly clear in the previous two

---

[16] *Prôtaton*, no. 1 (883); see also p. 48.
[17] *Prôtaton*, no. 2 (908).

documents.[18] Are we then here dealing with a clarification in more precise 'bureaucratese' of an existing situation or the interpretation of the word *epereia* in a different and more precise sense? It is impossible to be sure.

What points can be made so far? Firstly, if *epereia* is taken to mean all fiscal burdens *including* land tax, then the whole of the holy mountain of Athos and at least one property nearby was free of it by the mid-tenth century. The problem, however, is that nowhere is this explicitly stated and the means by which this might have come about are not at all clear. But freedom from all *epereiai* and *kakoseis* (lit. 'evilnesses', usually with a tax connotation) *was* reasserted by Constantine IX Monomachos (1042–55) in his *Typikon* (Regulations) and confirmatory chrysobull for the Athonites, dating to 1045 and 1046 respectively, and we possess no documents indicating that taxes and dues were paid for lands on Athos itself.[19] Secondly, whatever freedom from *epereiai* did mean, it is clear that it only applied to the area within the boundary of the Holy Mountain while lands held by Athonite houses outside Athos were (unless exempted) subject to taxation and the imposition of dues and services. Thirdly, it is, unfortunately, impossible to establish whether the other contemporary holy mountains of Asia Minor were also exempted from taxation (or levies), since no documents establishing such privileges in this period have survived from their archives.[20]

It is, however, much easier to find examples of exemptions from dues and services over and above the land tax and here the word *exkousseia* or its derivatives comes to be used. Documents from the archives of Iviron show that these were certainly being granted by the middle of the tenth century. A chrysobull of the Emperor Constantine VII Porphyrogennetos of 945/6 (but only known from its mention in another of the mid-eleventh century), exempted the monastery of the Prodromos of Leontia near Thessalonika, its lands and the *paroikoi* (dependent peasants) already settled there from

---

[18] *Prôtaton*, no. 3 (934). There is some controversy about the nature of the *kathedra ton geronton*. Papachryssanthou, *Prôtaton*, pp. 111–14, believes that it was a small-holding once possessed by monks (the 'old men' of the name), but it may have been an early meeting place of Athonite hermits.

[19] *Prôtaton*, nos. 8 (1045) and 9 (1046).

[20] For the other holy mountains of this period see, R. Morris, *Monks and Laymen in Byzantium 843–1118*, ch. 1.

extraodinary state demands and also added a gift of thirty-six *ateleis paroikoi* (tenants who did not pay tax – *telos* – to the *demosion*), who were also to be freed from extra charges and services.[21] In the confirmation of these privileges, issued by the imperial official Theodore Kladon in September 975, it is made clear that these services included various *corvées* and the need to supply food to military personnel. But the gift was there referred to not as that of thirty-six *ateleis paroikoi* freed from extra dues, but that of thirty-six *oikoi exkoussatoi*, a rather different kettle of fish not the least because there is controversy about what this term actually meant. For the editors of the *Acts of Iviron*, *oikoi exkoussatoi* were households of peasant *landowners* who did pay land tax, but whose tax was assigned to a third party. Michel Kaplan has seen them simply as *demosiarioi paroikoi* 'exemptés de certains impôts (les surtaxes)'. The implications of the apparent transmogrification of individuals into households will shortly be discussed.[22]

A similar process took place both in 957–8, when a chrysobull of Constantine Porphyrogennetos (mentioned in the same eleventh-century list of privileges as that referred to above) granted an *exkousseia* for the property owned by the monastery *tou Athonos* on the peninsula of Kassandra (S. Chalkidike) and in 959–60, when Romanos II exempted forty *ateleis paroikoi* which he had given to the monastery of Kolobos at Hierissos and on its other properties, from (if a confirmatory document of 995 is to be believed) *kastroiktisia* (construction and upkeep of fortresses), *chorton* (supply of forage), *prosodion* (charges for the upkeep of military officials) and *metaton*.[23] In 974, the imperial official Symeon, issued a document allowing the Great Lavra on Athos thirty-two *paroikoi* (who from the context were already *ateleis*) exemption from all requisitions (*epereiai*).[24] It seems clear that, at this period at least, the

---

[21] *Ivirôn*, vol. 2, no. 32 (probably 1059). The word *exkous[s]eia* is explicitly used.

[22] *Ivirôn*, vol. 1, no. 2 (975). The charges concerned are *blabe, epereia, zemia, angareia, aplekton, metaton*. The nature of the *oikos exkoussatos* is discussed pp. 111–12; see Kaplan, *Les hommes et la terre*, p. 270, for further comments. The translation of *demosiarios paroikos* also causes difficulties. Kaplan, *ibid.*, p. 265, n. 267, points out that it could refer both to peasant proprietors and to those farming lands belonging to the fisc; what they had in common was that both groups owed payments to the *demosion*. A. Harvey, 'Peasant categories in the tenth and eleventh centuries', *Byzantine and Modern Greek Studies*, 14 (1990), pp. 251–2, deals with other types of *exkoussatoi*.

[23] *Ivirôn*, vol. 2, no. 32; *Ivirôn*, vol. 1, no. 8 (995) and p. 153 for the fiscal charges. The act of Romanos II of 959–60 is lost, but is again mentioned and dated in *Ivirôn*, vol. 2, no. 32.

[24] *Lavra*, vol. 1, no. 6 (974).

exemptions seem to have been granted in a fairly specific region. The Bulgar attacks of the end of the tenth century and the associated 'militarization' of the northern themes of the Empire to cope with the threat, meant that the Athonite monasteries may have sought to lessen the effect of military requisitions on their lands and their peasantry and the granting of these exemptions were a mark of their success in this regard. But the exemptions were probably both specific and limited.[25]

What were the effects of these kinds of exemptions? In economic terms, the earliest exemptions (even if they did include the land tax) were of no great significance to the fortunes of the *demosion*, for the revenue obtainable from the remote areas first sought out by the tenth-century lavriote monastic founders was negligible. Byzantine land tax was, after all, based on an assessment of the *quality* of the land. In some cases, difficult circumstances made the exemptions almost worthless. The thirty-six *ateleis paroikoi* or, more likely, *oikoi exkoussatoi* granted to the monastery of the Prodromos at Thessalonika in 945–6 could not be found by Theodore Kladon in 975, for the hearths had disappeared because of barbarian invasions. The monastery was allowed to search out thirty-six 'suitable hearths' from anywhere in the theme (administrative district) with which to replace them. This probably meant that they could select another thirty-six *oikoi* for exemption from those that they possessed. By this stage, the privilege clearly meant *households* rather than individuals, even if it had not originally done so and was thus rather more beneficial. The imperial aim here was to compensate favoured houses for the loss of privileges which had previously been granted, but which dangerous physical circumstances had rendered temporarily worthless.[26]

In the eleventh century, however, it has been argued, the practice of tax exemption took on a much more serious aspect, especially when it was applied to the large, fertile and economically flourishing areas which by then had come into monastic hands.

---

[25] See *Ivirôn* vol. 1, p. 153, where the military nature of these late tenth-century exemptions is discussed.

[26] See *Ivirôn*, vol. 1, no. 2 (975). The process by which the authorities of Iviron were supposed to 'recover' the 'lost' *oikoi exkoussatoi* has not been given the attention it deserves, *pace* Harvey, 'Peasant categories', p. 252. If the households could not be found, then the descendents of the original *exkoussatoi* of 945 would have been equally difficult to trace. Surely the implication is that the monastery was to be allowed to *select* thirty-six suitable *oikoi*, a privilege in itself.

It is in this period, too, that the exemptions reached their most wide-ranging and elaborate form. A series of imperial chrysobulls, mostly concerning monastic houses, list the fiscal (and judicial) exemptions in much longer and more varied detail than anything found in the tenth century. The dues and services mentioned in the documents fall into three categories: money payments, labour services and dues payable in kind, such as the provision of food and lodging for imperial officials on the road and *matériel* of the imperial armed forces. But interesting though the scope of these lists is, they still do not, however, help with the solution of the most important problem, namely whether monastic houses were exempted from the basic land tax, the *demosios kanon*.[27]

The crux of the matter remains the interpretation of the word *epereia*. For some commentators, such as Ostrogorsky, this meant exemption from *all* fiscal burdens, including the *demosios kanon*, but for others, including Svoronos and, more recently, Kaplan, it referred to the extra charges and dues on land over and above the basic land tax plus supplementary taxes (*parakolouthemata*) levied according to the level of the *demosios kanon*: the *dikeraton, hexafollon, synetheia* and *elatikon*.[28] The problem is of paramount importance, since, if it is assumed that all the monastic houses which enjoyed *exkousseia kathara* ('complete exemption') paid no land tax, then the large and flourishing estates which many of them owned by the end of the eleventh century would have made no contribution whatsoever to the finances and resources of the central government.

There are two cases outside Athos where it seems clear that monastic lands *were* freed from the *demosios kanon*. In 1044, when Constantine Monomachos endowed the so-called Nea Mone on the island of Chios with lands in Asia Minor, he declared that the properties concerned were to be considered *idiostaton* and to have their own *isokodikes* (that is that they were noted in separate cadasters away from the existing fiscal units). This, in itself, was a privilege, but the emperor went further. The lands were to be granted a *sympatheia* (tax relief) on the '*demosion*' as well as *exkousseia* from a list of named services and dues. It is difficult to see what

---

[27] See A. Harvey, *Economic Expansion in the Byzantine Empire*, pp. 103–13.
[28] Ostrogorsky, 'Immunité'. See also Kaplan, *Les hommes et la terre*, p. 356, n. 513. For the *parakolouthemata*, see N. Svoronos, 'Recherches sur le cadastre byzantin et la fiscalité aux XIe et XIIe siècles: le cadastre de Thèbes', *Bulletin de Corréspondance Héllenique*, 83 (1959), pp. 81–3.

he could have meant other than the *demosios kanon*, especially since the relatively high figure of six *nomismata* was mentioned as the amount to be exempted.[29] It is likely that freedom from taxation was also applied to the lands of the Nea Mone on Chios itself, though this is nowhere explicitly stated. They certainly enjoyed considerable fiscal privileges. In 1049, all the Jews on the island, hitherto free men, were assigned as *paroikoi* to the monastery and were granted *exkousseia* from *epereia* and *angareia*. In addition, they were to pay the *kephaletikon* (a poll tax) directly to the Nea Mone. In a confirmatory chrysobull of 1053, the monastic lands on Chios were freed from the attentions of any *epereiastai* (collectors of dues and services), so that the monks should remain undisturbed 'to speak with God on behalf of the world'.[30] There are, in addition, no records from this period indicating that they paid taxes for their lands on the island.

A much stronger case, however, can be made for maintaining that the properties of the monastery of St John the Theologian on Patmos, founded by St Christodoulos in the late eleventh century, were freed from the *demosios kanon*. Imperial gifts of the lands on the neighbouring islands of Leipsos and Leros were made in 1087 on the understanding that they would not be subject to the *demosion*. They were not to be inscribed in either the *kodikes* (registers) of the *demosion* or those of the *sekreton* (administrative bureau) of the Myrelaion, the previous owner of the lands.[31] In April 1088, the same kind of complete fiscal immunity was granted for Patmos itself, for Alexios Komnenos ordered that they should be free from the demands of all imperial bureaux and that all returns should be cut and 'struck out' in cinnabar ink in the relevant records – a procedure very similar to that granting *prokatespasmena logisima*.[32] Further proof that exemption from the land tax was at issue here is provided by a document dated to May 1088, in which the empress-mother, Anna Dalassene, acting on behalf of her son, after

---

[29] *Jus graecoromanum*, ed. J. and P. Zepos, vol. 1, Appendix, doc. 4, esp. p. 616. For the difficulties in dealing with documents from the Nea Mone, see E. Vranoussi, 'Les archives de Néa Moni de Chio: Essai de reconstitution d'un dossier perdu', *Byzantinisch-neugriechische Jahrbücher*, 22 (1977–84).

[30] *Jus graecoromanum*, ed. Zepos, vol. 1, Appendix, docs. 10, 13; see esp. p. 636. For the nature of the *kephaletikon*, argued by some to be a specifically Jewish poll tax, see A. Scharf, *Byzantine Jewry. From Justinian to the Fourth Crusade*, p. 195.

[31] *BEMP*, vol. 1, no. 5 (May, 1087).

[32] *BEMP*, vol. 1, no. 6 (April, 1088).

receiving representations from Christodoulos, reiterated that the monastery was not subject to dues and that 'if any trace [of taxes or dues] remains by accident in the documents without having been noticed, these dispositions will be considered suppressed and will be crossed out in cinnabar ink'.[33]

What is noticeable about these cases, however, is that even when it is clear that exemption from the land tax was being granted, this was being done by special mechanisms – such as the striking out of fiscal records – which existed alongside the *exkousseia*, but were not the same as it. *Exkousseia* – the exemption from a greater or lesser list of dues and services – thus formed part of the 'package' of exemption, and even the term *kathara exkousseia* is best seen as applying to an extensive list of such dues rather than a complete exemption of all possible fiscal responsibilities. For on many monastic estates which enjoyed a considerable degree of fiscal exemption, the *demosios kanon* clearly *was* paid. At the end of the eleventh century, the monks of the Lavra on Athos were instructed to hand over the *telos* (tax payment) for their lands on Kassandra to Adrian Komnenos, the brother of the emperor (an indication, perhaps, that he had been awarded a grant of *solemnion logisimon*); the 'complete exemption' they had been awarded for these lands did not include the land tax.[34] Similarly, the monks were assured in 1092 that they had nothing to fear from the officials of another brother, Isaac Komnenos, if they continued to pay the *telos* for their property at St Andrew of Peristerai, near Thessalonika.[35] The page from the cadaster concerning the taxes paid by the small Athonite monastery of Kalliergou for its *metochion* (small subordinate house) at Hierissos was actually quoted in a document of 1079 by the *anagrapheus* (tax official) John Kataphloron, and indicates that they were paying *demosios kanon* and all the supplementary taxes as prescribed in the *Fiscal Treatise*. A similarly precise example also survives for the property of St Demetrios on Kassandra belonging to the Athonite monastery of St Panteleimon.[36]

Even in documents where a very comprehensive list of *exkousseiai* was given, the *demosios kanon* remained to be paid. The high official and monastic founder Michael Attaliates complained in

[33] *BEMP*, vol. 1, no. 49 (May, 1088), see Ostrogorsky, 'Immunité', p. 189.
[34] *Lavra*, vol. 1, no. 46 (1084).
[35] *Lavra*, vol. 1, no. 51 (1092).
[36] *Lavra*, vol. 1, no. 39 (1079); *Actes de Pantéléêmôn*, no. 3 (?1044).

1075 that his estates were being 'pillaged' by officials gathering
epereiai (certainly taxes in kind), and, as a consequence, was
granted a chrysobull freeing him from their attentions by the
Emperor Michael VII Doukas (1071–8). But he was still to give
his accustomed rate of *demosia* and other *telesmata*, a clear reference to land taxes and the other taxes calculated on them.[37]
Even when some of these lands were granted to his monastic
foundations, the arrangements remained the same. Nikephoros
III Botaniates (1078–81) confirmed the exemptions granted by
his imperial predecessor, but reiterated that land taxes must be
paid.[38] In the case of the layman Leo Kephalas, too, a grant of
exemption from taxes on some *klasma* lands at Derkos, granted
by Alexios Komnenos in 1082, did not include the *demosion*,
which he was still to pay at the rate of $4\frac{1}{2}$ *nomismata*.[39] In both
these cases, as in others, the *exkousseia* clearly referred to exemption from the dues in cash and kind and the labour services
which were levied in addition to the land tax. Only in a few,
very favoured cases, where the monastic houses concerned were
the subject of considerable imperial interest and patronage, can
we be sure that the *demosios kanon* was also remitted, for giving
up the land tax was tantamount to giving up one of the major
imperial prerogatives and was thus very rarely done.

But what were the financial and, indeed, political effects of the
granting of *exkousseia*? It could be that the comprehensive and lengthy lists of types of services contained in some – but not all –
eleventh-century charters are a reflection of the monetary crises
which swept the Empire especially in the period after about 1070
and which had, as a consequence, the need to increase the quantity
and extent of renders in kind and *corvées* in order to counter the
effects of a debased coinage.[40] And even if, as Alan Harvey believes,
these services were extensively commuted in the eleventh century
almost at the whim of the lay officials, it is understandable that
monastic landowners and their lay counterparts were more eager
to gain freedom from them than from the *demosios kanon* which,
after all, might remain unaltered for thirty years or longer and

---

[37] Chrysobull of Michael Doukas (March 1075): P. Gautier, 'La diataxis de Michel
Attaliate', *Revue des Études Byzantines*, 39 (1981), pp. 101–9, esp. p. 103.
[38] Chrysobull of Nikephoros Botaniates (April, 1079): Gautier, 'Diataxis', pp. 109–23.
[39] *Lavra*, vol. 1, no. 44 (1082).
[40] Haldon, 'Military administration', 59, n. 27 discusses the value of non-monetary renders.

thus, in a period of debased coinage, be a declining burden in real terms.[41]

There is some evidence to support this view. In mid-century, the Athonite house of Vatopedi had received a *solemnion* (annual imperial grant) of eighty *nomismata* under both Constantine Monomachos and Michael VI (1056–7), but it had been halved by Isaac I Komnenos (1057–9). It was raised again to seventy-two *nomismata* by Alexios Komnenos. The monks also owned two properties on Kassandra for which they paid nineteen *nomismata* in state taxes. In 1082, the monks requested the emperor to assign to them the nineteen *nomismata* (the process of *autourgon logisimon*) in place of the seventy-two *nomismata* of *solemnion*. At the same time they begged that he would forbid the local fiscal and judicial officials access to their possessions. For, they maintained, the judges often took twenty *nomismata* or even more from them as *chreia* (payments to support travelling officials) and *antikaniskion* (money in lieu of food dues to officials). They clearly felt that the freedom from dues in cash and kind payable to officials, and, more importantly, from the future attentions of the officials of the *demosion* would more than compensate for the loss of their *solemnion*, which suggests that the burden of extra levies and dues could often be considerable.[42]

But the fact remains that not all the grants of *exkousseia* surviving from the eleventh century are anything like as extensive in their scope as the most detailed of them, that in the chrysobull granted to the monastery of St John the Theologian on Patmos in 1088.[43] The explanation for this might be that the scope of the exemption was adjusted to suit the circumstances of each privilege or, indeed, that the diplomatic forms themselves demanded a variation. Different kinds of documents produced different sorts of formulas of greater or lesser length.[44] We must therefore be wary of assuming

---

[41] Harvey, *Economic Expansion*, p. 111. He argues for widescale commutation of obligations in kind and labour services in the eleventh century, though there is little direct evidence of this, *ibid.*, p. 109.

[42] M. Goudas, 'Byzantina engrapha tes en Atho hieras mones tou Batopediou', *Epeteris Hetaireias Byzantinon Spoudon*, 3 (1926); 4 (1927), no. 3 (1082), see also Ostrogorsky, 'Immunité', pp. 190–1.

[43] *BEMP*, vol. 1, no. 6 (April 1088).

[44] For a much shorter list of exemptions than that of the Patmos chrysobull, see that contained in *Lavra*, vol. 1, no. 55 (1102), also granted by the Emperor Alexios Komnenos. Both documents are, however, described as *chrysoboullos logos*. The exemptions granted to Chios in a *chrysoboullon sigillion* of 1044 (see p. 211 and n. 29, above) are of medium length.

that all *exkousseia* implied a tremendous loss of 'revenue' in cash or kind to the Byzantine state. Nor is it safe to assume that 'the growing number of exemptions granted by the emperors from the 1040s' should be associated with 'the growing strength, economically and politically, of the social elite of the empire' and that 'the granting of such immunities amounted to a very considerable loss indeed to the state in respect of disposable resources'.[45]

Certainly, the aim of all monastic houses and powerful lay individuals was to rid themselves of as many taxes and services as they could and thus entirely devote their resources to increasing the prosperity of their own estates. After all, the grant of an exemption or the diversion of a tax payment did not mean that the duty lapsed; what had hitherto been paid or supplied to the state was now appropriated by the landowner. This was a matter of just as much interest to monastic landowners as it was to their lay counterparts. Indeed, the archives of Athos bear eloquent witness at the end of the eleventh century to attempts at tax avoidance and to confrontation with officials on an epic scale.[46] But this is a situation in which the grant of *exkousseia* played only a part.

For it must firstly be recalled that *exkousseia* could only be granted by the emperor and thus the very act of making a grant was a mark of imperial strength and authority, not weakness and, secondly, that it cannot be proved that such grants were widespread. It is not safe to maintain that 'the number of exemptions granted to monastic foundations was paralleled by a similar number of exemptions to secular persons'. We simply do not know.[47] In the Athonite context, where our evidence is remarkably full, only certain highly favoured houses with strong imperial links (particularly the Lavra) were specifically granted *exkousseiai*, though the general exemption for Athos applied, of course, to all the houses there. Otherwise it is houses like those on Chios and Patmos, again enjoying all sorts of other imperial patronage, which have *exkousseia* added to their privileges. In the lay sphere too, the generals Leo Kephalas and Gregory Pakourianos, the founder of an important monastery at Bačkovo in the Balkan Mountains, who

---

[45] Haldon, 'Military administration', p. 59. And we cannot reasonably assume that 'the number of exemptions granted to monastic foundations was paralleled by a similar number of exemptions to secular persons'.

[46] See Morris, *Monks and Laymen*, ch. 10.

[47] Haldon, 'Military administration', p. 58.

enjoyed grants of *exkousseia* had performed extremely valuable service to the state and were (like Michael Attaliates) members of the closest imperial circle. We have no evidence that *exkousseia* were being extensively handed out; where we know they were given, it was usually to individuals and institutions already enjoying imperial favour[48].

We also have seriously to question how effective grants of fiscal *exkousseia* actually were. If the late eleventh-century case of Theophylact, Archbishop of Ohrid (again someone with considerable contacts at court), is anything to go by, those who held lands in militarily sensitive areas (as were those in his see in the northern Balkans) could expect a never-ending struggle with the agents of the *demosion* and even the ignoring of *exkousseiai* granted to houses under their control.[49] This kind of episode indicates that, far from enjoying undisturbed extensive privileges extorted by provincial elites from a weak central government, the holders of *exkousseiai* often faced a grim struggle with other members of the provincial 'powerful', such as tax farmers. The conflict of interest was on a local level.

For of far more significance than the simple exemption from the payment or performance of taxes and services was freedom from *introitus*: the entry of the fiscal and judicial officials of the Empire on to property, sometimes, but *not* always associated with *exkousseia*. This, like exemption, could be granted to a greater or lesser extent, but was, again, always in the gift of the emperor. The Holy Mountain of Athos, for instance, enjoyed a distinctive legal status within its boundaries, the monks generally settling disputes in hearings before the Protos and his council of *hegoumenoi*. This right had been granted to them by the end of the tenth century, when, after a series of disputes between the monks of the newly established Lavra and the eremitic groups already on the mountain, during which both parties had appealed to the imperial power, the Emperor John Tzimiskes (969–76) had intervened. According to the *Typikon*

---

[48] For Leo Kephalas, see G. Rouillard,'Un grand bénéficiare sous Alexis Comnène: Léon Kephalas', *Byzantinische Zeitschrift*, 30 (1930). For the career of Gregory Pakourianos: P. Gautier, 'Le typikon du sébaste Grégoire Pakourianos', *Revue des Études Byzantines*, 42 (1984), and for Michael Attaliates, Gautier, 'Diataxis'.

[49] M. E. Mullett, 'Theophylact through his letters: the two worlds of an exile bishop', and D. Obolensky, *Six Byzantine Portraits*, pp. 34–82 on Theophylact. See also A. Harvey, 'The land and taxation in the reign of Alexios I Komnenos: the evidence of Theophylakt of Ochrid', *Revue des Études Byzantines*, 51 (1993), esp. p. 146.

that he issued, all were agreed that such matters should not become the province of 'worldly courts' (*kosmika kriteria*). Euthymios, the *hegoumenos* of the celebrated Stoudios monastery in Constantinople, had investigated the disputes,

so that affairs should not be set in order by the representatives of the *archontes* (local officials) and matters discussed amongst themselves [the monks] or alleged against them should not become common knowledge. For the *kosmikoi* (men of the world) do not understand spiritual affairs.[50]

The *Typikon of Constantine Monomachos* (1045) further emphasized that the Protos and his council were to make up the body which should deal with conflicts on the mountain and deplored the fact that Athonites had been taking their grievances to lay judges.[51]

The Holy Mountain was thus withdrawn at an early period from the control of the lay and ecclesiastical jurisdictions of the region and both the Athonite monasteries and other famous houses also came to enjoy a certain degree of judicial exemption for their properties elsewhere. The chrysobulls granted to Michael Attaliates stipulated that the imperial judges were not to have access to his monastic lands and the monastic foundations of Gregory Pakourianos were also freed from the judicial as well as the financial control of the Metropolitan of Philippopolis.[52] The monks of the monastery of the Theotokos Eleousa at Stroumitza in Macedonia were 'not to be troubled by imperial or clerical judges, either those of the Archbishop of Bulgaria or of the Bishop of Stroumitza'.[53] But perhaps the most striking example of judicial immunity was that awarded by Constantine Monomachos to the Nea Mone on Chios in 1045. In order to preserve the monks *eremia* 'so that they may live the angelic life', no provincial judges were to have entry to the island:

The God-loving monks in the aforesaid monastery shall not be taken to any court for any reason concerning their lands and those on them. For only the imperial court (*bema*) shall issue judgements about such things.[54]

---

[50] *Prôtaton*, no. 7 (pre-summer 972).
[51] *Prôtaton*, no. 8 (1045).
[52] Gautier, 'Diataxis', pp. 103, 111; Gautier, 'Typikon du sébaste Grégoire Pakourianos', p. 45.
[53] L. Petit, 'Le monastère de Notre Dame de Pitié en Macédoine', *Izvestija Russkago Arheologičeskogo Instituta v Konstantinopole*, 6 (1900), docs. 1 (1085) and 2 (1106).
[54] *Jus graecoromanum*, ed. Zepos, vol. 1, Appendix, doc. 7, esp. p. 630.

The example of the Nea Mone is of great assistance in revealing the real aim of obtaining judicial (and indeed fiscal) exemptions. It certainly meant that, in the local sphere, monastic control over their lands and tenants was strong, but it did not mean that the monks were, or intended to be, beyond the reach or, indeed, the aid of the law. Rather, they sought to have their complaints heard and dealt with at the highest possible level. The monks of Chios were actually given permission to do this by the emperor, but recourse to him, and sometimes the patriarch, was common practice in other monastic establishments. As monastic founders pointed out in their *typika*, it was the duty of the emperor to protect the interests of the monastic houses and, as well as exercising this general guardianship, the ties of spiritual kinship or patronage often meant that the emperors involved themselves in conflicts on behalf of favoured houses or groups. It is significant that, when Athos was torn by a controversy concerning the presence of Vlach nomadic families on the mountain at the end of the eleventh century, the judicial organization of the Protaton was unable to make peace. The party in favour of the expulsion of the Vlachs, led by John Balmas, the *hegoumenos* of the Lavra, complained directly to the Emperor Alexios Komnenos and the Patriarch Nicholas Grammatikos. A similar example may be cited from Mount Latros, for when Christodoulos (the later founder of the monastery of St John on Patmos), then *hegoumenos* of the Stylos monastery on Mount Latros in western Asia Minor came under attack from his own monks and those of other houses, he appealed for help directly to the Patriarchs Kosmas, Eustratios Garidas and Nicholas Grammatikos.[55]

An interesting pattern emerges from these cases. Clearly, the monks of the holy mountains and other houses preferred, if possible, to administer justice for themselves. But if this proved impossible, they did not turn of choice to the secular or ecclesiastical justice of the surrounding areas, though they were sometimes forced into local courts by their neighbours. Instead, they made

---

[55] The Vlach dispute is described in the so-called *Diegesis Merike*, a muddled hotch-potch of memoranda compiled in Constantinople *c.*1180 and dealing with a number of problems troubling the Holy Mountain at the turn of the eleventh and twelfth centuries: *Diegesis merike tou epistolou Alexiou basileos kai Nicholaiou patriarches genomene kata diaphorous kairous*, in P. Meyer, *Die Haupturkunden für die Geschichte der Athos-Klöster*. For the disputes concerning Christodoulos, see F. Miklosich and J. Müller, *Acta et diplomata graeca medii aevi*, vol. 6, pp. 30–1.

use of the ties of patronage linking them to the capital to invoke the most influential assistance that they could, that of the emperor or the patriarch. In this sense there are distinct parallels with the motives for the search for exemptions in the West. The Cluniacs and their relationship with the papacy immediately spring to mind, but Jeffrey Denton has also written convincingly of the efforts of the English royal free chapels to escape from the clutches of the 'Argos-eyed bishops of the twelfth and thirteenth centuries'.[56]

For just as the Cluniac immunity was guarded by the keeper of the keys of heaven, the pope, who protected the monastery and its lands from the encroachments of local lay and ecclesiastical officials, both financial and judicial, so, too, did the imperial power protect favoured houses in Byzantium from local interests and ambitions.[57] And the 'freedom' of the English royal free chapels (just like favoured Byzantine monasteries) lay precisely in the fact that they were both 'isolated from the dioceses in which they were constituted' and, as in the case of the monks of the thirteenth-century church at Steyning in Sussex, were declared to be 'free from a domination of or subjection to barons, princes and all others. . .nor shall anyone intermeddle, except by their authority'.[58]

These similarities should not surprise us, since they ultimately derive from the same Roman law tradition passed down in two of ⁚ 's most important branches – the papacy and the Byzantine Empire. But Western parallels do help to provide balance to any interpretation of the significance of Byzantine exemption mechanisms especially when applied to monasteries. Just as the rights and freedoms accorded to Cluny were the exception rather than the rule, so too were those accorded to the 'charmed circle' of Byzantine monasteries such as those on Athos, Chios and Patmos. It cannot be argued that they were widespread. And just as Cluny wanted to increase its local power by keeping *local* officials at bay and gaining power over its local workforce and economic resources, so, too, the Athonite, Chiote and Patmiote monks defended their fiscal and judicial 'territory' from the encroachments of their neighbours, in which category must be included the tax officials and judges sent to hound them.

[56] See H. E. J. Cowdrey, *The Cluniacs and the Gregorian Reform* and J. H. Denton, *English Royal Free Chapels 1100–1200. A Constitutional Study*, p. 15.

[57] Cowdrey, *Cluniacs*, p. 13.

[58] Denton, *English Royal Free Chapels*, p. 73.

Any analysis of the importance of the varied exemptions enjoyed by tenth- and eleventh-century Byzantine monastic landholders (and their lay counterparts of whom we know so lamentably little) must take account of the fact that the process was neither new nor exclusive to Byzantium. Byzantine mechanisms of exemption and immunity, like those of the late Roman state or many western areas were not the same thing. In particular, *exkousseia*, existed alongside a whole range of other exemptions and formed only a part of the privileges that beneficiaries might enjoy. The precise 'mixture' of exemption and immunity was something which, in Roman as in Byzantine times, only the imperial power could administer and it was always in the power of the emperor to refuse to do so. Byzantine immunities reflected an aspect of imperial power and patronage, not weakness, a power which was deployed in the favour of those monastic houses and powerful individuals who most contributed to the spiritual and physical protection of the empire.[59]

[59] I should particularly like to thank John Haldon and Alan Harvey for providing copies of recent articles which have stimulated many of the thoughts in this paper and Jeffrey Denton for his insights into the subject of papal immunities. J. C. Morris, has, as ever, provided invaluable assistance with German material.

CHAPTER 9

Property ownership and signorial power in twelfth-century Tuscany

Chris Wickham

One of the crucial moments of social and political change in Western Europe has come to be seen as the years around the year 1000. Before it, we have the large, if crumbling, edifice of the Carolingian state, with its public structures, however rudimentary, and its interregional hierarchies of power. These hierarchies ultimately depended, it is true, on the landed wealth of kings, but they were firmly enough rooted in custom to allow considerable authority to be wielded by people who had royal favour, whether they themselves had local land or not. After it, the equation land=power was much more direct; power became limited by the number of armed men one could feed from one's land, and by one's capacity to control them once one had them there – considerable, if one was ...he duke of Normandy or (after a hiccup) the count of Barcelona; much less, if one was the count of Mâcon or the abbot of any one of a hundred miserable and newly impoverished monastic houses, menaced by the depredations of their armed neighbours and dependants. In recent years this shift has been theorized as the 'feudal revolution', and the early eleventh century, in particular, has been seen as a classic time of violence, as the new order set in, indeed took power by force; only in the late eleventh century, or perhaps in the twelfth, did this more small-scale and (above all) more military society begin to acquire its own rules: its own etiquette and ritual, but also an aristocratic moral code that came more and more to have the force of law, sufficient to marginalize the most uncontrollably violent members of the military elite and, in the end, to allow larger-scale political units to re-establish themselves on the basis of new rules.[1]

---

[1] See P. Bonnassie, *From Slavery to Feudalism in South-Western Europe*, pp. 104–31; J.-P. Poly and E. Bournazel, *The Feudal Transformation, 900–1200* – both translations of major French analyses from a decade earlier; T. Bisson, 'The "feudal revolution" ', *Past and Present*, 142 (1994), ably sums up the wider issues. The two classic accounts should also be cited

This theory has its problems. The first is that it only really properly works in France; indeed, one could argue that its Europe-wide influence as a model can best be seen as proof of the continuing dominance of France over the historiography of the central middle ages.[2] One can change the dates to make it work in Castile, at a pinch; Italy does not entirely fit, however, as we shall see; and Henry I of England and Frederick Barbarossa, notwithstanding their use of fiefs and vassals, arguably ruled more like Charlemagne than like Philip I – or even Philip II – of France. And recently the idea of the 'feudal revolution' or 'mutation' has come under attack in France as well. Dominique Barthélemy has argued that the changes around the year 1000 were merely terminological; that there was no real new nobility; that there was not significantly more violence; and, above all, that the new 'private' castle-based political systems were much like the old 'public' ones in their internal structures. Against the idea, for example, that Carolingian public courts judged according to law, with winners and losers, whereas seigneurial justice was based on feud and compromise, he introduces more anthropological ideas of the way disputes are settled, relying on the work of Stephen White and Patrick Geary, as well as our own earlier volume, to show that judgment and compromise usually go together to end cases, both before and after 1000. In both systems there was violence and injustice, but, set against this, there were also always rules.[3]

Some of this last critique I would happily accept. Barthélemy's point about justice and rules is important; so is his stress on the continuity of medieval Europe's essential division, between lords and peasants, throughout both periods. And my experience as an Italian historian leads me, like him, to doubt the universality of the idea of a sharp change, whether around 1000 or at any other time. In Italy, the shifts took place over a far longer period, as well as never being complete – there is not very much of a chronological gap, in most of central-northern Italy (the medieval kingdom of Italy, that is to say), between the public power of the Lombard–Carolingian tradition and that of the developing city states of the twelfth century. In Italy, too, one of the major aspects

---

here: M. Bloch, *Feudal Society*; G. Duby, *La société aux XIe et XIIe siècles dans la région mâconnaise.*
[2] See above, pp. 7–8.
[3] D. Barthélemy, 'La mutation féodale a-t-elle eu lieu?', *Annales E.S.C.*, 47 (1992).

of the 'feudal revolution', the eclipse of the landowning peasantry, never fully occurred; this relatively autonomous social stratum survived into the late middle ages (and, in some areas, longer still) to mediate between the naturally opposed interests of lords and their tenants. (Even in Old Catalonia, a cornerstone of the 'revolutionist' theory, it has recently been convincingly argued that such a stratum lasted a lot longer than was previously thought, up to 1200 in fact.)[4] Nonetheless, looking at Europe from the standpoint of Italy, it seems to me that it would be wrong to deny the existence of this shift entirely, by claiming for example that the political system in, say, 1150 was merely an updating of that in existence in, say, 900. Some things had indeed changed, and sharply, even if not all at the same time. And the sharpest changes were in the relationship between land and power.

Of these changes, I would single out three that were particularly important in Italy. One was what one could call the patrimonialization of public power. In the Carolingian world, major landed families of course controlled most public life, and, in particular, the local administrative circumscriptions, marches or counties, that legitimized the local exercise of power. In the tenth-century Italian kingdom, however, and still more in the eleventh, comital and marchesal power increasingly came to be seen as an attribute of families themselves; the titles of marquis and count could often be attached to all the male members of such a family, for instance (as with the Giselbertingi counts of Bergamo from the 1010s at the latest), and, after 1000, we sometimes find the very words county and march, together with the legal powers attached to them, applied to the *ad hoc* assemblages of land, whether held allodially or in lease or in fief, of such families. The old idea of the county remained, to become the legitimate area of expansion (*contado*) of the twelfth-century cities; but other areas of *de facto* landed power were themselves legitimized, precisely through the continuance of that idea.[5] Linked to this was the sharp growth in visibility of private relationships of dependence

---

[4] On the survival of free landowners and for further references see C.J. Wickham, *The Mountains and the City: The Tuscan Appennines in the Early Middle Ages*, pp. 242–68; compare, for Catalonia, P. Freedman, *The Origins of Peasant Servitude in Medieval Catalonia*, pp. 69–118; and, for Languedoc, M. Bourin-Derruau, *Villages médiévaux en Bas-Languedoc*, vol. 2, e.g. pp. 225–31.

[5] See most recently, for all these developments, the articles in *Formazione e strutture dei ceti dominanti nel medioevo*, vol. 1. Essential for this and what follows is the survey in G. Tabacco, *The Struggle for Power in Medieval Italy*, pp. 151–76, 191–208.

between the various levels of the aristocracy. Early medieval lords already had their *fideles*, their sworn dependants, on whom they in practice relied in order to exercise power both legally and illegally. But as public office became more and more the right of specific families, so did the personal links between them and their dependants become more formalized. We hear a great deal more about the *militia* of lords, their military following, and in the eleventh century this emerged as a definable social stratum in itself, linked through a network of increasingly explicit hierarchies to the greatest families and their ecclesiastical equivalents (the archbishop of Milan, most famously, had not one stratum of military dependants but two, *capitanei* and *valvassores*).[6]

The second change was in the definition of the aristocracy itself; for, in the eleventh century, military activity came for the first time to be formally recognized as a privilege rather than a burden, and thus began to define a boundary between the aristocratic and the non-aristocratic free, the *milites* and the *rustici*. Such a definition came to be based not on the links of dependence just mentioned, but, more and more, on autonomous criteria, that is to say criteria that were developed by the lesser ranks of *milites* themselves rather than by their lords: rituals of military behaviour which could be recognized by one's peers, and, above all, the possession of castles, which proliferated in Italy as much as anywhere else in Europe. By 1050, indeed, it was virtually essential that any aspiring aristocrat in the Italian kingdom should control a castle. This new military stratum was not better-behaved in Italy than in France; its lords – particularly its ecclesiastical lords – found it hard to control, and lamented its violence at their expense, sometimes at graphic length.[7] The military stratum also ended up powerful in city politics, for cities remained major centres of Italian political life; the twelfth-century victories of cities over their *contadi* often simply represented the final victory of urban *milites* over their old superiors (as well as over those *milites* who decided to stay with their own castles rather than with city politics).

The third change was the appearance of signorial rights as a major element in the way that power was exercised. I will discuss

---

[6] See e.g. H. Keller, *Adelsherrschaft und städtische Gesellschaft in Oberitalien*, pp. 251–302.

[7] Keller, *Adelsherrschaft*, pp. 342–79; A. A. Settia, *Castelli e villaggi nell'Italia padana*, pp. 168–76, 399–406; Wickham, *Mountains*, pp. 283–306.

this at length in what follows, for it is the major focus of the empirical material in this chapter. Here, however, it can be said that what is meant by signorial rights is the network of legal powers of coercion that military lords could have over their weaker neighbours: rights to call them to court as disputing parties or as bystanders; and rights to exact dues from them for certain public, ex-public or quasi-public services, such as the obligation to feed soldiers, or to do (or pay for) guard duty, or to build fortifications, or to go to the castle market, or – more rarely in north-central Italy – to use the lord's mill. These rights sometimes derived from the *de facto* powers over land that great owners had always had (there were some private landlords' courts, even for free tenants, already in the ninth century, for example); they were sometimes the devolved or usurped powers of Carolingian counts, as in Georges Duby's conception of the French equivalent of the *signoria*, the *seigneurie banale*; they were sometimes new burdens that were the specific product of the new boundary between a military aristocracy and the rest. But, as a package, they were new in the eleventh century: it is then that they became accepted as custom, even if they were bitterly resented (*mali usi* was a standard term for them in Italy as elsewhere, 'evil customs'). They were sometimes restricted to the landed properties of a lord, that is to his tenants; but increasingly – by 1100 in most of Italy – tended to be over specific territories, with defined boundaries, and over tenants and small owners (and sometimes rival lords) alike. The formation of such 'territorial *signorie*' was a recognized development at the time, for they had names (*dominatus loci*, the term used in Lombardy, is the best known); they could be bought and sold, and formally divided; and their boundaries are recorded in documents.[8]

All three of these political shifts are in the outer form rather than in the content of power. The public world of the Carolingians had, after all, been run by militarized aristocrats and their entourages, who had a virtually free hand in the provinces of the Empire. And that world, in Italy, had not entirely ended, particularly in the most urbanized parts of the peninsula, for the world of the city is a public

---

[8] For this and what follows see Tabacco, *Struggle for Power*, pp. 193–200; C. Violante, 'La signoria "territoriale" come quadro delle strutture organizzative del contado', in W. Paravicini and K. F. Werner (eds.), *Histoire comparée de l'administration*; *idem*, 'La signoria rurale nel secolo X', *Settimane di studio*, 38 (1991); Wickham, *Mountains*, pp. 105–9, 307–30; compare Duby, *Société dans la région mâconnaise*, pp. 174–9.

world almost by definition – it is too complex to be run as an *ad hoc* lordship, given its networks of competing and overlapping interest groups, always happy to fight. But the change in form was a huge one. The private exercise of power by great lords in the Carolingian world occurred, but it was illegal, in the sense that royal capitularies inveighed against it and tried to reverse it. Now, however, local private power was accepted by all, including by surviving public authorities, as itself *constituting* legality, in the framework of signorial customs. The takeover of cities by their local notables, which we call 'the rise of the commune', was an analogous process, of the illegal turning itself into the legal, even though cities were genuinely different in type from signorial lordships. Whether in the city or in the country, then, the oppression of the weak by the strong was a consistent feature of the whole period 800–1200, as indeed before and after; but the manner in which the power of the strong could be justified and, indeed, structured, had changed very considerably, as had the way this power related to landholding.

These pages must suffice as an introduction to the themes of this chapter. They are very general; it was, everywhere, more complicated than that, as we shall see. But they can serve as a framing for these complexities in the more specific context of one twelfth-century Tuscan city, Lucca. Actually, in north-west Tuscany (notably around Lucca and Pisa), where public power of a classic Carolingian type had remained firmly in the hands of the Canossa marquises right up to the wars of the Investiture Dispute in the 1080s, and the cities were large and militarily active, both locally and (in the case of Pisa) throughout the Mediterranean, signorial powers were relatively weak in the twelfth century, and urban justice was influential very early. But the developments I have just outlined had taken place nonetheless, especially in the second half of the eleventh century. The separation between the landowner's dominance of his tenants by proprietorial right and the signorial lord's dominance of his subjects by signorial right had occurred, here as elsewhere. (I use the word 'his' as a specific, not as a generic; with few exceptions, such as marquises, women could exercise few legal rights without the mediation of men.) Let us see what this meant, and how it worked, through some specific examples.

The affirmation of local power on the part of the military aristocracy in the eleventh century is ill-documented everywhere, for charters tend to record signorial rights only after they were already established. Our evidence about the slow extension of signorial powers comes largely from the complaints of churches whose own local control was being undermined; we have almost no eleventh-century material that tells us about the process from the standpoint of its chief victims, the peasantry. Two rare examples come, however, from the territory of Pisa (see Map 4), which is only 20 km. from Lucca and was fairly similar in its social structure. We shall look at the material from Lucca later. Both Pisan documents date from the 1090s, the precise moment in which the public structures of the March of Tuscany were in terminal decline.[9]

The first of the two, from *c.*1092, comes from the marshlands between Pisa and Lucca, and is in the form of an agreement between the local inhabitants and their lords:

Since grave injuries and miserable contumelies and much wretchedness through rapine took place in the Valdiserchio and its territory to the insult and damage of all its inhabitants and of some citizens of Pisa, it was arranged through divine clemency and the concern of good men, that, meeting together, they should find the best counsel about so many evils. So they elected consuls from the Pisans [seven are listed, some of them important city aristocrats] and other good men of the Valdiserchio, comforted by whose counsel and help they extirpated these ills by the roots, that is to say: that the common marshlands and pastures, which [the inhabitants] had lost without reason, they should hold as the aforesaid consuls set out; that they should remain wholly free of the protection (*comandiscia*), by which they were oppressed against their will; that they should be injured no more by the wretched rapine, which they suffered from some of the men of the *longubardi* [by now a standard term for the small military aristocracy],[10] regarding their grain, linen and other goods; that no-one should impose guard duty (*guardia*) or take anything for guard duty on their allods or lease-hold tenures (*tenimentum*) without the will of the holders of the latter; concerning the wood-dues (*silvaticum*) for the woods, whereof they suffered many evil customs (*malas consuetudines*) against the good old customs (*usus*), it was agreed that henceforth they should only give two *denarii* per cart yearly. [The 'Pisan *longubardi*' signed

---

[9] I use the edition of both texts in R. D'Amico, 'Note su alcuni rapporti tra città e campagna nel contado di Pisa tra XI e XII secolo', *Bollettino storico pisano*, 39 (1970), pp. 28–9, comparing the reading of the second with the edition by G. Garzella in M. Pasquinucci et al., *Cascina*, vol. 2, pp. 161–2. For commentary, see D'Amico, 'Note'; G. Rossetti, 'Società e istituzioni nei secoli IX e X. Pisa, Volterra, Populonia', in *Atti del 5° congresso internazionale*, pp. 320–37; G. Garzella in Pasquinucci et al., *Cascina*, vol. 2, pp. 73–5. For background, G. Volpe, *Studi sulle istituzioni comunali a Pisa*, pp. 6–65.

[10] G. Volpe, 'Lambardi e Romani nelle campagne e nella città', *Studi storici*, 13 (1904).

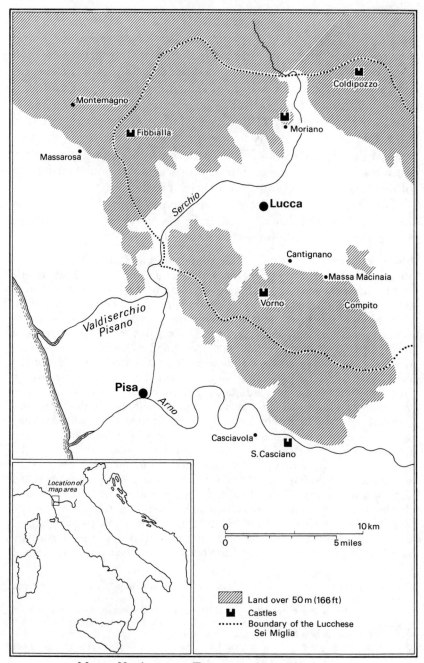

Map 4. North-western Tuscany in the twelfth century

this, and it was ratified by the Pisan *populus* (people) and the bishop of Pisa.]

The second text, from *c.*1100, is in the form of a plea to the cathedral and the consuls of the city by the inhabitants of the small Arno village of Casciavola, some 10 km. east of the city, against the lords of neighbouring S. Casciano:

We the men of Casciavola, recently made dependants (*fideles*), with our persons and possessions, of God and the cathedral of St Mary, make a proclamation to God and St Mary and the whole clergy and the consuls and the whole people (*populus*) of Pisa concerning the impiety and cruelty which the *longubardi* of S. Casciano do to us. Know and believe truly that we were always free men, and always lived on our allods, and we had a refuge and houses in the castle of S. Casciano when it was whole, and we never did any service (*servitium*) to any of these *longubardi* except for the castle and the houses we had in it. Our custom (*usus*), which we did for the castle, was this: we did guard duty (*waita*) when they told us to by messenger, and for each plot we gave them two carts of wood, and they defended us in the woodland. But afterwards they changed the wood due into a due in money, and we gave 16d per plot. Then with false prayers and trickery they got us to give them three carts of wood, throughout the village. This was our *usus*, and they had nothing else from us in any way, nor did we ever hold allods or fiefs from them. After the castle was destroyed, we should have been free from any *servitium*; but, before the destruction, they began to do rapine against our property, not by custom or by our will. So we came in anger to the palace at Pisa before the lady Beatrice [marquise of Tuscany, i.e. before her death in 1076], so that we might make a proclamation to her. Then Ungarello came with his associates [these were the lords of S. Casciano] and formally agreed to our fathers that they would do them no more evil, against a penalty of a thousand pounds [a huge sum of money], and the proclamation remained thus. Afterwards, when all power lost its strength, and justice was dead and perished in our land, they began to do us all evil, as if they were pagans or Saracens. They began to attack our houses, to assault our wives as they lay in bed and beat them, to take all our goods from our houses, to strike our children and roll them in water and mire, to take all our animals, to devastate our fields, to despoil our gardens of all their fruits, and to take all our possibilities of life. Whence we flee to God and St Mary, and throw ourselves at the feet of the victorious and glorious Pisans, that you take us from the power and cruelty of the pagans, so that they may not do us so many ills, and so that we may live faithful to the honour of God and St Mary.

These texts are classic accounts, and well-known to Pisan historians, for they fit into the period of formation of Italy's first city commune, and contain some of the earliest references to the city consuls of Pisa.[11] They also, however, derive from the formative period, the violent 'revolutionary' period, of the establishment of signorial rights, when lords were turning ad hoc and temporary concessions into stable resources, all over Europe (though here, in Pisa, a century later than in most of France). We do not have to accept them as wholly accurate and unbiased, particularly the second, which is explicitly only one side of the dispute; but even the second, in order to be plausible, had to depict a possible reality, and we can take both as representative of what people recognized *could* happen in the period. They present some notable similarities. In each case, local military lords were violently extending quite small traditional dues, notably on woodland, which had been owed by their free neighbours, both allodial landowners and (in the case of the Valdiserchio agreement) tenants. In both cases this had something to do with 'protection' (the Mafia overtones which this word has come to have, give a good sense of its meaning around 1100), which castle-holding military lords were particularly well-equipped to offer; one of the obligations in return was to perform, or pay for, guard duty in the castle(s) of the lords. Such guard duty was traditional in the second case; a new imposition in the first. But in both cases these dues were backed by more generalized attacks, presumably aimed at securing more stable and substantive sets of dues that would be recognitive of the political authority of the military aristocracy in specific territories. Pisa, in fact, succeeded in preventing this in each case, and in the twelfth century these areas were not notable at all for strong signorial rights. We should be wary of attributing this too easily to the anti-signorial attitudes of city communes, however, for the *longubardi* of each case came from major city families, and were active in the commune; they had, in effect, chosen to exert their dominance over the countryside via the city rather than independently of it.

I cite these texts at length because of their intrinsic interest; it was very often just like this that military lords extended their powers over their previously independent neighbours – by brute force, even if often doubtless on the basis of networks of pre-existing

---

[11] See Rossetti and Volpe, cit. n. 8 above; the most recent analysis, with bibliography, is G. Rossetti, 'Il lodo del vescovo Daiberto sull'altezza delle torri', in *Pisa e la Toscana occidentale nel Medioevo*, 2.

rights. Such activity was in these cases still 'illegal', and could be prevented or at least contained, but 'when justice was dead' this prevention could not always be achieved, and the new powers could already be called 'customs'; if ever they were not stopped, that is just what they would become. We cannot, unfortunately, be entirely sure of their context in these particular instances; the Valdiserchio area covers several villages, and how wide the troubles in the first text extended is unclear; and, although the immediate context is very clear in the second, it happens that Casciavola is a very small and ill-documented village, and we know almost nothing more about it until the 1170s.[12] For a context, let us move slightly later, and into the territory of Lucca. Here, we will look at greater length at two fully formed, fully 'legal', networks of signorial rights, to see how they worked. Their origins are obscure; Pisan texts of the type just cited are, as already noted, highly uncommon. But the local working of signorial power was in each case different, and in neither case does its most likely origin seem to have been exactly the same as the Pisan examples we have just looked at. We will in fact end up with three images of the development of signorial rights; on the basis of this diversity, we can then begin to generalize more firmly about the relationship between landholding and the exercise of power.

In the twelfth century, the six-mile territory around Lucca, called the Sei Miglia, was almost devoid of territorial *signorie*, much in the same way as the immediate hinterland of Pisa. Some aristocratic families held scattered signorial powers over some of their lands; in addition, some highly dependent tenants (*manentes*) owed specific dues to their landlords that represented a subjection that was political, not just economic.[13] But there were only three or four villages that had any sort of signorial territory attached to them, of a type that was totally normal in the rest of Italy. The two we will look at, Massa Macinaia, 6 km. south of the city and Moriano, 7 km. to its north, controlled respectively by the cathedral canons

---

[12] See Pasquinucci et al., *Cascina*, vol. 2, *sub indice*.

[13] See, in general, C. J. Wickham, 'Economia e società rurale nel territorio lucchese', in C. Violante (ed.), *Sant'Anselmo vescovo di Lucca*; Wickham, '*Manentes* e diritti signorili durante il XII secolo', in *Studi in onore di Cinzio Violante*; idem, *Comunità e clientele nella Toscana del XII secolo*; for a classic economic analysis see P. J. Jones, 'An Italian estate, 900–1200', *Economic History Review*, 7 (1954).

and the bishop of Lucca, were thus locally exceptional, although representative of a wider reality (see Map 4). They were weak *signorie* by Italian (still more by French) standards, but had some usefully typical features. As villages, they are both very well documented (Massa Macinaia has some eighty twelfth-century charters, and Moriano nearly 150); their internal structures are thus unusually clear. We cannot look at them in full detail, but we can put sample signorial documents into a much better context than was possible for our Pisan examples.

I begin with extracts from a list of testimonies, dating from 1160. Thirty-seven tenants in Massa Macinaia were interrogated as to the dues they had owed to Enrico di Sigefredo, lord of the castle of Vorno, in the hills some 5 km. west of Massa Macinaia. They are mostly short and repetitive; I translate the first and the twenty-fourth:

Manasse said on oath that he was accustomed to render to Enrico di Sigefredo, eight days before the latter went overseas, first: to bring with his donkey hay and grain and grass, wherever [Enrico] wanted, Vorno or Compito or Massa or Castelnuovo, and if it was ever necessary to take his donkey, Enrico's messenger took it and returned it safe and sound to his house; and he was accustomed to render a chicken each year, and two loaves, and two eggs and two linen cloths; and he gave guard duty (*guadia*) and hospitality. He also said that all his neighbours did the same, except the households of Bonciattoro and of Bornetto Cacacci who did not do guard duty; he did not know what others did, although he had heard that the household of Giovannico Vernacci did not do this obedience.

Corso said on oath that Enrico di Sigefredo and [his son] Rustichello had nothing from his house except that he did guard duty when asked, and gave hospitality, and fed two men there; he said that the men of Custogiore went to [the lord's] court (*ad placitum*) and gave hospitality but not guard duty; that the men of Colle neither went to court nor did guard duty, but did give the chicken, eggs, bread, linen and the donkey; that the men of the canons did guard duty and gave all the above; that the men of the sons of Riccio did not give guard duty or the chicken, but they did everything else.[14]

These testimonies, and the others, are consistent; the men of Massa Macinaia knew what their position was. The consuls of Lucca, who were hearing them, confirmed these obligations at the end,

[14] *Regesto del capitolo di Lucca*, ed. P. Guidi and O. Parenti (henceforth *RCL*, cited by charter no.), 1188.

stating that Rustichello di Enrico and his nephews the sons of Tignoso should continue to receive them – they were not, that is to say, controversial in the eyes of the city. The obligations were, however, quite substantial: they included guard duty, army service (which was added as an afterthought at the end of the list of testimonies), the duty to feed the lord's men, forced requisitions of animals and private justice.

These signorial obligations are different from those in our Pisan examples in one crucial way: they are all from tenants, not from landowners. Corso, for instance, held a mill in the village from the cathedral canons in 1187; and most of the next generation of dependants of the sons of Tignoso are called the canons' *manentes* in court cases of 1184 and 1188, when the canons managed to gain (or regain) from the Vorno family the right to subject tenants to private justice. From 1160 to the end of the century, these dependants appear over and over again as the canons' tenants, in leases or in rent lists. It is clear that the canons managed to take over the local signorial rights of the lords of Vorno by the 1180s; and this is confirmed by a somewhat sanctimonious contemporary dorsal note to the 1160 text, presumably written by the canons in whose archive it survives, which calls it 'The attestations by which our men of Massa Macinaia were subject to the lords of Vorno; and this church freed them from their fears'.[15]

It seems at first sight odd that the Vorno family should have managed to gain such rights over tenants who were, in all our other documents, stable tenants of the canons. The processes were probably fairly straightforward, however, as a political narrative will show. The canons got their biggest estate in Massa Macinaia, the *curtis* of S. Petronilla, from the royal family in the early tenth century. Across that century and later, they leased portions of it away to families of urban notables, including three families of city judges, Leone, Flaiperto and Rolando. The first of these, the *casa Lei iudicis*, moved out of the city in the later eleventh century, and is found controlling the castle of Vorno by the 1120s, as well as a private rural monastery at Cantignano. Relations with the canons remained good enough; there is no sign, for example, that the

---

[15] Corso: *RCL* 1568; court cases: *RCL* 1521, 1575; the *manentes* of *RCL* 1521 as the canons' tenants in *RCL* 1187, 1316, 1325, 1400, 1529, 1568, 1614, 1700; cf. also 1582 (AD 1188), an oath of obedience to the canons.

Vorno family tried to turn their Massa Macinaia lease into full ownership at the church's expense, as other noble families often did. Indeed in 1126 Enrico di Sigefredo gave up some of his residual claims over another castle, Fibbialla, which the canons had recently acquired, in return for a renewal of his family's leases, and agreed to protect the canons whenever they needed it in his castle at Vorno, against their enemies. The extension of the signorial powers of the Vorno family over those tenants in Massa Macinaia which they controlled probably came about in the context of the militarization of the family, which was probably then recent: the castle at Vorno is not known before this text.[16] One may guess that the canons were prepared to allow the transfer of such rights into the hands of military tenants because of their political alliance. But the Vorno family aimed too high; they got involved in the wars between Pisa and Lucca. In 1144, Enrico transferred his castle to Pisa; in the succeeding years the Lucchesi besieged it three times, until in 1150 they bought out the Vorno family and destroyed it. One may suppose that it was then that Enrico 'went overseas'; at any rate, in 1158 his son and grandsons agreed to return to Lucca and never to rebuild the castle. Although the Lucchesi confirmed their signorial rights in Massa Macinaia in return in 1160, as we have seen, their local control must have slipped along with their political power; hence the success of the canons in getting control of their rights, and maybe even their leases, by the mid-1180s.[17]

Although we cannot be sure about the origins of the *signoria* in Massa Macinaia, for we have no documents, it may be that they were less violent than in our two Pisan texts. The *curtis* of S. Petronilla was a Carolingian estate, and remained a unit with that name in the 1180s, with an unusually stable internal structure. *Curtes* of this type had always had highly dependent tenants; some of them in the early tenth century had been servile, and, although slave status had vanished in the Lucchese countryside in the meantime, the descendants of such slaves could have owed heavy obligations

[16] The main texts are *RCL* 6, 12, 34, 52, 359, 445, 542, 800, 826–7 (cf. 1352). For the family, see H. M. Schwarzmaier, *Lucca und das Reich*, pp. 284–91, 384–7; for the recent date of the signorial powers of this family and others see Wickham, 'Economia e società', pp. 409–11.

[17] For the political activities of Enrico and his descendants, see Bernardo Maragone, *Gli Annales pisani*, ed. M. Lupo Gentile, pp. 10–13; *Tholomei lucensis annales*, ed. B. Schmeidler, *MGH SRG*, ns. vol. 8, pp. 53–5, 288–9; V. Tirelli, 'Il vescovato di Lucca tra la fine del secolo XI e i primi tre decenni del XII', in *Allucio da Pescia*, pp. 87–8.

of all kinds. In addition, ecclesiastical landowners often had judicial powers over even free tenants in the ninth century, and the *placitum* of our 1160 text could well be its direct successor; the recognitive gifts of chickens and eggs in that text, too, had their equivalents in leases to cultivators in every century from the eighth to the twelfth. It would be a mistake to conclude from this that twelfth-century signorial-type obligations over tenants normally derived from the Carolingian world. In the Lucchesia, tenure was too fragmented in the intervening centuries to ensure the continuity of such powers over dependent cultivators, and they are undocumented in surviving leases.[18] Even in Massa Macinaia, the canons' estate was by no means the only property, although it was by far the largest; their tenants also held land from other landowners in the twelfth century, in divided plots that interpenetrated the lands of the canons' *curtis* (itself divided, as were nearly all Italian estates, into hundreds of pieces), and all this made it harder to control them.[19] But it is at least likely that the crystallization of signorial rights over the most dependent strata of tenants in the years around 1100, in a place like Massa Macinaia, may have partially represented the regularization and updating of obligations the tenants already owed. Ad hoc obligations previously simply attached to tenure, like gifts of chickens and donkey service, became part of a network of political burdens, guard duty and army service and hospitality and, most important, justice (all of which had Carolingian antecedents, but probably a largely new form by the twelfth century). These were now seen as wholly separate from rent-paying; the 1160 text mentions no standard rents – grain, wine or oil – at all.

On the largest and most traditional estates of the Lucchesia, then, signorial rights developed out of older patterns of dependence, and perhaps not always by brute force. But they were not simply a continuation of older traditions; they became separate from rents, and many of their features were new. It is interesting that the canons, when dealing with their own *manentes* on the Massa Macinaia estate, whether reclaimed from the Vorno family or controlled directly, did not ever refer to to the military duties that the

---

[18] See Jones, 'Italian estate'; Wickham, *'Manentes'*.

[19] Some examples: Gemignano di Albertino, a *manens* in *RCL* 1521 but apparently a land-owner in *RCL* 1161 (AD 1157); Bellando di Martino, another of the 1521 set, holding a lease from laymen in *RCL* 1826 (AD 1200).

1160 document stresses; they were almost exclusively interested in judicial rights, and a more generalized obedience to the canons' instructions – the canons, who did not have the same military pretensions, saw their signorial rights differently. Different lords took their chances in different ways in the early twelfth century, and ended up with different rights as a result, even over their most subject dependants. It is interesting, in fact, that the canons actually exerted less control over their *manentes* than many lords did, at least in one respect, for in Massa Macinaia such tenants do not seem to have been tied to the land, a (generally) new obligation that can be found almost universally for twelfth-century *manentes* elsewhere in the diocese. Perhaps on a big and stable estate such a requirement was unnecessary; but its absence is at least worth noting.[20] And the canons' *signoria* over its Massa Macinaia estate never turned into a territorial *signoria* over the whole village, either; here, too, they were either less ambitious or less successful than many lords further from the city.[21]

The canons and the lords of Vorno were not the only powers in control of sections of the *curtis* of S. Petronilla. As already noted, several families of notables had leased there from the canons. One of these was called the *filii Riccii*, the sons of Riccio, in the 1160 text and elsewhere; it was descended from Rolando *iudex*, who was active in Lucca a century earlier. Unlike the Vorno family, it had stayed in city politics; Gerardino di Riccio was a *consul maior* of Lucca in 1181. The *filii Riccii* were not, however, one of the largest families in the city, and indeed are not well-documented outside the Massa Macinaia area, where they were both landlords (on a small scale) and tenants. It is clear from Corso's 1160 testimony cited above that their dependants were subject to the Vorno *signoria;* either they were sub-tenants of the Vorno lords for at least part of their land (a common pattern in the Lucchesia) or else the Vorno family had managed to gain rights over the leases which the *filii Riccii* held direct from the canons. Either alternative makes the political situation in the village somewhat more complicated,

---

[20] For the canons' signorial interests, see *RCL* 1186, 1582; for example of tenants not tied to the land, *RCL* 1215, 1700. Jones, 'Italian estate', p. 20, points out that the canons also exacted no *fodrum*, an increasingly common signorial ground tax elsewhere.

[21] The canons were themselves more ambitious outside the Sei Miglia, at Massarosa, where they had a wide and coherent signorial territory: see G. Dinelli, 'Una signoria ecclesiastica nel contado lucchese', *Studi storici*, 23 (1915).

with a family of city notables to an extent dependent on a family
of rural lords; Gerardino actually used this dependence as a defence
in court against the canons in 1179, so his family was evidently
happy with it.[22] And the sense of complexity is further emphasized
by the fact that there was no consistency in the signorial burdens
listed in the 1160 text: not only the men of the *filii Riccii*, but also
several other families, owed fewer dues than others. It is as if each
family negotiated its duties separately, inside an overall framework
of subjection. We can also, occasionally, see tenant families building up their own lands, as with the son of one of the 1160 witnesses,
Benenato di Bonfiglio, who bought up canonical leases between
1172 and 1191, and sub-let to other cultivators, before willing his
possessions back to the canons in 1193; entire political careers
could be created through the 'land market' of tenures, and this
must have made the real content of signorial subjection more complex still.[23]

It should be clear by now that the development by major landholders (either owners or stable military tenants) of local political
rights over their lands was not at all straightforward. Even where
the process was, arguably, simply an extension of the powers that
lords already had over peasants, the network of levels of possession,
together with the different political interests of each landholder,
produced different results. The *filii Riccii* had no signorial rights at
all, perhaps because as a city family they had not sought them;
the lords of Vorno, with well-documented military activities based
on their castle, developed them most extensively – more indeed
than their own lords the canons, who were more prepared to accept
the hegemony of the city. It would be wrong to conclude that the

---

[22] For this family see *RCL* 359, 437, 542, 693, 789, 975, 1150–1, 1161, 1188, 1228, 1240,
1331, 1337, 1400, 1441, 1454 (these two are for Gerardino as consul), 1507, 1525, 1627,
1755. In *RCL* 1400 (AD 1179) Gerardino and his brother claim the *signoria* of the Vorno
family as a safeguard against being removed as the canons' lessees of a house in Massa
Macinaia in a court case, unsuccessfully. For Rolando *iudex*, see Schwarzmaier, *Lucca*,
pp. 324–5. One final comment on the *filii Riccii*. Commercial interests are almost entirely
undocumented in twelfth-century Lucca; it may well be that families like the *filii Riccii*,
of consular status but with a very small landed base, were already gaining their wealth
and influence from trade. This is a mark of the new world of twelfth-century Italian
cities; the countryside, however, was much less changed – there, the family's status
remained rather lower.

[23] *RCL* 1292, 1305–6, 1630, 1633–4, 1698 (cf. also 1184, 1240). Compare the ninth- and
tenth-century tenurial politics of the Gundualdi family in Campori, in the mountains
north of Lucca: Wickham, *Mountains*, pp. 45–51.

more urban a family (or a church) was, the less it was interested
in signorial rights; the most powerful urban family of all in the
twelfth century, the Avvocati (descendants of the judge Flaiperto),
had a small but clearly demarcated signorial territory around the
castle of Coldipozzo, conceded to them around 1160 by Frederick
Barbarossa. But one can certainly say that the extent and political
importance of signorial powers was dependent both on the local
political (and economic) opportunities, and on the wider political
aspirations, of landholders. Italy maintained in its cities a more
complex political arena than survived in most parts of Europe,
which remained attractive to all sorts of landowners in the countryside. How determined lords were to turn power over land into
power over its inhabitants was closely linked to what sorts of things
they wanted to do with power in that wider arena.[24]

My final, briefer, example is an illustration of this last point,
through the material for the bishop's *signoria* in Moriano north of
the city. Moriano was a large village with an episcopal estate scattered across it; this estate only covered about a fifth of the village,
but it was the only substantial property in the entire area of the
settlement, and was focussed on a castle on the hill above from the
early tenth century onwards. Moriano's inhabitants were largely
small and medium landowners, that is peasant owners and petty
notables with a few tenants; these strata also provided most of the
tenants of the bishop, for most people held land in lease as well as
in full property. This pattern, of a local autonomous peasantry set
against a single large landowner with a castle, looks like a richer
version of that found at Casciavola; we could expect the bishop,
given the absence of locally powerful rivals, to turn his predominance in this village into a *signoria*, perhaps by force. And indeed

---

[24] For Coldipozzo, see *RCL* 1259, 1284; Archivio arcivescovile di Lucca (henceforth AAL),
    ++G18 (AD 1175); Archivio di stato di Firenze, fondo diplomatico Strozziane Uguccioni,
    dic. 1220; Archivio del Capitolo di Lucca, fondo Martini, 12 magg. 1243. For Flaiperto
    and his descendants, see Schwarzmaier, *Lucca*, pp. 309–17. It is important to stress that
    the rules governing the relationship between local power and the urban arena were
    different from city to city as well; Milan, for example, was a strong and aggressive city
    in the twelfth century, but the rural lords around it (many of them city-dwellers) were
    far more interested in signorial rights than they were in Lucca, and the city did not ever
    object – indeed, its judges were happy to spend much of their time moderating signorial
    disputes. See, for this, the cases in *Gli atti del comune di Milano*, ed. C. Manaresi; and see
    e.g. A. Padoa Schioppa, 'Aspetti della giustizia milanese', in *Atti dell'XI° Congresso italiano
    di studi: sull'alto medioevo*, pp. 518–28.

Moriano is the first area in the diocese of Lucca to have a documented territorial *signoria*, that is to say an area with clear boundaries in which everyone owes certain obligations to a lord; the
bishop defended it against his nearest aristocratic rivals, the lords
of Montemagno, in a court case dating from the late 1070s, thanks
to local witnesses.[25] He was soon forced to defend his castle as well,
for Bishop Anselmo II was a major figure in the Gregorian side of
the Investiture Dispute, and was expelled from Lucca in 1080 by
the citizens; a combined city and imperial army besieged the Moriano castle in 1081–2, though ultimately without success. This
defeat, and the return of a reformist bishop to the city in the late
1090s, probably ensured the survival of the signorial territory of
Moriano, for the latter covered a surprisingly large area, given how
close to the city it was. In 1121, Moriano's adult male inhabitants,
all 293 of them, each swore an oath of loyalty to the bishop, and
the text of this oath will be the focus of what follows:

From this moment on, I so-and-so will make no association, or have it
made, and if I have done so I will not maintain it, against the honour of
St Martin [the cathedral saint] and the bishop of Lucca, or to divide the
commune (*communis populi*) of Moriano. And in the estate and castles of
Moriano I will make no deliberate theft (or have it made), or rapine, or
fire, or exaction, except by the word of the bishop or his certain representative. And concerning all the property the bishop (or his representatives)
has, puts, or has put in the castles or estate of Moriano, I will not take
it or contest it (or have it taken or contested) against Bishop Benedetto
of Lucca or his successors or his representatives. And I will not offend
any person who comes to the bishop in the castles or estate of Moriano,
either coming, staying, or leaving, either in his property or his person,
except in self-defence or in defence of my property. [There then follows
provision for the bishop to exact informal penalties.][26]

This text is the first loyalty oath for Moriano (and, indeed, is
among the first known from the diocese), but not the last. Later
ones were longer, and included more elements: military service, for
example, appears in 1159, as does explicit reference to the bishop's
placitum.[27] We should not consider these to be new in 1159, however,
as the bishop had established his judicial rights already in the

---

[25] The court case is AAL +K16; it has a very poor edition in *Memorie e documenti per servire
all'istoria della città e stato di Lucca*, vol. 4, ed. F. Bertini, *Appendice* 84. For all this section,
see the chapters on Moriano in Wickham, *Comunità e clientele*, cc. 4, 5.
[26] AAL +L91; incomplete edition in *Memorie*, ed. Bertini, *Appendice* 99.
[27] AAL ++B36.

1070s, and the *Morianenses* had defended his castle in 1081. What the bishop could claim throughout this period, in fact, stably and with little contestation, was a wide overall hegemony in Moriano: political, military, and judicial, including (as it emerges by the thirteenth century) judicial powers over capital crimes. This is what all signorial lords wanted, whether over tenants (as in Massa Macinaia) or over poorer neighbours (as at Casciavola); the bishop in Moriano had it over both.

This *signoria* was certainly, unlike at Massa Macinaia, a wholly new development in the late eleventh century; no lords in this part of Italy had any sort of analogous powers over free owners before the 1070s. But, unlike at Casciavola, it does not seem to have represented a forcible imposition from above. Not only did local inhabitants not take the risk of contesting the bishop's lordship, but they supported it in court and, indeed, by arms, from the start. The numerous documents for Moriano show that by the 1110s, if not earlier, the more prosperous Morianesi were episcopal feudatories, and attended him when he came to his castle; they also dominated the early rural commune of Moriano, which is indeed first documented in the text just cited. The bishop had, that is to say, a network of locally influential local supporters. But they were not, as often elsewhere, an elite military stratum, of aspiring petty aristocrats; peasant cultivators, too, held fiefs from the bishop, and the whole population swore to him in 1121.

Although there are fewer documents for Moriano from the eleventh century, and so we can be less certain about its history before 1070 or so, what seems to have happened is that the bishop had long been, as the major local owner, the centre of a clientele that stretched through all the social strata of the village, from local notables to tenant cultivators. (Perhaps it was not the only clientele in Moriano, but it was certainly the dominant one.) This informal patronage and protection, in the more privatized climate of the 1070s, turned into a much more formal set of signorial rights, focussed on justice and army service, stretching by now over the whole population. Whether or not this was sought by those who had not previously been part of the bishop's political network, it was certainly acceptable to episcopal clients, who could see their privileged access to the bishop crystallized into a set of rights and duties that could, and did, last. In this way, the bishop extended his powers as a landowner into powers as a political lord, but through patronage rather than coercion. And this cohesion between episcopal interest and local interest remained; as the city commune expanded its powers in the late twelfth century, the episcopal *signoria* became an area, not of particular economic exactions, but of tax privileges, which the Morianesi consistently sought to defend. Even in the area of rights over justice, we find by the end of the twelfth century that the personnel who controlled local justice for the bishop were actually the leaders of the commune of Moriano, who ran cases autonomously, and simply gave the bishop half the profits. And these two almost exhaust our references to signorial powers, apart from occasional military obligations (for the bishop was a more forceful political player than the cathedral canons ever were). The bishop took some wood-rights and river-bank tolls (shared with the local commune); but we have no reference at all to the array of menial duties we have seen in other villages. The role of the bishop in Moriano remained, in fact, one of rich neighbour and political patron, rather than ruler or lord; the new signorial politics permitted this rather traditional pattern to continue, and even to be reinforced.

The image of the development of signorial rights is generally one of violence; of armed warlords, finally unleashed, happily terrorizing peasants and churchmen up and down the lands of Western Europe. This image, although it does reflect the discontinuities of the process, is excessively romantic. It is actually quite hard to impose a new legal and political system exclusively by force over the huge majority of a region, even with modern technology, never mind that available in 1100. The imposition of signorial rights was effortful, and was achieved in inconsistent and piecemeal ways, over long periods. We have seen that it did not result in uniform rules of subjection even in a place like Massa Macinaia, where tenants were highly subject already. And, although we may feel for the peasants of Casciavola, we should note that they seem to have won; even had they lost, as was more normal, we must remember that the armed men of S. Casciano would have had their work cut out to terrorize more than a couple of villages at once. Under these circumstances (as, indeed, in all circumstances), the easiest means of gaining power is by achieving *consent* to that power, or at least resignation to its effects. This is why the documentation for Moriano is interesting, for it shows how, in a specific case –

and, of course, specific circumstances – consent could be constructed, and what for. But, in the end, consent for signorial powers was quite common, at least for a while, whether along the lines of the Moriano oaths or along those of the Massa Macinaia testimonies. They were not agreed to everywhere in Italy; the twelfth and (especially in Tuscany) thirteenth centuries were also periods in which rural communities and cities regarded signorial rights as illegitimate, and sought to remove them, often by force.[28] But this tended to be a subsequent development, a reaction to already established rights, which had previously, however unwillingly, been accepted. We would at any rate be unwise to conclude that signorial rights were *normally* always resisted, from the time of their imposition to the time of their abolition; far from it, in fact, or else they could hardly have existed as rights at all.

This consent was normally constructed through the acceptance of the extension of long-established patterns of dominance, either of lords as landowners or as aristocratic tenants/feudatories of whole estates, or of lords as rich neighbours and patrons, or both at once. We have seen the first in Massa Macinaia; the second in Moriano. In each case, the way the dominance worked changed, by becoming more formalized, more politicized, and probably more ritualized (in both villages we see rituals of subjection in our twelfth-century texts: the performance of menial duties for the more subject, the repetition of collective oaths for the more autonomous). It also involved economic obligations that were more precise, more generalized, and that were normally heavier. Lords hoped to get away with this, simply because the acceptance of the dominance of the rich was traditional; when the rich defined themselves in new ways, as an autonomous military aristocracy for example, so their dominance changed in style, and the poor were simply going to have to adapt. At Casciavola, they did not adapt, but rather resisted, bringing on themselves violent retribution. We could see this as a standard response, revealed to us by the lucky survival of a document. But I would guess that variants of the Moriano experience were more common: here, neighbours of a great lord accepted his *signoria*, and indeed in large part took it over. They were doubtless mindful of the dangers of resistance (the bishop

---

[28] See, for a good recent survey, A. Castagnetti, 'Il potere sui contadini', in B. Andreolli et al. (eds.), *Le campagne italiane prima e dopo il Mille*.

certainly had his own armed men); but their acceptance was made easier because he was *already* their patron. And he was not unique; the violence of the lords of S. Casciano in Casciavola was the retribution of people who had clearly always been patrons, and whose patronage was now rejected. The obligations were new, for society and the political system had changed, but the patronage, at least, was old.

This brings us back to the basic theme of this book, the relation between land and power. The new political system in Italy was a transformation of patterns of power that had very long roots in the past, and those patterns were, throughout, based largely on the control of land, even if the relationship altered. In the Carolingian period, land brought you wealth, and thus clients (military or political), and thus access to the spoils of public office, where power really lay; after the changes of the eleventh century, it brought you wealth, and thus armed clients (if you could control them), and thus strong bargaining rights over weaker neighbours, unarmed clients, which could be turned into more formal, signorial, relationships, immediate power on the ground. The second period might seem to show a more direct link between land and power as a result. The aim of the powerful in the second period was, however, not simply to establish such new relationships, but to legitimate them, through a new customary framework, which represented both a generalized consent to these relationships and an effective political barrier to their subsequent rejection. The framework of signorial rights seems to have lifted political power away from direct landholding, for such rights were separable from rents, and were often over people who were not tenants; they created a new arena for political practice that was often physically separate from landed power. (There were, indeed, some powerful signorial lordships in Italy which covered areas where the lords in question held little or no land directly.) Land remained at the base of signorial power, but, in the end, the interaction between land and power remained as complex as under the Carolingians. And finally, how it worked in detail depended on what lords wanted to use it for politically; for lords were, of course, interested in wider political stages than the villages they controlled most tightly. We have seen this at Massa Macinaia, for example, where signorial powers varied according to the military interests – and, to an extent, the urban political involvement – of each political actor. This can be generalized more widely: power *over* people was, and is, always conditioned by what that power is ultimately intended to be *for*. And how it derives from land – as, today, with money – always depends on the rules by which power is recognized to be legitimate, which are always complex, whether in the world of Italian city states or in that of Norman barons, or in that of Charlemagne.

Northern Italy can be said to be atypical of eleventh- and twelfth-century Western Europe: in its domination by cities, and thus by a more complicated and less directly military politics, as well as by a more continuously public political framework, with justice remaining largely in the hands of city courts – Lucchese city courts could be found judging cases, for example, even in a *signoria* as politically coherent as Moriano. Signorial politics were thus more limited in Italy: smaller-scale, more fragmented and, again, more complicated. But, largely as a result, in some respects they are more transparent: we can see what real relationships of power they represented. It is for this reason, for example, that we can link signorial powers to other forms of patronage, which mediated the basic opposition between lords and peasants; indeed, networks of political relationships between these two classes were probably commoner in much of the rest of Europe, too, than has sometimes been thought. If we want to look for these networks elsewhere, then the Italian experience can serve not as an exception to Western European developments but, with care, as a model for them.

CHAPTER 10

Conclusion: property and power in early medieval Europe

MODELS

'Dodo was the *domesticus* (leading administrator) of Prince Pippin, and he had many estates (*possessiones*) and many armed men (*pueri*) in his following.'[1] This is how the mid-eighth-century author of the 'Life of St Landibert' chose to emphasize the power of a dangerous enemy. No less than modern commentators he understood that Dodo's power lay in a combination of office and property, which together provided the resources to support the armed force necessary to protect his interests. Chris Wickham uses a similar formulation to characterize the basis of power in the Carolingian period.[2] Unlike moderns, however, medieval writers were rather more concerned with the effects than with the origins of power. They thought of power in terms of morality and social convention, that is, according to how it was used. Their view of property likewise concentrated upon use, and consequently the question of *ownership* was generally of less interest to medieval people than the issue of possession and use of property. Here David Ganz's chapter is essential as a guide to the ways in which some medieval people thought about the acquisition and use of property: principally, how they justified it in moral terms. The notion that who possessed and used property was as important as who owned it is one which is partially retained in modern generic definitions of the term 'property', for they include both possession and ownership. We have maintained this open-ended definition throughout our discussions in order to deal with the variety and complexity of the medieval use of property. In this our concluding discussion we will first look

---

[1] *Vita Landiberti Episcopi Traeiectensis Vetustissima*, ch. 11, ed. B. Krusch, *MGH SRM*, vol. 6, p. 365.
[2] See above, Wickham, p. 243.

at how modern views of the relationship between property and power have evolved, and consider what effect these views or models of history have had on our own researches. In the next section we will draw together observations about the nature and extent of our source material in order to see how these condition our understanding of property and power. We shall then examine the issue of how control over space developed in our different areas. In the fourth section of the conclusion we will discuss the effects of rulers or the 'state' upon the relationship between property and power, and in the final section we will close with an overview of the cultural dimension of our subject.

In the course of the seventeenth and eighteenth centuries the moralistic view of power gave way to a more materialistic analysis, and there developed a keen interest in how power was constituted, as well as in how it was exercised. At the same time, concern to redefine property ownership in order to stress individual rights of disposal led to a growing sense of difference between modern and earlier forms of property holding, the medieval form now being seen as comparatively precarious, or incomplete. As Susan Reynolds has recently demonstrated, it was the lawyers' view of medieval landholding as essentially different from the modern which came to be the basis on which medieval property relations in general, and in turn the whole of society, were seen by historians as distinct.[3] 'Feudal', an adjective for the whole of medieval society and for each of its constituent aspects, was a term historians borrowed from the lawyers. Modern views of medieval property and power thus have their roots in the notion that 'feudal' property relations were the basis of a distinctive kind of power, whether defined in constitutionalist or economistic terms. Over the last century a series of models has been advanced to explain the nature and development of this power according to those aspects seen as most significant for the long-term development of European society, namely, the history of particular European states, the growth of the state in general, and the development of the economy. Most influential of all has been the Francocentric model, which Chris Wickham outlines at the beginning of his chapter.[4] In this

---

[3] S. Reynolds, *Fiefs and Vassals. The Medieval Evidence Reinterpreted*, pp. 7–8.
[4] See above, Wickham, p. 221.

scheme, public authority is said to have declined across the early medieval period. By about the year 1000, it is argued, property had become the simple basis of power, which was consolidated through the exercise of judicial rights over that property and the surrounding population. According to the model, though such 'seigneurial' rights and power had typically been established by force, they would eventually become the platform upon which state institutions and public authority could be painstakingly rebuilt. The ramifications of this model have had an influence upon all of our discussions, even if our response has mostly been to point out its shortcomings as a tool for understanding the situation on the ground. Let us see how the Francocentric model has been treated in this volume.

Discussions about immunity, in the introduction and in the chapter by Paul Fouracre, were concerned with the question of whether the granting of certain judicial rights to ecclesiastical land-holders was an essential stimulus to the decline of public authority, prefiguring, as it were, the rise of 'private' or seigneurial justice and power. Here it was seen that immunities developed in quite specific Frankish contexts, which actually had nothing to do with the breakdown of public authority. Or, from another viewpoint, that from Wales, the development of immunities was shown in part to be a reaction to the *growth* of royal authority, that is, the opposite of what in the traditional view was meant to have happened on the continent. Ian Wood tackled another Frankish phenomenon closely identified with the development of 'feudal' society, namely the grant of land in *precaria*. Precarial tenure has been seen to lie at the heart of 'feudal' property relations: it concerned land granted on easy terms in return for military or political service which could be translated into power. At the same time precarial tenure was seen to illustrate the way in which possession rather than owner-ship had become the key feature of property holding. Here the institutional phenomenon is inseparable from the political history which gave birth to it: the Frankish leader Charles Martel (d.741) needed land to reward his followers and this allegedly led him to use *precaria* as a device through which to appropriate church lands. The institutional, social, economic and military implications of this thesis were spelled out by Heinrich Brunner in the late nine-teenth century, and like other clear and apparently comprehensive

explanations of complex historical change, it remains seductive.[5]
Ian Wood, however, demonstrates how the political history of
Charles Martel's period has recently been rewritten in a way which
questions both the timing and the scale of the appropriation of
church land. His close examination of one of the best-known
examples of precarial expropriation shows it to be exceptional, with
ecclesiastical institutions more normally letting out lands to their
own clients rather than to the followers of warrior leaders.[6] Chris
Wickham too had to engage with some of the main tenets of the
Francocentric model in his case studies of seigneurial power in
Italy. Here he focussed on the process by which lords imposed
their authority on local communities, and he was concerned to see
to what extent conditions in Italy fitted the currently prominent
notion of a feudal revolution which turned through a cycle of violence as lords forced peasants to accept their demands. His answer
was equivocal in that he shared the model's perception of a sharp
change in the relationship between land and power across the
period 900–1150, but he also identified a consensual element in
the imposition of seigneurial authority, and emphasized a greater
variety of relationships between lords and peasants than the classic
model of feudal revolution allows for. In his discussion of the evidence of the *Vita Meinwerci* Timothy Reuter addressed what one
might term the German branch of the Francocentric model. This
variant attempts to explain the apparent strength of public authority in Ottonian and Salian Germany by stressing the use of
bishops and abbots as instruments of central government. At the
same time, it is argued, magnates of all kinds amplified their power
by consolidating their hold over a coherent terrritory. The suppo-
sition is that the bishops and abbots used their territorial power
in effect to conserve central authority; this acted as a brake against
the privatization of authority, which would have been the consequence had lay magnates been left as the only ones to build up
territorial power. This kind of counterweighted power structure is
now seen as unnecessarily convoluted. Reuter shows that it bears
little relation to Meinwerk's situation, in which one sees a symbiotic power relationship between ruler and bishop and between

---

[5] The seminal work was H. Brunner, 'Der Reiterdienst und die Anfänge des Lehnwesens',
in his *Forschungen zur Geschichte des deutschen und französischen Rechts* (1894).
[6] See above, Wood, pp. 46–8.

bishop and lay magnate, rather than the strictly interdependent or antagonistic relationships forecast by the conventional model.

Patrick Wormald, too, was concerned to refute the dominant model's application to England, by showing that there is no evidence from late Saxon England to suggest that private justice was making inroads into public authority as it was supposedly doing on the continent in the same period. Wormald examines in detail the 1086 Domesday Book entry for the area of Oswaldslow in the diocese of Worcester, which is the main piece of evidence quoted in support of the view that judicial immunities of continental type were being established in England before 1066. He demonstrates that the Domesday entry, far from being at the end of a long tradition of granting immunity, was in fact part of a recent process of reinforcing the privileges of the church of Worcester in the light of continental practice imported after 1066 and in the face of unwelcome demands from unpleasant Norman sheriffs.[7] As Rosemary Morris explains, the idea that immunities weakened the state is, or ought to be, a point of debate for historians of Byzantium just as it is for those studying the West. Rather as in the case of Anglo-Saxon England, it has been supposed that in the eleventh century the granting of immunities in the Byzantine Empire sapped the strength of a hitherto resilient central authority. Here we see the convergence of two models of history, that is, the Francocentric version of the emergence of a newly empowered 'feudal' aristocracy in the period after 900, and the Byzantine historians' model of inexorable decline in the strength of the state in the post-Macedonian period. Morris shows that what can be said about the granting of *exkousseia* fits neither model. Byzantine emperors were not obviously giving away their main sources of revenue in the eleventh century, nor can *exkousseia* be associated with the growing strength of a social elite in the Empire. Exemptions were from incidental charges and services rather than from the main burden of taxation, and should be understood from the point of view of local arrangements of power and control over territory, rather than in the context of 'state-decline'.[8]

In all of these discussions, it was necessary to engage the basic model of feudal development because its central theme, that power

[7] See above, Wormald, pp. 133–4.
[8] See above, Morris, pp. 212–20.

came to rest increasingly, and eventually exclusively, on the holding of land, is one which reaches to the heart of our subject. As it
happens, since it is not our primary concern, this book does not
deal directly with the core Francocentric issue of what did change
and what did not change in power structures of the Frankish kingdom at the end of the Carolingian period. What we have done is
to provide reassessments of the period before and after this change.
In each case the model had to be amended or disregarded because
its overall scheme was too abstract to work with on the ground.
Firstly, the finding that immunities had been too simply identified
with long-term change in the political structure removed one of
the main planks in this overview of history. Secondly, the model
presented an analysis of power in relation to the long-term development (or, usually in our period, decline) of the state which made
little sense when approached from the point of view of case studies.
Lastly, the strong opposition between notions of 'public authority'
and 'private power' which is axiomatic to the concept of 'feudal
revolution' we found misleading when applied to our own fields
of study. We shall return to these important points later in this
conclusion.

Wendy Davies's discussion of the development of immunities in
early medieval Wales provides a good example of how misleading
models can be: the situation in Wales, far from looking anomalous
(as it tends to when viewed against the criteria for the development
of large states like England or Francia), appeared as variant within
a pattern which is seen throughout Christian culture, East and
West, namely, the drive by ecclesiastical institutions to protect
their space and privilege according to local pressures and opportunities.[9] In many ways, of course, models are invaluable, and we
have all benefited from having the Francocentric model as a point
of orientation. Janet Nelson engages with newly emergent models
of gender in history, and Patrick Wormald's discussion keys into
a model for the development of Anglo-Saxon central authority
which he himself has done a great deal to promote. There are also
anthropological models which underlie our unstated assumptions
about such phenomena as gift and counter-gift. We all share the
view that reciprocity was a fundamental principle of social conduct,
and that it was through the giving and receiving of gifts that a

[9] See above, Davies, pp. 140–7.

wide range of social relationships was expressed. The chapter which most clearly focusses on transactions and the 'continuing relationships' they underpinned, is Timothy Reuter's, but the theme is present at various levels in all our writing. The construction of social being through participation in sacred ritual and contribution to holy power is another anthropological theme which has been absorbed into historians' thinking. Again, it has influenced us all, but is particularly relevant to Paul Fouracre's discussion of the provision of lighting for the church. We have profited from the general insights that anthropology provides, but as historians concerned with specific cases it has not been our brief to enter into a critical evaluation of our anthropological models. Nonetheless we hope that our observations will be of use to anthropologists. In particular, Janet Nelson's remarks about the factor of gender in property relations, and Timothy Reuter's examination of the rationale of giving gifts to bishops in eleventh-century Saxony, are of direct relevance to current debate about the significance of reciprocity.[10] What emerges from our discussions in this volume is that to understand how people used property to exercise power, we have to start on the ground and work outwards. The advantage of charter evidence is that it draws our attention towards specific instances. It is from these that we may draw ideas about general developments, or build models, but we cannot seriously believe that medieval people shared these ideas.

THE DOCUMENTS

We are largely dependent on written sources for considering property in the early middle ages and we are unlikely to forget that the quantity of documentation at our disposal is often meagre and always variable. While there is relatively little surviving from sixth-century Francia or from Wales at any period, there is relatively

---

[10] Historians tend to draw on a canon of classic anthropological works, such M. Mauss, *The Gift*, or on the even older work of E. Durkheim, *The Elementary Forms of the Religious Life*. As A. Weiner, *Inalienable Possessions. The Paradox of Keeping-While-Giving*, pp. 28–30, has recently argued, these early models are in need of critical re-evaluation, not least on the subject of gift-giving and social reciprocity. Historians do not usually have the training to make such a challenge, but their observations may still be of relevance to the task, even when informed by traditional thinking, rather as Weiner draws on the work of S. D. White, *Custom, Kinship and Gifts to Saints, the* Laudatio Parentum *in Western France, 1050–1150*, who used Mauss, apparently without reservation.

much from twelfth-century Italy. But even within northern Italy we have noticed that there are many texts from, for example, Moriano but few from the neighbouring villages.[11] Whatever the reasons for these differences (and they will depend as much on record-keeping as on record-making, as much on political interest as on sudden disasters), the spread available to us is in practice haphazard. We do not have 'coverage', even in 'well-covered' areas; and we know *nothing* about a large proportion of property in the early middle ages, in all parts of Europe. This will always have a bearing on our assessments.

The quality of the documents is also variable. They can be cryptic, obscure or inconsistent; they can be rich in detail about every aspect other than the one you want to discover; they can be full but misleading, or brief but conclusive. So much is commonplace. No early medievalist expects to work from a dossier of total information and it would be naive to expect to find answers to everything in a set of texts 800 to 1,500 years old. Rather, we work with what we have.

Our starting point in this study lies with charter texts, although they do not form the foundation of every paper in this volume. The authors have drawn from narratives, laws, tracts, wills, surveys and the curious mixture of the formulaic and the particular which constitutes the Frankish formularies. However, many of them have examined the detail of specific charter texts to illuminate their points. The broad term 'charter' covers records that deal with more than conveyancing; it includes records of disputes, of surveys of estates, tenants and dependants, of dues expected, of special favours and privileges granted, many of which are acts designed to perpetuate the memory of donors. Charters can be brief or lengthy, but whatever their length they have especial value as texts recording the *particularities* of the transfer of property rights. They deal with named localities and named persons, in other words with individual people and particular places; thereby we can glimpse, despite the limitations, the way relationships and institutions worked and the way principles were applied. Although, then, the charter may show us only one piece of a complex narrative, a frozen moment in a network of continuing exchanges, the glimpse

---

[11] See above, Wickham, p. 232.

is especially valuable.[12] It allows us to make sense of the generalizations of the lawyer and the annalist; above all, it allows us to bring them down to earth.

We have, then, to acknowledge the limitations of the data but proceed nevertheless. One tool is the – on the surface purely technical – analysis of the relationship between the form and purpose of the texts, which reveals for example that a given form of document could be used to record transactions of a different type from that for which the form was originally intended, as forms of immunity were used in Ottonian East Francia. So, too, words for originally distinctive transactions were applied to an increasing range of different business, as *precarium* was used already by the seventh century, as words for fiscal exemptions were used in eleventh-century Byzantium and as the new lords in late eleventh-century England used old words with new meanings. Thus the use of once-distinctive language spread to cover a multiplicity of less specific purposes.[13] Unravelling the distinctions which are concealed rather than revealed by the language is one of the primary tasks of the specialist. This specialized work allows us to attribute meaning to the particular texts under the microscope; but it also allows us to see the process by which behaviour changed and to see the conceptual frameworks within which early medieval writers operated. In Germany sales were described as gifts; in Wales gifts were recorded as sales.[14] This is the language of reciprocity, and serves to underline the role of exchange in the web of continuing relationships that so many of the contributors to this book have emphasized.

Unravelling levels of meaning in the document is one of our primary tasks today, but in the early middle ages the document could of itself stimulate action and counter-action, as if it were itself an actor in the network of transactions; the very particularity of the written (charter) text injected an element that was different from the pure interplay of persons – as clerics and women knew. Writing and record-keeping were a conscious part of the ecclesiastical armoury against forceful neighbours. Early medieval people

---

[12] See above, Reuter, pp. 167–71.

[13] See above, Wood, pp. 42–7, Fouracre, pp. 66–8, Morris, pp. 209–13, and Wormald, pp. 133–5; also Introduction, pp. 12–14.

[14] See above, Reuter, pp. 180–1; *The Text of the Book of Llan Dâv*, ed. J. G. Evans with J. Rhys, nos. 201–203b.

used documents for real and immediate purposes, as well as for making permanent records. Some used a standard procedure and its accompanying documentary form for a purpose other than that for which they were formally intended; so, Erkanfrida used her bequest not only to make provision for affairs after her death but to secure her own protection in life; and eleventh-century Saxon lords made donations not so much to benefit the church as to control who would hold benefices in the neighbourhood.[15] Others changed a document, changed the text itself, for present or for future gain. So Llandaff clerics edited the texts they collected in their archive, for immediate use in their disputes with Norman lords and neighbouring bishops; Worcester clerics did the same in their argument with the abbey of Evesham; and perhaps they influenced the oral evidence that came to be recorded in the English Domesday Book.[16] This is precisely why all surviving charter texts are valuable, whether 'authentic' or 'forged'. They do not present a mere record of what happened, for they could themselves be instruments for securing control. We have the benefit of being able to analyse the instrument as well as the record.

CONTROLLING SPACE

The right of any free adult male to give protection to another was common in European societies and applied just as much to clerics as it did to laymen; it was therefore taken up by Christian religious bodies as they became established. In the case of some religious institutions, round about the eighth and ninth centuries the right became territorialized to produce the *noddfeydd*, gyrths, *termonn* lands and chartered sanctuaries of Wales, Scotland, Ireland and England.[17] These are very distinctively insular contexts. While the notion that a man had the power to give protection was certainly as much continental as it was insular in the very early middle ages,[18] we are not sure that the power to protect was ever

---

[15] See above, Nelson, pp. 108–9, and Reuter, pp. 171–2.

[16] See above, Wormald, pp. 121–8, and Davies, pp. 152–7.

[17] See above, Davies, pp. 144–5. The Scottish development could well be later; the English development is not evidenced at this early date; it could therefore also be later, but was not necessarily so.

[18] Cf. the Lombard legal collections, e.g. Rothari, ch. 35, Liutprand, ch. 37, and so on, in *The Lombard Laws*, trans. K. Fischer Drew, pp. 59, 162.

territorialized on the continent in the same way and to the same degree that it was in Britain and Ireland.

The Welsh *noddfa*, the area in which the special power of a given church's protection was exercised, was a place where people could expect to be safe and unharmed. It could be as big as three miles around the church, and could include houses of the laity as well as farmland. The church directly benefited by the public acknowledgement of such a territory and did so in an explicitly financial way: if offences were committed in the *noddfa*, of whatever type and against whomever, fugitive or not, then the church received an especially high compensatory payment. However, although the benefit was financial, this was in essence a legal and judicial privilege. It was the physical expression of the status and independence of the protector.

The development of protected ecclesiastical territories in Britain and Ireland was clearly influenced by the Old Testament notion of the safe haven and probably influenced by the canon law of sanctuary, a comparable but more limited idea of ecclesiastical protected space, for fugitive criminals and others. Ecclesiastical sanctuaries can in practice be found in many parts of the continent in the early middle ages, and some of these are recorded as extending to the cemetery wall, to the buildings around the church, to thirty paces beyond it, and so on. They could be clearly differentiated from the surrounding area, as were the *sagreres* (from *sacraria*, holy places) of Catalonia.[19] (Sanctuaries are sometimes called – by German scholars in particular – the 'narrow immunity', a refuge or asylum, a type of immunity with few financial implications.) In the early eleventh century, in the particular context of the Peace of God movement, oaths of peace and conciliar legislation emphasized the protected status ('peace') of the church building, and sometimes of the surround, by dwelling on the dire penalties that those who attacked or stole from it would suffer.[20] These ideas are certainly similar to the insular expressions but there are differences too. One difference between continental and insular territorial sanctuaries lies in their scale: insular protected territories were characteristically large and could be extremely large. Another

[19] R. Martí, 'L'Ensagrerament: l'adveniment de les *sagreres* feudals', *Faventia*, 10 (1988).
[20] H. Hoffmann, *Gottesfriede und Treuga Dei*, especially pp. 24–69; T. Head and R. Landes (eds.), *The Peace of God: Social Violence and Religious Response in France around the Year 1000*.

difference lies in the scale and form of the judicial consequences of violation. Penalties for violating sanctuary were built into insular secular law and had the force of the lay community behind them as well as ecclesiastical sanction. Financial profits to the offended church could be considerable. Continental penalties were sometimes purely spiritual. Moreover, they were primarily applied to attacks on the church and its property, although the protection might be extended to unarmed clergy and the defenceless, as also to food supplies.[21] Although the continental sanctuary was a safe haven, the consequences of violation were altogether different from the consequences of violating sanctuary in Britain and Ireland.

In the case of the Welsh document 'Braint Teilo', the idea of the *noddfa* was expanded in the early eleventh century into a full territorial immunity – a place not merely specially protected but exempted from obligations to the laity. The essential notion inherent in the immunity, exemption from a ruler's demands on his or her subjects, can be found throughout the areas we have discussed, from Ireland to the Byzantine Empire.[22] Desire to have such exemptions is easy to understand, and their widespread appearance and development does not need elaborate explanations, although there are late Roman precedents in many of the areas discussed (in particular the fourth-century attempts of Roman emperors to favour the Christian church, and clerical attempts to encourage this favour).[23] Exemptions were sometimes – as in the Byzantine Empire and the Frankish kingdom – in theory applicable to both laity and clerics, but keeping them and developing them was largely an ecclesiastical process. Over the period of the sixth and seventh centuries in Francia, and somewhat later to east and west, the emphasis of the exemptions shifted from being essentially fiscal to being largely judicial: immunities were exempted from the entry of public officials to hear disputes as well as to collect dues.[24] Though the reasons for this shift to the judicial

---

[21] Excommunication featured prominently; see H.-W. Goetz, 'Protection of the church, defense of the law, and reform: on the purposes and character of the Peace of God, 989–1038', in Head and Landes, *Peace of God*, at pp. 264–70.

[22] For Ireland see 'Liber Angeli' and 'Additamenta' to Tírechán's Life, in *The Patrician Texts in the Book of Armagh*, ed. L. Bieler, pp. 172, 174, 186.

[23] Whatever the precedents, however, it should be noted that application of the concepts changed over the early middle ages.

[24] See above, Fouracre, pp. 58–60, Morris, pp. 216–19, Wormald, pp. 134–5, Davies, pp. 150–1. See Introduction, n. 20, for comment on the views of A. Murray (who has argued for a stronger judicial element at an earlier period).

may well have been primarily financial, they serve to emphasize the physical consequence, the immunist's right to exclude officials from his space.

Major churches therefore in effect created territories which were free from state officials, from their physical entry, their presidency over public gatherings and their practical demands. They controlled the space occupied by some or all of their lands such that it became, as one Breton monk put it, 'like an island in the sea' and as if it had been picked up and 'put in a sack across his shoulders'.[25] This was a real and considerable political power. Moreover, once established, these islands of control were not merely areas exempt from rulers' interference; they were areas free from the interference of all kinds of neighbour, be he local official or local lord, lay or religious. By the ninth century Frankish immunists were as much, if not more, concerned to preserve this local aspect of the benefit of immunity as they were concerned about the ruler; rulers themselves began to take on the protection of immunities against intruders and spelled this out in their documents. As Paul Fouracre points out, by then it was the protection against the power of others *by* the ruler rather than the exemption *from* the ruler's own power that was the more highly valued by the immunist.[26]

In East Francia immunities were increasingly in practice run by the lay advocates who had to speak for the ecclesiastical immunist in court. Whereas in the ninth century these were spokesmen appointed on an ad hoc basis, by the twelfth century they were laymen holding permanent appointments for administration of the immunity, deriving considerable personal benefit and power from the office, and sometimes assisted by a network of sub-advocates.[27] To the extent that rulers influenced the selection of advocates, as some seem to have done in the twelfth century, the advocates almost became a type of state official.

Whatever we think of Francocentric models of 'feudal revolution', we can see that in the new world of the central middle ages, signorial/seigneurial rights and powers were developed by some

---

[25] *Cartulaire de Redon*, ed. A. de Courson, no. 136.

[26] See above, Fouracre, pp. 58, 65; see also Morris, pp. 216–19. Cf. the lands of the monastery of Redon in the later ninth century, where objections were forcefully and successfully made when the local machtierns Gredworet and Ratfred tried to encroach; *Cartulaire de Redon*, nos. 105, 261.

[27] E. E. Stengel, *Die Immunität in Deutschland*, pp. 512–24.

people in many parts of Europe and contributed a further stage in the acquisition of political power by major landlords. Regular annual payments, and payments in respect of specific lordly functions like protecting the harvest, were demanded from all who lived in a given territory; physical obligations were imposed – castle guard duty, fetching and carrying, ploughing mowing and threshing; restrictions on the peasant's freedom to marry and pass on his property to his heirs were introduced; seigneurial courts were established to deal with some categories of offence. This was far from being a distinctively ecclesiastical characteristic, and laymen were as prominent as clerics in developing seigneurial powers. Whether lay or ecclesiastical, the characteristic early medieval mode of controlling space by way of exemptions ('freedoms') in general gave way in the central middle ages to controlling the people who lived on it. As Chris Wickham puts it, the development of signorial rights in Italy is the means by which power over land was turned into power over its inhabitants.[28] What happened was that some landlords expanded their powers by expecting obligations from the (sometimes willing) local population, whether they lived on the landlord's own property or not.[29] It is a quite different means of controlling space – of expressing power over property – from that of earlier centuries. Indeed, the developed seigneurial territory did not have to coincide with the extent of the *seigneur*'s personal landed property.

This is too late a development for many of the papers in this book but it was nevertheless a development that was widespread. Our discussions have drawn attention to the *seigneuries banales* of western Francia in the tenth and subsequent centuries and focussed in this respect on late eleventh- and twelfth-century Wales and Italy.[30] From the eleventh century some of the great landlords of East Francia also acquired powers over free and unfree peasants

---

[28] See above, Wickham, pp. 221–6, 238.

[29] See above, Wickham, pp. 241–4, Davies, pp. 150–7. The summary in G. Duby, *Rural Economy and Country Life in the Medieval West*, pp. 224–31, remains both pertinent and useful.

[30] See above, Fouracre, pp. 66–7, Wickham, pp. 223–44, Davies, pp. 150–64. Cf. the abbot of Redon in eastern Brittany who already in the 890s exercised seigneurial control over a block of territory 10 × 20km., in which he could levy special dues, control vacant lands, hold a court at which he presided and imposed penalties, and – above all – expected the *loyalty* of the population, even above their loyalty to their landlords within the territory; W. Davies, *Small Worlds. The Village Community in Early Medieval Brittany*, pp. 188–200.

in lands outside their personal properties, having added so-called 'comital' or 'ducal' powers to their landlordship.[31] Hence the powers, for example, of the bishops of Würzburg by the early twelfth century. This is the *Bannherrschaft* of German scholars and its development is a process directly comparable to the seigneurial/signorial development of France and Italy.[32] We could have added comparable developments in the 'Castilo-Leonese ban' of northern Spain, and could have stressed some similar tendencies (though lacking the seigneurial courts) in Byzantium.[33]

Creation of the *seigneurie* did not depend on the presence of some pre-existing immunity and the immunity did not invariably become the *seigneurie*; indeed, some forms of immunity continued into the modern world – witness the Isle of Man and the Channel Islands; and some eleventh-century immunists remained exempt from the new seigneurial jurisdictions established around them.[34] However, sometimes royal grants of *districtus* and *bannus* necessarily added another layer to the power of some immunists, a layer that derived directly from the delegation of royal authority – known as *Bannimmunität* to German historians.[35] Hence freemen came under the jurisdiction of advocates in East Francia.[36] Where that happened the immunity could indeed become the core of the *seigneurie/signoria*. However, such cases did not necessarily progress to the full range of powers enjoyed by the Italian *signor*; indeed, in East Francia this only sometimes seems to have been the case. Power relationships were complex and do not fit tidily into a single model.

In the central middle ages power over property increasingly meant power over the people who lived on it – a power that was expressed in a multiplicity of detailed ways. Of course, major landlords had always had power over people in some sense but that

---

[31] Such powers did not have to be authorized by the ruler, but they were perceived to be the sort of powers that counts or dukes might exercise; B. Arnold, *Princes and Territories in Medieval Germany*, pp. 112–20.

[32] Arnold, *Princes and Territories*, pp. 62–3, 72.

[33] P. Bonnassie, *From Slavery to Feudalism in South-Western Europe*, pp. 122, 268–9; cf. pp. 109, 312–22.

[34] Duby, *Rural Economy*, pp. 188–9; cf. the example of 974 in Catalonia cited by Bonnassie, *From Slavery to Feudalism*, p. 250.

[35] Stengel, *Die Immunität in Deutschland*, pp. 589–98; cf. tenth- and eleventh-century village communities in Catalonia subject to abbots in whose immunities they lived; Bonnassie, *From Slavery to Feudalism*, p. 246.

[36] Arnold, *Princes and Territories*, p. 116; O. Brunner, *Land and Lordship. Structures of Governance in Medieval Austria*, p. 258.

power became more detailed and more practical, more close at hand; it came to make more of a difference to daily life. This need not imply, as classically supposed, a diminution of the power of the 'state' for these were increasingly new and local rather than transferred powers. They have as much to do with changing aristocratic attitudes to territory as with the role and power of the state: landlords were more inclined to dominate (physically) a stretch of land than sit at home and eat the income.

THE STATE AND PROPERTY

The influence of royal authority upon the relationship between property and power is an issue of common importance to all of the discussions in this volume. As our introduction explains, the collective power vested in the institutions of royal authority or 'state' would in theory function as a medium through which those holding property could acquire wide-ranging influence and achieve high status. At its strongest, that is, in the most favourable conditions, that collective power would be able to shape the institutional structures of society: hence the central place given to the history of the state in those models of history which we discussed earlier in this conclusion. Although it is in general likely that the holding of high office and participation in the high politics of a large state would have allowed landholders access to resources greater than those available from the income of their land alone, the studies in this volume make it clear that in practice the effect of royal authority upon property relations varied considerably according to time and place. As ever, what looks rather neat in abstract terms appears somewhat messy on the ground, and using the term 'state' to cover all of the elements of public and central authority poses problems. The term 'state' was seldom used by early medieval people, and rarely are historians clear about what they mean by it, for there is confusion between the term as it is applied to particular territorial entities and as it is used to refer to the collection of institutions and prerogatives through which the public authority vested in the ruler was exercised. Nowhere in Western Europe at this time did kings have a monopoly of power, nor were they anywhere in full control of public institutions, and law was determined as much by custom as it was by royal decree. Although early medieval people did distinguish between what was 'public' and what was 'private' in terms of both property and power, they did not have the strong sense of opposition between 'public' and 'private' which informs a modern understanding of the state. Our discussions about Frankish immunities pinpointed these issues, for they dealt directly with the question of the transfer of power from public officials to private corporate bodies and related this to the effects upon royal authority. The answer, that the effect of granting immunities was largely neutral in this respect where royal authority was concerned, makes the point that there was here no decisive shift in power, precisely because those who received the benefits of immunity were groups who generally used their power in support of royal authority.

In the later part of our period, when there was in some areas a more radical change in power relations, this, in Chris Wickham's words, amounted to 'shifts in the outer form rather than in the content of power'.[37] That is to say, since power had always been in the hands of local landholders, the removal of central authority sometimes made little difference. Nevertheless, although the term 'state' is one perhaps best avoided, the issue of central authority (nearly always, in practice, royal authority) remains important. Rulers did exist, and a precondition for their authority was that they could make demands upon the resources of others. With the probable exception of very early Wales, all the property mentioned in this volume was subject to burdens of a fiscal, military or judicial nature which, at least in origins, had been owed to rulers. In Frankish lands up to the late ninth century, generally in England, and always in Byzantium, rulers did exercise (or at least claim) some rights over all land. Frankish legislation, for example, makes it clear that even the greatest magnate did not have complete power in his own territory (*potestas*), for he was required to deliver up major criminals for judgment in the public court.[38]

The old textbook opinion is that royal authority was in general the loser in what was a trade-off of rights and resources in return for service from its aristocracy.[39] According to this view, periodically rulers or regimes emerged which had the vigour to recoup that loss, and thus redress the balance of power in favour of the centre. On the other

---

[37] See above, Wickham, p. 225.
[38] See above, Fouracre, p. 62, n. 23.
[39] For a textbook example, H. Mitteis, *Der Staat des hohen Mittelalters*.

hand, the theme here has been that in Francia and Italy the theoretical position of central authority as a mediator between property and power seems in practice to have been limited, basically because that authority was weak and was brought into play as much by the demands of others as by its own determined efforts. Ian Wood's discussion deals with Francia in the mid-eighth century, when it is said that the balance of power was dramatically altered in favour of the ruler, but he suggests that even at a time of apparent change in property holding and power relations brought about by the ruler's forceful actions, the monastery of St Wandrille, an institution which claimed to have been beggared by the change, actually kept most of its holdings intact. Although at this time the leasing of land in *precaria* was explicitly associated with the build up of military resources by the Frankish leaders, the vast majority of surviving precarial grants have nothing to do with this. Typically they reveal the arrangements by which people donated land to a local monastery or church but retained that right of usufruct needed to maintain wealth and status. In other words, the precarial grant was not an instrument through which the rulers transformed the nature of property holding to the benefit of their own power. Frankish rulers in fact said remarkably little about property and its use, and Frankish law is largely silent in this area too. It is significant that the remarks about the military use of *precaria* were expressed in an ecclesiastical context and concerned a form of land-holding associated only with the church.[40] It seems to have been the church which articulated views about property, and as David Ganz argues, the church was concerned above all to justify its own ownership of property in terms of its use on behalf of the whole Christian community. It was morally very difficult for the church to alienate property, although it tended to acquire more property than it could manage directly. The leasing of land was one solution to this problem, as long as the ecclesiastical ownership of that land could be formally recorded and regularly re-enacted through the payment of – often token – rent. Ganz shows how the church called on Carolingian rulers to safeguard its property in this way, and it was this ecclesiastical initiative rather than any 'policy' of the rulers which had the effect of making it more difficult for direct possession to be used as proof of the ownership of land.[41]

[40] The remarks were made at the Council of Estinnes: see above, Wood, p. 35.
[41] See above, Ganz, p. 26.

At the same Council at which the church had called on the ruler to safeguard its benefices (Paris 829), the bishops also gave instructions for the veiling of widows. These instructions, as Janet Nelson explains, were of direct relevance to power over property, for widows who took the veil in their own home could avoid remarriage and exercise control over their own property. If they entered convents, however, they lost control, and if they remarried there was a danger that control of their property would pass to the new husband.[42] Rulers were asked to consider these issues, but any intervention seems not to have been decisive, either in protecting widows from abductors, or in discouraging them from remaining veiled in their own homes. Here, as in the case of the development of *precaria*, royal authority was reacting to conditions, rather than creating them.

Chris Wickham examined what happened when the influence of central authority faded away, 'when all power lost its strength and justice was dead', as the villagers of Casciavola in Tuscany put it at the turn of the eleventh century.[43] In northern Italy at this time local lords with military power extended traditional dues taken from the peasantry to oppressive levels. As Wickham demonstrates with another example, the village of Massa Macinaia, seigneurial domination could develop out of older patterns of dependence, for the land of this village had been part of a Carolingian estate likely to have had servile tenants.[44] It was this element of continuity which led him to judge that the shift in power was in outward form rather than content. Whereas in the past, agents of central authority may have provided a source of redress against oppressive lords, now peasants sought help from powerful cities, and still, as before, an element of consensus made the relationship between villagers and lord workable.

Did the rulers have more influence over the relationship between property and power in Byzantium and England, two areas said to have had relatively strong central authority in this period? Central authority in the Byzantine Empire operated through a hierarchy of salaried officials, and historians freely use the term 'state' to refer to this government, which not only taxed its citizens heavily,

---

[42] See above, Nelson, pp. 90–4.
[43] See above, Wickham, p. 229.
[44] *Ibid.*, pp. 234–5.

but also continued and developed the Roman rhetoric of common-wealth. It is interesting in this context to note the sometimes ambiguous attitude of the Athos monastic establishment towards central government in the tenth and eleventh centuries. As Rose-mary Morris tells us, there is no doubt that the monks were devoted to the Empire's spiritual protection. They coveted and cherished direct access to the emperor, and paid their land tax, but found the officials of the state burdensome and intrusive. Some impositions or *munera* (the sort of services of labour and provision familiar in the West too) they deemed oppressive, even at a time of military crisis. In the later eleventh century, a time of sustained crisis, there was confrontation with officials and tax avoidance by the monasteries 'on an epic scale'.[45] As Morris argues, this resistance was not the fruit of the earlier granting of exemptions (*exkousseia*) but rather the result of the state trying to hang on to resources it was tempor-arily finding difficult to realize. In part it was because the Byzan-tine state was so inflexible in its mediation between land and power that despite a great deal of cultural and religious solidarity between rulers and subjects, there was also a degree of hostility towards central government. We must not forget that general consensus for widespread taxation is a phenomenon only of very modern, and relatively very wealthy, states.

In England, by the end of the tenth century, the king's influence over property relations was remarkably strong. Nearly all land was subject to his judicial control, and to certain fiscal burdens and military obligations. As Patrick Wormald argues with some vigour, the notion that in the late Saxon period kings began to relax their judicial control is false. England was not, however, like Byzantium, even though central government at times did tax heavily, for Eng-land was scarcely bureaucratic in organization, local landowners forming the backbone of government. The power of office thus complemented, and was in part derived from, the economic and social power of the landlord. Wormald gives the example of Abbot Æthelwig of Evesham who in the 1070s accumulated property in the West Midlands by virtue of his position as the king's leading representative in the area. Or, when Bishop Wulfstan defended his property in a public court he lined up his clients as witnesses.[46]

---

[45] Morris, above, p. 215.
[46] See above, Wormald, pp. 122–4.

Rulers did manipulate the courts to advance their interests, but what Wormald calls 'the tendency to integrate lordship into administration' meant that in practice, as with the Carolingians, there was often little difference between the public power wielded on behalf of the ruler, and the private power of the great lord which was based, ultimately, on property.

Wendy Davies shows the bishop of Llandaff in south-east Wales acting in the late eleventh century in a way rather similar to that of Wulfstan of Worcester a few years earlier. Both bishops attempted to strengthen the independence of their churches in the face of vigorous and intrusive Norman lordship. The Welsh evidence discussed by Davies is particularly valuable in demonstrating that this resentment towards the intrusion of rulers into church lands had a long history in Wales. There are hints of resentment elsewhere too, for example in the Byzantine context, as we have just seen. Nowhere but Wales, however, do we see the basic demands of rulers challenged as an affront to status and honour. Davies's example of King Brochfael being judged in the bishop's court for breaking the bishop's peace seems to be the inverse of what one would find elsewhere.[47] Whereas in the other areas discussed in this volume there was clearly a degree of partnership between landholders and rulers, which worked to their mutual advantage, in Wales rulers do not seem to have had the institutional basis to do much more than bring trouble to those outside their own region. The Welsh material is invaluable in reminding us of this hostile aspect of rulership, for elsewhere in Europe, too, rulers throughout our period did occasionally attempt to boost their power by raiding the property of others. The ravaging of Anglo-Saxon kings, for example in Worcestershire in 1041, shows how brittle the partnership between king and locals could be.[48]

We have seen that the power of rulers was everywhere a significant element in the relationship between property and power, but also that nowhere was it the sole arbiter of that relationship. It was generally essential for rulers to persuade those with power in the locality to act as their representatives. The suitability of bishops for this task had the effect of enhancing their importance in local power structures. Timothy Reuter shows this in some detail for

---

[47] Davies, above, p. 146.
[48] The narrative of the Worcester episode is in the chronicle known as *Florence of Worcester*, trans. D. Whitelock, *English Historical Documents*, vol. 1, 2nd edn, pp. 318–19.

Bishop Meinwerk of Paderborn in Saxony in the early eleventh century. His point, that the bishop's prominence as spiritual leader, judge and centre of a territorially defined community would make him a key figure throughout early medieval Europe is one this volume as a whole strongly supports.[49] Meinwerk's transactions illustrate his key position, with access to a wide range of resources which he could use with some flexibility to dispense an equally wide variety of services, both material and spiritual. Paul Fouracre too drew attention to the advantage church leaders had in building up a variety of resources which enhanced their already considerable economic power.[50] As Reuter suggests, however, the power of such people did not simply depend on their material wealth and on the support they received from rulers, for their spiritual, even charismatic, leadership was also an important factor maintaining their power over others. This non-material aspect of power we shall now examine, for it lies at the heart of this culture no matter how much it was based on property.

CULTURAL ASPECTS OF POWER

The moral justification for the ecclesiastical ownership and acquisition of property which David Ganz discussed, was not simply an ideological construct, for it helped in a practical way to articulate the giving of gifts to the church. This is evident in the countless charters of donation to the church in which the act of giving was introduced by a statement of the purpose and hoped-for result of the gift, namely, the desire to aid the church in return for spiritual salvation. This statement of intent and commitment in the preamble of charters is more than a pious formula, for it is clear that spiritual protection was highly valued, but as it was not for sale in a formal sense, it had to be earned aiding the church in its work. Giving could be targeted at specific ecclesiastical need or functions, such as paying for prayers to be said, for lighting, for alms to be distributed to the poor, or for food and clothing for the clergy. Supporting the church in its basic functions in this way was a means of quite literally turning property to spiritual use, of converting 'this worldly generosity, via monastic consumption, into

[49] See above, Reuter, p. 193.
[50] See above, Fouracre, pp. 78–9.

divine favour and next worldly benefit' as Janet Nelson describes payment for commemorative meals.[51] Paul Fouracre makes the same point in relation to the provision of lighting which was the stated aim of granting immunities in late seventh-century Francia. He argues that this gift of lighting should be seen as highly valuable in both a material and a spiritual sense because it focussed on a commodity of high economic value and great liturgical significance.[52]

The high value placed upon the spiritual made it an important factor in the world of material property and power. As was emphasized earlier in this conclusion, religious institutions could demand their own exclusive space on the basis of the need to maintain their spiritual purity, to remain undisturbed 'to speak with God on behalf of the world' as an imperial confirmation of a privilege for the monks of Chios put it in 1053.[53] Throughout Europe spiritual protection could mean actual physical protection in the form of sanctuary, and the ability to protect was an important attribute of anybody's power. It was also an exclusively male attribute.

As Reuter points out, it was not possible to argue with the principle of giving to the church, a principle which had the effect of creating a wide range of possible donors to it. This may also have meant that by giving to the church a wide section of people exercised, or at least attempted to exercise, the power to alienate their property. That this did involve growing numbers of less wealthy people seems to be indicated by the mushrooming numbers of charters recording small-scale donations from the mid-eighth century onwards.[54] Janet Nelson discusses the extent to which this development helped to empower women to exercise control over property. Her emphasis on the complexity of the issue shows that it is often simplistic to imagine (as some have done) that the church could legitimate women's control to its own advantage.[55] Women like the ninth-century Frankish widow Erkanfrida faced pressures from a number of interested parties – kindred, church and lords – and their control over land varied according to what kind of land it

---

[51] Nelson, above, p. 99.
[52] See above, Fouracre, p. 78.
[53] Morris, above, p. 211.
[54] The spread in the use of charters which illustrates this phenomenon is discussed with particular reference to the evidence from the monastery of St Gallen by R. McKitterick, *The Carolingians and the Written Word*, pp. 77–134.
[55] See above, Nelson, p. 83.

was, that is, whether inherited or acquired from the husband or others in various ways. Erkanfrida's main aim was simple enough, and it was one that donors generally shared: to secure the spiritual support of a number of monasteries and churches for the souls of herself and her dead husband. Mobilizing the resources to do this, however, was a complex process, even more so for women than for men, which showed that individuals' hold over property was in general far too precarious for the church to engineer the right for them to dispose of it at will, even for purposes which no one could gainsay.

Erkanfrida's attempts to build material and spiritual security for herself demonstrate the interaction of gender, family, lordship and religion upon property relations. In making transactions all of these elements had to be taken into account, and the framework for this reckoning was one of social obligations and cultural conventions. All of these factors together determined how property could be used. Legality did not necessarily determine social acceptability when it came to dealing with property. Relatives of donors often challenged what was the perfectly legal alienation of property and received some sort of compensation. At stake in such cases was not merely the family fortune, but also a loss of status and honour. Compensation acknowledged status and repaired honour. These social norms transcended the lay/religious divide. Churchmen, and saints, had honour and status just as much as lay persons. Religious values may have been mobilized around the prospect of eternity in another world, but on a mundane level, they actively reinforced the existing social system. This Wendy Davies demonstrates in the Welsh context, where major ecclesiastical landowners could expect compensation for offences committed in the *noddfa* on the basis that the patron saint's honour had been insulted and affronted.[56] Timothy Reuter shows how these values were woven into Meinwerk's transactions. We see the bishop making counter-gifts to families in order to make their gifts to him more acceptable, with the record of the transaction itself having a liturgical function and public importance. According to Reuter, moments of transaction reveal property as 'a medium through which relations of friendship, kinship and enmity, as well as of patronage and deference, can find public and highly ritualized expression precisely

---

[56] See above, Davies, pp. 145–6.

at those points at which rights in it are being granted away or modified'.[57]

It was through these social relations that property was channelled into power, but power could be used in a hostile manner to break these very rules when military victory or local crisis put rulers in a position to seize property and bring about a change of personnel. Both Ian Wood and Patrick Wormald refer to the use of power in such contexts: the establishment of the Carolingian regime in Francia and the building of Norman power in England. In both cases we see the deployment of military force, followed by the use of the law courts, the one to destroy the armed power of opponents, the other to effect a less disruptive transfer of resources to their own supporters.[58] The use of conflict to extend power was in fact exceptional, for normally the legitimation of power depended on the maintenance, not the disruption, of the social network based upon property ownership. The social customs and cultural conventions through which such networks operated were fundamental to the mediation between property and power, and they give us an insight into the important question of *why* people with property should have used their wealth to build up power of various kinds over others.

West European society was aggressively competitive, and status was a focus of competition. To protect one's social status it was necessary to honour social and religious obligations, and it was, as we have seen, through dealings with others that wealth was converted into power. Generosity, sumptuous display, the provision of patronage and the furnishing of aid were all ways of expressing status, and they all required wealth. In return they brought that loyalty and material and spiritual support which was the basis of power. Since the conversion of property into power entailed the circulation of wealth from lord to followers, there was not only competition to serve the lords, but social pressure on lords to increase their power. A primary motive in the accumulation of power was thus the need to satisfy the aspirations of followers. The needs of the followers themselves were equally pressing. As work

---

[57] Reuter, above, p. 172.

[58] Wormald's discussion, above, pp. 121–8, is set against the background of Norman expropriation. For discussion of the Carolingian use of the courts in this way, P. Fouracre, 'Carolingian justice: the rhetoric of improvement and contexts of abuse', *Settimane di Studio*, 42 (1995).

on precarial grants in eighth- and ninth-century southern Germany has shown, some members of less well-off families might sink in status (from 'noble' to 'free') over successive generations unless they could find some way of preventing the dissipation of their wealth amongst the growing numbers of family members.[59] One strategy for achieving this was to make a precarial arrangement through which it was possible to designate some, rather than all, of the family as landholders. Another possibility was to increase wealth and status through service to some powerful person or institution. Here demand in all probability far outstripped opportunity, and this factor has a bearing on the development of seigneurial lordship which Chris Wickham discussed, for it helps to explain the capacity of newly independent lords to recruit the lesser nobility as supporters.

It was because property was turned into power through activities which were seen as socially both desirable and necessary that the accumulation of power itself was generally seen in a good light: when people did express doubts, what they disliked was the misuse of, rather than the accumulation of, power. The legitimation of power should be understood in this cultural context. Things appeared rather different in Byzantium, famously so in the eyes of Anna Comnena. There, power was something which was supposed to be derived from, and exercised on behalf of, the emperor, not something built up from one's own property and wielded to protect the status of self, family and clients.[60] Not surprisingly the Westerners in the main appeared to the Byzantines as insatiably greedy. What was a vice to one culture was a virtue to the other.

The essays in this volume have examined four main areas: the meaning of power over property; the ways in which property conveyed power; the nature of immunities; and the power of royal authority to affect property relations. Our discussions as a whole have revealed and reinforced some obvious truths: power over others could be constructed through a variety of often complementary means, not only by making use of landed wealth, but also by

---

[59] See the works by Jahn and Hartung, cited by Reuter, above. p. 171, n. 21.

[60] In practice, the power of the Byzantine noble in the provinces lay in a combination of property and office, and in the course of the twelfth century the importance of office declined in relation to other forms of local influence. Nevertheless, the perception was that legitimate power was derived from the emperor, and when that power was contested it was challenged on the basis of misuse rather than on the grounds of its nature or origins. See J.-C. Cheynet, *Pouvoir et contestations à Byzance (963–1210)*, esp. pp. 207–48.

exercising rights through office, via spiritual leadership, or by the successful management of social obligations. Nonetheless, mediation between property and power was a normal operation of the social order. To challenge the principle that those with property should have power, was inconceivable. People did challenge specific abuse of their rights in the courts, and there was a strong sense that an abuse of power constituted injustice, but not only did the judicial system protect the privilege of the powerful, judicial rights were in themselves a source of power. Nor, on the whole, did the church provide a source of alternative values. As we have just seen, it was very much part of the property culture. In our earlier volume on the settlement of disputes we emphasized the prominence of the clergy in litigation about property, both lay and ecclesiastical, and narrative church sources are full of the language of law, property and power. Charters, with their anathemas protecting property, with their implied or literal links between earthly property and spiritual power, their call upon public witness and social obligation, and (when available) the aid of central authority, express all of these elements of spiritually sanctioned proprietary rights. Across Europe, and throughout the period we have studied, charters which recorded property transactions were basically similar in form, content and purpose. The similarity is testimony to the central place of property in European culture. It was the barefaced competition for property which everywhere gave shape to power.[61]

---

[61] For the way in which competition led to 'a rhetoric of expansionary violence' in the central middle ages, see R. Bartlett, *The Making of Europe. Conquest, Colonization and Cultural Change 950–1350*, pp. 85–90.

Glossary

* indicates a word that features in this glossary.

Advocate (Latin *advocatus*) Man appointed to carry out judicial functions on behalf of someone else, especially the church, and in some areas, women. In Francia, Carolingian legislation stipulated that all immunities should have advocates. As the position of advocate became powerful, it could in some cases turn into independent lordship, especially in Germany from the tenth century onwards.

Allod (also **alod**) Land held in full proprietorial right, though sometimes with restrictions on alienation (see *hereditas**). First documented in *Lex Salica*, and always common in the Frankish world, it spread to the rest of Latin Europe from the tenth century in contrast to *beneficium** or *feudum*, i.e. fief, land held in precarious (military) tenure. See also *proprietas**.

Angareia From Latin *angaria*. Compulsory labour service in the Byzantine Empire.

Angild In Old English, 'single payment', and in origin, therefore, probably the simple restitution of goods stolen; it perhaps acquired a more general sense of the payment owed as compensation by its perpetrator to the victim of an offence. Grants of the right to take *wite** for offences committed on a property stipulated that *angild* was to be paid to injured parties regardless.

Archon (pl. *archontes*) Local chief layman, in the Byzantine Empire; often also imperial officials or titleholders.

Ateleia Greek translation of Latin *immunitas*; see immunity*.

Ateleis paroikoi Byzantine peasants who held no land of their own, or who did not cultivate land belonging to the fisc*, and were thus not liable for dues or payments to it.

Bannus, *bannum* In the Frankish and Frankish-influenced world, public orders (e.g. to come to the army or to a law court); so, by extension, public jurisdiction, the king's peace, and public authority in general. Already by the sixth century it also meant a fine paid for offences against the public power. This terminology became associated with private lords, along with the powers themselves; see *seigneurie banale**.

Bema Byzantine imperial court of law.

Beneficium Literally, a good deed, a favour; in the Merovingian period, a gift of property in land or money; from the eighth century, the property given. Also, grant of land in return for rent. In the Carolingian period, all the above meanings, but increasingly often, land granted by a lord to men in return for military or other service. (See also *precarium**.) In principle revocable, or a life-grant, but usually heritable and throughout the Carolingian period frequently hereditary.

Braint Welsh word meaning 'privilege', and specifically the legal privilege due to a person in accordance with status; hence, in legal texts, equating to 'status'. Often but not exclusively translated *dignitas* in Latin versions of Welsh law texts. See further, pp. 146–7 above.

Camerarius Keeper of the dressing room, an important officer in a royal household with a wide range of administrative duties, but often associated with supervision of the ruler's treasure.

Cancellarius In Merovingian and Carolingian Francia, a public charter-writer, someone who can draw up a record of a property transaction (cf. notaries in Italy); such men are not documented after the end of the ninth century. The word is used, however, for the official responsible for authenticating documents in a wide variety of contexts.

Canon A decree issued by a church council; also a member of a collegiate church such as a minster church in Anglo-Saxon England or a cathedral church, normally in priestly orders. Especially before the eleventh-century reforms, canons varied widely in the extent to which they followed a quasi-monastic rule enforcing chastity and the common life (shared meals and living-quarters, no individual property).

Cartulary A book or books containing copies of the diplomata*, privileges, charters and *notitiae** pertaining to the property of a single holder (in the period covered by this volume almost invariably an ecclesiastical institution); in most cases it is the cartulary which has survived rather than the original material. The compilation of cartularies often involved editing in a variety of ways, ranging from simple shortening to systematic falsification and invention.

Censuales (pl.) People who paid tribute (*census**) to the church on a yearly basis. The same class of people is also referred to as *tributarii**, and they appear in charters from the eleventh century onward, especially in Germany, as the subject of gifts whereby their lords transferred their rents to the church.

Census Rent or tax. In Frankish sources it often has a specific meaning as the token rent which was paid for land leased under a precarial arrangement.

Cerarii (pl.) Hereditary payers of tribute to the church, who paid their dues in wax (*cera*), or cash, to provide lighting. First mentioned in eighth-century Carolingian legislation, they appear in ninth-century polyptychs* as indistinguishable from the *luminarii**, with both groups paying four pence a year for lighting. From the tenth century onwards *cerarii* are mentioned in charters as being given to the church by their lords, which suggests that by this time they were regarded as unfree in status.

Chrysobull (Greek *chrysobullon*). Gold seal used only by the Byzantine emperor. It gives its name to a type of imperial document.

Comes Count. Royal officer invested with public authority in a district, of which he was the head of the civil and military administration, and also in charge of the judicial arrangements. Cf. *pagus**.

Comes palatii Count of the palace. In Francia he was the officer responsible for managing the business of the royal court, with the specific duty of overseeing judicial proceedings.

Commune The organized collective leadership of city or village, or, by extension, a city or village so ruled. Its principals, often called consuls or *sindici* or *scabini*, tend to be attested from *c*.1100.

Concordia Agreement. Hence often a written statement of the terms of an agreement meant to conclude a dispute.

Consuetudo Payments and services customarily due to a king or lord; see also *malus usus**, *servitium**.

Convivium In western Europe between the seventh and twelfth centuries, a ritual feast commemorating an important event (saints' days, church dedications) or reinforcing social bonds (marriage, friendship, entry into religion).

Curtis Courtyard, enclosure, royal residence. The range of meanings in this word is paralleled by modern uses of its derivative, 'court'. Its meaning extended in medieval Latin to refer to the estate centred on the court.

Defensio The right to call upon royal protection. In grants of immunity* from the mid-eighth century onwards, *defensio* was coupled with *tuitio**, another term for the personal protection of the king; together they referred to royal protection of the immunist's rights of exclusion. Breach of the privilege carried a fine for illegal entry into the immunity. By the late tenth century the right to fine illegal entrants had become one of the most valued elements of the immunity privilege.

Demesne See *dominium**.

Demosiarioi paroikoi Dependent peasants in the Byzantine Empire, owing dues or payments to the fisc*, either because they held land of their own or because they cultivated land belonging to the fisc.

Demosios kanon or **demosion** Basic land tax in the Byzantine Empire.

Dikeraton Supplementary tax in the Byzantine Empire; paid at the rate of one-twelfth of the *demosios kanon**.

Diploma A charter issued by a king or emperor which can be dispositive (the act of drawing up and handing over the charter is itself the transfer of rights and does not merely record it) and evidentiary (the production of the charter in court proceedings is in itself proof of right). The term is used by historians for more than one form of document produced by rulers.

Districtio From Latin *distringere*, meaning, in early medieval legal texts, to prosecute, to punish. Punishment or penalty, or legal coercion. In the later ninth and tenth centuries, it has a more general sense, jurisdiction, such as that exercised by counts. *Districtus*, very rare earlier, frequent from the tenth century, means coercive action, distraint, then jurisdiction, and thence an area of jurisdiction, especially considered as a source of revenue – so, a governmental 'district'.

Dominium In Classical Roman law, absolute ownership of property as distinct from possession; in Vulgar Roman law, right of ownership of land; thence the land itself, and increasingly from the Carolingian period onwards, the lord's reserve ('demesne') as distinct from peasant tenements or lands granted out. Also, lordship over men.

Dos, also **dotalicium** Any kind of gift associated with marriage. In

Classical Roman law, and in early medieval southern Italy, parental endowment of a daughter at marriage; dowry. In early medieval Frankish formularies, a groom's gift to his bride, of land and/or movables; dower, retained by a widow for her life, then passed to husband's heirs. By extension, landed endowment given to a church.

Dower See *dos**.

Elatikon Supplementary tax in the Byzantine Empire, added at a flat rate to the *demosios kanon**.

Epereiai Extraordinary state requisitions in cash or kind. Used in the Byzantine Empire from the tenth century.

Euages oikoi 'Pious houses'; the term usually refers to charitable institutions in the Byzantine Empire.

Exkous[s]eia See pp. 200–4, above.

Fideiussores (pl.) Roman law term used in the early middle ages for sureties, that is, those who guaranteed fulfilment of obligations by other parties, and thus (rarely) the executors of a will. The provision of *fideiussores* was often a legal requirement, made in order to guarantee that people turned up to court.

Fisc (Latin *fiscus*). In antiquity, imperial treasury, later, a ruler's treasury. In Frankish contexts the term could refer both to royal estates ('fiscal land') and to the office which gathered revenue from a variety of sources.

Fiscalini In the Carolingian period the word has two distinct senses: peasants on royal lands (the fisc*); and, increasingly commonly, managers of royal estates.

Flymena fyrmth In Old English, harbouring of fugitives, so being accessory to the crime committed by the fugitive, and so in turn liable to the fine due for this offence; hence, the penalty paid for this offence, or the privilege of collecting it as landlord; see Wormald, above, pp. 116–19.

Formulary Collection of documents, or parts of documents, relating to land, dowry, immunity, rights of attorney etc., for use as models.

Forstal In Old English, obstruction; thus the offence of assaulting someone when going about their business, and so (as with *flymena fyrmth**) the penalty paid for this offence, or the privilege of collecting it as landlord; see Wormald, above, pp. 116–19.

Fyrdwite In Old English, army fine (see also *wite**); hence the penalty for failure to perform military service owed, and perhaps for military indiscipline of other sorts. Hence, the penalty paid for this offence, or the privilege of collecting it as a landlord.

Geld The Anglo-Saxon levy on each hide*, first used to pay the tribute required by Danish raiders under King Æthelred II, and often called 'Danegeld' thereafter. By the mid-eleventh century, when it was (temporarily) abolished, it was known as *heregeld* (army tax), and was evidently a regular, even annual, tax on property. Like other royal rights, the right to collect it could be granted to beneficiaries.

Grithbryce In Old English, breach of protection; thus the offence of breaking a specially created peace like a sanctuary and potentially that of disrupting the 'king's peace' wherever it applied, but in practice no more than 'breach of peace' as understood in modern law. Like *flymena fyrmth**, it acquired the extra meaning of the financial penalty paid for the offence, and so of the privilege of receiving this sum in the king's place; see Wormald, above, pp. 116–19.

Hamsocn Old English 'seeking at home', so assaulting someone on their property, or effectively indoor assault; this word (like *flymena fyrmth**) came to denote what was payable for the offence, or the privilege of collecting it as landlord; see Wormald, above, pp. 116–19.

Hegoumenos Head of a Byzantine monastic house or community, like a Western abbot.

Hereditas In early medieval texts, land owned by inheritance or otherwise, in contradistinction to property (such as *precaria** or *beneficium**) held conditionally. Much commoner than, but sometimes synonymous with, *allodium* (allod*).

Hexafollon Supplementary tax in the Byzantine Empire, added at a flat rate to the *demosios kanon**.

Hide Repeatedly described by the Englishman Bede (e.g. *Hist. Eccl.* I. 25) as 'the land of one family', and 'according to the English method of reckoning', the hide was evidently the amount of land whose produce could be expected to support a single family, probably the *close* family of an ordinary free man. As a unit of the yield appropriate for one family, it was also ideally suited to calculating the share of produce or reserve of labour that lords could expect to draw on; hence its appearance in grants of land or privilege as the normal means of reckoning throughout the Anglo-Saxon period and as a unit of assessment for taxation or services due in later Old English sources, notably *Domesday Book*.

Hlaford The normal Anglo-Saxon word for lord from the later seventh century; its etymology, 'loaf-giver', underlines the material basis of early lordship. *Landhlaford* in later Anglo-Saxon sources is simply 'landlord'.

Honor In the Carolingian period, deriving from Late Antique usage, official power, office; also social rank more generally, with associated rights and legal position, and thence landed endowment attached to office. By the tenth century, commonly, lands granted by a lord to his man.

Hundred The standard sub-division of English local government below the shire. In the mid-tenth century it appears, probably under Frankish influence, as the name for a court of first instance and a unit of policing. In records of dispute, it is normally encountered as a body of 'several' or 'many' hundreds lending support to a party, or giving evidence.

Idiostaton Rural properties removed from existing fiscal units and noted in separate tax lists in the Byzantine Empire.

Immunity (from Latin *emunitas, immunitas*) A privilege granted to a person or church which frees the recipient from various kinds of intervention by public authority, notably in respect of taxation and jurisdiction. For full discussion, see above, pp. 12–15.

Infangtheof In Old English 'catching of thieves', so very probably a term for theft detected *in flagrante*, which gave its victim the right to kill the thief without subsequent liability to vengeance. The appearance of this term (or Latin *furis comprehensio*) in grants of judicial privilege (see also *angild**, *flymena fyrmth**) probably means that a grantee was entitled to the forfeited chattels of thieves despatched in this way; see Wormald, above, pp. 116–19.

Isokodikes Special tax lists noting rural properties which had been removed from existing fiscal units in the Byzantine Empire.

Ius In Roman law relating to landed property, a right of ownership, enforceable against any wrongful possessor, distinguished from usufruct* by being without time limit and involving the power to alienate. It also retains a broader sense, what is morally right or just, and is hence linked with justice.

Kakoseis 'Evilnesses', usually referring to excessive fiscal demands. Compare *malus usus**.

Klasma Land abandoned for more than thirty years, taken over by the Byzantine state, detached from the village fiscal unit and leased, regranted or sold.

Landhlaford See *Hlaford**.

Logisimon Attribution by the Byzantine state of fiscal revenues to a private individual or an institution such as a monastery.

Luminaria (pl.) Lamps burned in Christian churches after the tradition of the Jewish temple. The term sometimes has the wider meaning of lighting in general, or even the provision of lighting.

Luminarii (pl.) Hereditary tribute payers of free but relatively low status who appear in Carolingian polyptychs*, whose tribute was paid in cash or wax in order to provide lighting (*luminaria**). Like the *cerarii** they appear to have paid four pence a year. Unlike the other terms for tribute payers of this kind, the term *luminarii* does not appear after the ninth century.

Maior domus/maior palatii Chief officer of the Merovingian palace, with vice-regal powers which made him the most powerful non-royal leader in the kingdom.

Mallus The official meeting place of a local community in the Frankish world, and thus also the place at which legal issues were settled.

Malus usus, mala consuetudo Common terms for seigneurial/signorial obligations (see *seigneurie**). Meaning 'evil custom', the phrases had an obviously negative connotation when they came in in the eleventh century, but soon became standard terms, used by lords and peasants alike. See also *consuetudo**.

Mancipium (pl. *mancipia*) In classical Latin, a slave. In the medieval period usually a dependent peasant of servile status.

Manentes (pl.) Tenants. Often, under the Carolingians, unfree tenants; by the twelfth century, in Italy, a free tenant tied to the land and subject to 'servile' obligations such as cart-service and enforced hospitality for the lord's representatives.

Mansio Latin term used in immunity privileges to refer to the count's* right of lodging or hospitality on the land.

Mansus Peasant holding, with land and dwellings. In Frankish contexts it became a common term of reference to the units of production and settlement which were the components of estates, and which were assessed as providers of revenue in Carolingian polyptychs*.

Matricula List of those entitled to receive alms from a church. It could also refer to the recipients themselves.

Metaton (mitaton) Compulsory billeting of soldiers in the Byzantine Empire.

Metochion Byzantine term for a monastery subordinate to another, more powerful one.

Miles (pl. *milites*) In classical Latin the word means 'soldier, fighting-man'. In the Carolingian successor-states it came increasingly from the late tenth century onwards to mean 'man' or 'follower' of a lord; hence the later extensions of meaning between the eleventh and thirteenth centuries to denote 'knight', 'noble'.

Nawdd Welsh word meaning 'protection', and specifically the legal power of protection which a freeman could offer another person; translated *refugium* in Latin versions of Welsh law texts. The power to protect was originally for a specified period but it was territorialized in the early middle ages. Hence *noddfa*, '*nawdd* place', the area in which *nawdd* could legally be exercised. Cf. *grith* in Anglo-Saxon law (see *grithbryce**). See further, pp. 144–6 above.

Noddfa (pl. *noddfeydd*) See *nawdd**.

Nomisma Byzantine gold coin.

Notitia Record, often of legal proceedings.

Pagus Administrative area; in Frankish contexts usually, but not always, the area ruled by a count, thus 'county'.

Parakolouthemata Supplementary taxes in the Byzantine Empire, usually calculated on the base of the *demosios kanon**.

Patrimonium (pl. *patrimonia*) Literally 'inheritance'; in the early middle ages used especially of lands held by a church, and in particular by the Roman church (hence 'the Patrimony of St Peter' as a term for the 'papal state').

Patrocinium In Classical Latin, patronage or protection, especially of a master over a freed slave. In Late Antiquity and the early middle ages, more generally, personalized protective power.

Pauperes (pl.) (sing. *pauper*) Literally, the poor. Generally in the early middle ages, the lowly, those lacking social power, not always with the meaning 'poor' in an economic sense, and hence those in need of protection, including monks, women and children. Often in paired contrast with *potentes**.

Placitum (pl. *placita*) A word generally used by historians to refer to a specific type of document recording the final composition at the end of a law suit; for example, a mutual agreement or a formal royal permission. This usage is attested in early medieval sources, although the word had a very much wider range of meanings in classical and late Latin. The document now called a *placitum* appears to have developed only in the sixth century. By the eighth century in Francia and Italy, the meaning was extended to that of a public court hearing ('an agreement to appear in court' or a 'royal licence for a public hearing') and later to the whole of a public court-case, across many hearings; and to the document recording the case.

Polyptych From a Greek word meaning 'many-leaved', a written inventory of an estate's resources, including people, generally organized according to *mansi**. Polyptychs were the product of a distinct phase of ecclesiastical estate management in Carolingian Francia.

Possessio In Vulgar Roman law, which assumes that possession and ownership coincide, legal and permanent ownership; the meaning continues through the early middle ages.

Potens (more commonly used in the plural, *potentes*) Literally, persons having power, in a social and political as well as an economic sense. Generally in early medieval literary texts and also capitularies, magnates as distinct from lesser aristocrats. Often with the specific sense of men with direct access to the king. Despite its appearance in the Magnificat (Luke 1: 52), seldom explicitly pejorative. Often contrasted with *pauperes**.

Potestas In classical Latin and earlier medieval usage, power of command, also public office, and in the plural, highest magistrates. It also had the concrete meaning of an area within which power is exercised.

Praedium (pl. *praedia*) Essentially a synonym for allod*; to be contrasted with *beneficium**.

Praepositus In ecclesiastical contexts, prior of a monastery, second-in-command to the abbot; in the Carolingian period, also head of a chapter of canons. Also a layman entrusted with the material affairs of a church. In secular contexts, in the Carolingian period, a public official; from the tenth century especially, bailiff of a lord or of the king (cf. French *prévôt*).

Precarium, -ia In Francia and Italy, a grant of land on terms of revocable tenure, usually but not always in return for rent or service (often military); and also, by extension, a charter making such a grant. How far such grants were in practice revocable certainly varied from case to case. See Wood, above, pp. 43–9.

Proprietas Lands owned, without time limit and without renders owed to a lord, but on which, according to Carolingian legislation, tithe had to be paid. Distinct from more conditional forms of tenure. In the Carolingian period, often in contradistinction to *beneficium**. Also, the estate itself, 'the property'.

Publicus/-a/-um Pertaining to state office, royal; pertaining to royal lands or movable wealth. *Publicum*: the fisc*, into which fines and confiscations were paid, as distinct from *proprium*, 'private'. *Res publica* was occasionally used in the Carolingian period for the royal fisc, also the state.

Res privatae In Roman imperial law, the emperor's personal property, as distinct from his property *ex officio*. Extremely rare in the early middle ages, but the concept was familiar to Wipo in the eleventh century.

Quitclaim A charter or *notitia** referring to a dispute, which records that one party has renounced or abandoned their claims or has been defeated in court proceedings.

Reconciliation The restoration of a state of peace and friendship following the settlement of a dispute, often marked by a *convivium** or gift, or both, given by the winner to the loser.

Sake and soke Old English, 'dispute and suit (of court)'; hence, in sources from either side of the Norman Conquest of England, the normal formula for the privilege of holding jurisdiction, although this did not apparently involve anything more than the right to collect fines payable in the local court.

Sanctuary A place of safety for a limited period for criminals and other fugitives, protected by the Christian church. By the middle of the fifth century the safe area was normally held to extend to the walls of a church precinct, including the church and sometimes houses of the clergy. This was variously interpreted in the succeeding centuries, to extend to 30–5 paces beyond the walls, or from the church door, and so on. Some types of fugitive, such as debtors, murderers and adulterers, were excluded by ecclesiastical and secular laws governing sanctuary.

Sarhaed Welsh word meaning 'insult'; in medieval texts it denoted the Welsh legal offence of insult, and secondarily the compensation due to the person who suffered legal insult. The legal offence of insult occurred when honour was besmirched. Often but not invariably translated *iniuria* in Latin texts. See further, pp. 146–7 above.

Seigneurie (banale) (Fr.), **signoria** (It.) Modern terms that denote a local lordship based on a network of quasi-public rights, such as a private law court, tolls on roads and rivers, or the power to exact *servitia**. The range and heaviness of such rights varied very greatly. *Seigneuries/signorie* could be restricted to (all or part of) the landholdings of a lord, or could be extended to a defined territory, covering tenants of the seigneurial lord, tenants of other lords and independent owners alike.

Servitium (pl. *servitia*) Service, usually the specific set of services due from dependants to lords, in return for land or maintenance. For military dependants, this would characteristically include army service; for peasants, it would include guard-duty in castles, cart service, road repairs and other public works, as well as demesne labour and rent. See also *consuetudo**, *malus usus**.

Signoria See *seigneurie**.

Soke Old English *socn* means 'seeking', hence 'suit of court'. In *Domesday Book* soke denotes a lordship over an area that may have originated in the right to command its inhabitants' attendance at the court held in the lord's manor; but it also comes to designate the area throughout which such lordship was exercised; see Wormald, above, pp. 116–20.

Sympatheia Relief from taxation in the Byzantine Empire on rural property which had been abandoned. The next stage (after thirty years) was to declare the land *klasma**.

Synetheia Supplementary tax in the Byzantine Empire, added at a flat rate to the *demosios kanon**.

Synod, diocesan In Francia and in England, a meeting of the clergy and prominent laymen of a diocese presided over by the bishop, in theory to be held once or twice a year, and in practice certainly held more frequently than the records would suggest.

Telesmata Byzantine term for tax payments.

Telos Byzantine term for totality of tax payments.

Toll and team The formula associated with 'sake and soke'* and *infangtheof** which expressed lordship over market transactions within the area of a granted property. *Toll* is simply the sum owed for transactions of business to a market's lord, while *team* (literally 'line') is a term applied to the process of 'vouching to warranty', i.e. tracing stolen goods back through a line of buyers and sellers; also the privilege of collecting the sum as landlord.

Tractoria Document of late Roman origin, issued to those travelling on behalf of the ruler, which orders the ruler's agents to supply the bearer with provisions *en route*. In Merovingian

Francia the document was issued by rulers to church persons travelling on ecclesiastical business.

Traditio (pl. *traditiones*) Primarily 'handing over'. In medieval Latin the term refers to the public transfer of a piece of property or property rights; also the record of such a transfer, either as a *notitia** or, in the east Frankish/German kingdom, as an entry in a book kept by a body of public standing, such as a monastery.

Tributarii (pl.) People who owed tribute to the church on a yearly basis. The same class of people is also known as *censuales**. They appear in south German charters from the eleventh century onwards as unfree people who were given to the church, that is, whose rents were transferred to the church.

Tuitio Royal protection. See *defensio**.

Ususfructus Usufruct. In Late Roman law, a qualified type of possession of property, limited in time (usually a life interest) and scope (usually to consumable goods), and without power of alienation. In the early middle ages, generally clearly distinguished from *possessio**. Often, life interest, as in property given to a church, or in a widow's *dos**.

Villa Primary meaning is estate. Hence also, a village inhabited by the tenants of an estate; sometimes specifically a royal estate, hence royal residence.

Wite In Anglo-Saxon law, strictly the fine, i.e. payment owed to an authority for an offence, as opposed to the compensation due to the injured party. Anglo-Saxon kings from the later eighth century often included the right to take *wite* for offences committed on a piece of property in a grant of the property itself, while insisting that offenders should still compensate their victims (*angild**).

Writ In Anglo-Saxon usage, a sealed letter, usually in the vernacular, from the king or otherwise established authority to an individual subject or collective institution, generally on issues of property, including disputes.

Zemia Term meaning fiscal exactions, in the Byzantine Empire.

Works cited

MANUSCRIPT SOURCES

Archivio archivescovile di Lucca, diplomatico, +K16, +L91, ++G18, ++B36.
Archivio del Capitolo di Lucca, fondo Martini, 12 magg. 1243.
Archivio di stato di Firenze, fondo diplomatico Strozziane Uguccioni, dic. 1220.
Münster, Staatsarchiv, Fürstbistum Paderborn, Urkunden 43, 44.

PRINTED PRIMARY SOURCES

Acta et diplomata graeca medii aevi, F. Miklosich and J. Müller, 6 vols., Vienna, 1860–90.
Actes d'Ivirôn, vols. 1 and 2, ed. J. Lefort, N. Oikonomidès, D. Papachryssanthou, with A. Métrévéli and V. Kravari, *Archives de l'Athos*, vols. 14, 15, Paris, 1985, 1990.
Actes de Lavra, vol. 1, ed. A. Guillou, P. Lemerle, N. Svoronos, D. Papachryssanthou, *Archives de l'Athos*, vol. 5, Paris, 1971.
Actes du Prôtaton, vol. 1, ed. D. Papachryssanthou, *Archives de l'Athos*, vol. 7, Paris, 1975.
Admonitio ad Omni Regni Ordines 823–825, in *Capitularia Regum Francorum*, vol. 1, pp. 303–7.
Agobard of Lyons, 'Epistolae', in *Epistolae Karolini aevi (III)*, ed. E. Dümmler and K. Hampe, *MGH Epistolae*, vol. 5, Berlin, 1898–9.
Anglo-Saxon Wills, D. Whitelock, Cambridge, 1930.
Anglo-Saxon Writs, ed. and trans. F. Harmer, 2nd edn, Stamford, 1989.
Annales de S. Bertin, ed. F. Grat, J. Vieillard, S. Clemencet, Paris, 1964.
Annales Fuldenses, ed. F. Kurze, *MGH SRG*, vol. 7, Hannover, 1891.
Annales Mettenses Priores, ed. B. von Simson, *MGH SRG*, vol. 10, Berlin, 1905.
Gli Annales pisani, B. Maragone, ed. M. Lupo Gentile, *Rerum italicarum scriptores nova editio*, vol. 6, pt 2, Bologna, 1930–6.
The Annals of Fulda, trans. T. Reuter, Manchester, 1992.

Arator, *De Actibus Apostolorum, Corpus Scriptorum Ecclesiasticorum Latinorum*, vol. 72, Vienna, 1951.

Archives de l'Athos, P. Lemerle, G. Dagron, S. Circovi, vol. 12, Paris, 1982.

Astronomer, *Life of Louis the Pious*, ed. G. Pertz, *MGH Scriptores*, vol. 2, Hannover, 1829.

Gli atti del comune di Milano fino all'anno MCCXVI, ed. C. Manaresi, Milan, 1919.

Augustine, *Confessiones, Corpus Christianorum, Series Latina*, vol. 27, Turnhout, 1981.

    De Civitate Dei, Corpus Christianorum, Series Latina, vols. 47, 48, Turnhout, 1955.

    'De Moribus Ecclesiae Catholicae', *Patrologia Latina*, vol. 32, Paris, 1877, cols. 1300–77.

    Enarrationes in Psalmos, Corpus Christianorum, Series Latina, vol. 33, Turnhout, 1958.

    Regula tertia, ed. L. Verheijen, Paris, 1967.

    'Sermones', *Patrologia Latina*, vol. 38, Paris, 1841.

    Tractatus in Joh., Corpus Christianorum, Series Latina, vol. 36, Turnhout, 1954.

Basilicorum, libri lx, series A, Textus, ed. H. J. Scheltema, D. Holwerda and N. van der Wal, 8 vols., Gröningen, 1953–88.

Bede, *Commentaries, Corpus Christianorum, Series Latina*, vol. 120, Turnhout, 1969.

    De Tabernaculo, Corpus Christianorum, Series Latina, vol. 119A, Turnhout, 1969.

    Historia Ecclesiastica Gentis Anglorum, in *Venerabilis Bedae Opera Historica*, ed. C. Plummer, Oxford, 1896.

Benedict, *Regula*, ed. A. de Vogue, *Sources Chrétiennes*, vol. 182, Paris, 1970.

Die Briefe des heiligen Bonifatius und Lullus, ed. M. Tangl, *MGH Epistolae Selectae*, vol. 1, Berlin, 1916.

Brut y Tywysogion, Red Book of Hergest version, ed. T. Jones, *Board of Celtic Studies History and Law Series*, no. 16, Cardiff, 1955.

'Byzantina engrapha tes en Atho hieras mones tou Batopediou', M. Goudas, *Epeteris Hetaireias Byzantinon Spoudon*, 3 (1926), pp. 113–34; 4 (1927), pp. 211–48.

Byzantina Engrapha tes Mones Patmou, vol. 1, *Autokratorika*, ed. E. Vranoussi; vol. 2, *Demosion Leitourgon*, ed. M. Nystazopoulou-Pelekidou, *Ethnikon Hidryma Ereunon*, Athens, 1980.

Canu Llywarch Hen, ed. I. Williams, Cardiff, 1935.

Capitula de Diversis Causis, 807, in *Capitularia Regum Francorum*, vol. 1, pp. 135–6.

Capitula Italica, in *Capitularia Regum Francorum*, vol. 1, pp. 335–7.

Capitula Missorum vel Synodalia, in *Capitularia Regum Francorum*, vol. 1, pp. 182–2.

Capitula Missorum in Theodonis villa datum primum mere ecclesiasticum, in *Capitularia Regum Francorum*, vol. 1, pp. 121–2.

Capitulare de Functionibus Publicis, in *Capitularia Regum Francorum*, vol. 1, pp. 294–5.

Capitulare Haristallense, in *Capitularia Regum Francorum*, vol. 1, pp. 46–51.

Capitulare de Latronibus, in *Capitularia Regum Francorum*, vol. 1, pp. 180–1.

Capitulare Legibus Additum 803, in *Capitularia Regum Francorum*, vol. 1, pp. 113–14.

Capitulare Missorum Generale, in *Capitularia Regum Francorum*, vol. 1, pp. 91–9.

Capitulare Missorum Suessionense, in *Capitularia Regum Francorum*, vol. 2, pp. 267–70.

Capitulare Olonnense Mundanum 825, in *Capitularia Regum Francorum*, vol. 1, pp. 329–31.

Capitularia Ecclesiastica ad Salz data 803–4, in *Capitularia Regum Francorum*, vol. 1, pp. 119–20.

Capitularia Regum Francorum, vol. 1, ed. A. Boretius; vol. 2, ed. A. Boretius, V. Krause, *MGH LL in quarto*, sectio 2, vols. 1–2, Hannover, 1883, 1897.

Cartae Senonicae, in *Formulae Merowingici et Karolini Aevi*, ed. K. Zeumer, pp. 185–207.

Cartulaire de Redon, ed. A. de Courson, Paris, 1863.

Cartulary of Worcester Cathedral Priory, ed. R. R. Darlington, *Pipe Roll Society*, new series, vol. 38, London, 1962–3.

Cassian, *Conlationes*, *Corpus Scriptorum Ecclesiasticorum Latinorum*, vol. 13, Vienna, 1886.

Cassien, Jean, 'Institutions Cénobitiques', ed. J.-C. Guy, *Sources Chrétiennes*, vol. 109, Paris, 1965, pp. 64–8.

Cassiodorus, *In Psalmos*, *Corpus Christianorum, Series Latina*, vol. 98, Turnhout, 1959.

Chartae Latinae Antiquiores, ed. A. Bruckner, M. Marichal; vol. 14, ed. H. Atsma, J. Vezin, Zurich, 1982; cited by document number.

Chronicarum quae dicuntur Fredegarii scholastici libri IV, ed. B. Krusch, *MGH SRM*, vol. 2, Hannover, 1888, pp. 1–194.

Chronicles of the Picts, Chronicles of the Scots, ed. W. F. Skene, Edinburgh, 1867.

Chronicon Abbatiæ de Evesham, ed. W. D. Macray, *Rolls Series*, vol. 29, London, 1863.

Clotharii Edictum, in *Capitularia Regum Francorum*, vol. 1, pp. 20–3.

Clotharii Praeceptio, in *Capitularia Regum Francorum*, vol. 1, pp. 18–19.

Concilia aevi Karolini, ed. A. Werminghoff, 2 vols., *MGH LL in quarto*, sectio 3, *Concilia*, vol. 2, pts 1, 2, Hannover and Leipzig, 1906, 1908.

Concilia Galliae A. 511–695, ed. C. de Clercq, *Corpus Christianorum, Series Latina*, vol. 148A, Turnhout, 1963.

Concilios Visigoticos e Hispano-Romanos, ed. J. Vives, T. M. Martínez and G. Martínez Díez, *España Christiana*, vol. 1, Madrid and Barcelona, 1963.

'Concilium Aquisgranense a 836', in A. Werminghoff (ed.), *Concilia aevi Karolini*, vol. 2, pp. 709–67.

'Concilium Aurelianense', in C. de Clercq (ed.), *Concilia Galliae*, pp. 4–19.

'Concilium Cabillonense 813', in A. Werminghoff (ed.), *Concilia aevi Karolini*, vol. 2, pp. 274–85.

'Concilium Meldense-Parisiense 845–6', in *Capitularia Regum Francorum*, vol. 2, pp. 395–421.

'Concilium Romanum a 761', in A. Werminghoff (ed.), *Concilia aevi Karolini*, vol. 2, pp. 65–72.

Constitutio de Hispanis in Francorum Regnum Profugis Prima, in *Capitularia Regum Francorum*, vol. 1, pp. 261–3.

Councils and Synods and other documents relating to the English Church, vol. 1, pt 1, ed. D. Whitelock, Oxford, 1981.

Crónica mozárabe de 754: edición crítica y traducción, ed. E. López Pereira, Zaragossa, 1980.

Decretales Pseudo-Isidorianae et Capitula Angilramni, ed. P. Hinschius, Leipzig, 1863.

Desiderius, 'Epistolae', ed. W. Arndt, *MGH Epistolae in quarto*, vol. 3, *Epistolae Merowingici et Karolini Aevi (I)*, Berlin, 1892, pp. 191–214.

Dhuoda, *Manuel pour mon fils*, ed. P. Riché, Paris, 1975.

'La diataxis de Michel Attaliate', P. Gautier, *Revue des Études Byzantines*, 39 (1981), pp. 5–143.

MGH Diplomata Karolinorum, vol. 1, ed. E. Mühlbacher, Hannover, 1906; vol. 3, ed. T. Schieffer, Berlin, 1966.

Diplomata Ottonis I, see *Die Urkunden Konrad I.*.

MGH Diplomata regum et imperatorum Germaniae, vol. 1, ed. T. Sickel, Hannover, 1879–84.

Diplomata regum Francorum e stirpe Merowingica, in *MGH Diplomatum Imperii*, vol. 1, ed. K. Pertz, Hannover, 1872.

MGH Diplomata regum Germaniae ex stirpe Karolinorum, vol. 1, ed. P. Kehr, Berlin, 1934; vol. 2, ed. P. Kehr, Berlin, 1936–7.

Domesday Book, general eds. A. Williams and R. W. Erskine, London, 1988.

Domesday Book, 14: Worcestershire, ed. and trans. F. and C. Thorn, *Domesday Book*, general ed. J. Morris, Chichester, 1982.

Early Scottish Charters, ed. A. C. Lawrie, Glasgow, 1905.

Edictum Pistense, in *Capitularia Regum Francorum*, vol. 2, pp. 311–28.

English Lawsuits from William I to Richard I, ed. and trans. R. C. van Caenegem, 2 vols., *Selden Society*, vols. 106–7, London, 1990–1.

Episcopum ad Hludowico Imperatorem Relatio, 829, in *Capitularia Regum Francorum*, vol. 2, pp. 26–51.

Epitaphium Arsenii, ed. E. Dümmler, *Abhandlungen der kaiserlichen Akademie der Wissenschaften zu Berlin, phil.-hist. Klasse*, 1900.

Formulae Andecavenses, in *Formulae Merowingici et Karolini Aevi*, ed. K. Zeumer, pp. 1–25.

Formulae extravagantes, in *Formulae Merowingici et Karolini Aevi*, ed. K. Zeumer, pp. 533–71.

Formulae Merowingici et Karolini Aevi, ed. K. Zeumer, *MGH LL in quarto*, sectio 5, Hannover, 1886.

Fredegar, see *Chronicarum quae dicuntur Fredegarii scholastici libri IV*.

Gerald of Wales, *The Description of Wales*, trans. L. Thorpe, Harmondsworth, 1978.

Die Gesetze der Angelsachsen, ed. F. Liebermann, 3 vols., Halle, 1903–16, rep. Aalen, 1961.

Gesta Dagoberti, ed. B. Krusch, *MGH SRM*, vol. 2, Hannover, 1888, pp. 399–425.

Gesta episcoporum Autissiodorensium, ed. G. Waitz, *MGH Scriptores*, vol. 13, Hannover, 1881, pp. 393–400.

Gesta sanctorum patrum Fontanellensis coenobii, ed. F. Lohier and R. P. J. Laporte, Rouen, 1936.

Gregorii I papae Registrum epistolarum. Libri VIII–XIV, ed. P. Ewald and L. M. Hartmann, *MGH Epistolae*, 2 vols., 1892–9.

Gregory of Tours, *Decem Libri Historiarum*, ed. B. Krusch and W. Levison, 2nd edn, *MGH SRM*, vol. 1, pt. 1, Hannover, 1951.

Liber Vitae Patrum, ed. B. Krusch, *MGH SRM*, vol. 1, pt. 2, Hannover, 1885.

Hariulf, *Chronique de l'abbaye de St Riquier*, ed. F. Lot, Paris, 1894.

Die Haupturkunden für die Geschichte der Athos-klöster, ed. P. Meyer, Leipzig, 1894.

Hemingi Chartularium Ecclesiae Wigorniensis, ed. T. Hearne, 2 vols., Oxford, 1723.

Hincmar of Rheims, *Collectio De Ecclesiis et Capellis*, ed. M. Stratmann, *MGH Fontes Iuris Germanici Antiqui in usum Scholarum separatim editi*, vol. 14, Hannover, 1990.

De Divortio Lotharii Regis et Theutbergae Reginae, ed. L. Böhringer, *MGH LL in quarto*, sectio 3, *Concilia*, vol. 4, Supplementum 1, Hannover, 1992.

Hincmari archiepiscopi Remensis epistolae, pt 1, ed. E. Perels, *MGH Epistolae in quarto*, vol. 8, *Epistolae Karolini aevi (VI)*, Berlin, 1939.

Isidore, *De Ecclesiasticis Officiis*, *Patrologia Latina*, vol. 83, Paris, 1850.

Isidori Hispalensis episcopi etymologiarum sive originum libri xx, ed. W. M. Lindsay, 2 vols., Oxford, 1911.

Jerome, 'Adversus Jovinianum', *Patrologia Latina*, vol. 23, Paris, 1883, cols. 221–352.

'Adversus Rufinum', *Corpus Christianorum, Series Latina*, vol. 79, Turnhout, 1985.

Jonas of Orléans, *Patrologia Latina*, vol. 106, Paris, 1864.

Julianus Pomerius, *De Vita Contemplativa*, *Patrologia Latina*, vol. 59, Paris, 1862, cols. 411–515.

Jus graecoromanum, ed. J. and P. Zepos, 8 vols., Athens, 1931–6, rep. Aalen, 1962.

Justinian, *Digest*, ed. T. Mommsen and P. Krueger, trans. A. Watson, 4 vols., Philadelphia, 1988.

Novellae, ed. R. Schöll and W. Kroll, *Corpus Iuris Civilis*, vol. 3, Berlin, 1959.

Karoli Magni Capitulare Primum, 769, in *Capitularia Regum Francorum*, vol. 1, pp. 44–6.

Die Konzilien der karolingischen Teilreiche 843–859, ed. W. Hartmann, *MGH LL in quarto*, sectio 3, *Concilia*, vol. 3, Hannover, 1984.

Leges Saxonum und Lex Thuringorum, ed. C. von Schwerin, *MGH Fontes iuris Germanici antiqui in usum scholarum separatim editi*, vol. 4, Hannover, 1918.

Leges Visigothorum, ed. K. Zeumer, *MGH LL in quarto*, sectio 1, vol. 1, Hannover, 1902.

Lex Ribuaria, ed. F. Beyerle and R. Buchner, *MGH LL in quarto*, sectio 1, vol. 3, pt. 2, Hannover, 1954.

Liber Eliensis, ed. E. O. Blake, *Camden Society*, 3rd ser., vol. 92, London, 1962.

Liber Historiae Francorum, ed. B. Krusch, *MGH SRM*, vol. 2, Hannover, 1888, pp. 215–328.

The Lombard Laws, trans. K. Fischer Drew, Philadelphia, 1973.

Llyfr Colan, ed. D. Jenkins, *Board of Celtic Studies History and Law Series*, no. 19, Cardiff, 1963.

Llyfr Iorwerth, ed. A. R. Wiliam, *Board of Celtic Studies History and Law Series*, no. 18, Cardiff, 1960.

Mansi, J.-D. *Sacrorum Conciliorum Nova et Amplissima Collectio*, 31 vols., Florence, 1957–98.

Marculfi Formularum Libri Duo, ed. and French trans. A. Uddholm, Uppsala, 1962; also *Marculfi Formularum Libri Duo*, in *Formulae Merowingici et Karolini Aevi*, ed. K. Zeumer, pp. 36–106.

Memorie e documenti per servire all'istoria della città e stato di Lucca, vol. 4, ed. F. Bertini, Lucca, 1818–36.

'Le monastère de Notre Dame de Pitié en Macédoine', L. Petit, *Izvestija Russkago Arheologičeskogo Instituta v Konstantinopole*, 6 (1900), pp. 1–153.

Die alten Mönchslisten und die Traditionen von Corvey, ed. K. Honselmann, Paderborn, 1982.

Notitiae as Leabhar Cheanannais 1033–1161, ed. G. MacNiocaill, Dublin, 1961.

Pactus Legis Salicae, ed. K. A. Eckhardt, *MGH LL in quarto*, sectio 1, vol. 4, pt. 1, Hannover, 1962.

Pardessus, J. M. *Diplomata, Chartae, Epistolae, Leges ad res Gallo-Francicas spectantia*, 2 vols., Paris, 1843–9.

Passio Praejecti, ed. B. Krusch, *MGH SRM*, vol. 5, Hannover and Leipzig, 1910, pp. 225–48.

The Patrician Texts in the Book of Armagh, ed. L. Bieler, *Scriptores Latini Hiberniae*, vol. 10, Dublin, 1979.

Paul the Deacon, *Gesta episcoporum Mettensium*, see *Pauli Warnefridi*.

Pauli Warnefridi liber de episcopis Mettensibus, ed. G. H. Pertz, *MGH Scriptores*, vol. 2, Berlin, 1829, pp. 260–8.

Pippini Capitulare Italicum, 801–10, in *Capitularia Regum Francorum*, vol. 1, pp. 209–10.

Pippini Italiae Regis Capitulare 782–786, in *Capitularia Regum Francorum*, vol. 1, pp. 191–3.

Le Polyptique de St Bertin (844–859). *Édition Critique et Commentaire*, F. Ganshof, Paris, 1975.

Polyptique de St Germain des Prés, ed. A. Longnon, 2 vols., Paris, 1885, 1895; rep. Geneva, 1978.

Possidius, *Vita Augustini*, see *Vita Possidio*.

Recueil des Actes de Charles II le Chauve, ed. G. Tessier, 3 vols., Paris, 1943–55.

Recueil des Actes de Lothaire et de Louis IV, rois de France (954–87), ed. L. Halphen and F. Lot, Paris, 1908.

Recueil des chartes de l'abbaye de Cluny, ed. A. Bernard and A. Bruel, 6 vols., *Collection des documents inédits sur l'histoire de France*, Paris, 1876–1903.

Recueil des chartes de l'abbaye de St-Benoît-sur-Loire, ed. M. Prou and A. Vidier, *Documents publiés par la société historique et archéologique du Gâtinais*, vol. 5, Paris and Orléans, 1900.

Regesta Historiae Westfaliae, accedit Codex diplomaticus, H. Erhard, 2 vols., Münster, 1847–51.

Regesta Regum Scottorum, vol. 1, *The Acts of Malcolm IV King of Scots 1153–65*, ed. G. W. S. Barrow, Edinburgh, 1960.

Regesta Regum Scottorum, vol. 5, *The Acts of Robert I*, ed. A. A. M. Duncan, Edinburgh, 1988.

Regesto del capitolo di Lucca, ed. P. Guidi and O. Parenti, 3 vols., Rome, 1910–39.

Registrum vulgariter nuncupatum 'The Record of Caernarvon', ed. H. Ellis, London, 1838.

Regula Basilii, Patrologia Graeca, vol. 31, Paris, 1885, cols. 890–1300.

Regula Magistri, ed. and French trans. A. de Voguë, in *La Règle du Maître*, *Sources Chrétiennes*, vols. 105–7, Paris, 1964.

Rhigyfarch's Life of St David, ed. J. W. James, Cardiff, 1967.

The Text of the Book of Llan Dâv, ed. J. G. Evans with J. Rhys, Oxford, 1893; cited by number.

Theodosian Code, trans. C. Pharr, Princeton, 1952.

Thietmar of Merseburg, *Chronicon*, ed. R. Holtzmann, *MGH SRG*, ns., vol. 9, Berlin, 1935.

Tholomei lucensis annales, ed. B. Schmeidler, *MGH SRG*, ns. vol. 8, Berlin, 1930.

Die Traditionen des Hochstifts Regensburg und des Klosters S. Emmeram, ed. J. Widemann, Munich, 1943; rep. Aalen, 1968.

'Le typikon du sébaste Grégoire Pakourianos', P. Gautier, *Revue des Études Byzantines*, 42 (1984), pp. 5–145.

Urkunden- und Quellenbuch zur Geschichte der altluxemburgischen Territorien, C. Wampach, vol. 1, Luxemburg, 1935.

Urkundenbuch zur Geschichte der Mittelrheinischen Territorien, ed. H. Beyer, Coblenz, 1860.

Die Urkunden Heinrichs II. und Arduins, ed. H. Bresslau, H. Bloch and R. Holtzmann, *MGH Diplomata regum et imperatorum Germaniae,* vol. 3, Vienna, 1900–3.

Die Urkunden Konrad I., Heinrich I., und Otto I., ed. T. Sickel, *MGH Diplomata regum et imperatorum Germaniae,* vol. 1, Hannover, 1879–84.

Die Urkunden Konrads II., ed. H. Bresslau, *MGH Diplomata regum et imperatorum Germaniae,* vol. 4, Vienna, 1909.

Die Urkunden Lothars I und Lothars II, ed. T. Schieffer, *MGH Diplomata Karolinorum,* vol. 3, Berlin, 1966.

Die Urkunden Ludwigs des Deutschen, ed. P. Kehr, *MGH Diplomata regum Germaniae ex stirpe Karolinorum,* vol. 1, Berlin, 1934.

Die Urkunden Otto des II., ed. T. Sickel, *MGH Diplomata regum et imperatorum Germaniae,* vol. 2, pt 1, Vienna, 1888.

Die Urkunden Otto des III., ed. T. Sickel, *MGH Diplomata regum et imperatorum Germaniae,* vol. 2, pt 2, Vienna, 1893.

Venantius Fortunatus, *Opera Poetica,* ed. F. Leo, *MGH AA,* vol. 4, pt 1, Berlin, 1881.

'Vie de Saint Paul de Léon', ed. Ch. Cuissard, *Revue Celtique,* 5 (1881–3), pp. 417–59.

Visio Baronti, ed. B. Krusch, *MGH SRM,* vol. 5, Hannover and Leipzig, 1910, pp. 377–94.

Vita Ansberti episcopi Rotomagensis, ed. B. Krusch, *MGH SRM,* vol. 5, Hannover and Leipzig, 1910, pp. 613–43.

Vita Balthildis, ed. B. Krusch, *MGH SRM,* vol. 2, Hannover, 1888, pp. 482–508.

'Vita Sancti Cadoci', in Wade-Evans, *Vitae Sanctorum Britanniae,* pp. 24–140.

Vita Corbiniani ab auctore Arbeone, ed. B. Krusch, *MGH SRM,* vol. 6, Hannover and Leipzig, 1913, pp. 560–93.

Vita Eucherii, ed. W. Levison, *MGH SRM,* vol. 7, Hannover and Leipzig, 1919–20, pp. 41–53.

'Vita Sancti Gundleii', in Wade-Evans, *Vitae Sanctorum Britanniae,* pp. 172–92.

'Vita Juliani', in *Actus pontificum Cenomannis in urbe degentium,* ed. G. Busson and A. Ledru, *Archives historiques du Maine,* vol. 2, Le Mans, 1901.

Vita Landiberti Episcopi Traeiectensis Vetustissima, ed. B. Krusch, *MGH SRM,* vol. 6, Hannover and Leipzig, 1913, pp. 353–84.

Vita Lantberti abbatis Fontanellensis, ed. W. Levison, *MGH SRM,* vol. 5, Hannover and Leipzig, 1910, pp. 606–12.

Vita Meinwerci episcopi Patherbrunnensis, ed. F. Tenckhoff, *MGH SRG,* vol. 59, Hannover, 1921.

'Vita Sancti Paterni', in Wade-Evans, *Vitae Sanctorum Britanniae*, pp. 254–68.

Vita Philiberti, ed. B. Krusch, *MGH SRM*, vol. 5, Hannover and Leipzig, 1910, pp. 583–604.

Vita Possidio, Vita de S. Agostino, ed. M. Pellegrino, Alba, 1955.

Vita Rigoberti, ed. W. Levison, *MGH SRM*, vol. 7, Hannover and Leipzig, 1919–20, pp. 54–80.

Vita Segolenae viduae, Acta Sanctorum, July 5, Antwerp, 1727, pp. 630–2.

Vita II Wandregisili, Acta Sanctorum, July 5, Antwerp, 1727, pp. 272–81.

Vita Wulfstani, ed. R. R. Darlington, Camden Society 3rd series, vol. 40, 1928.

Vitae Sanctorum Britanniae et Genealogiae, A. W. Wade-Evans, *Board of Celtic Studies History and Law Series*, no. 9, Cardiff, 1944.

Die Vorakte der älteren St Galler Urkunden, ed. A. Bruckner, St Gallen, 1931.

Whitelock D. (ed. and trans.), *The Will of Æthelgifu. A Tenth-Century Anglo-Saxon Manuscript*, Oxford, 1968.

William of Malmesbury, *De Gestis Pontificum Anglorum*, ed. N. E. S. A. Hamilton, *Rolls Series*, vol. 52, London, 1870.

Wulfstan, Sammlung der ihm zugeschriebenen Homilien, ed. A. Napier, Berlin, 1883.

SECONDARY WORKS

Adams, H. (ed.) *Essays in Anglo-Saxon Law*, Boston, 1876.

Althoff, G. *Verwandte, Freunde und Getreue. Zum politischen Stellenwert der Gruppenbindungen im frühen Mittelalter*, Darmstadt, 1990.

'Demonstration und Inszenierung. Spielregeln der Kommunikation in mittelalterlicher Öffentlichkeit', *Frühmittelalterliche Studien*, 27 (1993), pp. 27–50.

Amt, E. *Women's Lives in Medieval Europe*, London, 1993.

Angenendt, A. 'Theologie und Liturgie der mittelalterlichen Toten-Memoria', in K. Schmid and J. Wollasch (eds.), *Memoria. Der geschichtliche Zeugniswert des liturgischen Gedenkens im Mittelalter*, Munich, 1984, pp. 79–199.

Archer, R. J. 'Rich old ladies: the problem of late medieval dowagers', in T. Pollard, *Property and Politics: Essays in Later Medieval English History*, Gloucester, 1984, pp. 15–35.

Arnold, B. *Princes and Territories in Medieval Germany*, Cambridge, 1991.

Atsma, H. (ed.) *La Neustrie. Les Pays au Nord de la Loire de 650 à 850, Beihefte der Francia*, vol. 16, 2 vols., Sigmaringen, 1989.

Aurell i Cardona, M. 'Ermessinde, Comtesse de Barcelona', in M. Parisse (ed.), *Veuves et veuvage dans le haut moyen âge*, pp. 201–32.

Baltrusch-Schneider, D. 'Klosterleben als alternative Lebensform zur Ehe?', in H.-W. Goetz (ed.), *Weibliche Lebensgestaltung im Mittelalter*, Cologne and Vienna, 1991, pp. 45–64.

Balzer, M. *Untersuchungen zur Geschichte des Grundbesitzes in der Paderborner Feldmark, Münstersche Mittelalter-Schriften,* vol. 29, Munich, 1977.

'Zeugnisse für das Selbstverständnis Bischof Meinwerks von Paderborn', in N. Kamp and J. Wollasch (eds.), *Tradition als historische Kraft: Interdisciplinäre Forschungen zur Geschichte des früheren Mittelalters,* Berlin, 1982, pp. 267–96.

Bannasch, H. *Das Bistum Paderborn unter den Bischöfen Rethar und Meinwerk (983–1036), Studien und Quellen zur westfälischen Geschichte,* vol. 12, Paderborn, 1972.

'Fälscher aus Frömmigkeit: Der Meinwerkbiograph – ein mittelalterlicher Fälscher und sein Selbstverständnis', *Archiv für Diplomatik,* 23 (1977), pp. 224–41.

Barrow, J. 'How the twelfth-century monks of Worcester perceived their past', in P. Magdalino (ed.), *The Perception of the Past in Twelfth-Century Europe,* London, 1992, pp. 53–74.

Barthélemy, D. 'La mutation féodale a-t-elle eu lieu?', *Annales E.S.C.,* 47 (1992), pp. 767–77.

La Société dans le comté de Vendôme de l'an Mil au XIVᵉ siècle, Paris, 1993.

Bartlett, R. *The Making of Europe. Conquest, Colonization and Cultural Change 950–1350,* London, 1993.

Bates, D. 'The land pleas of William I's reign: Penenden Heath revisited', *Bulletin of the Institute of Historical Research,* 51 (1978), pp. 1–19.

Normandy Before 1066, London, 1982.

Bennett, J. ' "History that stands still": women's work in the European past', *Feminist Studies,* 14 (1988), pp. 269–83.

'Widows in the medieval English countryside', in L. Mirrer (ed.), *Upon My Husband's Death. Widows in the Literature and Histories of Medieval Europe,* Michigan, 1992, pp. 69–114.

Berger, A. *Encyclopedic Dictionary of Roman Law, Transactions of the American Philosophical Society,* n.s. vol. 43/2 (1953).

Bernhardt, J. W. *Itinerant Kingship and Royal Monasteries in Early Medieval Germany, c. 936–1075,* Cambridge, 1993.

Bisson, T. 'The "feudal revolution" ', *Past and Present,* 142 (1994), pp. 6–42.

Blecker, M. P. 'Roman law and consilium in the *Regula Magistri* and the *Regula Benedicti*', *Speculum,* 47 (1972), pp. 1–28.

Bleiber, W. *Naturalwirtschaft und Ware-Geld-Beziehungen zwischen Somme und Loire während des 7. Jahrhunderts,* Berlin, 1981.

Bloch, M. *Feudal Society,* 2 vols., trans. L. Manyon, London, 1961–2.

Blok, D. P. *De oudste particuliere oorkonden van het klooster Werden. Een diplomatische studie met enige uitweidingen over het onstann van did soort oorkunden in het algemeen,* Assen, 1960.

Bonnassie, P. *From Slavery to Feudalism in South-Western Europe,* trans. J. Birrell, Cambridge, 1991.

Bori, P. *Chiesa primitiva. L'immagine della communita delli origini – Atti 2, 42–47; 4, 32–37 – nella storia della chiesa antica,* Brescia, 1974.

Bouchard, C. B. *Holy Entrepreneurs. Cistercians, Knights, and Economic Exchange in Twelfth-Century Burgundy*, Ithaca, 1991.

Bourdieu, P. *The Logic of Practice*, Eng. trans. London, 1990.

Bourin-Derruau, M. *Villages médiévaux en Bas-Languedoc*, 2 vols., Paris, 1987.

Brand, C. M. 'Two Byzantine treatises on taxation', *Traditio*, 25 (1967), pp. 35–60.

Brandt M. and Eggebrecht A. (eds.) *Bernward von Hildesheim und das Zeitalter der Ottonen*, 2 vols., Hildesheim, 1993.

Brooke, C. N. L. 'St Peter of Gloucester and St Cadoc of Llancarfan', in N. K. Chadwick et al., *Celt and Saxon*, Cambridge, 1963, pp. 258–322.

Brooks, N. P. 'The development of military obligations in eighth- and ninth-century England', in P. Clemoes and K. Hughes (eds.), *England before the Conquest. Studies presented to Dorothy Whitelock*, Cambridge, 1971, pp. 69–84.

Brooks, N. P. and Cubitt, K. (eds.), *St Oswald of Worcester: Life and Influence*, Leicester, 1994.

Brown, P. *The Body and Society*, New York, 1988.

Brunner, H. 'Der Reiterdienst und die Anfänge des Lehnwesens', in *idem*, *Forschungen zur Geschichte des deutschen und französischen Rechts*, Stuttgart, 1894.

  Deutsche Rechtsgeschichte, 2 vols., Leipzig, 1887–92; 2nd edn, by C. F. von Schwerin, Leipzig-Munich, 1906–28; rep. Berlin, 1961.

Brunner, O. *Land and Lordship. Structures of Governance in Medieval Austria*, 4th edn, trans. H. Kaminsky and J. van Horn Melton, Philadelphia, 1984.

Cam, H. *Law-finders and Law-makers in Medieval England*, London, 1962.

Campbell, J. 'Was it infancy in England? Some questions of comparison', in M. Jones and M. Vale (eds.), *England and her Neighbours, 1066–1453. Essays in Honour of Pierre Chaplais*, London, 1989, pp. 1–17.

Castagnetti, A. 'Il potere sui contadini', in B. Andreolli et al. (eds.), *Le campagne italiane prima e dopo il Mille*, Bologna, 1985, pp. 219–51.

Charles-Edwards, T. M. 'The pastoral role of the church in the early Irish laws', in J. Blair and R. Sharpe (eds.), *Pastoral Care before the Parish*, Leicester, 1992, pp. 63–80.

Cheynet, J.-C. *Pouvoir et contestations à Byzance (963–1210)*, Byzantina Sorbonensia, vol. 9, Paris, 1990.

Classen, P. (ed.) *Recht und Schrift im Mittelalter, Vorträge und Forschungen*, vol. 23, Sigmaringen, 1977.

Claude, D. 'Untersuchungen zum frühfränkischen Comitat', *Zeitschrift der Savigny-Stiftung für Rechtsgeschichte, germanistische Abteilung*, 42 (1964), pp. 1–79.

  'Der Handel im westlichen Mittelmeer während des Frühmittelalters', in K. Düwel, H. Jankuhn, H. Siems and D. Timpe (eds.), *Untersuchungen zu Handel und Verkehr der vor- und frühgeschichtlichen Zeit im Mittel- und Nordeuropa*, Göttingen, 1985.

Claussen, M. 'Community, tradition and reform in early Carolingian Francia: Chrodegang and the canons of Metz cathedral', unpublished Ph.D. thesis, University of Virginia, 1992.

Collins, R. J. *The Arab Conquest of Spain*, Oxford, 1989.

Constable, G. '*Nona et decima*, an aspect of Carolingian economy', *Speculum*, 35 (1960), pp. 224–50.

Coué, S. 'Acht Bischofsviten aus der Salierzeit – neu interpretiert', in S. Weinfurter (ed.), *Die Salier und das Reich*, vol. 3, *Gesellschaftlicher und ideengeschichtlicher Wandel im Reich der Salier*, Sigmaringen, 1991, pp. 347–413.

Cowdrey, H. E. J. *The Cluniacs and the Gregorian Reform*, Oxford, 1970.

Cox, J. C. *The Sanctuaries and Sanctuary Seekers of Medieval England*, London, 1911.

D'Amico, R. 'Note su alcuni rapporti tra città e campagna nel contado di Pisa tra XI e XII secolo', *Bollettino storico pisano*, 39 (1970), pp. 15–29.

Davies, R. R. 'Kings, lords and liberties in the March of Wales, 1066–1272', *Transactions of the Royal Historical Society*, 5th ser., 29 (1979), pp. 41–61.

Conquest, Coexistence and Change: Wales 1063–1415, Oxford, 1987.

Davies, W. '*Liber Landavensis*: its construction and credibility', *English Historical Review*, 88 (1973), pp. 335–51.

'Braint Teilo', *Bulletin of the Board of Celtic Studies*, 26 (1974–6), pp. 123–37.

'The consecration of bishops of Llandaff in the tenth and eleventh centuries', *Bulletin of the Board of Celtic Studies*, 26 (1974–6), pp. 53–73.

An Early Welsh Microcosm, London, 1978.

The Llandaff Charters, Aberystwyth, 1979.

'Property rights and property claims in Welsh "Vitae" of the eleventh century', in E. Patlagean and P. Riché (eds.), *Hagiographie. Cultures et Sociétés*, Paris, 1981, pp. 515–33.

Wales in the Early Middle Ages, Leicester, 1982.

'Clerics as rulers: some implications of the terminology of ecclesiastical authority in early medieval Ireland', in N. P. Brooks (ed.), *Latin and the Vernacular Languages in Early Medieval Britain*, Leicester, 1982, pp. 81–97.

'The Latin charter-tradition in western Britain, Brittany and Ireland in the early mediaeval period', in D. Whitelock, R. McKitterick and D. Dumville (eds.), *Ireland in Early Mediaeval Europe*, Cambridge, 1982, pp. 258–80.

Small Worlds. The Village Community in Early Medieval Brittany, London, 1988.

Patterns of Power in Early Wales, Oxford, 1990.

'The myth of the Celtic church', in N. Edwards and A. Lane (eds.), *The Early Church in Wales and the West*, Oxford, Oxbow Monograph vol. 16, 1992, pp. 12–21.

Davies, W. and Fouracre, P. (eds.) *The Settlement of Disputes in Early Medieval Europe*, Cambridge, 1986.

Denton, J. H. *English Royal Free Chapels 1100–1300. A Constitutional Study*, Manchester, 1970.

Devisse, J. 'L'influence de Julien Pomère sur les clercs carolingiens', *Revue d'Histoire de l'Église de France*, 61 (1970), pp. 285–95.

Hincmar, Archévêque de Reims 845–882, 3 vols., Geneva, 1975.

Devroey, J.-P. 'Réflexions sur l'économie des premiers temps Carolingiens (768–877): grands domaines et action politique entre Seine et Rhin', *Francia*, 13 (1985), pp. 475–88.

Dinelli, G. 'Una signoria ecclesiastica nel contado lucchese dal sec° XI al sec° XIV', *Studi storici*, 23 (1915), pp. 187–291.

Dölger, F. *Beiträge zur Geschichte der byzantinischen Finanzverwaltung besonders des 10. und 11. Jahrhunderts, Byzantinisches Archiv*, vol. 9, Leipzig/Berlin, 1927.

Duby, G. *La société aux XIe et XIIe siècles dans la région mâconnaise*, Paris, 1953; 2nd edn, Paris, 1971.

Rural Economy and Country Life in the Medieval West, trans. C. Postan, London, 1968 [*L'économie rurale et la vie des campagnes dans l'occident médiéval*, 1962].

Early Growth of the European Economy: Warriors and Peasants from the Seventh to the Twelfth Century, trans. H. Clarke, Ithaca, 1974.

Du Cange, *Glossarium mediae et infimae Latinitatis*, ed. G. A. L. Henschel, 7 vols., Paris, 1843–60.

Durkheim, E. *The Elementary Forms of the Religious Life*, trans. J. Swain, New York, 1965.

Durliat, J. *Les Finances Publiques de Dioclétien aux Carolingiens (284–888)*, *Beihefte der Francia*, vol. 21, Sigmaringen, 1990.

Ebling, H. *Prosopographie der Amtsträger des Merowingerreiches von Chlothar II (613) bis Karl Martel (741)*, Munich, 1974.

Edwards, J. G. 'The Normans and the Welsh March', *Proceedings of the British Academy*, 42 (1956), pp. 155–77.

Emanuel, H. D. 'An analysis of the composition of the "Vita Cadoci"', *National Library of Wales Journal*, 7 (1951–2), pp. 217–27.

Engels, O. 'Der Reichsbischof in ottonischer und frühsalischer Zeit', in I. Crusius (ed.), *Beiträge zu Geschichte und Struktur der mittelalterlichen Germania Sacra*, Göttingen, 1989, pp. 135–75.

Erler, A. 'Ecclesia non sitit sanguinem', in A. Erler (ed.), *Handwörterbuch zur Deutschen Rechtsgeschichte*, vol. 1, *Aachen – Haustür*, Berlin, 1973, cols. 795–8.

Ewig, E. 'Milo et eiusmodi similes', in H. Büttner (ed.), *Sankt Bonifatius: Gedenkengabe zum 1200 Todestage*, Fulda, 1954, pp. 215–41.

Fichtenau, H. *Living in the Tenth Century*, Eng. trans., Chicago, 1990.

Fischer-Drew, K. 'The immunity in Carolingian Italy', *Speculum*, 37 (1962), pp. 182–97.

Fisher, D. J. V. 'The anti-monastic reaction in the reign of Edward the Martyr', *Cambridge Historical Journal*, 10 (1952), pp. 254–70.

Formazione e strutture dei ceti dominanti nel medioevo: marchesi conti e visconti nel regno italico (secc. IX–XII), vol. 1, Rome, 1988.

Fouracre, P. 'Merovingians, mayors of the palace and the notion of a "low-born" Ebroin', *Bulletin of the Institute of Historical Research*, 57 (1984), pp. 1–14.

'Observations on the outgrowth of Pippinid influence in the "regnum Francorum" after the battle of Tertry (687–715)', *Medieval Prosopography*, 5 (1984), pp. 1–31.

' "Placita" and the settlement of disputes in later Merovingian Francia', in W. Davies and P. Fouracre (eds.), *The Settlement of Disputes in Early Medieval Europe*, pp. 23–43.

'Cultural conformity and social conservatism in early medieval Europe', *History Workshop Journal*, 33 (1992), pp. 152–61.

'Carolingian justice: the rhetoric of improvement and contexts of abuse', *Settimane di Studio*, 42 (1995).

Freedman, P. *The Origins of Peasant Servitude in Medieval Catalonia*, Cambridge, 1991.

Fuhrmann, H. *Einfluß und Verbreitung der pseudoisidorischen Fälschungen*, 3 vols., *MGH Schriften*, vol. 24, Stuttgart, 1972–4.

Ganshof, F. 'L'Immunité dans la monarchie Franque', in *Les liens de vassalité et les immunités*, Recueil de la société Jean Bodin, vol. 1, 2nd rev. edn, Brussels, 1956, pp. 171–216.

Ganz, D. 'The *Epitaphium Arsenii* and opposition to Louis the Pious', in P. Godman and R. Collins (eds.), *Charlemagne's Heir. New Perspectives on the Reign of Louis the Pious*, Oxford, 1990, pp. 537–50.

Ganz, D. and Goffart, W. 'Charters earlier than 800 from French collections', *Speculum*, 65 (1990), pp. 906–32.

Geary, P. J. *Aristocracy in Provence. The Rhône Basin at the Dawn of the Carolingian Age*, Philadelphia, 1985.

'Vivre en conflit dans une France sans état', *Annales E.S.C.*, 41 (1986), pp. 1107–33.

Gerberding, R. A. *The Rise of the Carolingians and the Liber Historiae Francorum*, Oxford, 1987.

Goebel, J. *Felony and Misdemeanor*, rep. with introduction by E. Peters, Philadelphia, 1976.

Goetz, H.-W. 'Protection of the church, defense of the law, and reform: on the purposes and character of the peace of God, 989–1038', in T. Head and R. Landes (eds.), *The Peace of God*, pp. 259–79.

Goffart, W. *The Le Mans Forgeries. A Chapter in the History of Church Property in the Ninth Century*, Cambridge, Mass., 1966.

'From Roman taxation to medieval seigneurie: three notes', *Speculum*, 47 (1972), pp. 165–87, 373–94.

'Old and new in Merovingian taxation', *Past and Present*, 96 (1982), pp. 3–22.

Goody, J. *The Development of the Family and Marriage in Europe*, Cambridge, 1982.

Gottlieb, B. 'The problem of feminism in the fifteenth century', in J. Kirshner and S. Wemple (eds.), *Women of the Medieval World*, pp. 337–64.

Grégoire, H. 'Un édit de l'empereur Justinien II', *Byzantion*, 17 (1944–5), pp. 119–23.

Haenchen, E. *The Acts of the Apostles*, Philadelphia, 1971.

Hägermann, D. 'Der Abt als Grundherr. Kloster und Wirtschaft im frühen Mittelalter', in F. Prinz (ed.), *Herrschaft und Kirche*, Stuttgart, 1988, pp. 345–85.

Haldon, J. F. 'The army and the economy: the allocation and redistribution of surplus wealth in the Byzantine state', *Mediterranean Historical Review*, 7/2 (1992), pp. 133–53.

  The State and the Tributary Mode of Production, London, 1993.

  'Military administration and bureaucracy: state demands and private interests', *Byzantinische Forschungen*, 19 (1993), pp. 43–63.

Hall, D. 'The sanctuary of St Cuthbert', in G. Bonner, D. Rollason and C. Stancliffe (eds.), *St Cuthbert, his Cult and his Community to AD 1200*, Woodbridge, 1989, pp. 425–36.

Harries J. D. and Wood I. N. (eds.) *The Theodosian Code*, London, 1994.

Hartmann, W. 'Der Bischof als Richter. Zum geistlichen Gericht über kriminelle Vergehen von Laien im früheren Mittelalter', *Römische Historische Mitteilungen*, 28 (1986), pp. 103–24.

  Die Synoden der Karolingerzeit im Frankenreich und in Italien, Paderborn, 1989.

Hartung, W. 'Adel, Erbrecht, Schenkung: Die strukturellen Ursachen der frühmittelalterlichen Besitzübertragungen an die Kirche', in F. Seibt (ed.), *Gesellschaftsgeschichte. Festschrift für Karl Bosl zum 80. Geburtstag*, vol. 1, pp. 417–38.

Harvey, A. *Economic Expansion in the Byzantine Empire*, Cambridge, 1989.

  'Peasant categories in the tenth and eleventh centuries', *Byzantine and Modern Greek Studies*, 14 (1990), pp. 250–6.

  'The land and taxation in the reign of Alexios I Komnenos: the evidence of Theophylakt of Ochrid', *Revue des Études Byzantines*, 51 (1993), pp. 139–54.

Head, T. and Landes, R. (eds.) *The Peace of God: Social Violence and Religious Response in France around the Year 1000*, Ithaca and London, 1992.

Heidrich, I. 'Die Verbindung von Schutz und Immunität', *Zeitschrift der Savigny-Stiftung für Rechtsgeschichte, germanistische Abteilung*, 90 (1973), pp. 10–30.

Hellfaier, D. 'Früher Besitz des Klosters St Michael zu Hildesheim im 11. Jahrhundert', in M. Brandt and A. Eggebrecht (eds.), *Bernward von Hildesheim und das Zeitalter der Ottonen*, vol. 2, Hannover, 1993, pp. 477–80.

Hennebicque, R. 'Structures familiales et politiques au IXe siècle: un groupe familial de l'aristocratie franque', *Revue historique*, 265 (1981), pp. 289–333.

Herlihy, D. 'Land, family and women in continental Europe, 701–1200', *Traditio*, 17 (1961), pp. 89–120, reprinted in S. M. Stuard (ed.), *Women in Medieval Society*, Philadelphia, 1976, pp. 13–45.

Herold, H. 'Der Dreissigste und die rechtsgeschichtliche Bedeutung des Totengedächtnisses', *Zeitschrift für Schweizerisches Recht*, neue Folge 57 (1937), pp. 375–420.

Hochstetler, D. *A Conflict of Traditions. Women in Religion in the Early Middle Ages 500–840*, Lanham, Maryland, 1992.

Hodgson, A. 'The Frankish church and women', unpublished Ph.D. thesis, University of London, 1992.

Hoffmann, H. *Gottesfriede und Treuga Dei, Schriften der MGH*, vol. 20, Stuttgart, 1964.

'Grafschaften in Bischofshand', *Deutsches Archiv für Erforschung des Mittelalters*, 46 (1990), pp. 375–480.

Mönchskönig und rex idiota. *Studien zur Kirchenpolitik Heinrichs II. und Konrads II.*, Hannover, 1993.

Holt, J. C. 'Feudal society and the family in medieval England, I', *Transactions of the Royal Historical Society*, 5th ser., 32 (1982), pp. 193–212.

Honselmann, K. *Von der Carta zur Siegelurkunde. Beiträge zum Urkundenwesen im Bistum Paderborn, 862–1178, Paderborner Studien*, vol. 1, Paderborn, 1939.

'Der Autor der Vita Meinwerci vermutlich Abt Konrad von Abdinghof', *Westfälische Zeitschrift*, 114, pt. 2 (1964), pp. 349–52.

Hughes, D. O. 'From brideprice to dowry', *Journal of Family History*, 3 (1978), pp. 262–96.

Hurnard, N. D. 'The Anglo-Norman franchises', *English Historical Review*, 64 (1949), pp. 289–322, 433–60.

Irsigler, F. '*Divites* und *pauperes* in der Vita Meinwerci. Untersuchungen zur wirtschaftlichen und sozialen Differenzierung der Bevölkerung Westfalens im Hochmittelalter', *Vierteljahresschrift für Sozial- und Wirtschaftsgeschichte*, 57 (1970), pp. 449–99.

'Bischof Meinwerk, Graf Dodiko und Warburg: Herrschaft, Wirtschaft und Gesellschaft des hohen Mittelalters im östlichen Westfalen', *Westfälische Zeitschrift*, 126–7 (1976–7), pp. 181–200.

Jahn, J. 'Tradere ad Sanctum: Politische und gesellschaftliche Aspekte der Traditionspraxis im agilolfingischen Bayern', in Seibt (ed.), *Gesellschaftsgeschichte. Festschrift für Karl Bosl zum 80. Geburtstag*, vol. 1, pp. 400–16.

James, E. A. '*Beati pacifici*: bishops and the law in sixth-century Gaul', in J. Bossy (ed.), *Disputes and Settlements*, Cambridge, 1983, pp. 25–46.

Le Jan-Hennebicque, R. 'Aux origines du douaire médiéval', in M. Parisse (ed.), *Veuves et veuvage dans le haut moyen âge*, Paris, 1993, pp. 107–22.

Jarnut, J., Nonn, U. and Richter, M. (eds.) *Karl Martell in seiner Zeit*, Sigmaringen, 1994.

Jenkins, D. and Owen, M. E. 'The Welsh marginalia in the Lichfield Gospels, Part I', *Cambridge Medieval Celtic Studies*, 5 (1983), pp. 37–66; 'Part II', *ibid.*, 7 (1984), pp. 91–120.

Jenkins, D. and Owen, M. E. (eds.) *The Welsh Law of Women*, Cardiff, 1980.

Johanek, P. *Die Frühzeit der Siegelurkunde im Bistum Würzburg, Quellen und Forschungen zur Geschichte des Bistums und Hochstifts Würzburg*, vol. 20, Würzburg, 1969.

'Zur rechtlichen Funktion von Traditionsnotiz, Traditionsbuch und früher Siegelurkunde', in P. Classen (ed.), *Recht und Schrift im Mittelalter, Vorträge und Forschungen*, vol. 23, pp. 131–62.

'Die Corveyer Traditionen als Gedenküberlieferung', in K. Schmid and J. Wollasch (eds.), *Der Liber Vitae der Abtei Corvey. Studien zur Corveyer Gedenküberlieferung und zur Erschließung des Liber Vitae*, Wiesbaden, 1989, pp. 124–34.

'Die Erzbischöfe von Hamburg-Bremen in der Salierzeit', in S. Weinfurter (ed.), *Die Salier und das Reich*, vol. 2, *Die Reichskirche in der Salierzeit*, Sigmaringen, 1991, pp. 79–112.

John, E. *Land Tenure in Early England*, Leicester, 1960.

'War and society in the tenth century: the Maldon campaign', *Transactions of the Royal Historical Society*, 5th ser., 27 (1977), pp. 173–95.

Jones, P. J. 'An Italian estate, 900–1200', *Economic History Review*, 2nd ser., 7 (1954), pp. 18–32.

Jussen, B. 'Der "Name" der Witwe. Zur "Konstruktion" eines Standes in Spätantike und Frühmittelalter', in M. Parisse (ed.), *Veuves et veuvage dans le haut moyen âge*, pp. 139–75.

'On church organisation and the definition of an estate. The idea of widowhood in late antique and early medieval Christianity', *Tel Aviver Jahrbuch für deutsche Geschichte*, 22 (1993), pp. 25–42.

Kaiser, R. 'Royauté et pouvoir épiscopale au Nord de la Gaule VIIe – IXe siècles' in H. Atsma (ed.), *La Neustrie. Les Pays au Nord de la Loire de 650 à 850*, vol. 1, pp. 141–60.

Kaplan, M. *Les hommes et la terre à Byzance du VIe au XIe siècle*, Byzantina Sorbonensia, vol. 10, Paris, 1992.

Kasten, B. 'Erbrechtliche Verfügungen des 8. und 9. Jhdts', *Zeitschrift für Rechtsgeschichte, Germ. Abt.*, 107 (1990), pp. 236–338.

Kaster, R. *Guardians of Language*, Berkeley, 1988.

Kazhdan, A. P. et al. (eds.) *Oxford Dictionary of Byzantium*, 3 vols., New York and Oxford, 1991.

Keller, H. *Adelsherrschaft und städtische Gesellschaft in Oberitalien*, Tübingen, 1979.

Ker, N. R. 'Hemming's Cartulary', in R. W. Hunt, W. A. Pantin and R. W. Southern (eds.), *Studies in Medieval History Presented to Frederick Maurice Powicke*, Oxford, 1948, pp. 49–75.

Kienast, W. *Die fränkische Vassallität*, Frankfurt, 1990.

Kiessling, R. *Bürgerliche Gesellschaft und Kirche in Augsburg im Spätmittelalter. Ein Beitrag zur Strukturanalyse der Oberdeutschen Reichsstadt*, Augsburg, 1971.

Kirshner, J. and Wemple, S. (eds.) *Women of the Medieval World*, Oxford, 1986.

Koselleck, R. 'The historical-political semantics of asymmetric counter-concepts', in *idem, Futures Past, on the Semantics of Historical Time*, London, 1985, pp. 159–97.

Koziol, G. *Begging Pardon and Favor: Ritual and Political Order in Early Medieval France*, Ithaca, 1992.

Kroell, M. *L'Immunité Franque*, Paris, 1910.

Laistner, M. W. *Bedae Venerabilis Expositio Actuum Apostolorum et Retractatio*, Cambridge, Mass., 1939.

Lawson, M. K. 'The collection of Danegeld and Heregeld in the reigns of Æthelred II and Cnut', *English Historical Review*, 99 (1984), pp. 721–38.

Lauranson-Rosaz, C. 'Douaire et *Sponsalicium*', in M. Parisse (ed.), *Veuves et veuvage dans le haut moyen âge*, pp. 99–104.

Lemaire, A. 'Les origines de la communauté de biens entre époux dans le droit coutumier français', *Revue historique de droit français et étranger*, 4th ser., 7 (1928), pp. 584–93.

Lesne, E. *Histoire de la Propriété Ecclésiastique en France*, 6 vols., Lille, 1910–38.

Levillain, L. *Examen critique des chartes Mérovingiennes et Carolingiennes de l'abbaye de Corbie, École des Chartes, Mémoires et Documents*, vol. 5, Paris, 1902.

    'Note sur l'immunité Mérovingienne', *Revue historique de droit français et étranger*, 6 (1927), pp. 38–67.

Levison, W. 'Sigolena', *Neues Archiv*, 35 (1910), pp. 219–31.

    England and the Continent in the Eighth Century, Oxford, 1946.

Levy, E. *West Roman Vulgar Law. The Law of Property*, Philadelphia, 1951.

    Weströmisches Vulgarrecht, vol. 1, *Das Obligationenrecht*, Weimar, 1956.

Lewis, C. T. and Short, C. *A Latin Dictionary*, Oxford, 1879.

Leyser, K. *Rule and Conflict in an Early Medieval Society. Ottonian Saxony*, London, 1979.

    'Henry I and the beginnings of the Saxon Empire', in *idem, Medieval Germany and its Neighbours, 900–1250*, London, 1982, pp. 11–42.

    'The crisis of medieval Germany', in *idem, Communications and Power in Medieval Europe: The Gregorian Revolution and Beyond*, ed. T. Reuter, London, 1994, pp. 21–49.

Little, L. K. 'Spiritual sanctions in Wales', in R. Blumenfeld-Kosinski (ed.), *Images of Sainthood in Medieval Europe*, Ithaca, 1991, pp. 67–80.

Loengard, J. S. ' "Of the gift of her husband": English dower and its consequences in the year 1200', in J. Kirshner and S. Wemple (eds.), *Women of the Medieval World*, pp. 215–55.

Lot, F. *Études critiques sur l'abbaye de Saint-Wandrille, Bibliothèque de l'École des Hautes Études*, vol. 204, Paris, 1913.

Magnou-Nortier, E. 'Les Évêques et la paix dans l'espace franc (VIe–XIe siècles)', in *L'Évêque dans l'histoire de l'église*, Angers, 1984, pp. 33–50.

'Étude sur le privilège d'immunité du IVe au IXe siècle', *Revue Mabillon*, 60 (1984), pp. 465–512.

'Les "Pagenses" notables et fermiers du fisc durant le haut moyen âge', *Revue Belge de Philologie et d'Histoire*, 65 (1987), pp. 237–56.

'La gestion publique en Neustrie: Les moyens et les hommes (VIIe–IXe siècles)', in H. Atsma (ed.), *La Neustrie. Les Pays au Nord de la Loire de 650 à 850*, vol. 1, pp. 271–320.

Maitland, F. W. *Domesday Book and Beyond* (with introduction by E. Miller), London, 1960.

Malherbe, A. J. *Social Aspects of Early Christianity*, Philadelphia, 1983.

Markus, R. *The End of Ancient Christianity*, Cambridge, 1990.

Martí, R. 'L'Ensagrerament: l'adveniment de les *sagreres* feudals', *Faventia*, 10 (1988), pp. 153–82.

Martindale, J. 'The nun Immena and the foundation of the abbey of Beaulieu: a woman's prospects in the Carolingian church', *Studies in Church History*, 27 (1990), pp. 27–42.

Marx, J. 'Das Testament der lotharingischen Gräfin Erkanfrida', *Trierer theologische Zeitschrift Pastor bonus*, 6 (1894), p. 141.

'Das "Testament" Erkanfridas', *Jahrbücher der Gesellschaft für lothringische Geschichte und Altertumskunde*, 7 (1895), pp. 180–93.

Maund, K. L. *Ireland, Wales, and England in the Eleventh Century*, Woodbridge, 1991.

Mauss, M. *The Gift*, trans. I. Cunnison, Glencoe, 1954.

Mayer, T. *Fürsten und Staat*, Weimar, 1950.

Mayr-Harting, H. 'The church of Magdeburg: its trade and its town in the tenth and eleventh centuries', in D. Abulafia, M. Franklin and M. Rubin (eds.), *Church and City 1000–1500, Essays in Honour of Christopher Brooke*, Cambridge, 1992, pp. 129–50.

McKitterick, R. *The Frankish Kingdoms under the Carolingians 751–987*, London, 1983.

The Carolingians and the Written Word, Cambridge, 1989.

McNamara, J. A. and Wemple, S. 'The power of women through the family in medieval Europe', in M. Erler and M. Kowaleski (eds.), *Women and Power in the Middle Ages*, Athens, Georgia, 1989, pp. 83–101.

Meeks, W. *The First Urban Christians: The Social World of the Apostle Paul*, Yale, 1983.

Melovski, H. 'Einige Probleme der exkusseia', *Jahrbuch der österreichischen Byzantinistik*, 32/2 (1981), pp. 361–8.

Mietke, G. *Die Bautätigkeit Bischof Meinwerks von Paderborn und die frühchristliche und byzantinische Architektur*, Paderborn, 1991.

Miller, E. *The Abbey and Bishopric of Ely*, Cambridge, 1951.

Miller, M. *The Saints of Gwynedd*, Woodbridge, 1979.

Miller, W. I. *Bloodtaking and Peacemaking. Feud, Law and Society in Saga Iceland*, Chicago, 1990.

   Humiliation; and Other Essays on Honor, Social Discomfiture, and Violence, Ithaca, 1993.

Mirrer, L. (ed.) *Upon My Husband's Death. Widows in the Literature and Histories of Medieval Europe*, Michigan, 1992.

Mitteis, H. *Der Staat des hohen Mittelalters*, 2nd edn, Weimar, 1948.

Morris, R. *Monks and Laymen in Byzantium 843–1118*, Cambridge, forthcoming.

Mullett, M. E. 'Theophylact through his letters: the two worlds of an exile bishop', unpublished Ph.D. thesis, University of Birmingham, 1981.

Murray, A. C. 'Immunity, nobility and the edict of Paris', *Speculum*, 69 (1994), pp. 18–39.

Nelson, J. L. *Politics and Ritual in Early Medieval Europe*, London, 1986.

   'Dispute settlement in Carolingian West Francia', in Davies and Fouracre (eds.), *The Settlement of Disputes in Early Medieval Europe*, pp. 45–64.

   'Les femmes et l'évangélisation dans le haut moyen âge', *Revue du Nord*, 68 (1986), pp. 471–85.

   'Kommentar', in W. Affeldt (ed.), *Frauen in Spätantike und Frühmittelalter*, Sigmaringen, 1990, pp. 325–32.

   Charles the Bald, London, 1992.

Niermeyer, J. F. *Mediae Latinitatis Lexicon Minus*, 2nd edn, Leiden, 1984.

Nonn, U. 'Das Bild Karl Martells in den lateinschen Quellen vornehmlich des 8. und 9. Jahrhunderts', *Frühmittelalterliche Studien*, 4 (1970), pp. 70–137.

   'Merowingische Testamente', *Archiv für Diplomatik*, 18 (1972), pp. 1–129.

'Erminethrud – eine vornehme neustrische Dame um 700', *Historisches Jahrbuch*, 102 (1982), pp. 135–43.

Obolensky, D. *Six Byzantine Portraits*, Oxford, 1988.

Ó Corráin, D. 'Nationality and kingship in pre-Norman Ireland', in T. W. Moody (ed.), *Nationality and the Pursuit of National Independence*, Belfast, 1978, pp. 1–35.

Oikonomides, N. 'Das Verfalland im 10. und 11. Jahrhundert: Verkauf und Besteuerung', *Fontes Minores*, vol. 7, *Forschungen zur Byzantinischen Rechtsgeschichte*, vol. 14, Frankfurt, 1986, rep. in *Byzantium from the Ninth Century to the Fourth Crusade*, Aldershot, 1992, V.

Olsen, G. 'The idea of the *Ecclesia Primitiva* in the writings of the twelfth-century canonists', *Traditio*, 25 (1969), pp. 61–86.

'Bede as historian: the evidence from his observations on the life of the first Christian community at Jerusalem', *Journal of Ecclesiastical History*, 33 (1982), pp. 519–30.

Olson, L. *Early Monasteries in Cornwall*, Woodbridge, 1989.

Omont, H. 'Le Testament d'Erkanfrida, veuve du comte Nithadus de Trèves', *Bibliothèque de l'École des Chartes*, 52 (1891), pp. 573–7.

Ostrogorsky, G. 'Pour l'histoire de l'immunité à Byzance', *Byzantion*, 28 (1958), pp. 165–254.

Padoa Schioppa, A. 'Aspetti della giustizia milanese dal X al XII secolo', in *Atti dell'XI° Congresso italiano di studi sull'alto medioevo*, Spoleto, 1989, pp. 459–549.

Parisse, M. (ed.) *Veuves et veuvage dans le haut moyen age*, Paris, 1993.

Pasquinucci, M., Garzella, G. and Ceccarelli Lemut, M. L. *Cascina*, vol. 2, Pisa, 1986.

Pelt, J.-B. (ed.) *Études sur la liturgie de Metz*, Metz, 1937.

Perrin, Ch. *Recherches sur la Seigneurie Rurale en Lorraine d'après les plus anciennes Censiers (IXe–XIIe siècles)*, Paris, 1935.

Phythian-Adams, C. 'Rutland reconsidered', in A. Dornier (ed.), *Mercian Studies*, Leicester, 1977, pp. 63–84.

Pollock, F. and Maitland, F.W. *History of English Law*, 2 vols., 1898, rep. ed. S. F. C. Milsom, Cambridge, 1968.

Poly, J.-P. and Bournazel, E. *The Feudal Transformation, 900–1200*, London, 1991.

Pope, J. 'Ælfric and the Old English version of the Ely privilege', in P. Clemoes and K. Hughes (eds.), *England Before the Conquest. Studies in Primary Sources Presented to D. Whitelock*, Cambridge, 1971, pp. 85–113.

Popkes, W. 'Gemeinschaft', in *Reallexikon für Antike und Christentum*, vol. 9, Stuttgart, 1976, cols. 1100–45.

Pryce, H. 'Ecclesiastical sanctuary in thirteenth-century Welsh law', *Journal of Legal History*, 5 (1984), pp. 1–13.
  Native Law and the Church in Medieval Wales, Oxford, 1993.
  'The church of Trefeglwys and the end of the "Celtic" Charter-tradition in twelfth-century Wales', *Cambridge Medieval Celtic Studies*, 25 (1993), pp. 15–54.
Reuter, T. 'The "imperial church system" of the Ottonian and Salian rulers: a reconsideration', *Journal of Ecclesiastical History*, 33 (1982), pp. 347–74.
  'Plunder and tribute in the Carolingian Empire', *Transactions of the Royal Historical Society*, 5th ser., 35 (1985), pp. 75–94.
  'Gedenküberlieferung und -praxis im Briefbuch Wibalds von Stablo', in K. Schmid and J. Wollasch (eds.), *Der Liber Vitae der Abtei Corvey. Studien zur Corveyer Gedenküberlieferung und zur Erschließung des Liber Vitae*, Wiesbaden, 1989, pp. 161–77.
  Germany in the Early Middle Ages, c. 800–1056, London, 1991.
  'Unruhestiftung, Fehde, Rebellion, Widerstand: Gewalt und Frieden in der Politik der Salierzeit', in S. Weinfurter (ed.), *Die Salier und das Reich*, vol. 3, *Gesellschaftlicher und ideengeschichtlicher Wandel im Reich der Salier*, Sigmaringen, 1991, pp. 297–325.
  'The medieval German *Sonderweg*? The empire and its rulers in the high middle ages', in A. Duggan (ed.), *Kings and Kingship in Medieval Europe*, London, 1993, pp. 179–211.
  'Pre-Gregorian mentalities', *Journal of Ecclesiastical History*, 35 (1994), pp. 465–74.
  '*Filii matris nostrae pugnant adversum nos*: bonds and tensions between prelates and their *milites* in the German high middle ages', in G. Picasso (ed.), *Chiesa e mondo feudale nei secoli X–XII*, Milan, forthcoming.
Reynolds, R. E. 'Unity and diversity in Carolingian canon law collections: the case of the *Collectio Hibernensis* and its derivatives', in U. R. Blumenthal (ed.), *Carolingian Essays*, Washington, 1983, pp. 99–135.
Reynolds, S. 'Bookland, folkland and fiefs', *Anglo-Norman Studies*, 14 (1992), pp. 211–27.
  Fiefs and Vassals. The Medieval Evidence Reinterpreted, Oxford, 1994.
Roffe, D. 'Nottinghamshire and the North: a Domesday study', Unpublished Ph.D. thesis, University of Leicester, 1987.
Rösener, W. *Peasants in the Middle Ages*, trans. A. Stützer, Cambridge, 1992.

Rosenwein, B. H. *To Be the Neighbor of St Peter: The Social Meaning of Cluny's Property, 909–1049*, Ithaca, 1989.

Rossetti, G. 'Società e istituzioni nei secoli IX e X. Pisa, Volterra, Populonia', in *Atti del 5° congresso internazionale di studi sull'alto medioevo*, Spoleto, 1973, pp. 209–338.

'Il lodo del vescovo Daiberto sull'altezza delle torri', in *Pisa e la Toscana occidentale nel Medioevo, 2*, Pisa, 1991, pp. 25–47.

Rouche, M. 'Les repas de fête à l'époque carolingienne', in D. Menjot (ed.), *Manger et boire au moyen âge, Actes du Colloque de Nice (15–17 octobre 1982)*, vol. 1, *Aliments et Société*, Nice, 1984, pp. 265–96.

Rouillard, G. 'Un grand Bénéficiare sous Alexis Comnène: Léon Képhalas', *Byzantinische Zeitschrift*, 30 (1930), pp. 44–50.

Rowland, J. *Early Welsh Saga Poetry: A Study and Edition of the Englynion*, Cambridge, 1990.

Sahlins, M. *Stone Age Economics*, London, 1974.

Samson, R. 'Economic anthropology and Vikings', and 'Fighting with silver: rethinking trading, raiding, and hoarding', in *idem* (ed.), *Social Approaches to Viking Studies*, Glasgow, 1991, pp. 87–96 and 123–33.

Sauerland, H. V. 'Das "Testament" der lotharingischen Gräfin Erkanfrida', *Jahrbücher der Gesellschaft für lothringische Geschichte und Altertumskunde*, 7 (1894), pp. 288–96.

'Das "Testament" Erkanfridas', *Jahrbücher der Gesellschaft für lothringische Geschichte und Altertumskunde*, 8 (1896), pp. 205–34.

Sawyer, B. *Property and Inheritance in Viking Scandinavia: The Runic Evidence*, Alingsaås, 1988.

Sawyer, P. H. *Anglo-Saxon Charters: An Annotated List and Bibliography*, London, 1968.

'Charters of the reform movement: the Worcester archive', in D. Parsons (ed.), *Tenth-Century Studies*, Chichester, 1982.

'1066–86: A tenurial revolution?', in P. H. Sawyer (ed.), *Domesday Book. A Reassessment*, London, 1985, pp. 71–85.

Scharf, A. *Byzantine Jewry. From Justinian to the Fourth Crusade*, London, 1971.

Schieffer, R. *Die Entstehung von Domkapiteln in Deutschland*, Bonn, 1976.

Schmitt, C., Romer H. and Maksimovi, Lj. 'Immunität', *Lexikon des Mittelalters*, vol. 4, *Erzkanzler-Hide*, Munich, 1987–9, cols. 390–3.

Schröder, R. *Geschichte des ehelichen Güterrechts*, 2 vols., Stettin, 1871.

Schuffels, H. J. 'Bernward Bischof von Hildesheim. Eine biographische Skizze', in M. Brandt and A. Eggebrecht (eds.), *Bernward von Hildesheim und das Zeitalter der Ottonen*, vol. 1, Hannover, 1993, pp. 29–43.

Schütte, L. *Die alten Mönchslisten und die Traditionen von Corvey*, vol. 2, *Indices und andere Hilfsmittel*, Paderborn, 1992.

Schwarzmaier, H. M. *Lucca und das Reich bis zum Ende des 11. Jahrhunderts*, Tübingen, 1972.

Scott, J. W. 'Gender: a useful category of historical analysis', *American Historical Review*, 91 (1986), pp. 1053–75.

Seibt, F. (ed.) *Gesellschaftsgeschichte. Festschrift für Karl Bosl zum 80. Geburtstag*, 2 vols., Munich, 1988.

Semmler, J. 'Traditio und Königsschutz', *Zeitschrift der Savigny Stiftung für Rechtsgeschichte, kanonistische Abteilung*, 45 (1959), pp. 1–30.

'Chrodegang Bischof von Metz. 747–766', in *Die Reichsabtei Lorsch: Festschrift zum Bedenken an die Stiftung der Reichsabtei Lorsch 764*, Darmstadt, 1973, vol. 1, pp. 229–45.

'Mönche und Kanoniker im Frankenreiche Pippins III. und Karls des Großen', in *Untersuchungen zu Kloster und Stift*, Veröffentlichungen des Max-Planck-Instituts für Geschichte, vol. 68, Göttingen, 1980, pp. 78–111.

'Benedictus II, Una Regula–Una Consuetudo,' in W. Lourdaux and D. Verhelst (eds.), *Benedictine Culture 750–1050*, Medievalia Louvanensia, vol. 11, Louvain, 1983, pp. 1–49.

Senn, F. *L'Institution des avoueries ecclésiastiques en France*, Paris, 1903.

Settia, A. A. *Castelli e villaggi nell'Italia padana*, Naples, 1984.

Sickel, T. *Beiträge zur Diplomatik*, vols. 3, 5, *Sitzungsbericht der Akademie der Wissenschaften zu Wien, Philosophisch-Historische Klasse*, 47, 49 (1864, 1865).

Skinner, P. 'Women, wills and wealth in medieval southern Italy', *Early Medieval Europe*, 2 (1993), pp. 133–52.

Smith, J. M. H. *Province and Empire. Brittany and the Carolingians*, Cambridge, 1992.

Spreckelmeyer, G. 'Zur rechtlichen Funktion frühmittelalterlicher Testamente', in P. Classen (ed.), *Recht und Schrift im Mittelalter, Vorträge und Forschungen*, vol. 23, pp. 91–113.

Stacey, R. Chapman. 'Ties that bind: immunities in Irish and Welsh law', *Cambridge Medieval Celtic Studies*, 20 (1990), pp. 39–60.

Stafford, P. *Queens, Concubines, and Dowagers. The King's Wife in the Early Middle Ages*, Athens, Georgia, 1983.

Unification and Conquest. A Political and Social History of England in the Tenth and Eleventh Centuries, London, 1989.

'Women and the Norman Conquest', *Transactions of the Royal Historical Society*, 6th ser., 4 (1994), pp. 221–49.

Stengel, E. E. *Die Immunität in Deutschland bis zum Ende des 11. Jahrhunderts*, vol. 1, *Diplomatik der deutschen Immunitäts-Privilegien*, Innsbruck, 1910.

Strayer, J. *On the Medieval Origins of the Modern State*, Princeton, 1970.

Svoronos, N. G. 'Recherches sur le cadastre byzantin et la fiscalité aux XIe et XIIe siècles: le cadastre de Thèbes', *Bulletin de Corréspondance Héllenique*, 83 (1959), pp. 1–166, rep. in *Études sur l'organisation intérieure, la société et l'économie de l'empire byzantin*, III, London, 1973.

Tabacco, G. 'La connessione tra potere e possesso nel regno franco e nel regno longobardo', *Settimane di studio*, 20 (1972), pp. 133–68.

The Struggle for Power in Medieval Italy, Cambridge, 1989.

Tabuteau, E. Z. *Transfers of Property in Eleventh–Century Norman Law*, Chapel Hill, 1988.

Taylor, P. 'The endowment and military obligations of the see of London: a reassessment of three sources', *Anglo-Norman Studies*, 14 (1992).

Tirelli, V. 'Il vescovato di Lucca tra la fine del secolo XI e i primi tre decenni del XII', in *Allucio da Pescia (1070 c.a.–1134)*, Rome, 1991, pp. 55–146.

Troeltsch, E. *The Social Teaching of the Christian Churches*, trans. O. Wyon, London, 1931.

Vacandard, E. 'Saint Wandrille, était-il apparenté aux rois mérovingiens et carolingiens?', *Revue des questions historiques*, 67 (1900), pp. 214–28.

van der Wal, N. and Lokin, J. H. A. *Historiae iuris graeco-romani delineatio. Les sources du droit byzantin de 300 à 1453*, Gröningen, 1985.

Verheijen, L. 'Spiritualité et vie monastique chez St. Augustin. L'utilisation monastique des Actes des Apôtres 4, 31, 32–35 dans son oeuvre', in C. Kannengiesser (ed.), *Jean Chrysostome et Augustin*, Paris, 1975, pp. 83–123.

Saint Augustine's Monasticism in the Light of Acts 4, 32–35, Villanova, 1979.

Victoria County History of Worcestershire, ed. W. L. Page, 4 vols., London, 1901–26.

Violante, C. 'La signoria "territoriale" come quadro delle strutture organizzative del contado nella Lombardia del secolo XII', in W. Paravicini and K. F. Werner (eds.), *Histoire comparée de l'administration (IVe–XVIIIe siècles)*, *Beihefte der Francia*, vol. 9, Munich, 1980, pp. 333–44.

'La signoria rurale nel secolo X: proposte tipologiche', *Settimane di studio*, 38 (1991), pp. 329–85.

Voigt, K. *Die karolingische Klosterpolitik und der Niedergang des westfränkischen Königtums*, Stuttgart, 1917.

Volpe, G. 'Lambardi e Romani nelle campagne e nella città', *Studi storici*, 13 (1904), pp. 53–81, 167–82, 241–315, 369–416.

Studi sulle istituzioni comunali a Pisa, 2nd edn, Florence, 1970.

Voltelini, H. 'Prekarie und Benefizium', *Vierteljahresschrift für Social und Wirtschaftsgeschichte*, 16 (1922), pp. 259–306.

von Gierke, O. *Das Deutsche Genossenschaftsrecht*, 4 vols., Berlin, 1868–1913.

Vranoussi, E. 'Les archives de Néa Moni de Chio: Essai de reconstitution d'un dossier perdu', *Byzantinisch-neugriechische Jahrbücher*, 22 (1977–84), pp. 267–84.

Wacht, M. 'Gütergemeinschaft', in *Reallexikon für Antike und Christentum*, vol. 13, Stuttgart, 1986, cols. 1–59.

Waitz, G. *Deutsche Verfassungsgeschichte*, 8 vols., vols. 1–3 3rd edn, vols. 4–6 2nd edn, Berlin, 1876–96.

Waitz, G. 'Urkunden aus Karolingischer Zeit', in *Forschungen zur deutschen Geschichte*, 18 (1878), pp. 181–7.

Wallace-Hadrill, J. M. *The Long-Haired Kings*, London, 1962.

The Frankish Church, Oxford, 1983.

Wampach, C. (ed.) *Geschichte der Grundherrschaft Echternach*, Luxembourg, 1929.

Weidemann, M. *Das Testament des Bischofs Berthramn von Le Mans vom 27. März 616: Untersuchungen zu Besitz und Geschichte einer fränkischen Familie im 6. und 7. Jahrhundert*, Mainz, 1986.

Weiner, A. *Inalienable Possessions. The Paradox of Keeping-While-Giving*, Berkeley, Los Angeles and Oxford, 1992.

Weinfurter, S. 'Die Zentralisierung der Herrschaftsgewalt im Reich durch Kaiser Heinrich II.', *Historisches Jahrbuch*, 106 (1986), pp. 241–97.

Weinrich, L. *Wala, Graf, Mönch und Rebell: Die Biographie eines Karolingers*, Lübeck, 1963.

Wemple, S. *Women in Frankish Society. Marriage and the Cloister 500–900*, Philadelphia, 1981.

Werner, K.-F. 'Observations sur le rôle des évêques dans le mouvement de paix aux Xe et XIe siècles', in *Medievalia Christiana XIe–XIIe siècles. Hommage à Raymonde Foreville*, Paris 1990, pp. 155–95.

Werner, M. *Adelsfamilien in Umkreis der frühen Karolinger. Die Verwandtschaft Irminas von Oeren und Adelas von Pfalzel*, Sigmaringen, 1982.

White, S. D. '*Pactum . . . legem vincit, et amor iudicum*: the settlement of disputes by compromise in eleventh-century western France', *American Journal of Legal History*, 22 (1978), pp. 281–308.

'Feuding and peace-making in the Touraine around the year 1100', *Traditio*, 42 (1986), pp. 195–263.

'Inheritances and legal arguments in western France, 1050–1100', *Traditio*, 43 (1987), pp. 55–103.

Custom, Kinship and Gifts to Saints: the Laudatio Parentum *in Western France, 1050–1150*, Chapel Hill, 1988.

Whitelock, D. (ed.) *English Historical Documents*, vol. 1 *c.500–1042*, 2nd edn, London, 1979.

Wickham, C. J. 'The other transition: from the ancient world to feudalism', *Past and Present*, 103 (1984), pp. 3–36.

'Land-disputes and their social framework in Lombard–Carolingian Italy', in W. Davies and P. Fouracre (eds.), *The Settlement of Disputes in Early Medieval Europe*, pp. 105–24.

The Mountains and the City: The Tuscan Appenines in the Early Middle Ages, Oxford, 1988.

'European forests in the early middle ages', *Settimane di studio*, 37 (1989), pp. 479–545.

'Economia e società rurale nel territorio lucchese durante la seconda metà del secolo XI', in C. Violante (ed.), *Sant'Anselmo vescovo di Lucca (1073–1086)*, Rome, 1992, pp. 391–422.

'La Chute de Rome n'aura pas lieu. A propos d'un livre récent', *Le Môyen Age*, 99 (1993), pp. 107–26.

'*Manentes* e diritti signorili durante il XII secolo: il caso della Lucchesia', in *Studi in onore di Cinzio Violante*, Spoleto, 1993.

Comunità e clientele nella Toscana del XII secolo, Florence, 1994.

Wilks, M. '*Thesaurus Ecclesiae*', in *The Church and Wealth, Studies in Church History*, vol. 24, London, 1988, pp. xv–xlv.

Williams, A. '*Princeps Merciorum Gentis*: the family, career and connections of Ælfhere, ealdorman of Mercia', *Anglo-Saxon England*, 10 (1981), pp. 143–72.

'Introduction', in A. Williams (ed.), *The Worcestershire Domesday*, London, 1988.

Willoweit, D. 'Immunität', in A. Erler and E. Kaufmann (eds.), *Handwörterbuch der Deutschen Rechtsgeschichte*, vol. 2, *Haustür–Lippe*, Berlin, 1972–8, cols. 312–30.

Wisplinghoff, E. *Untersuchungen zur frühen Geschichte der Abtei S. Maximin bei Trier*, Mainz, 1970.

Wood, I. N. 'Saint-Wandrille and its hagiography', in I. N. Wood and G. A. Loud (eds.), *Church and Chronicle in the Middle Ages*, London, 1991, pp. 1–14.

The Merovingian Kingdoms 450–751, London, 1994.

Wolf, K. B. *Conquerors and Chroniclers of Early Medieval Spain*, Liverpool, 1990.

Wormald, P. 'A handlist of Anglo-Saxon lawsuits', *Anglo-Saxon England*, 17 (1988), pp. 247–81.

How do we Know so Much about Anglo-Saxon Deerhurst?, n.p., 1991.

'Domesday lawsuits: a provisional list and preliminary comment', in C. Hicks (ed.), *England in the Eleventh Century, Harlaxton Medieval Studies*, vol. 2, 1992, pp. 61–102.

' "*Quadripartitus*" ', in G. Garnett and J. Hudson (eds.), *Law and Government in Medieval England and Normandy: Studies presented to J. C. Holt*, Cambridge, 1994, pp. 111–47.

'*Engla Lond*: the making of an allegiance', *Journal of Historical Sociology*, 7 (1994), pp. 1–24.

Index

313